Mythologies of the World

A Guide to Sources

Ron Smith
Utah State University

National Council of Teachers of English
1111 Kenyon Road, Urbana, Illinois 61801

NCTE Editorial Board: Paul T. Bryant, Marilyn Hanf Buckley, Thomas J. Creswell, C. Kermeen Fristrom, Jane M. Hornburger, Robert F. Hogan, *ex officio*, Paul O'Dea, *ex officio*

Book Design: Tom Kovacs, interior; V. Martin, cover

NCTE Stock Number 32227

Library of Congress Cataloging in Publication Data

Smith, Ron, 1937–
  Mythologies of the world.

  1. Mythology—Bibliography. I. Title.
Z7836.S63   [BL311] 56   016.2911'3   81-666
ISBN 0-8141-3222-7   AACR2
                    32,836

Contents

Acknowledgments

At a dinner I attended not long before writing these words, a friend asked, "What book are you writing now?" "The same one I was last time you asked" was the only reply possible. As the months I planned for completion of the guide dragged on into years, I felt a growing responsibility to those who had been of so much help just in making the guide possible at all. They, above all others, deserve, in lieu of an end to it all, at least this evidence of what they've helped me to do—and by all means they are due my sincere thanks. First, there's Kathryn, my wife. She will never be the same after all the card catalogs she worshiped before. Then there's Lee, my daughter, whose question "Where's Daddy?" always had (and continues to have) the same dismaying answer. Then there's my college dean, Bill Lye, who surely has wondered more than once to what end he'd ventured money to enable me to spend time for research at the University of California at Berkeley. My department head, Ken Hunsaker, who found the money to *get* me to Berkeley and back, too has no doubt had reason since to think a hundred and fifty or so reams of ditto paper at 1976 prices would've been a wiser investment. Finally, Paul O'Dea, Director of Publications at NCTE, is in line for special thanks for his encouragement and just for remembering who I am over the years.

Introduction

As Brian Branston said at the start of his book, *Gods of the North*, "Mythology is every man's business." Indeed it is. As a teacher, I have become firmly convinced that any subject that deals with basic concerns as mythology commonly does—where we came from, why we're here, what or who started it all, how we're supposed to act, where we go when we die—is a subject no student can afford to miss.

That, however, is only my own reason why anyone should study mythology. I'm not foolish enough to believe it is the same reason that so many students enroll in the course. I've known scores of students, for instance, who, upon entering my basic mythology course, were startled to discover something more than three hours of laughs a week in class and three of hilarity assigned as homework. They had come to me with the conventional notion that mythology is a well-charted realm of frivolous and uninformed beliefs, with innumerable and repetitive stories that told the wild speculations of peoples too remote in time and place ever to be taken seriously. Certainly there is entertainment in the study of myths and, for that matter, some genuine belly laughs. But were the study of mythology no more than a simple and dilettantish game, there would be little need for studying it, and none at all for this guide.

On the Study of Mythology

Even if mythology needs a new image, its legitimacy as an area of study needs no new defense. H.R. Ellis Davidson, in her *Gods and Myths of Northern Europe*, comments, "the study of mythology need no longer be looked on as an escape from reality into the fantasies of primitive peoples, but as a search for the deeper understanding of the human mind. In reaching out to explore the distant hills where the gods dwell and the deeps where the monsters are lurking, we are perhaps discovering the way home." Given the contributions of psychology, the path to the way home is more clearly marked than ever before. Maps and guidance are also offered us by anthropologists, archaeologists, sociologists, linguists, philologists, comparative religionists, and folklorists. We have discovered that what once was the case in the study of mythology —a puddle-sized pool of reliable information and oceans of ill-conceived theory—no longer satisfies any serious student. Today, the study of mythology is an interdisciplinary effort in pursuit of the broadest of intellectual goals—understanding. And for the first time in its long and uneven history, we have the variety of methods equal to the task.

Before 1825, the available pool of myths from around the world was about one percent of the present size of that pool. Archaeology, which was just starting then, by today has given us an incredible amount of new information, including countless myths from civilizations we had known about only second hand through the records of other, usually neighboring civilizations. Most of the myths we now have of the ancient Egyptians, Phoe-nicians, Hittites, and Mesopotamian-area cultures, for example, are the result of archaeological finds and subsequent work by philologists and epigraphers. Like archaeology, anthropology began in the last century. Although prior explorations had brought some myths into the pool, it wasn't until anthropologists (or ethnographers) began systematically studying newly discovered cultures that new riches in the form of whole belief and myth "systems" were put before us.

The nineteenth century also saw the birth of psychology, sociology, the comparative study of religions, folklore, and many of the natural and physical sciences. Each made a contribution to the study of mythology. We learned that many of the myths of the ancient Near East were part of the heritage of western civili-zation. We learned how cultures grow and interact, not only in adjacent regions but around the world. Psychology taught us to consider myth by thinking about attitude. Sociology taught us, by contrast, about the collective mind and group behavior. And the other new disciplines reminded us to consider the power of belief and faith, the force of oral traditions, the connections between thought and language, and insights into the processes of nature.

In its long infancy, mythology was not organized and was accordingly vulnerable to high speculation. In the childhood of the discipline, all myths were perceived as rationalizations of physical phenomena, or else they were viewed as corruptions of biblical stories, or else they were elaborate allegories, or else they were the vestiges of ritual performances, and so on through a generally provocative list of theories, each autonomous and most clearly implying that myth was no more than fiction. Today, caution in the interpretation of myths is the byword. Too much information is at hand for safe pronouncements about how all myths originate or how their meanings may be construed. In the light of the findings of the established sciences, the sweeping generalizations of the past are now easily seen through. What is just as important, respect for all myths has grown. It no longer seems important to argue over whether or not *any* myth conveys events, lives, and history in *exactly* the way they are presented in the myths themselves. We know at last that the study of mythology never will be an exact science as such; inference and deduction will almost always be the way any conclusions about myths can be established. Yet we also know, with assurance, that our thinking about myths can be systematic without rigidity and reliable though cautious. Those are good kinds of knowing, given mythology's uneven past.

Today, more than ever before, myth study offers the sturdiest and most satisfying of outcomes for those who work at mythology with enthusiastic attention to detail. There is something genuinely exciting about studying mythology. It involves recognition that myths are all around us—even now. We must be willing to inspect all of them—past ones and present, our own as well as others'—on an equal and open-minded basis as our way of gaining that "deeper understanding of the human mind." We must be willing to take some pretty large risks in the process. The greatest one, of course, is in pooling our own myths with the world's for the sake of gaining insight into them all. It's just not easily done without a great deal of rationalizing on behalf of our own, since the tendency is to view all myths *except* our own as fabrications— which, by the way, is where the common usage of the word "myth" as fabrication, misconception, and the like came from quite a few centuries back. Mythologists long ago began steering clear of such rationalizing as nonproductive and contrary to the increasing body of evidence.

The proper study of mythology today thus involves taking advantage of the contributions of many branches of study and of what has become an enormous pool of myths from around the world. What we know of and about the human kind internationally, those living as well as those who lived earlier, comes into play. It gives us a way of viewing and thinking about a single myth in isolation as well as about whole classes of them—sacral myths, legends, and folktales. Looking into each of the classes separately also tends to illuminate, since each class has its own characteristics and spectrum of purposes, each drawing regularly from a broad group of types—creation myths, eschatological myths, heroic myths, genealogical myths, solar myths, beast myths, and many others identified principally (but not alone) by their content. Looking into a large group of creation myths, for instance, cannot help but be instructive about all creation myths and will end in the possibility of insights about the myth-making process, the origin of myths, and the like concerns of all people in all places and times. What is more, close inspection of creation myths, as with close inspection of any other myth type with wide distribution geographically, will yield key conclusions concerning parallels among myths, prevalent motifs, and, among other things, what constitutes important constants among myths and what constitutes equally important variables. Perhaps as significant as all of these, the proper study of mythology today involves appropriate use of past theories of myth and its meaning and/or origin. Not one of these theories is without flaws—often serious ones the result of a confusion of "possible" and "probable"; but not one fails to tell us something of importance in at least some instances. If we have learned that theories which undertake to explain *all* myths are as a rule overly ambitious, we have additionally learned that their impetus and core ideas are to be respected.

Pooling the world's myths in order to study mythology does not preclude the study of an individual culture's myths by using what is known of the culture as a frame for understanding its myths. In fact, there is no *sure* way of truly understanding any culture's myths without doing that. What can be generalized about the world's myths from a single culture's myths, however, is quite limited. It is usually more fruitful to generalize about an individual culture's myths from the world's myths. A good many students with past experience in myth study have entered my mythology classes thinking mythology to be "somebody else's religion"—a parochial view to say the least. That attitude comes from focusing on one or a few apparently alien cultures without considering the classes and types of myths which know no geographic boundary or examining the widespread parallels, motifs, and the variables and constants in all myths. As George William Cox said just about a hundred years ago at the start of his *An Introduction to the Science of Comparative Mythology and Folklore*, "The myth is a parasite which is ready to twine round any stem; and in each case it is the business of the mythologist to ascertain the nature of the stem, if he would account satisfactorily for the peculiar forms of its vesture." Pooling the world's myths, as all comparative mythologists and folklorists do, is the way to move toward ascertaining "the nature of the stem."

A story is told about the American philosopher-psychologist William James. He had just finished a lecture on the solar system when he was approached by an older woman from his audience. "Mr. James," she said, "that business about the solar system and this earth revolving around the sun is nonsense." James was, needless to say, at least mildly surprised by so direct an attack on science taking place in the twentieth century, but he let her have her say. "It so happens, Mr. James," she continued, "that this earth is spread across the back of an enormous turtle." James could no doubt have packed a considerable amount of scientific evidence into a rejoinder had he so wished, but instead he merely asked a question. "If that is so, my dear, on what is that turtle standing?" "Why, Mr. James, of course it's standing on the back of another, far larger turtle!" James thought for a second an asked another question: "And on what is that turtle standing?" The lady looked him straight in the eye and laughed at his apparent ignorance. "It's no use, Mr. James. It's turtles all the way down."

There are two myths operative in the story—the lady's version of "how it is," a version closely related to a number of American Indian creation myths, and James' scientific version. Neither version was so convincingly proven or disproven as to be beyond argument at the time. Understanding "the nature of the stem" in mythology is not likely when a single version of "how it is" is held to be correct. Confrontations, whether that between the lady and William James or between those long-time combatants, science and religion, are best left for other battlefields. When each side fails to see a myth for what it is—a traditional narrative the content of which is almost always impossible to prove or disprove, a single version of how it is among many others like it—serious myth study has stopped.

Truly serious study of mythology has the potential to be the work of a lifetime. While it may invite dabbling at the start, before long it demands commitment across the boundaries of many disciplines. Mary Barnard noted, in her book *The Mythmakers:*

> There is something to be learned from the simple fact that no enlightened university has established a Chair of Mythology. Mythology is not a field in itself, but a patchwork of the corners of other fields. The chair would have to be a bench long enough

to seat students of literature, linguistics, religion, archaeology, anthropology, psychology (two or three schools), folklore and philosophy. Besides that we need a stool somewhere for the poet.

Those who have gone all the way, that is those who could (or can) honestly call themselves "mythologists," have been few in number as a result. As a result, also, "mythology" has never received the kinds of organizing attention or been accorded recognition as an academic discipline the way its nearest of kin, folklore and comparative religions, have.

Back in 1921, in *An Introduction to Mythology*, still one of the few *truly* introductory mythology texts (as opposed to "mythographies," or collections of myths, of which there have been hundreds in English alone), Lewis Spence referred to "the present chaotic state of the science" and explained that "the two great drawbacks of mythology are lack of accepted definitions and of an historical and philosophical review of the subject on popular lines to coordinate the results of research." Since that time, mythology has reaped the benefits of being the sometimes step-child of folklore and comparative religions. Nevertheless, definitions are still disputed; terms are still used in different ways by different people; theories of myth and its origins that are the center of a kind of scholarly cult worship one day become the object of ridicule the next; and the results of research are still, for the most part, uncoordinated. The interested study of myths has been an on-and-off activity since the sixth century B.C., and regularly an avocational if not always professional pursuit since the first half of the nineteenth; but there is still much to be done.

The difficulties inherent in bringing together the diverse reaches of mythology are not insurmountable. Symposia could be the start —symposia much like, though concerned with a far broader problem than, those held at the University of California at Berkeley in 1976. Bearing the title "The Flood Myth: An Inquiry into Causes and Circumstances," the Berkeley symposia brought together thirteen experts in various disciplines which have some concern with the ancient Near-Eastern flood myths. The symposia I have in mind would tackle the nature of mythology: the limits and concerns of its substance would be discussed, relevant findings in each discipline would be elaborated upon and brought together with like findings from the other disciplines, appropriate terminology would once and for all be isolated and clarified for use in myth study, and guidelines would be set for the acceptable training of professionals in mythology and of those who will teach it in secondary and college classrooms. The order is a gigantic one without question.

Right now, English teachers do most of the teaching of mythology in the United States. At college level, historians of religion, folklorists, and classicists are also involved. Historians of religion have been training their people well enough in mythology; but unfortunately, few of them have the opportunity to teach mythology compared to the great numbers of English teachers who do. Folklorists, too, are often enough trained in mythology as a distinct part of their discipline, but they, too, have their own concerns. Classicists, almost needless to say, have little if any opportunity to teach anything other than Greco-Roman mythology and are no better trained in mythology generally than are English teachers.

English teachers, trained as they are in the teaching of narratives, are the ones who *should* teach mythology after all. Whatever else myths are, and whatever other disciplines may justifiably lay claim to them, myths are always literature, however oral and, at times, unliterary they may appear to be. However, there is far more to myths than approaching them as literature alone can possibly justify. Sad to say, narrow approaches to the teaching of mythology, simply uninformed approaches in fact, abound. Few English teachers have gone very far on their own in preparing to teach mythology.

About This Guide

That's where this guide comes in. With it, anyone who is so inclined may take some significant steps toward responsible preparation in mythology. It will not provide all the leads and direction possible, since I am myself at some stage (advanced, I keep hoping) along the way toward discovering them. What follows is a brief review of how I came to write it in the first place.

During the first seven years I taught mythology, I frequently wondered why I was unable to find a work written for serious myth students and teachers in which could be found the answer to a question I felt certain was being asked regularly around the country by others like me: Where next? Having gotten involved with ancient Egyptian myths, for instance, what are some sources in which the myths are elaborated upon or analyzed? What are some books or articles in which ancient Egyptian religion is discussed? In what works can useful background studies of the history and culture be found? How about works in which the archaeology of ancient Egypt is discussed? These, it so happens, are among the more easily answered questions a myth student might ask concerning ancient Egypt. The harder-to-answer ones bothered me most, and I was, as many others no doubt have been, too often frustrated in the attempt to locate the answers myself. Having come upon a reference to myth, ritual, and divine kingship in ancient Egypt, for example, in what works can coverage of the subject be found? What are some good comparative studies of creation myths in which Egypt's are placed in perspective? Are there any specialized studies of Set, Horus, and other deities? What sources are there for direct translations of relevant Egyptian texts? This overall group of questions involving ancient Egypt represents groups like them that could be asked of any mythology in the world, from ancient Mesopotamian to North American Indian, and the fact is, the more deeply one gets into mythology, the harder the answers are to come by. In my early years as a teacher of mythology, I turned up a good many books and articles useful in the study of the subject along the way to discovering there just wasn't a work available in which the run of "Where next?" questions were answered, a few conspicuously limited bibliographies being as close as I came to one at the time. The whole business had been for me hit and miss, to say the least.

Then came one of the happier experiences I've been enriched by—participation in the 1976 summer seminar for college teachers sponsored by the National Endowment for the Humanities and conducted by Dr. John Peradotto at the State University of New York at Buffalo. Entitled "Greek Myth and Modern Theories of Interpretation," the seminar exposed me to eight lively weeks of virtually uninterrupted thinking, talking, and writing about mythology and put me in contact with countless books and articles beyond those I'd already read during seven years of high interest in myth study. Equally important as concerns the genesis of this guide, I discovered Peradotto's superb *Classical Mythology: An Annotated Bibliographical Survey* (Urbana, Ill.: The American Philological Association, 1973). Designed for teachers of Classics who teach or wish to teach classical mythology, that valuable seventy-six page work eventually led me to undertake the further research for and writing of *Mythologies of the World: A Guide to Sources*, my own version of the answer to "Where next?" for anyone seriously interested in the overall study of mythology, for teachers of English who teach mythology especially but for intermediate to advanced students as well.

At some point while I was in the process of doing the additional research, for example—in the libraries of Utah State University, the University of Utah, and the University of California at Berkeley, and through a remarkably efficient interlibrary loan system—I read some remarks by Paul Jordan-Smith in a review he'd written for the Fall 1976 issue of *Parabola.* Having complained that the book he'd reviewed had a weak bibliography, he added, much to my anguish, "This is almost always the weakest part of any book. One's list is never complete and invariably reflects one's own prejudices." I'd already gotten far enough along on my research— whether 2,000 note cards or 4,000 by then I can't say—to know I was into a bottomless pit (the study of mythology being that way) and was beginning to understand why no one had ever published a guide attempting an answer to the "Where next?" question asked by myth students. Any who had tried just hadn't been heard from since, I was sure. All I needed at precisely that time, as a result, was to be reminded by Paul Jordan-Smith of what I'd come to realize on my own—that my work on what is essentially an extended bibliographical essay would never be complete and, in the end, would no doubt reflect my own biases and, worse yet, ignorance. As it so happens, I am just hard-headed enough not to be put off by the probability of shortfall *or* the accusation of ignorance. Therefore, I kept on with few regrets (albeit with a pretty troublesome assortment of nagging doubts), determined, wherever and whenever necessary, to hide behind the common knowledge (at least I hope it is) that a single worker in too large a vineyard is not likely to account for all the world's wine. And as for the accusation of ignorance, I trust it will be no more palliative to say I came into the world ignorant and, despite all efforts at change for the better, I will no doubt leave it with the situation only minimally remedied.

My initial plan for the guide was modest—a slender volume, perhaps, listing relevant works. Certainly no more than that. It was only in doing research of an extensive sort that I really learned one doesn't drink at the well of mythology without substantial risk of drowning. It is a subject broadened not only by its multi-disciplinary base but by boundless geographical and temporal ones as well. Just as it does not begin or end in ancient Egypt, it does not begin or end in any one period of time. This volume grew and grew in order to accommodate my conviction that the study of any one mythology ought never to be isolated from the related religion, history, culture, art, and whatever else will shed light on why the given myths are the way they are. A people's myths are simultaneously the result of and the inspiration for their values, their beliefs, their social institutions, their creativity, and their life-styles. All facets of a culture therefore illuminate the myths of the culture in varying ways and degrees, and all that could logically be included toward that illumination has been—again, given my limitations as a researcher. Rather than simply list works in categories, though, I have set up each geographical section as a bibliographical essay. Each of the geographically identified mythologies is prefaced by a short introduction—not necessarily for the purpose of discussing the individual mythologies, something done better and to more appropriate lengths in other books by other authors, but, rather, as enticement to the mythologies through varied kinds of background information. Close to thirty self-contained sections, each ballooning to its own peculiar limits (and mine, as I cannot overemphasize), thus came about to comprise "Mythologies of the World."

Mythologies of the World: A Guide to Sources as it now stands has long been needed. If it fills that need satisfactorily, if it handles the geographical "Where next?" questions—whenever and for whatever reasons they are asked—I'll after all be a little less haunted by Paul Jordan-Smith's remark about the invariable incompleteness of one's list and the way the list "reflects one's own prejudices."

How to Use This Guide

Despite the kindred nature of all myths, there is an individuality to each mythology of the world, an individuality that increases in importance as our focus moves from broad geographical areas toward individual cultures within those areas. At the broadest level where the mythologies of the world are considered collectively, the things we talk about are very general since we are talking about what is common to all mythologies. At the narrowest level, the mythology of a single culture, just the opposite pertains. At that level the intricacies of the ethical code and belief system of a single culture are involved, thus creating the need for specifics rather than generalizations. Obviously, both ways of looking at myths are essential in the proper study of mythology.

Subdividing the mythologies of the world into ever smaller geographical units can be accomplished in two basic ways: through the use of historical and geographical boundaries or through the sole use of geographical ones. I have chosen the latter way as the tidier. There is far more clarity in lumping the mythologies of Africa together as African than there is in trying to lump together the representatives of three continents—Egypt, Canaan, and Greece—as "ancient" and then wondering what to do with Middle American mythology, an ancient mythology from an entirely different time frame and yet another continent to boot. Besides, as a worldwide phenomenon, mythology *is* geographical rather than in any important sense historical, there being far more signs of the geographical backdrop in any culture's myths than there are of the historical. Myths are, in fact, singularly timeless and removed from the historical stream. Their time is indefinite except that they happen "in the past." They are seldom placeless, though; geographical clues poke through at every bend in the narrative.

This guide, then, is devoted to the geographical study of mythology, whether that geography be worldwide in scope or minute—as in, say, Japan. The one exception to this scheme comes in the section ahead called "Prehistoric Mythologies," a rather recently developed area thanks to archaeology. It, too, is worldwide, however, for its evidence is drawn from widely scattered parts of the world; what makes it time-organized rather than geographical is the relatedness of the evidence within that broad expanse of time called "prehistory."

What you will find in the guide's many sections ahead was dictated by a variety of factors, foremost among them the now pervasive thinking that mythology should not be studied in a vacuum. It is not enough simply to read through a collection of Egyptian myths to call oneself knowledgeable about Egyptian mythology. The questions of what beliefs and practices lay behind those myths must be answered. So, too, must the questions about everyday life in ancient Egypt, about Egyptian art, and about Egyptian history—to mention some obvious areas of concern. Anthropologists have long argued for the understanding of the whole culture toward understanding any single part of it, just as mythologists have recently argued for understanding the nature and origins of myth, for understanding the many ways of interpreting it, for understanding its relation to ritual and religion, and for understanding the extensive contributions of psychology, philosophy, and a host of other academic disciplines toward understanding the phenomena of mythology. The sections of the guide are, therefore, organized in accordance with the fairly recent thought that mythology is a portion of a larger cultural whole.

Each of the geographical sections has taken its own shape from the availability of works within the following broad pattern: collections of myths, works in which analyses or interpretations of the myths are undertaken, works on religion, works on cultural history, works on relevant archaeology, works on art and architecture, and, occasionally, works having to do with the language and its translation. This, however, is a broad pattern sometimes violated in order and in inclusiveness depending on the particular culture/mythology and what has been done in print with it. For some mythologies, much has been done in virtually all of the areas—Greek one of them, biblical another. For others, there is a shortage of works in one or more areas—Hittite, Finno-Ugric and some other ancient and medieval European among the more conspicuous examples. Also, the broader the region covered, as a rule, the less there is available in most areas. Finally, there are my own limitations as a researcher to account for still other weaknesses in how the pattern wasn't entirely fulfilled. How much I've yet to learn is surely one of the things I *did* learn in working with the cultures of the world and their mythologies!

Space limitations demanded that I not be too wordy about any single work, of course. This means there are limits to the usefulness of what I do say about most of them. A few rules of thumb to follow as you read through any section are therefore called for. First, books on cultural history are quite frequently fine sources of information about a culture's religion and mythology, so don't think of them only as "history." When you're studying such mythologies as Etruscan, Incan, Hittite, and a number of others for which there are few (or no) collections of myths and nothing much on religion, cultural histories are especially important. Second, pictures of artifacts, archaeological sites, temples, and the like are also something works on cultural history very often have to offer, so don't overlook them as sources of pictures that will help you better know the culture and mythology you're studying. Third, a culture's art may or may not be directly related to its mythology and religion. Greek art is closely tied to the mythology and religion of Greece, but Islam's art apparently has very little to do with its mythology and religion. Whether or not there is a helpful connection between the art and mythology/religion of the culture you happen to be studying, remember that a culture's art has much to say about its people, their way of life, their way of viewing the world around them, and other things. And just about anything of this sort you can learn about a culture will without doubt help you better understand the mythology involved.

Mythologies of the World

Worldwide Mythologies

Although the very idea that myth study can be approached from a "worldwide" angle does indeed seem ludicrous, there are a surprising number of works and series available that are broad enough in scope to make it seem at least plausible. Various kinds of such collections of myths will be covered first in this section, then dictionaries useful in myth study, and finally works suitable for background to myth study.

Collections of Myths—Geographically Organized

A colorful sixteen-volume *International Mythology* (ib) series was published between 1965 and 1973 by the Paul Hamlyn Group of London. Each volume has about 140 pages and over 200 illustrations, 24 of them in color, and all of the volumes have brief but useful bibliographies. The series includes John Gray's *Near Eastern Mythology* (Mesopotamia, Canaan, and Israel), John R. Hinnells' *Persian Mythology*, George Every's *Christian Mythology*, Felix Guirand's *Greek Mythology*, Stewart Perowne's *Roman Mythology*, Veronica Ions' *Indian Mythology*, *Egyptian Mythology* (no author given), Proinsias MacCana's *Celtic Mythology*, H.R. Ellis Davidson's *Scandinavian Mythology*, Anthony Christie's *Chinese Mythology*, Juliet Piggott's *Japanese Mythology*, Cottie Burland's *North American Indian Mythology*, Irene Nicholson's *Mexican and Central American Mythology*, Harold Osborne's *South American Mythology*, Geoffrey Parrinder's *African Mythology*, and Roslyn Poignant's *Oceanic Mythology*. Although there is some qualitative unevenness across the series, overall it is excellent—as are the professional credentials of most of the writers.

Pelham Books of London has recently (1976–78) completed publication of a four-volume worldwide mythography (collection of myths) called *Pears Encyclopedia of Myths and Legends* (ib)

The following symbols will be found, where applicable, in the bibliographic citation, usually following the date of publication: i = has useful illustrations; b = has a useful bibliography; p = has been published in paperbound edition.

3

written principally by Sheila Savill. Each volume is illustrated
and runs between 191 and 247 pages in length. There are eight
chapters all told in the four volumes: Volume I has a chapter on
the Ancient Near and Middle East and one on Classical Greece
and Rome; Volume II has a chapter on Northern Europe and one
on South and Central Africa; Volume III has a chapter on Ancient
Iran and the Indian Sub-Continent and one on Northern and
Eastern Asia (Tibet, China, Korea, Japan); Volume IV has a
chapter on the Oceanic Islands and one on the Americas. Each
chapter has a helpful introduction and is followed by a glossary,
short bibliography, and index. The *Encyclopedia* comprises
a sound but more compact international mythography than
Hamlyn's sixteen-volume series.

The classic multi-volume mythography, still commonly found
in libraries throughout the country despite its antiquity, is *The
Mythology of All Races*, a mammoth thirteen-volume work under
the general editorship of Louis Herbert Gray. First published in
Boston by the Marshall Jones Company between 1916 and 1932,
it has been made available since 1964 by Cooper Square Press of
New York in a reprinted edition. The fact that it hasn't been
re-edited in all those years to accommodate more recent scholarship limits its usefulness, of course, but it remains a valuable
source for myths. Volume I is *Greek and Roman* by William
Sherwood Fox, Volume II *Teutonic* by Axel Olrik, Volume III
Celtic and *Slavic* by John A. MacCulloch and Jan Machal, Volume
IV *Finno-Ugric* and *Siberian* by Uno Holmberg, Volume V *Semitic*
by R. Campbell Thompson, Volume VI *Indian* and *Iranian* by
A. Berriedale Keith and Albert J. Carnoy, Volume VII *Armenian*
and *African* by Mardiros Ananikian and George Foucart, Volume
VIII *Chinese* and *Japanese* by U. Hattori and Masaharu Anesaki,
Volume IX *Oceanic* by Roland Burrage Dixon, Volume X *American*
(North of Mexico) by Hartley Burr Alexander, Volume XI *Amer-
ican* (Latin) by Hartley Burr Alexander, Volume XII *Egypt, Far
East* by W. Max Müller, and Volume XIII *Index*. The list of
authors comes very near to reading like the Who's Who in myth
study during the first third of this century!

An even older series which appeared in a limited edition is the
Gresham Publishing Company's ten-volume *Myth and Legend in
Literature and Art* (i). Published in London in the years following
1913, the set is beautifully illustrated with engravings after works
of art (hence the series title). It includes *Classic Myth and Legend*
and *Romance and Legend of Chivalry* by A.R. Hope Moncrieff,

Celtic Myth and Legend, Poetry and Romance by Charles Squire, and, all by Donald A. Mackenzie, *Teutonic Myth and Legend, Egyptian Myth and Legend, Indian Myth and Legend, Myths of Babylonia and Assyria, Myths of Crete and Pre-Hellenic Europe, Myths of China and Japan,* and *Myths of Pre-Columbian America.* The series is, needless to say, dated by much research of the past fifty years, but for myths and pictures, it's still a beautiful set.

If I were to recommend a one-volume worldwide mythography from among the several that have in recent years been available, it would have to be the *Larousse World Mythology* (New York: Putnam, 1965/ib), edited by Pierre Grimal and translated by Patricia Beardsworth. In its 560 large-size pages are hundreds of illustrations (several dozen of them in color), a helpful bibliography, a good introduction called "Man and Myth" by Grimal and literally thousands of myths from around the world spread throughout twenty-two individual sections on myth systems or groups. Just about a score of experts were called upon to write chapters for the book within their own specialties, so there is some discontinuity from section to section and occasionally difficult reading for those who haven't read much in mythology before. But the book is, in my estimation, the best of its kind; its coverage is complete and extra attention is paid throughout to helping the reader understand mythology.

A close second is the *Larousse Encyclopedia of Mythology* (London: Paul Hamlyn, 1959/ibp), edited by Felix Guirand and translated by Richard Aldington and Delano Ames. It, too, is a big book, is thoroughly illustrated (black and white only), has a good (if not up to date) bibliography, and has a nice introduction written by Robert Graves. Its thousands of myths from around the world are spread through seventeen individual chapters on the main myth systems or groups, each written by an expert. It is, like the *Larousse World Mythology,* somewhat difficult at times for those inexperienced in myth study, but it is a fine book overall.

The rest of the single-volume worldwide works are weaker than the two Larousse volumes, but each has its merits. A book called *Encyclopedia of World Mythology* (no author given—New York: Galahad Books, 1975/i) compresses a lot of material into 252 large-format pages. The book is liberally illustrated in color and covers roughly the same territory as the two Larousse volumes. Unlike them, though, the coverage is overly brief—especially the space devoted to Oceanic, Hittite, Babylonian, and a number of others. What are especially helpful in the book are the chapters devoted to thematic areas—"The Mythology of Plants," "The Mythology of Animals," and "Common Mythological Themes" (creation myths, the hero, the mother goddess, the flood, etc.).

If the *Encyclopedia of World Mythology* comes close to being better classified as a "coffee table" volume because of its colorful layout, a book which *must* be classified that way is Veronica Ions' *The World's Mythology in Colour* (London: Paul Hamlyn, 1974/i). It has a good introductory essay by Jacquetta Hawkes, "Myth and Mankind," but the rest of the text is inadequate. The book has 366 pictures in color, the same ones that appear in Hamlyn's *International Mythology* series, and covers the standard run of myth systems and groups. Because the text relating to each myth section is minimal (something like a four to one ratio of space devoted to pictures and text prevails), the book is close to useless *except* as a picture-book companion to either Larousse volume.

Not quite a worldwide mythography but nonetheless worth considering because of its ready availability in paperback and because the chapters are written by experts is *Mythologies of the Ancient World* (Garden City, N.Y.: Doubleday Anchor, 1961/bp), edited by Samuel Noah Kramer. As its title suggests, it is concerned only with ancient mythologies—Egyptian, Sumerian-Akkadian, Hittite, Canaanite, Greek, Indian, Iranian, Chinese, Japanese, Mexican (Toltec and Aztec). Each of the ten chapters is accompanied by a good bibliography. Kramer's introduction on the problem of reliability in myth texts is worth reading, by the way, but as in the two Larousse books, there are some difficult passages for the neophyte to cope with.

There are a number of less ambitious collections of myths—not worldwide in scope but covering at least several systems each—which ought to be mentioned. They are much more suited as introductory texts than most of the books already described. Several paperback editions of *Bulfinch's Mythology*, for example, are still on the market. The standard abridged editions (such as Edmund Fuller's abridgement in Dell Laurel) include Greek, Roman, some Norse, Teutonic, Arthurian, and French (Charlemagne). Padraic Colum's *Myths of the World* (formerly *Orpheus* in the Macmillan 1930 edition; now New York: Grosset and Dunlop, 1959/ip) is an assortment of myths without any particular thematic or geographical unity; the myths are nicely retold, however, and there are some interesting illustrations in the text.

Mythology for the Modern Reader (the same as Cliff's Notes' *Mythology*, both published at Lincoln, Neb., 1973/p), by James Weigel, Jr., offers very brief coverage of Egyptian, Babylonian, Indian, Greek, Roman, Norse, and Arthurian mythologies. Julia W. Loomis' *Mythology: Greek, Roman, Norse, Babylonian, Indian* is in the "Monarch Notes and Study Guides" series (New York: Simon and Schuster, 1965); it is, of course, also very brief. James Burl Hogins' *Literature: Mythology and Folklore* (Chicago: Science Research Associates, 1973/p) is a short, more or less random collection of myths and folktales from around the world. Max J. Herzberg's *Myths and Their Meaning* (Boston: Allyn and Bacon, 1969/i) handles Greco-Roman, Norse, and Celtic myth in an introductory fashion, with guidance for the reader in the form of questions and a couple of helpful chapters on the nature of myth.

Finally, it should at least be noted in passing that there are worldwide anthologies of folktales which might be useful alongside any of the above mythographies. For instance, there are *A Harvest of World Folktales* (New York: Viking Press, 1975/p; also published as the *The Penguin Book of World Folktales*/p), edited by Milton Rugoff, and *One Hundred Favorite Folktales* (Bloomington: Indiana University Midland Book, 1976/p), edited by Stith Thompson, among the more recent ones.

Collections of Myths—Topically Organized

Just as those collections of myths which are geographically organized fill a definite need, so too do those mythographies which, though worldwide, are arranged by topic (creation myths, hero myths, solar myths, etc.). It is, in other words, instructive to study myths in the framework of the cultures and time periods in which they were produced and *also* to compare myths. Some would even say that our greatest understanding of mythology as a worldwide phenomenon comes from working with topical groupings. In part, at least, it is just such a notion that lies behind two very lovely books published in recent years, either one of which will serve as a fine introduction to mythology: *Myths* (New York: McGraw-Hill, 1976/ib), edited by Alexander Eliot, and *Mythology* (New York: Newsweek Books, 1976), by David Leeming. Eliot's is the grander and more expensive of the two—large in format and longer, written partially by such experts as Joseph Campbell and Mircea Eliade, beautifully illustrated throughout. Its chapters are for the most part thematic units which cut across many cultures:

"Creators of Nature and Mankind," "Bringers of Magic and the Arts," "Animals, Monsters, and Mythic Beasts," "Distant Quests and Mortal Tests," "Death and Rebirth," and others. Leeming's is also a beautiful, much shorter, book which has in it chapters not all so conspicuously theme-focused but nonetheless thematic in intent. He is after what lies behind the existence of myths and uses the several things he finds as his unifying thread. There are especially good sections on heroic and creation myths. Another work well worth considering is Derek and Julia Parker's *The Immortals* (London: Barrie & Jenkins, 1976/i). It is a combination of topically and geographically organized sections and is beautifully illustrated throughout. The longest chapter in the book, "A World Tour of Myth," is clearly geographical, the major myth systems and groups all represented in introductory form. The other chapters are topical—"Spirits of the Elements," "The Saints," "The Devil," and "An Immortal Bestiary" some of them. (See also the *Encyclopedia of World Mythology*, described above.)

Two older works by that titan among early twentieth-century mythologists, Sir James George Frazer, *The Golden Bough* and *Folklore in the Old Testament*, may still be considered for their topical gropings of myths even though the broad framework of each of the works is more ambitiously conceived than simply to present the groupings. The third edition of *The Golden Bough* (1911-15) reached twelve volumes (!), a set often found at better libraries but now more commonly available in its abridged, single-volume edition: *The New Golden Bough*, ed. Theodor H. Gaster (Garden City, N.Y.: Doubleday Anchor, 1961/p). Look in it especially for myths associated with vegetation, death/resurrection, and dying/reviving gods. *Folklore in the Old Testament* (reprinted edition; New York: Hart Publishing Co., 1975) is an even better source for some types of myths—creation of man, fall of man, flood myths, and some others.

If you're looking for a book devoted exclusively to creation myths, there are five that can especially be recommended. Maria Leach's *The Beginning: Creation Myths Around the World* (New York: Funk and Wagnalls, 1956) is a fine, straightforward survey of creation myths that begins with a variety of scientifc theories some former advocates would now disavow. Two fine later works are organized in much the same way Leach's book is, geographically, and are at least as complete: Barbara C. Sproul's *Primal Myths: Creating the World* (New York: Harper and Row, 1979/bp) and Raymond Van Over's *Sun Songs: Creation Myths from Around the World* (New York: N. A. L. Mentor Book, 1980/bp). Each has a good general introduction as well as introductions to the individual geographic sections. Philip Freund's *Myths of Creation* (New York: Washington Square Press, 1965/p) is a valuable book which includes a gaggle of worldwide creation myths interlaced with interpretation and speculation about myths generally. Freund is no expert, but his thinking about myths is reasonable as a rule. Finally, Charles H. Long, a well known comparative religionist, has assembled a good collection of creation myths from around the world and analyzed them by category—emergence, earth diver, world parent, etc.—in his book *Alpha: The Myths of Creation* (Toronto: Collier Books, 1963/ibp).

At the other end of the spectrum from creation myths are those called "eschatological," myths having to do with final things—death, judgment, resurrection. *The Wisdom of the Serpent: The Myths of Death, Rebirth, and Resurrection* (New York: Collier Books, 1971/ibp), by Joseph E. Henderson and Maud Oakes, is divided into two parts, the first a psychoanalytic analysis (by Henderson) of myths that have been inspired by man's knowledge that he will die and the second (by Oakes) a worldwide survey of myths of death, rebirth, and resurrection. The book is well illustrated and is well worth the reading, difficult though it be at times. Although neither *Reincarnation in World Thought* (New York: Julian Press, 1976), by Joseph Head and S.L. Cranston, nor S.G.F. Brandon's *The Judgment of the Dead* (New York: Scribner's, 1967) are mythographies as such, both have a great deal to offer in the way of eschatological myths. *Reincarnation in World Thought* offers comments on reincarnation from around the world and in virtually all times. It includes excerpts from sacred writings and from the writings of literary people. *The Judgment of the Dead* surveys most of the world's religions that include belief in judgment of the dead, starting with earliest Egypt.

Three books which cover the broad range of life topics from birth through death are Cottie A. Burland's *Myths of Life and Death* (New York: Crown Publishers, 1974/ib), Alan W. Watts' *The Two Hands of God* (New York: Collier Books, 1969/ip), and Barbara and Gene Stanford's *Myths and Modern Man* (New York: Pocket Books, 1972). Burland's book, loaded with myths and pictures, is centered on the "triple passage"—the path through life, the path of the seasons of the year, the path of the seven directions—and has throughout a special preoccupation with myths of death. Watts' *The Two Hands of God* deals with polarity or opposition in mythology and art—life and death, good and evil, etc. Each section in the book focuses on a different kind of myth, retelling and analyzing many from around the world in the process. The Stanfords' book is meant as a junior-senior high text, but because it groups myths in an interesting way, it deserves inclusion here. The titles of the five sections into which the book is divided tell all: "Where Did We Come From?" "How Do Men and Women Differ?" "What Is the Perfect Man?" "Can Men Live Together in Peace?" "Is Death the End?"

Myths of the hero form a large and impressive group among the world's myths. *Myths of the Hero* (New York: Orion Press, 1960/i), by Norma Lore Goodrich, offers a good collection of ancient and medieval heroic myths retold principally for the junior-senior high age group. David Adams Leeming's *Mythology: The Voyage of the Hero* (Philadelphia: J.B. Lippincott, 1973/bp) is organized around the phases of the heroic career, offering a broad cross-section of the world's heroic myths along the way.

Man's preoccupation with the sky and the heavenly bodies has also produced a sizable body of thematically related myths. William Tyler Olcott's *Myths of the Sun* (New York: Capricorn Books, 1967/p; originally 1914) is a delightful collection of myths, legends, and general lore about the sun as is his *Star Lore of All Ages* (New York: G.P. Putnam's Sons, 1911), about the other heavenly bodies. An interesting pictures-and-text volume related to the subject is Katherine Komaroff's *Sky Gods: The Sun and Moon in Art and Myth* (New York: Universe Books, 1977/ip) meant mainly for ten-to-fourteen year olds. Its only deficiency is that it just doesn't cover much ground. Raffaelle Pettazoni's *The All-Knowing God*, trans. by H.J. Rose, (London: Methuen, 1956/i) is, on the other hand, a first-rate survey of sky and astral dieties broken down into twenty-four geographical-national divisions but does not always recount the full content of the myths involved.

A good, representative sampling of the myths involving divine kingship, divided into four geographical units, is John Weir Perry's *Lord of the Four Quarters: Myths of the Royal Father* (New York: Collier, 1970/ibp).

Animals and monsters, so long a concern of humankind, have inspired a great many myths and folktales. A useful dictionary with over 400 entries is Paula Sedgwick's *Mythological Creatures:*

A Pictorial Dictionary (New York: Holt, Rinehart and Winston, 1974/ib). It is pretty elementary, written primarily for a youthful audience, but it does cover the subject reasonably. Angelo de Gubernatis' two-volume work called *Zoological Mythology: On The Legends of Animals* (London: Trubner and Co., 1872; reprinted in 1977 by Arno Press, New York) was at one time an authoritative work on the subject but now is hard to find and is severely dated by later scholarship. Another older work, reprinted and made available a while back, is C.J.S. Thompson's *The Mystery and Lore of Monsters* (New Hyde Park, N.Y.: University Books, 1968/ip). Like de Gubernatis' work, it needs updating, but there are some helpful chapters, and many myths are retold in it. Relatively few myths are recounted in P. Lum's *Fabulous Beasts* (New York: Pantheon Press, 1951/i); his method instead is to summarize what was said about the beasts—their activities, shapes, etc.—in myths.

Special within the animals-monsters category are myths and folktales that include serpents/dragons and birds. Ernest Ingersoll's *Dragons and Dragon Lore* (Detroit: Singing Tree Press, 1968/i; reprint of the 1928 New York edition) remains, after many years, the standard work on its subject. Francis Huxley's *The Dragon: Nature of Spirit, Spirit of Nature* (New York: Collier, 1979/ibp) is an interesting and well illustrated work on dragons, too, and would surely do in lieu of Ingersoll's book. Joseph Fontenrose has incorporated into his broader study called *Python: A Study of the Delphic Myth and Its Origins* (Berkeley: University of California Press, 1959) a pretty good run of worldwide myths of combat with dragons for those who don't mind hunting through the book's 616 pages to find them. A very old source of some serpent myths is *Serpent and Siva Worship* (London: Trubner and Co., 1876), by Hyde Clarke and C. Staniland Wake. R. van den Broek's *The Myth of the Phoenix According to Classical and Early Christian Traditions*, trans. Mrs. I. Seeger (Leiden: E.J. Brill, 1972/i), is a fine study of the phoenix myth in all its varieties in the ancient world. And, back to Ernest Ingersoll, his *Birds in Legend, Fable, and Folklore* (Detroit: Singing Tree Press, 1968/i; reprint of the 1923 edition) is still our main source on its subject matter.

In addition to the topics already mentioned, there are a number of others to consider. If you're interested in the mythology and folklore of volcanoes, land forms, floods—anything related to the "earth"—the place to find it is Dorothy Vitaliano's *Legends of the Earth* (Bloomington: Indiana University Press, 1973/ibp).

George Frederick Kunz's *The Curious Lore of Precious Stones* (Philadelphia: J.B. Lippincott, 1913; reprinted by Dover Publications in 1971/ip) has many myths scattered throughout for the finding. A nicely organized worldwide survey, *Myths of the Origin of Fire* (London: Macmillan and Co., 1930), by Sir James George Frazer, is still found on the shelves of a great many libraries and is the main source in its area. Alexander Porteous' *Forest Folklore, Mythology, and Romance* (Detroit: Singing Tree Press, 1968/i; reprint of the 1928 edition) provides a broad spectrum of the world's myths and folktales (superstitions principally) set in and about forests. Charles Skinner's *Myths and Legends of Flowers, Trees, Fruits and Plants* (Philadelphia: J.B. Lippincott, 1925) is equally worthwhile for myths that are botanical in focus. And finally, although it's not particularly good for myths as such, it's the only book-length source on its topic that I'm aware of— that is, Denis de Rougemont's *The Myths of Love*, trans. Richard Howard (London: Faber and Faber, 1961). Maybe it will prove useful to you.

Dictionaries Incorporating Several Mythologies

Unfortunately, there still has been no individual, or group of people, energetic enough to put at our disposal a dictionary (which would have to be multi-volume) in which the known myths of the world and/or characters in all of those myths could be found alphabetically ordered. That is not to say that there haven't been pretty broad dictionaries of mythology, for there have been quite a few. It's just that the success of any one of them ranges from "limited" to something like "forget it" and that even with a splendid collection of the available dictionaries at the disposal of the myth student there are peculiar shortcomings.

Far and away the most successful dictionaries have been *Myths and Legends of All Nations* (Totowa, N.J.: Littlefield Adams, 1976/p; originally published in 1950 and known in one edition as *The Encyclopedia of Myths and Legends of All Nations*), by Herbert Spencer Robinson and Knox Wilson, and the more recent *Mythologies of the World: A Concise Encyclopedia* (Garden City, N.Y.: Doubleday, 1979), eds. Max S. Shapiro and Rhoda A. Hendricks. Each covers over twenty of the world's mythologies, the Robinson/Wilson volume in individual geographical and non-alphabetical sections (but with a useful alphabetical index), the Shapiro/Hendricks volume alphabetically. The problem of missing names and even mythologies limits the helpfulness of both books, but their incompleteness is secondary to what they do accomplish as handy reference sources where nothing more extensive or comprehensive exists. One or the other should be included in every library of myth books.

One other dictionary is a near competitor to the Robinson/Wilson volume. Frank Chapin Bray's *The World of Myths: A Dictionary of Mythology* (New York: Thomas Y. Crowell, 1935) or, as known in another edition, *Bray's University Dictionary of Mythology*, covers the world's major myth systems with each system organized alphabetically. Some of what is missing in Robinson/Wilson or Shapiro/Hendricks can be found here as well as much of what isn't. A major problem, though, is finding the book!

A large group of dictionaries is made up of volumes which aren't quite as ambitious. Egerton Sykes' *Everyman's Dictionary of Non-Classical Mythology* (New York: Dutton, 1952) and Marian Edwardes' *Dictionary of Non-Classical Mythology* (London: J.M. Dent, 1912) both cover a good many of the world's myth systems, excluding Greco-Roman, and are nicely organized in alphabetical order. *Putnam's Concise Mythological Dictionary* (New York: Capricorn, 1964/p; revised from a 1931 book called *Gods, A Dictionary of the Deities of All Lands)*, by Joseph Kaster, includes Greek, Roman, Egyptian, Babylonian, Hindu, Norse, Middle and North American Indian, and some entries on the sacred books of principal religions. P.G. Woodcock's *Short Dictionary of Mythology* (New York: Philosophical Library, 1953) is a highly selective dictionary of classical, Scandinavian, Egyptian and Indian mythology—as is Alexander S. Murray's *Manual of Mythology* (New York: Charles Scribner's Sons, 1900/i). The latter was at one time a standard among myth reference works but is now dated; it *does* have lovely illustrations. Bergen Evans' *Dictionary of Mythology: Mainly Classical* (New York: Dell Laurel, 1972/p) is a beautifully written dictionary—principally of Greco-Roman mythology, but with a healthy sprinkling of Arthurian legends, Norse myths, and the major names from Babylonian and Egyptian mythology. Whatever its limitations, and they are many, Evans' love of language makes browsing through it a delight.

Still found in some libraries is Joseph Thomas' two-volume *Universal* (or *Lippincott's*) *Dictionary of Biography and Mythology* (Philadelphia: J.B. Lippincott, 1915) with its principally Greco-Roman, very brief entries for myth characters. Two works more commonly found in libraries, college-level ones especially, are Gertrude Jobes' three-volume *Dictionary of Mythology, Folklore and Symbols* (New York: Scarecrow Press, 1961–62) and Funk and Wagnalls' *Standard Dictionary of Folklore, Mythology, and Legend* (New York: 1949 as two-volumes, 1971 as one, revised), edited by Maria Leach. Jobes' work has a good representation of important characters from the mythologies of the world but falls substantially short of being a *reliable* source for names or information. The Funk and Wagnalls' dictionary is much more reliable for those names but not without an inconvenience: some are in the alphabetical listings but most aren't, and even when they are, they are often accompanied by cross-reference directions to the large entry on the myth system from which they come. At the end of the dictionary is a "Key to Countries, Regions, Cultures, Culture Areas, Peoples, Tribes, and Ethnic Groups" which ordinarily must be consulted in order to come up with some information about a particular mortal or god.

A dictionary unlike all others but useful as a general reference work and as a resource tool for the symbolic meanings and associations of many of the major names in mythology is G.A. Gaskell's *Dictionary of All Scriptures and Myths* (New York: The Julian Press, 1960). Its title suggests a great deal more than is delivered but it does have a lot of off-beat information in its 844 pages.

Background Works

There are obviously hundreds, possibly thousands, of works which could be included in so sweeping a category as "background" to the study of worldwide mythology. Because some should be—and cannot appropriately be accounted for elsewhere in the guide anyway—the category is necessary. However, because most that could be covered here are better included in other sections, this category is relatively small.

The great majority of those myth books described in the preceding sections of this part of the guide have background material—usually as introductions to the individual myth systems but sometimes in the form of a broad, general introduction prefacing all or many of the systems collectively. Otherwise, Joseph Campbell's four-volume series called *The Masks of God* (New York: The Viking Press/ip) is of great value as a background source for worldwide mythologies. While it has in it an abundance of myths—mainly myths alluded to or briefly synopsized—it is an interpretation and analysis rather than a mythography as such. The first volume, *Primitive Mythology* (1959), is excellent for prehistoric and contemporary primitive mythology as well as for the terms relevant to their study. Volume II, *Oriental Mythology* (1962), covers India, the Near East, China, and Japan principally, with much on myth theory, too. Volume III, *Occidental Mythology* (1964), covers generally, but not in clear-cut geographical sections, Hebrew, Greek, Roman, Norse, Celtic, and some Persian mythology. The fourth volume, *Creative Mythology* (1968), is hard to categorize except to say that Campbell's aim is to show the breakdown of traditional systems and emergence of a "new" syncretism.

For generally useful articles on individual myth systems or groups, Funk and Wagnalls' *Standard Dictionary of Folklore, Mythology and Legend* (New York: Funk and Wagnalls, 1949 and 1971) cannot be overlooked as a single-volume source. Its "Key to Countries, Regions, Cultures, Culture Areas, Peoples, Tribes and Ethnic Groups" should be used, rather than the alphabetical listings, as the aid to finding individual systems. Also, two books by Lewis Spence, *An Introduction to Mythology* (London: George K. Harrap & Co., 1921) and *The Outlines of Mythology* (Greenwich, Conn.: Fawcett Premier, 1961/p; originally 1944), contain chapters devoted to broad background for the world's myth systems. A magnificent volume by S.G.F. Brandon, *Man and God in Art and Ritual* (New York: Charles Scribner's Sons, 1975/i) should also be mentioned as highly worthwhile. In it, Brandon, a well known comparative religionist, attempts to view the religious in man strictly through art and ritual, rather than through sacred texts. It can be most helpful as very general background to the mythologies of the world as a result.

Several broad histories will also serve as background to mythology around the world. *Atlas of World History* (Chicago: Rand-McNally, 1957/p), is a useful but very brief introduction to the worldwide histories involved, its main virtue for myth students being the 128 maps, 92 of which are in color. Virtually the same holds true for *Historical Atlas of the World* (New York: Barnes & Noble, 1972/i; revision of a Norwegian edition), which is filled with maps in color, 108 of them all told. There's also an index of place names, historical events, names of peoples, military expeditions, and voyages of discovery. *An Encyclopedia of World History*, 5th edition (Boston: Houghton-Mifflin, 1972), edited by William L. Langer, is loaded with information that will be helpful as background. Much more useful for straightforward historical narrative is the grand six-volume set called *The History of Mankind* (New York: Harper and Row, 1963 and following) sponsored by UNESCO and handled by the International Commission for a History of Scientific and Cultural Development of Mankind. The first two volumes, which cover from prehistoric times through A.D. 500 will no doubt be of most use, but some of the later mythologies will necessitate use of other volumes. Cambridge University Press has three separate historical series which are excellent, two of them directly useful for background work: *The Cambridge Ancient History* (twelve volumes published between 1923 and 1939) and *The Cambridge Medieval History* (eight volumes published between 1913 and 1936). The ten-volume set written by Will and Ariel Durant, *The Story of Civilization* (New York: Simon and Schuster, 1935–67) is, with the exception of the first volume, focused on western civilization, but for anything thereto related, it's a beautifully written background source. *The Epic of Man to 1500* (Englewood Cliffs, N.J.: Prentice-Hall, 1970/p) is a good two-volume history edited by L.S. Stavrianos. The *Larousse Encyclopedia of Ancient and Medieval History* (New York: Harper & Row, 1963), under the general editorship of Marcel Dunan and translated by Delano Ames and Geoffrey Sainsbury, is worldwide in scope but emphasizes Europe and the Near East. Another single-volume source is *The Columbia History of the World* (New York: Harper & Row, 1972), edited by John A. Garraty and Peter Gay. (Virtually all of the atlases and histories noted above are commonly found in better libraries).

Not in the same league with these histories is the two-volume *Western Civilization* (bp) set written by Walter Kirchner for The College Outline Series published by Barnes and Noble (New York: 1960, etc.). Volume I (to 1500) will be the more useful of the two, and especially helpful is the "Tabulated Bibliography of Standard Textbooks" at the beginning, which Kirchner has keyed to the sections of his own volume, making it easy to look up further discussions in additional texts.

Three books on ancient and earlier history should also be considered here since so many of the mythologies we have come from those times. *The Dawn of Civilization: The First World Survey of Human Cultures in Early Times* (New York: McGraw-Hill, 1961/i) is a mammoth book—404 pages, 940 illustrations, 48 maps and chronological charts—that covers the ancient Near East, Egypt, ancient Europe, the pre-Columbian Americas, India, and China. Jacquetta Hawkes' *The Atlas of Early Man* (New York: Saint Martin's Press, 1976/i) embraces "concurrent developments across the ancient world from 35,000 B.C. to A.D. 500" and is most useful. John E. Pfeiffer's *The Emergence of Society: A Prehistory of the Establishment* (New York: McGraw-Hill, 1977/i), a sequel to the author's *The Emergence of Man*, will be valuable for those who wish to see the jigsaw puzzle of the distant past put together with an emphasis on how society emerged from the varied and disparate pieces.

There are also many useful series of books which embrace culture, history, art, religion, and just about anything else relevant to individual cultures. While these will not all be equal in cultures covered, or in what is covered in the cultures, they are wonderful sources for background information, illustrations, chronological charts, maps, and the like. Some of the more notable ones are as follows. *The Great Ages of Man* series (1967/ib) published by Time-Life has over twenty volumes, at least half of which will serve splendidly for background—*Ancient China, Early Islam, Ancient America, Classical Greece, Imperial Rome, Cradle of Civilization, Historic India* among them. As is the case with all Time-Life books, each volume is colorful and informative. *The World of . . .* series published by Minerva Editions of Geneva, Switzerland, is a colorful and inexpensive series of shorter volumes meant for general readers. It includes books on the Aztecs, Incas, Persians, Egyptians, Greeks, Romans, and many others. That series would do yeoman service for junior and senior high students, as would the *Early Culture* series (ib) published by McGraw-Hill. It, too, has lots of color and includes volumes entitled *The Medes and Persians, The Sumerians, The Early Romans*, and so on. *The Ancient Peoples and Places* series (1956/ibp) of Thames and Hudson (London) and Frederick A. Praeger (New York) has a long run of lovely volumes in it that includes individual titles on the Celts, the Etruscans, the Phoenicians, etc. I haven't yet seen many volumes in the series called *The Making of the Past* (ib) published under the Elsevier/Phaidon imprint by E.P. Dutton of New York, but the few I have indicated it will be a first-rate survey of the ancient world as revealed through archaeology. A. Rosalie David's *The Egyptians* is an excellent example from the series. Among the larger and more expensive series is one especially worth pointing out: *The Arts of Mankind* series (ib) published by the Golden Press of New York under the editorship of André Malraux and Georges Salles. The books are all large, exquisitely done affairs, and include such titles as *Ancient Iran*, *Sumer*, and *Ancient Mesopotamia*.

All of the series bring to mind that if you are especially interested in pictures related to any mythology as background, general encyclopedias and histories of art are not to be bypassed! Since any library will have a good selection of these, and since there are so many, there's not much point in specifying particular ones here.

Prehistoric Mythologies

If it is true that much of what we can say in general about myths and myth systems is speculative, it is decidedly the case with prehistoric mythology. Anywhere in the world the archaeologist digs and pieces together without the benefit of concurrent written records of *any* sort, the word "prehistoric" prevails; anywhere a mythology is deduced from the on-site evidence of burial customs, ritual centers, carvings, and the like—and from nothing else except possibly comparison with other similar sites and conditions—the mythology is deductively reconstructed and is prehistoric. It is possible to have such "prehistoric mythology" wherever the archaeological record precedes the written one.

Where the written record actually succeeds the unwritten archaeological one—that is, where there is ample evidence that a given site or group of them is historically continuous from prehistory through the introduction of written records later on—it is possible to infer things about the prehistoric period from the written records. A great deal of such inferring has gone on about Middle America, where the history we know of starts with later Aztec-Mayan principally but very probably is premised in earlier Olmec, Toltec, Zapotec, and others. Much Egyptian history is reconstructed in this way, too, as are many other areas. In the case where an earlier mythology is reconstructed from the later historical and mythological record, we also have "prehistoric mythology," as a result.

Very important to thinking about prehistoric mythology is the study of primitive cultures by anthropologists. Much that is "known" about prehistoric mythology has been inferred from the remains of prehistoric cultures by comparison with what is known about contemporary primitive cultures. The idea is that those modern primitive peoples have much to tell us about ancient primitive peoples. This may or may not be a valid approach, and there is still a great deal of controversy over such methodology and over the very word "primitive."

Works Which Discuss and Analyze the Myths

There are not as yet a great many sources to find help with prehistoric mythology as such, but there are some. Joseph Campbell's *Primitive Mythology* (New York: The Viking Press, 1959/bp), in his *The Masks of God* series, remains the most extensive and valuable of the sources despite its heavily psychoanalytic orientation. Very brief chapters are devoted to prehistoric mythology in both the *Larousse Encyclopedia of Mythology*, ed. Felix Guirand (London: Paul Hamlyn, 1959/ip), and the *Larousse World Mythology*, ed. Pierre Grimal (New York: Putnam, 1965/i); the pertinent chapter in the former book is by G.H. Luquet and the one in the latter book by A. Varagnac. Also, don't overlook as potential sources discussion of early myths and history in many myth books devoted to individual myth systems from around the world. Many times, what is known of a given myth system has traces in it of earlier religion, divinities, and myths, and these are, as a rule, reported on in a separate chapter devoted to such remote times as may be involved.

Two theories of the interpretation and origin of myth have been responsible for a great many works which deal theoretically with prehistoric myth and religion. The "Natural Theory" or "old philological" school saw myth as a corruption of language through which ancient mythologies could be traced further back to their prehistoric forms. Because the theory has been discredited, there is no point in including works representative of the approach employed by the Naturalists here. However, another theory—variously called "Dumézilian," "new philological," "new comparative," and "Indo-European"—originated by the French scholar Georges Dumézil has been employed on European materials quite successfully in this century and has attracted numerous followers.

Dumézil's theory attempts, through the archaeological and linguistic evidence available, to reconstruct prehistoric European mythology to establish which deities from, say, Norse and Roman mythology can be traced backwards to distant origins. For a good introduction to this fascinating but difficult theory, see *The New Comparative Mythology*, revised edition (Berkeley: University of California Press, 1973/bp) by C. Scott Littleton. For an interesting article in which the theory is employed, and discussed to some extent, see Bruce Lincoln's "The Indo-European Myth of Creation" in *History of Religions*, 15 (November 1975), pp. 121-45.

Also a theoretical, highly speculative work having much to do with prehistoric mythology, *Hamlet's Mill: An Essay on Myth and the Frame of Time* (Boston: Gambit, 1969/b), by Giorgio de

Santillana and Hertha von Dechend, should be looked into as background and for some good ideas as to how tentative *all* looks at what is prehistoric *must* be.

Works on Religion and Related Matters

Books having to do with prehistoric religion are the most useful background to prehistoric mythology, of course, and here there are several very good works at your disposal. Marija Gimbutas' *The Gods and Goddesses of Old Europe: 7000 to 3500 B.C.* (Berkeley: University of California Press, 1974/ib) is a dandy book with 252 illustrations, 171 text figures, and 8 maps. Concerned only with prehistoric Europe, it nonetheless gives a pretty good idea of the gods and goddesses that may well be in the background of ancient mythologies elsewhere as well. There's also *excellent* geographical and archaeological background in the book. Gertrude Levy's *The Gate of Horn* (London: Faber and Faber, 1948/ip) undertakes to uncover the "living unity of belief and practice, which underlies the religious, artistic and social development of the ancient world before the revolutions of the iron age" and, ultimately, how this unity appeared and influenced European thought. It covers the paleolithic period through the ancient Greeks and includes earlier Egypt, Sumer, Central America, and Palestine. E.O. James' *Prehistoric Religion* (New York: Barnes and Noble, 1957/bp) is a good archaeological reconstruction— from artifacts, graves, etc.—that covers Europe, Egypt, and Mesopotamia principally. Johannes Maringer's *The Gods of Prehistoric Man*, ed. and trans. Mary Ilford (New York: Alfred A. Knopf, 1960/i), is also a good reconstruction from the archaeological evidence.

Background Works

For what may be considered the "history" of prehistory, there are many excellent works, some of them broad in geographical coverage, others relatively localized to Europe alone. One of the broadest and latest is Grahame Clark's *World Prehistory: In New Perspective* (New York: Cambridge University Press, 1978/i). It is a popular rendering of all that is currently known about many areas of prehistory and, generally, man's rise around the world. Jacquetta Hawkes' *The Atlas of Early Man* (New York: St. Martin's Press, 1976/i) is a beautiful book in large format, loaded with maps and charts. It covers "concurrent developments across the ancient world 35,000 B.C.–A.D. 500" and is divided into eight chronological sections. John E. Pfeiffer's *The Emergence of Society: A Prehistory of the Establishment* (New York: McGraw-Hill, 1977/ib), more or less worldwide in scope, is directed at showing that it was the problems faced by peoples in prehistory that forced the development of "society" as we know it to have been. V. Gordon Childe's *The Dawn of Civilization*, 5th edition revised (London: Routledge and Kegan Paul, 1950), is a reasonable survey, Mediterranean-Middle East largely, through the Bronze Age. His *Prehistoric Migrations in Europe* (New York: Humanities Press, 1969/i) is the sort of book that would serve nicely as background to Indo-European myth (which is prehistoric, remember), as would Stuart Piggott's *Ancient Europe: From the Beginnings of Agriculture to Classical Antiquity* (Chicago: Aldine Publishing Company, 1965/i) and C.F.C. Hawkes' *The Prehistoric Foundations of Europe* (London: Methuen and Co., 1940/i).

Specifically devoted to prehistory in Europe are such works as Geoffrey Bibby's *The Testimony of the Spade* (New York: Alfred A. Knopf, 1956/i), a popular history of archaeological work in the northern half of Europe. It incorporates a "history" of mankind there from the Ice Age through the rise of agriculture and the Vikings. And speaking of Ice Age, there's an excellent little article you might look into for background to prehistoric mythology—Alexander Marshack's "Exploring the Mind of Ice Age Man," *National Geographic*, 147 (January 1975/i), pp. 64–89. It has excellent photographs *and* text and covers 10,000–37,000 years ago. Considerably more recent a time period, in Great Britain alone from 1700–450 B.C., is gone into in Sir Cyril Fred Fox's *Life and Death in the Bronze Age* (London: Routledge and Kegan Paul, 1959/i). It contains some particularly good commentary on burial, ritual, and belief during that period. Robert Wernick and the editors of Time-Life Books put together *The Monument Builders* (New York: Time-Life Books, 1973/ib), a beautiful volume in *The Emergence of Man* series. Not quite all of it deals with prehistory, but its visual and textual tour of the megaliths and monuments of prehistory makes it well worthwhile as background. "Who Were the Indo-Europeans?" is an excellent article by Robert Claiborne which deals, in an introductory way, with the main problems of the study of Europe's most ancient humans; you can find it in *Mysteries of the Past* (New York: American Heritage Publishing Co., 1977/i), ed. Joseph J. Thorndike, Jr.

Two older works that may still be looked into are George Renard's *Life and Work in Prehistoric Times* (London: Kegan Paul, Trench, and Trubner, 1929) and Herdonau Cleland's *Our Prehistoric Ancestors* (New York: Coward-McCann, 1928), both of which have some contents devoted to religion and myth in them. And certainly there's no need to overlook chapters in standard books of history that are concerned with a broader spectrum of time than just prehistory. The chapter by Jean Piveteau entitled "Man Before History" in the *Larousse Encyclopedia of Ancient and Medieval History*, trans. Delano Ames and Geoffrey Sainsbury (New York: Harper and Row, 1963/i) comes immediately to mind as does the chapter entitled "The First Achievements of Man" in Chester Starr's fine *A History of the Ancient World* (New York: Oxford University Press, 1965/ib). Many others could be mentioned, but the examples should be adequate to make finding others simple enough.

A very important thing to keep in mind with any work on prehistory older than a few years is that it is only recently that the radio carbon dating schedule was adjusted to correct an error that had all of the ancient and prehistoric dating out of line for many years. See Colin Renfrew's "Ancient Europe is Older Than We Thought" in *National Geographic*, 152 (November 1977/i), pp. 614-23, for a brief discussion of this. For a longer one, see his *Before Civilization* (New York: Alfred A. Knopf, 1973/ib). An excellent example of an otherwise fine article on "Prehistoric Archaeology" now rather seriously flawed by its reliance on the unadjusted scale is L.R. Nougier's on pp. 143-59 in the *Larousse Encyclopedia of Archaeology*, trans. Anne Ward (New York: G.P. Putnam's Sons, 1972). It can still be read as one of the best introductions to its subject, however.

Occasionally the comparative method, that is the method employed wherein the anthropologist's findings about primitive culture have effectively been used to deduce information about prehistoric areas, results in a work generally worthwhile as background to the study of prehistoric mythology. One of my favorites is Ivar Lissner's *Man, God and Magic* (New York: G.P. Putnam's Sons, 1961/i). Lissner's theories are not all widely accepted ones (particularly on "primitive" monotheism), but for use of that comparative method, the book is excellent. Leo Frobenius, one of the earlier great ethnologists, wrote a book called *The Childhood of Man* (New York: Meridian Books, 1960; originally published in English in 1909) which should be looked into as well—not so much for the excellence of the comparative results as for the amazing quality of the speculations for so early a date. The book is an attempt to trace into prehistory the origin and nature of man's institutions, customs, and myths. Paul Radin, a well known later anthropologist, also wrote an admirable book employing the method, *The World of Primitive Man* (New York: Henry Schuman, 1953).

West Asian Mythologies

"West Asian" here refers to that portion of Asia west of Afghanistan and Pakistan. The land mass involved includes the present-day countries of Iran, Iraq, Turkey, Syria, Jordan, Israel, Lebanon, and the countries on the Arabian peninsula.

In his book *The Silent Past*, Ivar Lissner says "One and all, the civilizations of the past live on in us, for our lives are rooted deep in the remote, mysterious and ancient civilizations of the past." At no time is that deep-rootedness more conspicuous to all of us in the modern western world than when we look into the events, cultures, and mythologies of ancient Western Asia. It is to the Mesopotamians, Hittites, Canaanites, and Persians who lived thousands of years ago that western civilization and religious thought owes it clearest debt. The debt is not alone to them, of course. As each passing year brings to light new discoveries about the contacts these ancient peoples had, with one another and elsewhere, and about their thought, it becomes more and more apparent that what we once knew of our civilized origins in the west was but the exposed tip of an iceberg of enormous proportions. As recently as 200 years ago, no such statement could have been made, let alone proven, since at the time, the *Bible* and ancient Greece were thought to be about all there was to even the deepest portions of the iceberg.

To see how little we still know of the depth and girth of that iceberg, a relatively recent discovery seems worth a moment's attention. It was in 1956 that word reached the wire services that in the course of excavating the ancient city of Ebla (in northern Syria about thirty-four miles south of Aleppo), archaeologists had discovered 15,000 clay tablets in the archives of the royal palace there. Such news is always exciting to those of us who follow the progress of archaeologists and philologists awaiting the latest finds and translations that may bear on myth

---

The following symbols will be found, where applicable, in the bibliographic citation, usually following the date of publication: i = has useful illustrations; b = has a useful bibliography; p = has been published in paperbound edition.

study. Previously, in this century, there had been similarly stunning news from Bogazkoy (Hittite), Ras Shamra (Canaanite), Qumran (Biblical), and other archaeological sites, and each time the artifacts found and works eventually translated had been of great significance to myth students. So, when the wire services carried word that on the tablets the names of some of the Hebrew patriarchs were inscribed and that if those references are actually to the patriarchs, they are the earliest known references—also that Ebla was the center of a great civilization, equal in third millenium B.C. importance to Egypt and Mesopotamia—what were we to think? Just how much of that iceberg has really been hidden? What then about the still-to-be-discovered and/or excavated sites elsewhere in Western Asia? What about the Elamites, the Kassites, the Chaldeans, the Lycians, the Lydians, the Hurrians and others who once lived in the Near and Middle East? Are there great discoveries yet to be made that will further modify our tentative knowledge of that iceberg? Will what is still to be done at Ebla and the finds there make any difference?

Just such questions as these are what make myth study in general an exciting activity and, for people with western civilization in their blood, what make study of the myths of ancient Western Asia particularly absorbing.

Works that cross the boundaries of several of the cultures and myth systems involved (as well as the boundaries of others such as Egyptian, Greek, Roman, and Indian) will be found in the separate West Asian sections that follow, but since so many of the broadest works should prove useful, discussion of some of them is first in order. (Islam is discussed only at the end of this chapter since it is not ancient while all the others are.)

Collections of the Myths; Translations

There are plenty of books of myths which have at least some coverage of the Western Asian myth systems—a group including Mesopotamian, Hittite, Phoenician, Persian, Biblical, and, later, Islamic. An old standard is S.H. Hooke's *Middle Eastern Mythology* (Harmondsworth, G.B.: Penguin, 1963/ibp). Written by an authority on the area, the book is especially good on how some myths were diffused in Mesopotamia, Egypt, Ugarit (Phoenicians), Anatolia (Hittites), and Palestine (Old and New Testaments). Gerald A. Larue's *Ancient Myth and Modern Man* (Englewood Cliffs, N.J.: Prentice-Hall, 1975/ip) considers "the impact of ancient Near Eastern myth on modern society" and is centered on biblical mythology as the ancient/modern intersection. It is a fine book, arranged by myth types, with a good sampling of all but Islamic myth. John Gray's *Near Eastern Mythology* (London: Paul Hamlyn, 1969/ib) is an even more comprehensive source for Mesopotamian, Canaanite, and Hebrew myths since the book was written by an expert on Hebrew and Semitic languages. Fred Gladstone Bratton's *Myths and Legends of the Ancient Near East* (New York: Thomas Y. Crowell, 1970/ib) does not cover Persian, Biblical, and Islamic but does include the others *plus* a healthy section on Egyptian. Theodore Gaster's *The Oldest Stories in the World* (New York: Viking Press, 1952; Beach Press, 1958/p) is a retelling of selected Babylonian, Hittite, and Canaanite myths for the junior and lower senior high, but it can be used as a fair reference tool as well. Then, too, the encyclopedic *Myths and Legends of All Nations*, by Herbert Spencer Robinson and Knox Wilson (Totawa, N.J.: Littlefield, Adams, 1976/p), is useful for several West Asian myth systems.

Among the mythographies I have called "worldwide," the following will be of most use for the West Asian groups. *Mythologies of the Ancient World* (Garden City, N.Y.: Doubleday Anchor, 1961/bp), edited by Samuel Noah Kramer, has good individual sections on Mesopotamian (Sumerian/Akkadian), Hittite, Canaanite, and Persian. So, too, does the *Larousse World Mythology* (New York: Putnam, 1965/i), ed. Pierre Grimal and trans. Patricia Beardsworth. The *Pears Encyclopedia of Myths and Legends* (London: Pelham Books, 1976–78/ib) has these systems also, but you'll need Volumes I and III to get at them if you wish to study Iranian. The *Larousse Encyclopedia of Mythology* (London: Paul Hamlyn, 1959/ip), ed. Felix Guirand and trans. Richard Aldington and Delano Ames, has excellent sections on Mesopotamian, Phoenician, and Persian only.

If you're after creation myths from the West Asian systems, a few other books will be helpful. Maria Leach's *The Beginning: Creation Myths Around the World* (New York: Funk and Wagnalls, 1956) has any you will be looking for. Samuel F.G. Brandon's *Creation Legends of the Ancient Near East* (London: Hodder and Stoughton, 1963/ib) has a first-rate interpretive chapter devoted to each of the Mesopotamian, Biblical, Persian (and Egyptian and Greek as well) "cosmogonies" and is well worth checking into. If you're looking for translations of the original creation texts, Charles Doria and Harris Lenowitz have put together an excellent book called *Origins: Creation Texts from the Ancient Mediterranean* (Garden City, N.Y.: Anchor Books,

1976/bp) which includes the Mesopotamian, Hittite, Phoenician, Persian, and Biblical creation texts (and the Egyptian, Greek, and Roman, too).

Speaking of original texts, James B. Pritchard's *Ancient Near Eastern Texts Relating to the Old Testament*, 3rd edition (Princeton: Princeton University Press, 1969, also available in abridged form as the two-volume *The Ancient Near East: An Anthology of Texts and Pictures*/ip) is the standard source for all sorts of original texts in translation from Mesopotamia, Anatolia (Hittites), and Ugarit (Phoenicians). In it, you'll find the complete *Epic of Gilgamesh* among other things. *Near Eastern Religious Texts Relating to the Old Testament* (Leiden: E.J. Brill, 1978), ed. W. Beyerlin, can also be of significant use. *Documents from Old Testament Times* (New York: Harper Torch Book, 1961/ip), ed. D. Winton Thomas, is not nearly as comprehensive as either Pritchard's or Beyerlin's book, but in it you'll find a fair offering of Mesopotamian, Hebrew, Aramaic, and Moabite documents in translation. Not many are related to myth study directly, but the book is still of value. An earlier multi-volume work in which you'll find plenty of original texts in translation is *The Sacred Books and Early Literature of the East* (New York: Parke, Austin and Lipscomb, 1917). Because of its early date, it lacks quite a few works that have since been translated, but it does have a good selection of Mesopotamian, Persian, Hebrew, and Arabian texts.

Works on Religion and Related Matters

There are some really fine works available that deal with religion in ancient West Asia. E.O. James' *Ancient Gods: The History and Diffusion of Religion in the Ancient Near East and the Eastern Mediterranean* (New York: Capricorn Books, 1964/bp) is superb despite the fact that many of his ideas are speculative and not necessarily accepted today. The book covers all but the Islamic. Also, Henri Frankfort's *The Problem of Similarity in Ancient Near Eastern Religions* (Oxford: Clarendon Press, 1951) and Helmer Ringgren's *Religions of the Ancient Near East* (Philadelphia: Westminster Press, 1973/b) are both useful for background to the religions of ancient Western Asia. Ringgren's book is especially good on Mesopotamian and Canaanite religions. *Ancient Religions* (New York: Citadel Press, 1965/bp; originally published in 1950 as *Forgotten Religions*), edited by Vergilius Ferm, has separate chapters, each written by an expert, on

Mesopotamian, Hittite, Phoenician, Persian, and many others. I've used the book often and recommend it highly! Joseph Campbell's *Oriental Mythology* and *Occidental Mythology*, Volumes II and III in *The Masks of God* (New York: Viking Press, 1962, 1964/ ibp), are somewhat more sweeping in scope than West Asian, but each has much excellent information about the myths and religions of ancient West Asia—Islam included (Volume III).

In addition, there a number of books available that will serve nicely in more specialized ways as background to ancient West Asian mythologies. William Foxwell Albright's *From Stone Age to Christianity: Monotheism and the Historical Process*, 2nd edition (Garden City, N.Y.: Anchor Press, 1957/p) is, for instance, superb in showing the origins and development of monotheism from its roots in Mesopotamia and Egypt through the later biblical periods. Two works on the interconnection of myth and ritual are also worthwhile background: editor S.H. Hooke's *Myth and Ritual* (London: Oxford University Press, 1933)—which has separate chapters on Egypt, Babylonia, Canaan, and Israel/ Palestine—and E.O. James' *Myth and Ritual in the Ancient Near East* (New York: Praeger, 1958/b). Closely related are studies of divine kingship in the area. I. Engnell's *Studies in Divine Kingship in the Ancient Near East* (Uppsala: Appelbergs Boktryckeriaktiebolag, 1953) is one of the more useful on as broad a geographical basis as "West Asian" signifies. E.O. James has also contributed other books of note—*The Cult of the Mother Goddess: An Archae- ological and Documentary Study* (New York: Praeger, 1959/b) and *Seasonal Feasts and Festivals* (New York: Barnes and Noble, 1963/bp), both of which embrace the geographical territory of interest here among others. An A.M.S. reprint edition of Walter A. Jayne's 1925 work *Healing Gods of Ancient Civilizations* was released in 1976 and has information you might wish to make use of at some time. Kurt Seligmann's "story of magical ideas and manifestations in the western world," *Magic, Supernaturalism and Religion* (New York: Pantheon Books, 1971/i; originally published as *The History of Magic* in 1948) devotes three early chapters to Mesopotamia, Persia, and the Hebrews. Paul Carus' *The History of the Devil and the Idea of Evil* (New York: Bell Publishing, 1969/i) traces his title topics back to earliest Mesopotamia and Persia before getting to the biblical adaptations. Leopold Sabourin's *Priesthood: A Comparative Study* (Leiden: E.J. Brill, 1973/b), *the* work on priesthood in Asia and Europe, has much on its origins, mani- festations, and functions in the ancient Near East. S.G.F. Brandon's

Time and Mankind: An Historical and Philosophical Study of Mankind's Attitude to the Phenomena of Change (London: Hutchinson and Co., 1951/b) is a fascinating and useful source for background of the more specialized sort; it has several sections devoted to the ancient West Asian area. John Ferguson's *Moral Values in the Ancient World* (London: Methuen, 1958/b) has much of value despite its heavy orientation toward the Greco-Roman worlds. And, finally, for a full-scale run-down on the phoenix myth in early West Asia and later, try R. van den Broek's *The Myth of the Phoenix According to Classical and Early Christian Traditions*, trans. Mrs. I. Seeger (Leiden: E.J. Brill, 1972/b).

Works on Historical/Cultural Background

Histories—of the cultures, traditions, politics, and the like—are where one sees most clearly how high interest has been in ancient Western Asia. The number of books devoted to this area is incredible. James Mellaart's *Earliest Civilizations of the Near East* (New York: McGraw-Hill, 1966/i) is a good prehistory of the Mesopotamian, Syrian, and Turkish-area cultures dating from 3,000 B.C. and earlier. It's excellent for seeing the common roots of the civilizations that gave us so many myths. Leonard Cottrell's *The Anvil of Civilization* (New York: New American Library, 1957/ibp) is a good overview of the area that includes the Egyptians and Greeks as well. It has two chapters directly related to myth study, too. Very brief surveys of the same territory and history are Siegfried J. Schwantes' *A Short History of the Near East* (Grand Rapids, Mich.: Baker Book House, 1965/p) and Milton Covensky's *The Ancient Near Eastern Tradition* (New York: Harper and Row, 1966/bp). *Peoples of the Old Testament* (Oxford: The Clarendon Press, 1973), ed. D.J. Wiseman, is a first-rate collection of essays by professionals, each of which is focused on a culture contiguous to and/or involved in the Old Testament. There are thirteen essays all told, covering all the West Asian cultures of the era. Sabatino Moscati's *Ancient Semitic Civilizations* (New York: Capricorn Books, 1960/ibp) is also first-rate historical background to the study of West Asian myth. Here, the Babylonians and Assyrians, Canaanites, Hebrews, Aramaeans, Arabs (Islam), and Ethiopians are all discussed at some length. In his fine earlier work, *The Face of the Ancient Orient* (Garden City, N.Y.: Anchor, 1956), the full range of ancient Near Eastern cultures is covered, Egyptian included.

There are also books that are primarily histories in which the tying together of the West Asian cultures is more conspicious— either because the authors see diffusion as a greater factor or because they are clearly oriented toward demonstrating the overall spread and flow of tradition in the ancient world. Gordon V. Childe's *New Light on the Most Ancient East* (New York: W.W. Norton, 1953/ip) deals with the archaeology of the Near East and India in the light of the diffusion of cultures. Cyrus H. Gordon's *Before the Bible: The Common Background of Greek and Hebrew Civilizations* (New York: Harper & Row, 1962) is a marvelous example of diffusionist thinking in which the influence of Egypt and the Near East on Greece and the *Bible* is considered at length. Ephraim A. Speiser's *Mesopotamian Origins: The Basic Population of the Near East* (Philadelphia: University of Pennsylvania Press, 1930) has the thesis that the Elamites, Sumerians, Lullu, Guti, Kassites, Hurrians, and Hittites were all genetically related and formed the basic stock of ancient West Asia. Speculative, of course, but fascinating! W.G. De Burgh's *The Legacy of the Ancient World* (Harmondsworth, G.B.: Penguin, 1961/p; originally published in 1923) is concerned with showing the contributions of Israel, Greece and Rome to Christianity and the Christian world, but chapter two is on the early civilizations of the ancient Near East, so the book ultimately ties together the ancient West Asian cultures. So, too, does William Foxwell Albright's *History, Archaeology, and Christian Humanism* (New York: McGraw-Hill, 1964/b) even though its principal concern is historical, philological, and archaeological research associated with the *Bible*. Chapters four and five, "How Well Can We Know the Ancient Near East?" and "The Ancient Near East and the Religion of Israel," deal marvelously with syncretism there and with the general emergence from cultures prior to and coexistent with the Israelites. *The Bible and the Ancient Near East* (Garden City, N.Y.: Doubleday, 1961/b), edited by Ernest G. Wright, is a collection of essays in honor of Albright that ought not to be overlooked since many of the essays assess the interconnections between Near Eastern cultures and detail the state of our knowledge of each of the major ones.

Broad histories of the ancient world—wherever "world" be in this case—are useful, too, as background sources. Sweeping coverage of many cultures tends often to involve pretty good perspective on the interrelatedness of the cultures, as a matter of fact. Volume

I of the UNESCO *History of Mankind—Prehistory and the Beginnings of Civilizations* (New York: Harper & Row, 1963), by
Jacquetta Hawkes and Leonard Woolley, is an especially good
example. It has in it a great deal of historical and cultural information about early Western Asia (including Islam) and even has
a fine chapter called "Religious Beliefs and Practices" (part two,
chapter eight) in which *all* of the principal ancient religions are
touched upon. James Henry Breasted's *The Dawn of Consciousness*
(New York: Chalres Scribner's Sons, 1933) is both historical *and*
centered on the moral development of man prior to the Hebrews.
There's quite a bit of myth-related information in it, a few good
chapters on solar myth included. *The Dawn of Civilization* (New
York: McGraw-Hill, 1961/i), edited by Stuart Piggott, is a handy
historical background source that does some good tying together
of the cultures of Western Asia, as is Volume I of *The Story
of Civilization—Our Oriental Heritage* (New York: Simon and
Schuster, 1935) by Will Durant. There's much more space devoted
to the separate cultures in *The Cambridge Ancient History*, 3rd
edition (Cambridge: Cambridge University Press, 1971/i), but
interrelatedness is not much a concern of the writers. Less space
is, on the contrary, given the individual cultures with much
greater consideration for their interrelatedness in Volume I of *A
History of Asia* (Boston: Allyn and Bacon, 1964), by Woodbridge,
Conroy, and Ikle. The same holds true for Richard Mansfield
Haywood's *The Ancient World* (New York: David McKay, 1971/
ib), Chester G. Starr's *A History of the Ancient World* (New York:
Oxford University Press, 1965/ib), and Michael Grant's *The
Ancient Mediterranean* (New York: Charles Scribner's Sons,
1969/ib)—three among many similarly organized works which
give most attention to Greco-Roman history.

For some shorter, introductory discussions of West Asian
cultures don't forget general encyclopedias (*Britannica, World
Book* especially), and by all means don't overlook a pretty useful
group of other encyclopedias, histories, and dictionaries that
include the following: *Encyclopedia Judaica*, sixteen volumes
and yearbooks (Jerusalem: Keter Publishing House, 1972/i); the
multi-volume *World History of the Jewish People* (Tel Aviv:
Massadah Publishing Company, 1964/i); *Dictionary of the Bible*
(New York: Charles Scribner's Sons, 1963), ed. James Hastings;
The New Westminster Dictionary of the Bible (Philadelphia:
Westminster Press, 1970), ed. Henry Snyder Gehman. All have
much to offer for brief background, as do works like C. McEvedy's

The Penguin Atlas of Ancient History (Harmondsworth, G.B.: Penguin, 1975/p) and Keith Branigan's *Atlas of Ancient Civilizations* (New York: John Day, 1976/i).

Fritz M. Heichelheim's enormous three-volume *An Ancient Economic History* (Leiden: A.W. Sitjhoff, 1958–70) is a great source for information on early trade around the world, Western Asia included, and is particularly fruitful for the diffusionist-minded. George Sarton's *History of Science: Ancient Science Through the Golden Age of Greece* (Cambridge: Harvard University Press, 1952; reprinted by W.W. Norton, N.Y., 1970/p) has more to do with myth study than might be thought, its first three chapters of special interest as background to West Asian. So, too, with Otto Neugebauer's *The Exact Sciences in Antiquity*, 2nd edition (Providence, R.I.: Brown University Press, 1970/i). Robert W. Ehrich's *Chronologies in Old World Archaeology* (Chicago: University of Chicago Press, 1965) now needs some revision to fit the adjusted radio-carbon dating scales, but it is good for seeing how chronologies of ancient Europe *and* Asia were arrived at. Not all of the West Asian civilizations are included, but enough are to make looking into it worth the effort. Immanuel Velikovsky's *Peoples of the Sea* (Garden City, N.Y.: Doubleday, 1977/i) speculates on a radically different possibility concerning chronology in the first and second millenia, much of it relevant to West Asian myth study. John Gray's *Archaeology and the Old Testament World* (New York: Harper Torchbooks, 1965/i) puts Old Testament Israel in context; Part I is devoted to cultures contemporaneous to it and Part II to the time of Judges through later Old Testament times.

Works on Art

Art is well covered in geographically broad works, too. Henry A. Frankfort's *The Art and Architecture of the Ancient Orient*, 4th edition (Harmondsworth, G.B.: Penguin, 1970/ip) has 289 pages of text and close to 200 glossy black and white photographs that deal with the art of ancient Western Asia. Leonard Woolley's *The Art of the Middle East* (New York: Crown Publishers, 1961/i) hasn't quite as many pictures, although there are a substantial number of color plates, but the text is superb on Persia, Mesopotamia, Palestine, and Anatolia. Lloyd Seton's *The Art of the Ancient Near East* (New York: Praeger, 1965/ip) surveys Egyptian, Mesopotamian, Anatolian, and Persian art—with 249 illustrations, some in color. Giovanni Garbini's *The Ancient World* (London:

Paul Hamlyn, 1967/i) is a run-through of the art and architecture mainly of Mesopotamia, Persia, Anatolia, and Egypt that has 200 illustrations, 102 of them in color. William Stevenson Smith's *Interconnections in the Ancient Near East* (New Haven: Yale University Press, 1965/i) is not as useful for pictures (about 80 of them) as for its thoroughly engaging "study of the relationship between the arts of Egypt, the Aegean, and Western Asia." (Diffusionists note!) And finally, the standard source for pictures of art and ruins of the ancient Mesopotamians, Phoenicians, and Hittites is James B. Pritchard's *The Ancient Near East in Pictures*, 2nd edition (Princeton: Princeton University Press, 1919/i). Of reasonable importance is the end section of interpretive notes since many are in fact little essays, with topics like "Gods and Their Emblems" represented.

Don't fail to look into art histories and encyclopedias for help, by the way—René Huyghe's *Larousse Encyclopedia of Prehistoric and Ancient Art* (New York: Prometheus Press, 1963 /i) one of many possibilities—and into illustrated mythographies such as the many noted in the earlier section on worldwide mythographies. Veronica Ions' *The World's Mythology in Colour* (London: Paul Hamlyn, 1974/i) is a sterling example.

Mesopotamian Mythologies

Within the boundaries of present-day Iraq, generally along and between the rivers Tigris and Euphrates, is the region once known as "Mesopotamia" (literally "between the rivers"). From about where Mosul is now in the north to Basra in the south, interrelated ancient Mesopotamian cultures developed and flourished, if with some interruptions, from the fourth millenium through the second half of the first millenium B.C. First in importance were the Sumerians (the biblical people of Shinar) whose principal cities were Uruk (the biblical Erech), Eridu, Ur, and Lagash—all of them to the south. Their dominance spanned the years 2900–2350 B.C., the latter date marks the establishment, under Sargon, of Accadian rule over the federation of city states called Sumer and Accad (sometimes spelled "Akkad" or "Agade"). "Babylonia" became the name of southern Mesopotamia around 1800 B.C. just as "Assyria" became the name of northern Babylonia about two centuries earlier. The center of the Mesopotamian region thereafter became Babylon, the city of great biblical importance, and despite various conquests, overrunnings, and captivities by the

Hittites, Persians, and Greeks, it remained central in the region—geographically and in importance—until the very end of the first millenium B.C.

Even before the rather sensational recovery of the Babylonian version of the biblical flood story (Genesis 6:5-9:17) by George Smith in the 1870s, the Mesopotamian-area ruins had attracted *Bible*-knowledgeable travellers as early as the twelfth century A.D. The numerous biblical references to the peoples of the area and their ways (particularly in such stories as that of The Tower of Babel, Genesis 11:1-9) inspired the travels and precipitated fairly early identification of the ruins of specific places, such as Babylon itself in 1761. The result of this interest is a fairly extensive knowledge, through archaeological excavation, of the history, culture, art, religion, and mythology of those peoples called Sumerians, Akkadians, Assyrians, and Babylonians.

The mythology of Mesopotamia is usually treated as seamless fabric in the available discussions. But as is the case with *any* mythology spanning serveral thousand years, a myth system, like the "Mesopotamian," is less "system" than an agglomeration resulting from different groups of people adding to and changing the collection of myths over a long period of time. The Semitic-speaking people who succeeded the Sumerians, for example, no doubt inherited much of the Sumerians' mythology, but what they did with the myths is hard to know with any assurance given the extant written sources.

Collections of the Myths

Fortunately for all of us who wish to look into the mythology of Mesopotamia, there are plenty of resources. As Silvestro Fiore said in his *Voices from the Clay*,

> it now becomes more and more apparent that both Israel and Hellas had their roots in the spiritual realm of Ancient Mesopotamia. The theological and ethical revolution of the Hebrew people, the message of Greek poets and philosophers, are not a *creatio ex nihilo*; they are milestones on the road of human evolution, a road which started five thousand years ago in the "land of the Two Rivers."

In my opinion, though, the *better* places just to find the myths are relatively few in number. About equal in quality of presentation and completeness are the sections devoted to them in John Gray's *Near Eastern Mythology* (London: Paul Hamlyn, 1969/i), Felix Guirand's *Larousse Encyclopedia of Mythology* (London:

Paul Hamlyn, 1959/ip), trans. Richard Aldington and Delano
Ames, and Samuel Noah Kramer's *Mythologies of the Ancient
World* (Garden City, N.Y.: Anchor, 1961/bp). All of the sections
have some depth to them, and in all there is some respect shown
for the long and changing lives of the myths involved—particularly
in Kramer's where the distinctions between Sumerian and Akkadian
myth are clearly delineated. Part II of Fred Gladstone Bratton's
Myths and Legends of the Ancient Near East (New York: Thomas
Y. Crowell, 1970/i) offers a reasonable run-through of "Sumero-
Akkadian" myths also, and there are quite good, if somewhat
brief, sections on Sumerian and Babylonian myths in the *Larousse
World Mythology* (New York: Putnam, 1965/i), edited by Pierre
Grimal. Volume I of the *Pears Encyclopedia of Myths and Legends*
(London: Pelham Books, 1976/i) also has a section on Mesopo-
tamian myths that, while fairly brief, is adequate for most purposes.
Briefest of any coverage of Mesopotamian area myth that is at
all recommendable, though, will be found in *Encyclopedia of
World Mythology* (New York: Galahad Books, 1975/i). From
there, it is downhill to such scant coverage as is offered, for
instance, in James Weigel's *Mythology for the Modern Reader*
(Lincoln, Neb.: Centennial Press, 1973/p) and Theodor Gaster's
The Oldest Stories in the World (New York: Viking Press, 1952/p).
In fairness, however, each of the last three volumes mentioned
have other purposes than to be complete in their attention to
any one mythology.

Several older mythographies ought not to be overlooked as
sources for the myths of ancient Mesopotamia. However, it
should be kept in mind that what has been found in the last
fifty or sixty years does mean the older mythographies will
necessarily be either incomplete in some ways or in error. The
best of the older ones is Lewis Spence's *Myths and Legends of
Babylonia and Assyria* (Detroit: Gale Research, 1975; reprint
of the 1916 edition). Spence was a wonder for his time, and
the level-headed quality of anything he wrote means good reading
and *general* reliability. L.W. King's *Legends of Babylon and Egypt*
(London: Oxford University Press, 1918), Donald A. Mackenzie's
Myths of Babylonia and Assyria (London: Gresham Publishing
Co., 1918), and R. Campbell Thompson's *Semitic Mythology*
(Boston: Marshall Jones Co., 1918), are all of limited value and
unquestionably misleading (because of later findings) except
as you already know something about ancient Mesopotamian
mythology. If you do, what is said about the myths may be
interesting.

A few other books deserve separate classification for various reasons. Samuel Noah Kramer's excellent volume called *Sumerian Mythology* (New York: Harper Torchbooks, 1961/ip) is really a fine introduction to Sumerian myths and literature (including numerous translated excerpts) by a Sumerologist of the first order. S.H. Hooke's *Middle Eastern Mythology* (Harmondsworth, G.B.: Penguin, 1963/ip) has a good section on Sumerian and Babylonian myths, but it is a book which demonstrates the nature of these myths in relation to the mythologies of the Near East rather than a place to find myths. Hooke is a Near Eastern scholar of note, so the volume has importance and authority. It's just not a collection of myths as such. Gerald A. Larue's *Ancient Myth and Modern Man* (Englewood Cliffs, N.J.: Prentice-Hall, 1975/p) is a fine book for seeing the interrelationship of ancient Near Eastern myth systems with each other and, more particularly, for insights concerning the relevance of the myths' subject matter in the twentieth century. However, the book is organized by myth types. Using it to find individual myths is pretty much a misuse of it, therefore. Joseph Campbell has some interesting and useful comments on Mesopotamian myth in his *Occidental Mythology* (New York: Viking Press, 1964/p); particularly worthwhile is the way he neatly puts the nature of these myths in a larger frame.

Works on Religion and Related Matters

Books and articles having to do more specifically with Mesopotamian religion than with myths are to be found quite easily too, these days. Two of the three chapters in Helmer Ringgren's *Religions of the Ancient Near East*, trans. John Sturdy (Philadelphia: Westminster Press, 1973), are devoted to Sumerian and Babylonian-Assyrian religion, and for those who want a nicely integrated source for religion *and* mythology, this excellent volume is it. The chapters by Samuel Noah Kramer ("Sumerian Religion") and A. Leo Oppenheim ("Assyro-Babylonian Religion") in *Ancient Religions* (New York: Citadel Press, 1965/bp; originally published as *Forgotten Religions* in 1950), ed. Vergilius Ferm, are excellent as introductions to the religious beliefs and practices involved. Thorkild Jacobsen has given us what is probably the most elaborate overview and interpretation of Mesopotamian religion in *The Treasures of Darkness: A History of Mesopotamian Religion* (New Haven: Yale University Press, 1976/i). An eminent Assyriologist and philologist, Jacobsen employs four religious

metaphors to characterize the four millenia in which Mesopotamian
civilizations began, flourished, and faded, thereby clarifying the
phases of the religions. There are also several essays that pertain
to religion and mythology included in his *Toward the Image of
Tammuz and Other Essays on Mesopotamian History and Culture*,
ed. William L. Moran (Cambridge: Harvard University Press,
1970); and by all means worth reading are his short but excellent
overview entitled "Ancient Mesopotamian Religion: The Central
Concerns" in *Proceedings of the American Philosophical Society*,
107 (December 20, 1963), pp. 473–84, and "Formative Tendencies
in Sumerian Religion" in *The Bible and the Ancient Near East*
(New York: Doubleday, 1961), ed. G. Ernest Wright. J.J.M.
Roberts addresses the problems of the "interpretation of Sumerian
and Semitic elements in 'Mesopotamian' religion" in a way that
shows the several chronological layers of Semitic religion in his
*The Earliest Semitic Pantheon: A Study of the Semitic Deities
Attested in Mesopotamia Before Ur III* (Baltimore: Johns Hopkins
University Press, 1972). It is difficult reading and definitely for
deeper background because, through a diachronic study of the
deities worshipped at Ur III, it attempts to unravel the still seamless fabric called Mesopotamian religion. Easier sledding and
perhaps more immediately useful background will be found in
the chapter on Mesopotamian religion in Cornelius Loew's *Myth,
Sacred History and Philosophy: The Pre-Christian Religious
Heritage of the West* (New York: Harcourt, Brace and World,
1967), a book intended to clarify the religious background to
the Old and New Testaments. S.H. Hooke's *Babylonian and
Assyrian Religion* (New York: Hutchinson's University Library,
1953/b) is a short and somewhat older study that remains one
of the most impressive introductions to its subject matter.

There are a good many even older studies of Mesopotamian-
area religion and special aspects of it that continue to have some
limited value as background. Among them are Leonard W. King's
Babylonian Religion and Mythology (New York: AMS, 1976;
reprint of the 1899 edition), Morris Jastrow's *The Religion of
Babylonia and Assyria* (Boston: Ginn and Company, 1898)
and *Aspects of Religious Belief and Practice in Babylonia and
Assyria* (New York: G.P. Putnam's Sons, 1911), S. Langdon's
*Tammuz and Ishtar: A Monograph upon Babylonian Religion
and Theology* (Oxford: Clarendon Press, 1914) and Robertson W.
Smith's *The Religion of the Semites* (New York: Meridian Books,
1956/p; reprint of the 1889 edition). This last work is concerned

with Phoenicia and the Hebrews as well as Babylonia and Assyria. Langdon's work is pretty remarkable for its extensive information on the deities Tammuz, Ishtar, Geshtinanna, and some others.

Studies of the Myths and Religion

There have been a surprising number of special studies of Mesopotamian area myths and religions. One of the more exciting ones is that done by J.V. and Herman Vantisphout, *The Rebel Lands: An Investigation into the Origins of Early Mesopotamian Mythology* (Cambridge: Cambridge University Press Oriental Publications No. 29, 1978). G.S. Kirk's *Myth: Its Meaning and Functions in Ancient and Other Cultures* (Berkeley: University of California Press, 1970/p) has a provocative chapter entitled "The Nature of Myths in Ancient Mesopotamia" and, additionally, some discussion of Gilgamesh. "The Epic of Gilgamesh" is chapter ten in S.G.F. Brandon's *Religion in Ancient History* (New York: Charles Scribner's Sons, 1969). It provides excellent discussion of the eschatological "ethos" in the poem that tells one of the three principal Sumero-Assyrian myths. The same matter is addressed in chapter two of John Armstrong's *The Paradise Myth* (New York: Oxford University Press, 1969)—although here only briefly —and in Samuel Noah Kramer's "Dilmun, the Land of the Living" in the *Bulletin of the American Schools of Oriental Research*, 96 (1944), pp. 18-28. Kramer's "The Epic of Gilgamesh and Its Sumerian Sources," in *Journal of the American Oriental Society*, 64 (1944), pp. 7-23, gives good background information on the antiquity of the Gilgamesh story and its sources.

For a fine explanatory discussion of the creation myth of the Mesopotamians, see S.G.F. Brandon's *Creation Legends of the Ancient Near East* (London: Hodder and Stoughton, 1963). The myth is included in translation, as it is also in *Origins: Creation Texts from the Ancient Mediterranean* (Garden City, N.Y.: Anchor Books, 1976).

The Sumerian King List (Chicago: University of Chicago Press, 1939), by Thorkild Jacobsen, is a fascinating book to read as deep background into the philological and dating problems concerning that important genealogical myth. David P. Henige's *The Chronology of Oral Tradition* (Oxford: Clarendon Press, 1974) deals broadly with mythological versus historical time and includes an excellent appendix on the king list; the book might serve overall as background to that list *and* genealogical myth in the Near East even though it is concerned primarily with African materials. Thomas C. Hartland's "Some Thoughts on the Sumerian King List and Genesis 5 and 11B" in the *Journal of Biblical Literature*, 91 (March 1972), pp. 25–32, concludes that biblical writers did *not* draw upon the king list as a model—should the possibility that they did ever occur to you. And speaking of the matter of oral tradition as a factor in the dissemination of a myth—even where disparate possibilities like the king list from Mesopotamia ending up in the Genesis genealogies are involved—there's a fine discussion called "The Origin of Sumerian Mythology" buried away as chapter ten in Beatrice Goff's *Symbols of Prehistoric Mesopotamia* (New Haven, Conn.: Yale University Press, 1963). It's a clear statement concerning what can be said about myths when a long period of oral tradition lies behind their "final" form for posterity. The book otherwise is useful only in deepest background study, though.

"Myth-Ritual" is the umbrella term covering another batch of books and articles which could prove useful. C.J. Gadd's article on myth and ritual in Babylonia in the book called *Myth and Ritual* (London: Oxford University Press, 1933), ed. S.H. Hooke, is excellent. (The book's first chapter is a good general overview of myth-ritual as a concept.) E.O. James' *Myth and Ritual in the Ancient Near East* (New York: Praeger, 1958) also has a useful chapter devoted to the Mesopotamian area, and in S.H. Hooke's *The Labyrinth: Further Studies in the Relation Between Myth and Ritual in the Ancient World* (London: Society for Promoting Christian Knowledge, 1935), Eric Burrows' article, "Some Cosmological Patterns in Babylonian Religion," is worth reading. Sidney Smith's "The Practice of Kingship in Early Semitic Kingdoms" in *Myth, Ritual and Kingship* (Oxford: Clarendon Press, 1958), ed. S.H. Hooke, is a good place to see how the concept embraces kingship in Mesopotamia, as is Henri Frankfort's discussion in *Kingship and the Gods* (Chicago: University of Chicago Press, 1948). Ivan Engnell's *Studies in Divine Kingship in the Ancient Near East*, 2nd edition (Oxford: B. Blackwell, 1967), can be consulted *after* a few of the preceding works have been digested.

Closely related to those myth-ritual works are some others you may wish to work with. Leopold Sabourin's *Priesthood: A Comparative Study* (Leiden: E.J. Brill, 1973) looks into priesthood in the ancient world generally, the Mesopotamian version included. E.O. James' *Seasonal Feasts and Festivals* (New York:

Barnes and Noble, 1963) has a fine chapter in it on the New Year's festival in Babylon, an important religious occasion and most certainly a significant enactment of myth according to myth-ritual theorists. David Johnson's "The Wisdom of Festival," *Parabola*, 2 (Spring 1977), pp. 20–23, uses that occasion as its main example. The cosmological myth involved in the festival (called "Enuma Elish") is worth reconsidering for its value for living says J.J. Finkelstein in "The West, The Bible and the Ancient East: Apperceptions and Categorizations," *Man*, New Series 9 (December 1974), pp. 591–608.

According to many, as I have suggested elsewhere, the roots of western tradition go back far into ancient West Asia. It is not at all surprising, therefore, to see that much has been done to show either the indebtedness of later peoples to the Mesopotamians or to deal with the correspondences of myths and religious ideas in several cultures. Alexander Heidel's *The Gilgamesh Epic and Old Testament Parallels* (Chicago: University of Chicago Press, 1949) and *The Babylonian Genesis* (Chicago: University of Chicago Press, 1951) contain translations of the epic and Enuma Elish respectively and are very much concerned with the parallels between those works and what can be found in the Old Testament. André Parrot's *Babylon and the Old Testament*, trans. B.E. Hooke (New York: Philosophical Library, 1958), C. Leonard Woolley's *The Excavations at Ur and the Hebrew Records* (London: George Allen & Unwin, 1929), Gerald A. Larue's *Babylon and The Bible* (Grand Rapids, Mich.: Baker Book House/p), and Robert William Rogers' *Cuneiform Parallels to the Old Testament* (New York: Gordon Press, 1977) all tackle the archaeological evidence to explicate biblical references to Babylon and/or to deal with myth parallels of the two cultures. P. Walcot has taken the literary evidence from Mesopotamia and Anatolia to suggest possible influence on the later *Theogony* of Hesiod (Greek), and religious parallels between ancient Greece and Mesopotamia are dealt with in Lewis R. Farnell's *Greece and Babylon* (Edinburgh: T. & T. Clark, 1911) and Vassilios Christides' *Greek Goddesses in the Near East: A Study in Religious Syncretism* (New Rochelle, N.Y.: Caratzas Brothers Publishers, 1977). The latter work is more a study of the merging of goddesses from ancient Greece with those of Near Eastern cultures (Ishtar among them) than a study of Mesopotamian influence, though. Volume II of George Widengren's *King and Savior—Mesopotamian Elements in Manichaeism* (Upsala: Upsala Universitet Arsskrift, 1946) shows similar interest with Persian religion and myth. Sir James George Frazer deals with the interrelatedness of surface-different agricultural myths and rituals in his *Adonis, Attis, Osiris: Studies in the History of Oriental Religion* (London: Macmillan, 1906); the Mesopotamian parallels are dealt with at length. Irving Jacobs' "Elements of Near Eastern Mythology in Rabbinic Aggadah," which can be found in *Journal of Jewish Studies*, 28 (Spring 1977), pp. 1–11, has some useful treatment of Mesopotamian myth in later narrative contexts. Hyland A. Drew traces *The Origins of Philosophy* (New York: G.P. Putnam's Sons, 1973/p) right back to the Mesopotamian sources, Gilgamesh epic included, even though its main emphasis is on Greek origins. And how about this for a prospect: "Are the Sumerians and the Hungarians or the Uralic Peoples Related?" That's a short article by István Fodor in *Current Anthropology*, 17 (March 1976), pp. 115–18.

Translations

Sources in which you can find translations of the original Meso-potamian area texts are fairly accessible these days. Until recently, James B. Pritchard's *Ancient Near Eastern Texts Relating to the Old Testament*, 3rd edition (Princeton: Princeton University Press, 1969/p) was the best single-volume one. It has in its Babylo-nian section the Enuma Elish, Epic of Gilgamesh, and Kings List among other things. However, Samuel Noah Kramer's *From the Poetry of Sumer: Creation, Glorification, Adoration* (Berkeley: University of California Press, 1979/i) has supplanted it—not because of more translations as much as for Kramer's learned commentaries and the book's interesting illustrations related to the translations. Additionally, N.K. Sandars' translations, *The Epic of Gilgamesh* and *Poems of Heaven and Hell from Ancient Mesopotamia*, were both published by Penguin (Harmondsworth, G.B., 1962, 1971/p). Herbert Mason's *Gilgamesh* (New York: N.A.L., 1972/p) is a colorful retelling of the Gilgamesh story in verse rather than a direct translation of it, but it should be mentioned here even so. In *Documents from Old Testament Times* (New York: Harper Torchbooks, 1961/p), ed. Thomas D. Winton, you'll find the Enuma Elish and flood story in translation. Daniel David Luckenbill's two-volume *Ancient Records of Assyria and Babylonia* (Chicago: University of Chicago Press, 1926) has in it all of the translations of historical records available through the first quarter of this century. *Papyrus and Tablet* (Englewood Cliffs, N.J.: Prentice-Hall, 1973), ed. A. Grayson and D. Redford, has in it a small selection of translations of Mesopotamian and Egyptian texts that throw light on various phases of both cultures. In the multi-volume *The Sacred Books and Literature of the East* (New York: Parke, Austin and Lipscomb, 1917) you'll find some good translations, although as with the Luckenbill, the early date of the work means incompleteness. Silvestro Fiore's *Voices from the Clay: The Development of Assyro-Babylonian Literature* (Norman: University of Oklahoma Press, 1965) is split about equally between translations and the author's commentary, but it's a fairly useful book for the translations it contains. Isaac Mendelsohn's *Religions of the Ancient Near East* (New York: Liberal Arts Press, 1955) has a good number of primary source readings in the poetry, epics, rituals, and other religious writings from Mesopotamia and Ugarit (Phoenicia).

Works on Historical/Cultural Background

There is a special abundance of books and articles which treat the cultural and political history of the ancient Tigris-Euphrates region, some of them broadly, others just in part. Often there is some attention paid in them to religion and/or myth.

To begin with, there are three excellent chapters by Thorkild Jacobsen in *The Intellectual Adventure of Ancient Man* (Chicago: University of Chicago Press: 1946; reprinted in part as *Before Philosophy* in 1949/p) which provide an important overview of Mesopotamia's cultural "mood." Chapters seven and eight in *Peoples of the Old Testament* (Oxford: Clarendon Press, 1973), ed. D.F. Wiseman, are H.W.F. Saggs' "The Assyrians" and W.G. Lambert's "The Babylonians and Chaldaeans." Chapter four in Sabatino Moscati's *Ancient Semitic Civilizations* (New York: Capricorn Books, 1960/p) is a nice once-over of the Babylonians and Assyrians. Jacquetta Hawkes devotes a healthy portion of her *The First Great Civilizations: Life in Mesopotamia, the Indus Valley, and Egypt* (New York: Alfred A. Knopf, 1973) to Mesopotamia. There are pretty nice discussions of Babylon as such in Robert Silverberg's *Lost Cities and Vanished Civilizations* (New York: Bantam, 1974/ip; originally in hardbound—Chilton Book Co., 1962) and L. Sprague de Camp's *Great Cities of the Ancient World* (Garden City, N.Y.: Doubleday, 1972). Also, the discussions in many broader histories should be considered as brief possibilities; a great many of these exist, but as examples, Richard Mansfield Haywood's *Ancient Greece and the Near East* (New York: David McKay, 1964) and *The Near East: The Early Civiliza-*

tions (New York: Delacorte Press, 1967), by Bottero, Cassia, and Vercoutta can be mentioned.

Whole books on the subject abound. Martin A. Beek's *Atlas of Mesopotamia*, trans. D.R. Welsh (London: Nelson, 1962/i) has in it a series of fine articles on the Mesopotamian cultures from earliest times through the fall of Babylon and is especially good for its color maps. H.W.F. Saggs' *The Greatness That Was Babylon* (New York: N.A.L. Mentor, 1963/ibp; originally London 1962) is the one book I would be most inclined to give highest recommendation to as a single-source comprehensive introduction to Mesopotamian culture and history. Filled with pictures, drawings, charts, maps, and good reading, this book "has it all." Chapter ten is even devoted to religion. Certainly not to be considered very far away in overall sweep and contents is the book called *Cradle of Civilization* (New York: Time-Life Books, 1967/ib) by the editors of Time-Life and Samuel Noah Kramer, a foremost Sumerologist. Chapter five is called "Faith, Myth and Rites." The book has a great many pictures in color. A.L. Oppenheim's *Ancient Mesopotamia: Portrait of a Dead Civilization* (Chicago: University of Chicago Press, 1964/p) and Georges Roux's *Ancient Iraq* (London: George Allen and Unwin, 1964/i) are both also fine sources for history and cultural background.

H.W.F. Saggs' *Everyday Life in Babylonia and Assyria* (New York: G.P. Putnam's Sons, 1965) and Georges Contenau's *Everyday Life in Babylon and Assyria* (London: E. Arnold, 1954) are both somewhat more limited in both historical and cultural scope, but both have some good information on religion and myth. Similarly limited are Charles Seignobos' *The World of Babylon, Ninevah, and Assyria*, trans. David Macrae (New York: Leon Amiel, 1975/i); James Wellard's *Babylon* (New York: Saturday Review Press, 1972/ib); James G. MacQueen's *Babylon* (London: Hale, 1964); and Jorgen Laessoe's *People of Ancient Assyria*, trans. F. S. Leigh-Browne (London: Routledge & Kegan Paul, 1963). These are narrower in historical coverage, focusing, as they do, on post-Akkadian Babylon and Assyria. In the case of Laessoe's book, historical inscriptions are used to draw conclusions about the people and uncover the "reality" of the Assyrians. Older books such as A.T. Omstead's *History of Assyria* (New York: Charles Scribner's Sons, 1923) and Leonard W. King's *A History of Babylon* (New York: F.A. Stokes & Co., 1915) are severely restricted to a smaller pool of information available to the authors at the time the books were written.

Concerned only or mainly with the Sumerians are a group of additional works. Samuel Noah Kramer's *The Sumerians: Their History, Culture, and Character* (Chicago: University of Chicago Press, 1963/ib) is as wonderfully complete a history for adult reading as Elizabeth Lansing's *The Sumerians: Inventors and Builders* (New York: McGraw-Hill, 1978/ib) is colorful for adolescents. A couple of earlier works by Kramer are also worth looking into: *History Begins at Sumer* (London: Thames & Hudson, 1961/ib) for fairly full coverage, and "The Sumerians," an article in *Scientific American*, 197 (October 1957), pp. 70–83, for a brief introduction. Leonard Cottrell's *The Land of Shinar* (London: Souvenir Press, 1965/i) describes an adventurer-writer's fascination and experience with Sumerian archaeology and history, but it is certainly one of the most *delightful* books I've read on Sumer. Older volumes like C. Leonard Woolley's *The Sumerians* (Oxford: Clarendon Press, 1928) and Leonard W. King's *A History of Sumer and Akkad* (New York: F.A. Stokes & Co., 1910), though written by experts in their times (Woolley, the renowned archaeologist of Ur, for instance), are now so dated as to be almost worthless *except* in deep background study once other histories have been digested.

Several books concerned primarily with the earliest history of the region may be of use, though probably not for any but deepest background. Henri Frankfort's *The Birth of Civilization in the Near East* (Garden City, N.Y.: Anchor Books, 1959/p) goes far enough back into Near Eastern beginnings that half the book is gone before Mesopotamian cultures are gotten to, for instance. *The Sumerian Problem* (New York: John Wiley & Sons, 1969), ed. Tom Jones, contains essays by Assyriologists which point toward the problems of Sumerian origins and whether or not the Sumerians were the originators of culture. The essays span close to a hundred years so there's a pretty good history of "Sumerology" in it. M.E.L. Mallowan's *Early Mesopotamia and Iran* (London: Thames and Hudson, 1965) is generally good on archaeological evidence and studies. Books like Ephraim Speiser's *Mesopotamian Origins: The Basic Population of the Near East* (Philadelphia: University of Pennsylvania, 1930) and Sidney Smith's *Early History of Assyria to 1,000 B.C.* (London: Chatto, 1928) are just too early to be of value—except that in Speiser's book, the thesis that the Sumerians were part of the overall "genetically" related population of the Near East makes the speculative value still as good (or bad) as it was fifty years ago.

Works on Archaeology

Works having to do with Mesopotamian-area archaeology may
also be of help as background and are fairly abundant. Seton
Lloyd's superb synthesis of what has been done in Iraq to uncover
the ancient Mesopotamians, *The Archaeology of Mesopotamia:
From the Old Stone Age to the Persian Conquest* (London:
Thames and Hudson, 1978/ibp), heads the list. If you're interested
in a single-volume source, it has to be this one. Hans Baumann's
In the Land of Ur: The Discovery of Ancient Mesopotamia, trans.
Stella Humphries (New York: Pantheon Books, 1969/i) is a
beautifully color-illustrated work which tells the story of the
Mesopotamian archaeological discoveries and includes lists of
the principal archaeologists and major sites. Brian Fagan's more
recently published *Return to Babylon: Travelers, Archaeologists,
and Monuments in Mesopotamia* (Boston: Little, Brown, 1979/ib)
covers much the same territory in equally pleasant-to-read fashion.
In Glyn Daniel's *The First Civilizations: The Archaeology of Their
Origins* (New York: Apollo Editions, 1970/p) you'll find a good
overview chapter as well. Robert Koldewey's *The Excavations at
Babylon*, trans. Agnes St. Johns (London: Macmillan, 1914),
although old, is good reading involving a major complex of sites.
C. Leonard Woolley's *Ur of the Chaldees* (London, 1950)—later
updated as *Excavations at Ur: Record of Twelve Years' Work*
(New York: Apollo Editions, 1965/ip)—or, if you've the desire
for a more comprehensive work, his multi-volume *Ur Excavations*
(London: Oxford University Press, 1927/i, etc.), are all excellent
on their subject. Also, Shirley Glubok edited the *Ur Excavations*
work into *Discovering the Royal Tombs at Ur* (London: Macmillan, 1969/i); it has a hundred or so marvelous photographs in
black and white and has a very readable text. Geoffrey Bibby's
Looking for Dilmun (New York: Alfred A. Knopf, 1969/ip)
isn't properly Mesopotamian, but because Dilmun is the "Paradise"
of the Epic of Gilgamesh, the book may well prove of high interest
once looked into!

Quite a number of books have chapters in them which record
particular Mesopotamian "digs" and the finds there. C.W. Ceram's
Gods, Graves, and Scholars, 2nd edition (New York: Alfred A.
Knopf, 1951; Bantam, 1972/ip), has a good batch of such chapters
in part three, and in his *Hands on the Past* (New York: Alfred A.
Knopf, 1966/ip), the archaeologists' own reports on their finds
are included as separate chapters. The two books make good

companion volumes. Chapter two of William Foxwell Albright's
Archaeology and the Religion of Israel (Baltimore: Johns Hopkins
Press, 1942) has some useful information on Mesopotamian-area
archaeology, religion, and mythology. J. Mellaart's *The Chalcolithic
and Early Bronze Ages in the Near East and Anatolia* (Beirut:
Khayats, 1966), as a broad introduction to archaeology there,
has some good discussion of Mesopotamian-area finds and work.

If the deciphering of cuneiform—the step which once accomplished opened up Mesopotamian mythology to the world—
interests you, see A.J. Booth's authoritative discussion in *The
Discovery and Decipherment of the Trilingual Cuneiform Inscriptions* (London: Longmans, Green and Co., 1902). Shorter, but
nonetheless interesting, introductory discussions can be found in
many other books. The following all recommended as possibilities:
Ernst Doblhofer's *Voices in Stone: The Decipherment of Ancient
Scripts and Writings*, trans. Mervyn Savill (New York: The Viking
Press, 1961/i); Leo Deuel's *Testaments of Time: The Search for
Lost Manuscripts and Records* (New York: Alfred A. Knopf,
1965/i); and Maurice Pope's *The Story of Archaeological Deci-
pherment: From Egyptian Hieroglyphs to Linear B* (New York:
Charles Scribner's Sons, 1975/ip).

Since "The Flood" has been a most significant story translated
from the cuneiform, I might also add that articles, films, books,
and even symposia proceedings have been appearing regularly on
it for years—from most recently as in Fred Warshofsky's "Noah,
The Flood, The Facts," in *Reader's Digest*, 111 (September 1977),
pp. 129-34, to articles like C. Leonard Woolley's "The Flood" in
Myth or Legend? (New York: Capricorn Books, 1968/p), to a
series of seven audio cassettes entitled *The Flood Myth: An
Inquiry into Causes and Circumstances* put out in 1976 by the
University of California at Berkeley's Media Extension Service
(Set no. AT 335-41). While all seven tapes are of interest ultimately, only the first deals directly with the Mesopotamian
sources. Experts discuss the evidence for a flood and work with
parallels (Old Testament).

Works on Art

The art of Mesopotamia has been well covered in books. James B.
Pritchard's *The Ancient Near East in Pictures*, 2nd edition (Princeton: Princeton University Press, 1969/ip) covers, in hundreds of
pictures, the arts of Mesopotamia, Egypt, Ugarit, and Anatolia.
Lloyd Seton's *The Art of the Ancient Near East* (New York:

Praeger, 1969/i) has in it many pictures of Mesopotamian art
in color and black and white. Eva Strommenger's *5000 Years of
the Art of Mesopotamia*, trans. Christina Haglund (New York:
Harry N. Abrams, 1964/i), is certainly one of the most exciting
of the sources—both for pictures *and* text. Two large volumes by
André Parrot in the *Arts of Mankind* series, *Sumer: The Dawn of
Art* (New York: Golden Press, 1961/ib) and *Ninevah and Babylon*
(London: Thames and Hudson, 1969/ib) are both gorgeous
volumes filled with photographs in color and black and white,
maps, and the like. I highly recommend them.

Hittite Mythologies

The Hittites were an Indo-European people who around 2000 B.C.
settled in Asia Minor in what is now Turkey, Northern Syria, and a
small portion of northern Iraq. Their empire grew and flourished
until about 1200 B.C., when it fell to invaders. It flourished
roughly concurrently with the period of the biblical patriarchs
through the Israelite settlement, Egypt's middle and new kingdoms, the Minoan and Mycenaean empires on Crete and in Greece,
the heyday of the Canaanites, and the first Babylonian empire
through the first two rulers of the Assyrian empire.

Although the Hittites have long been known about from biblical references (Genesis 15:20, Deuteronomy 7:1, Judges 3:5,
Joshua 1:4, etc.), it is only during the second quarter of this
century that any clear understanding of their culture and mythology was made possible through a number of earlier archaeological
excavations and subsequent translations of Hittite hieroglyphs.
Of particular importance among the excavations is the site of
the ancient Hittite capital, Hattusas, near Bogazkoy, a Turkish
village west of Ankara in the region called Anatolia. Systematic
archaeological work there began in 1906 and has been continuing
intermittently ever since. Some 10,000 tablets have been found
at Bogazkoy, among which are many relating to Hittite religion
and ritual.

Because the Hittites were politically a group of nations (perhaps
"confederation" would be a more appropriate designation), it is
not surprising that the existing Hittite religion and mythology is
syncretist, with deities of Sumerian, Canaanite, and, particularly,
Hurrite origin present. It is also not surprising that with so late
a start on understanding the Hittites, we are not blessed with
quite the abundance of works in English that we are with the
Mesopotamian cultures.

Works on the Myths and Religion

By far the best sources for the myths and religion of the Hittites are two articles by Hans G. Guterbock, one entitled "Hittite Mythology" in *Mythologies of the Ancient World* (Garden City, N.Y.: Anchor books, 1969/ip), ed. Samuel Noah Kramer, and "Hittite Religion" in *Ancient Religions* (New York: Citadel Press, 1965/p; also published as *Forgotten Religions* in hardbound), ed. Vergilius Ferm. O.R. Gurney's *Some Aspects of the Hittite Religion* (Leiden: E.J. Brill, 1977), which was a Schweich Lecture at the British Academy in 1976, is also one of the better sources on Hittite religion and mythology. The *Larousse World Mythology*, trans. Patricia Beardsworth (New York: Putnam, 1965/i), ed. Pierre Grimal, has a section on the Hurrites and Hittites, but it is not as cogent as Guterbock's two articles. Chapter one in Volume I of the *Pears Encyclopedia of Myths and Legends* (London: Pelham Books, 1976/i) also has a section on Hittite mythology, as does Fred Gladstone Bratton's *Myths and Legends of the Ancient Near East* (New York: Thomas Y. Crowell, 1970). Both are adequate only. The chapter on Hittite mythology in S.H. Hooke's *Middle Eastern Mythology* (Harmondsworth, G.B.: Penguin, 1963/p) is very brief but does cover the three main myths—those of Ullikummis, Illuyankas, and Telepinus—and does some tying in of the myths of the Hittites with those of other Near Eastern cultures. The section devoted to "Hittite Stories" in Theodor H. Gaster's *The Oldest Stories in the World* (New York: Viking Press, 1952; Boston: Beacon Press, 1958/p) is quite good, despite the book's being for younger readers, and his commentaries on the myths are incisive. "The Hittites" in the *Encyclopedia of World Mythology* (New York: Galahad Books, 1975) is pretty brief, but in a pinch it will do.

Works on Historical/Cultural Background

Fortunately, there are several first-rate books which combine at least some discussion of Hittite religion and mythology with an overall concern for history, archaeology, and culture. *The Empire Builders* (New York: Time-Life Books, 1974/ib), by Jim Hicks and the editors of Time-Life, is definitely the most colorful and possibly the most useful to beginners. The pictures alone are worth the price, but the text, which includes a section called "An Illustrated Sampler of Hittite Myths," is readable and informative as well. Johannes Lehmann's *The Hittites: People of a Thousand Gods*, trans. J. Maxwell Brownjohn (New York: Viking Press, 1977/i) hasn't the color, but it does have the most up-to-date and well researched text I've seen, *and* it has a good deal on the myths and religions of the Hittites. J.G. McQueen's *The Hittites and Their Contemporaries in Asia Minor* (Boulder, Colo.: Westview Press, 1975/ib), which is Volume 83 in that ever useful series called *Ancient Peoples and Places*, has lots of drawings and black and white pictures. It's written by an expert in Anatolian studies and includes a fine chapter on the religion of the Hittites. O.R. Gurney's superb *The Hittites*, 2nd edition (Harmondsworth, G.B.: Penguin, 1954/ibp) was for some years the standard work on the Hittites and will still serve well in lieu of a later book. Chapter seven is on Hittite religion. C.W. Ceram's *The Secret of the Hittites*, trans. Richard and Clara Winston (New York: Alfred A. Knopf, 1956/ibp) is also worth considering, but not so much for the history and religion as for its cultural survey and record of archaeological and philological work. H.A. Hoffner's chapter entitled "The Hittites and Hurrians" in *Peoples of the Old Testament* (Oxford: Clarendon Press, 1973) is a good, brief introduction to the Hittites—as will be most articles in major encyclopedias, including religious encyclopedias and dictionaries. Older books like John Garstang's *The Hittite Empire* (London: Constable and Co., 1929) should be considered unreliable for the reason that Hittite hieroglyphs were first deciphered in 1915 and because there have been several major additions to our knowledge of the Hittite language and culture since 1929. A good review of the status of Anatolian studies, Hittite included, was written by Albrecht Goetze and is included in *The Bible and the Ancient Near East* (Garden City, N.Y.: Doubleday, 1961/i). It is fast becoming dated, but for a good, concise review it is still of use.

Studies of the Myths and Religion

Not a great deal has been done in English on Hittite myth and religion that is of special help to myth students. However, there are a few things that can be mentioned. For instance Arvid S. Kapelrud's *Baal in the Ras Shamra Texts* (Copenhagen: G.E.C., Gad, 1952) investigates Canaanite texts and nicely relates the findings to Hittite and other myth groups/systems. S.H. Hooke's *Myth, Ritual and Kingship* (Oxford: Clarendon Press, 1958) has an excellent article in it by O.R. Gurney, "Hittite Kingship," that should be read by those deepening their understanding of Hittite myth and religion. Theodor H. Gaster's *Thespis: Ritual, Myth, and Drama in the Ancient Near East*, new edition (Garden City, N.Y.: Doubleday, 1961; New York: W.W. Norton, 1977/p) has, in the course of its exploration of the remains of seasonal drama-ritual, some useful discussion of the Hittites' part in it. Chapter five of E.O. James' *Seasonal Feasts and Festivals* (New York: Barnes and Noble, 1963/p) is on the Hittites and Greeks. There's also a good deal of helpful information in his *The Ancient Gods: The History and Diffusion of Religion in the Ancient Near East and the Eastern Mediterranean* (New York: Capricorn Books, 1964/p). And if you're ever interested in a rationalist explanation of the Ullikummis myth, see chapter thirteen in Jan Schoo's *Hercules' Labors: Fact or Fiction?* (Chicago: Argonaut, 1969); it's interesting and fun to read—as is the whole book otherwise, but in connection with Greek myth or as an example of rationalist interpretation.

Translations, Archaeology, and Art

The best place to look for translations from Hittite works is J. Pritchard's *Ancient Near Eastern Texts Relating to the Old Testament*, 3rd edition (Princeton: Princeton University Press, 1969/p). Even here, though, you will not find as much as has been translated into German, the main language (and country) for Hittite scholarship. Charles Doria and Harris Lenowitz have included the translated text of the Hittite creation myth in their *Origins: Creation Texts from the Ancient Mediterranean* (Garden City, N.Y.: Anchor Books, 1976).

There is evidence that the Hittites and earliest Greeks had strong ties. For some of the evidence, see G.L. Huxley's *Achaeans and Hittites* (Oxford: Vincent-Baxter, 1960), which handles both the linguistic and myth connections pretty well. Simon Davis, in *The Decipherment of Minoan Linear A and Pictographic Scripts* (Johannesburg: Witwaterstrand University Press, 1967), concludes "that the language spoken by the Minoans [Crete] is Hittite." The book is a good one for seeing how philological evidence is used and arrived at. On the other hand, there are plenty of scholars who would argue through the myth sources alone. Two such arguments, though not overly ambitious, are Hans G. Guterbock's "The Hittite Version of the Hurrian Kumarbi Myths: Oriental Forerunners of Hesiod," *American Journal of Archaeology*, 52 (1948), pp. 122–34, and P. Walcot's *Hesiod and the Near East* (Cardiff: University of Wales, 1966). The latter work considers the potential influence on the *Theogony* of the Hittites, Babylonians, and Egyptians.

Good chapters on the archaeology and deciphering of Hittite hieroglyphs are contained in Maurice Pope's *The Story of Archaeological Decipherment* (New York: Charles Scribner's Sons,

1975/i) and Ernst Doblhofer's *Voices in Stone: The Decipherment of Ancient Scripts and Writings*, trans. Mervyn Savill (New York: The Viking Press, 1961/i). There are three good articles by the people directly involved in Hittite archaeology and philology included in C.W. Ceram's *Hands on the Past* (New York: Alfred A. Knopf, 1966/p). U. Alkim's *Anatolia I: From the Beginnings to the End* (London: Barrie & Rockliff, 1970/i) is the most authoritative source for information on the archaeological work done on the Hittites and other ancient Anatolian cultures, but you'll also find some help in George E. Bean's *Aegean Turkey: An Archaeological Guide* (London: Ernest Benn, 1966/i) and Dora Jane Hamblin's *Buried Cities and Ancient Treasures* (New York: Simon and Schuster, 1973/i). The best sources otherwise are the cultural histories listed above. James Mellaart's *The Chalcolithic and Early Bronze Ages in the Near East and Anatolia* (Beirut: Khayats, 1966) is a good survey of Assyrian, Egyptian, and Anatolian archaeology, so it should be considered, too, as should his fine *The Archaeology of Ancient Turkey* (Totowa, N.J.: Rowman and Littlefield, 1978/i).

In addition to the discussions and pictures of Hittite art that you'll find in other books already mentioned, Ekrem Akurgal's *The Art of the Hittites* (New York: Harry N. Abrams, 1962/i) is filled with photographs of artifacts and other archaeological remains—many of them in color. The text is also worthwhile since there's much of interest to myth students in it. Also of use is M. Vieyra's *Hittite Art: 2300–750 B.C.* (London: A. Tiranti, 1955/i), although it's not quite as well illustrated or as useful to myth students in what it has to say. James B. Pritchard's *The Ancient Near East in Pictures* (Princeton: Princeton University Press, 1969/i) has a fair run of pictures on Hittite subjects and should be considered a useful source.

Canaanite Mythologies

As early as the third millenium B.C., the land of Canaan was a crossroads between the Mediterranean world, Egypt included, and the Middle East. Canaanite homeland settlements—after about 1500 B.C., "Phoenician"—were scattered up and down the eastern Mediterranean coast, in the north from about where Adana is in modern Turkey to where Gaza still is at the southern tip of Israel. In 574 B.C. Tyre fell to Nebuchadnezzar of Babylonia, ending the Phoenicians' control of their homeland, but as late as the second century B.C., settlements abroad were still thriving.

A seafaring people, the Canaanites travelled far and wide establishing colonies throughout the Mediterranean (Carthage on the north coast of Africa a principal one), venturing into the Atlantic Ocean, no doubt journeying around Africa and possibly sailing as far as the Americas. The likelihood of such broad contact makes the Canaanites and their mythology especially important as a link between various cultures and mythologies in the ancient world.

Until the exciting discovery of ancient Ugarit (on the coast in Syria) in 1928 at a site called Ras Shamra, very little was known about Canaanite mythology. Phoenician inscriptions and the *Bible* had long been a principal source of Canaanite myths. However, while the palace in Ugarit was being excavated, archives were uncovered in which were found cuneiform tablets in Accadian, Hittite, and Hurrian, and a language related to Hebrew and Phoenician. Great chunks of mythology were included that immediately became important not only as missing links in Canaanite mythology, but which as well provided reasonable proof of the interconnections of Canaanite with biblical myth, and possibly with other mythologies in the Near and Middle East.

Needless to say, such interesting finds and speculations have had their effect in works available to myth students. There are plenty of sources for the myths, religion, history, cultural background, and translated texts of the peoples now called just about interchangeably "Phoenicians" or "Canaanites."

Collections of the Myths

I personally like John Gray's *Near Eastern Mythology* (London: Paul Hamlyn, 1969/ib) as a source for Canaanite myths and religion. It's nicely organized and beautifully illustrated—as are the two other sections in the book devoted to ancient Mesopotamian and Israeli mythology. Cyrus Gordon's chapter on Canaanite myth in *Mythologies of the Ancient World* (Garden City, N.Y.: Anchor, 1961/bp) includes some translated excerpts and is a helpful if brief source for the myths. L. Delaporte's "Phoenician Mythology" in the *Larousse Encyclopedia of Mythology* (London: Paul Hamlyn, 1959/ip) is also a brief but helpful source as are the sections devoted to them in Fred Gladstone Bratton's *Myths and Legends of the Ancient Near East* (New York: Thomas Y. Crowell, 1970/i) and in Volume I of the *Pears Encyclopedia of Myths and*

Legends (London: Pelham Books, 1976). S.H. Hooke nicely outlines some of the myths found on the tablets at Ugarit in his *Middle Eastern Mythology* (Harmondsworth, G.B.: Penguin, 1963/p), noting their importance to the western world in saying that they "show clear evidence of the influence of both Egyptian and Babylonian mythology" and that "Canaanite mythology has left marked traces in Hebrew poetry and mythology." Smaller sections yet are devoted to the myths in Pierre Grimal's *Larousse World Mythology*, trans. Patricia Beardsworth (New York: Putnam, 1965/i); the *Encyclopedia of World Mythology* (New York: Galahad Books, 1975/i); and Theodor Gaster's *The Oldest Stories in the World* (New York: Viking Press, 1952; Boston: Beacon Press, 1958/p). Gaster has only three myths he deals with, but perhaps they should be looked at for the valuable commentaries that follow each. R. Campbell Thompson's volume called *Semitic Mythology* in *The Mythology of All Races* series (Boston: Marshall Jones Company, 1916-32) came along too early to incorporate the Ugaritic material and is therefore quite limited in value.

Works on Religion and Related Matters

Another fine source for information about the religion of the Canaanites—in addition to that found in John Gray's *Near Eastern Mythology*, that is—is Theodor H. Gaster's article in *Ancient Religions* (New York: Citadel Press, 1965/ip; originally in hardbound as *Forgotten Religions* in 1950), ed. Vergilius Ferm. It is excellent, as is Gray's chapter entitled "The Religion of Canaan" in his book *The Legacy of Canaan* (Leiden: E.J. Brill, 1957). Briefer summaries can be found in Helmer Ringgren's *Religions of the Ancient Near East*, trans. John Sturdy (Philadelphia: Westminster Press, 1973) and in many of the encyclopedias, atlases, and texts devoted to the world's religions.

Works having immediate relevance as background to the study of Canaanite mythology and religion are too numerous to cover completely. For instance, chapter three in William Foxwell Albright's *Archaeology and the Religion of Israel* (Baltimore: The Johns Hopkins Press, 1942) is very good on Canaanite mythology as such and on the related archaeological evidence. Chapters two and three in a work by John Gray mentioned earlier, *The Legacy of Canaan* (Leiden: E.J. Brill, 1957), are great for Canaanite "Myths of the Fertility Cult" and "Saga and Legend." There's a lot in E.O. James' *The Ancient Gods* (New York: Capricorn Books, 1960/p) that you'll find useful, too. Julian Obermann's

Ugaritic Mythology: A Study of Its Leading Motif (New Haven, Conn.: Yale University Press, 1948), Arvid S. Kapelrud's *Baal in the Ras Shamra Texts* (Copenhagen: G.E.C., Gad, 1952), and Maurice H. Pope's *El in the Ugaritic Texts* (Leiden: E.J. Brill, 1955) will all challenge the reader due to their technical (and sometimes obscure) content, but each is a *superb* background source for those interested. J.C.L. Gibson's "Myth, Legend and Folk-Lore in the Ugaritic Keret and Aghat Texts," on page 60 and following in *Supplements to Vetus Testamentum: Congress Volume* (Leiden: E.J. Brill, 1975), is much easier, definitely worthwhile reading. William Culican's "Phoenician Demons" in *Journal of Near Eastern Studies*, 35 (January 1976), pp. 21-24, is a good study of horned and other Phoenician demons that antedate adoption of the Egyptian Bes in Phoenicia. Islwyn Blythin's "Magic and Methodology" is good toward a definition of "magic" but especially so since Canaanite religion is used as an example.

The myth-ritual school has had its say as regards Canaanite myth and religion, too. Chapter four in the book he edited called *Myth and Ritual* (London: Oxford University Press, 1933) is by S.H. Hooke and is on Canaanite myth and ritual. R. De Langhe's "Myth, Ritual, and Kingship in the Ras Shamra Tablets" in *Myth, Ritual and Kingship* (Oxford: Clarendon Press, 1958), ed. S.H. Hooke, is excellent, as is the section devoted to Canaan in *Myth and Ritual in The Ancient Near East* (London: Praeger, 1958) by E.O. James. James devotes chapter four to Canaanite and Palestinian seasonal feasts and festivals in the book he also wrote entitled, aptly enough, *Seasonal Feasts and Festivals* (New York: Barnes & Noble, 1963/p), and you'll find the Canaanites treated in Theodor H. Gaster's *Thespis: Ritual, Myth, and Drama in the Ancient Near East*, new edition (Garden City, N.Y.: Doubleday, 1961; New York: W.W. Norton, 1977/p).

The interconnections of Canaanite civilization with others in the ancient world, as suggested before, are much speculated on. Generally of most interest to myth students are those works dealing with what may be said of Canaanite myth and Old Testament parallels. E.A. Leslie's *Old Testament Religion in the Light of Its Canaanite Backgrounds* (New York, 1936) is one of the earlier works on the subject, as is J.W. Jack's *The Ras Shamra Tablets: Their Bearing on the Old Testament* (Edinburgh: Clark, 1935). Both are good "ways into" the matter of parallels. Arvid S. Kapelrud's *The Ras Shamra Discoveries and the Old Testament*, trans. G.W. Anderson (Norman: University of Oklahoma Press,

1963) is a more recent, if short, discussion. It's an important book, though, and most chapters will prove of interest, particularly the fourth, "The Deities of Ras Shamra: Old Testament Parallels." Frank M. Cross' *Canaanite Myth and Hebrew Epic* (Cambridge: Harvard University Press, 1973) and William Foxwell Albright's *Yahweh and the Gods of Canaan* (Garden City, N.Y.: Doubleday, 1968) will both be useful studies; the latter one incorporates as fine an introduction to Canaanite religion as will be found anywhere. Also comparative studies are Norman C. Habel's *Yahweh versus Baal: A Conflict of Religious Cultures* (New York: Bookman Associates, 1964) and Gunnar Osborn's *Yahweh and Baal* (Lund: Lunds Universitets, 1956). Kathleen M. Kenyon's *Amorites and Canaanites* (London: Oxford University Press, 1966/i) goes as far back as the peoples in possession of "the promised land" in the intermediate and middle bronze periods "to assess the effect of this culture upon the infiltrating Israelites"—a fine and certainly recommended book.

The contacts and spread elsewhere of the Phoenicians are investigated in some other books, at least a few of them pretty fascinating. "Ugaritic literature has bridged the gap between Homer and the Bible," says Cyrus H. Gordon in his three-way comparison of Biblical, Ugaritic, and Minoan texts and other sources, *Ugarit and Minoan Crete* (New York: W.W. Norton, 1966). "Thanks to Minoan texts we know that from about 1800 to about 1100 B.C., Greece was dominated by Northwest Semites ('Phoenicians'), who linked it linguistically and culturally with the whole Semitic Levant." A good archaeologically-oriented version of the same general track may be found in Adolphe G. Horon's "Canaan and the Aegean Sea: Greco-Phoenician Origins Reviewed," *Diogenes*, 58 (Summer 1967), pp. 37–61. If you really like fast and furiously dealt-out speculation, though, try Hugh Fox's *Gods of the Cataclysm: A Revolutionary Investigation of Man and His Gods Before and After the Great Cataclysm* (New York: Harper's Magazine Press, 1976/i) and/or James Bailey's *The God-Kings & The Titans: The New World Ascendancy in Ancient Times* (New York: St. Martin's Press, 1973/i). Both books link Phoenicia with North America quite energetically. (There are times when I say to myself that arrant guessing, such as is sometimes the case in these books, is the sort of foolishness I ought not to encourage, but at about those times I read of a Carthaginian coin found in Arkansas or an inscribed stone in Cape Cod discovered to be Phoenician in origin. Such finds always remind me of the "wild" speculations about Old and New World contacts that were so popular during the first half of the nineteenth century—*without* the proof of Phoenician artifacts—and I become more indulgent until shown reason not to be.)

Translations

Quite a few good sources of Canaanite literature in translation exist as the result of its importance for connections with other cultures. Cyrus H. Gordon's *Ugaritic Literature: A Comprehensive Translation of the Poetic and Prose Texts* (Rome: Pontificium Institutum Biblicum, 1949) is a superb primary source for Ugaritic myths and legends in translation—The Baal and Anat cycle, the birth of the gods myth, the wedding of Nikkal and the moon, and others. His *The Loves and Wars of Baal and Anat and Other Poems* (Princeton: Princeton University Press, 1943) includes a poem called "The Saga of Aghat, Son of Daniel"—probably the same Daniel mentioned in Ezekiel 14:14—among many other interesting ones. G.R. Driver's *Canaanite Myths and Legends* (Edinburgh: Clark, 1956/p) is excellent, too. On facing pages are the transliterated Canaanite and English translation, and the book does have almost all of the known myths and legends. J. Gibson recently brought out a completely revised version of Driver's second edition of *Canaanite Myths and Legends*. It's published by E.J. Brill of Leiden, Netherlands (1978). Most of the significant myth-related texts from Ugarit are also included in James B. Pritchard's *Ancient Near Eastern Texts Relating to the Old Testament*, 3rd edition (Princeton: Princeton University Press, 1969; in abridged paperbound edition as *The Ancient Near East: An Anthology of Texts and Pictures*). Isaac Mendelsohn's *Religions of the Ancient Near East* (New York: Liberal Arts Press, 1955) has several translations, as does *Documents from Old Testament Times* (New York: Harper Torchbook, 1969/p), ed. Thomas D. Winton. Also, you'll find the Canaanite creation myth in translated version in *Origins: Creation Texts from the Ancient Mediterranean* (Garden City, N.Y.: Anchor Books, 1976/p).

Works on Historical/Cultural Background

There are many books and introductory articles in which the history, culture, and religion of the Phoenicians are dealt with. First of all, I would recommend highly that, if possible, William

Foxwell Albright's "The Role of the Canaanites in the History of
Civilization" be read as a primer. It is in *The Bible and the Ancient
Near East* (Garden City, N.Y.: Doubleday, 1961), ed. Ernest G.
Wright, and will frame the study of Canaanite mythology nicely.
From there it's a choice from among several excellent books, all
of which are suitable for developing the broad background to
the Phoenicians you may wish to have and all of which have
some good information on Phoenician religion. There's Gerhard
Herm's *The Phoenicians: The Purple Empire of the Ancient
World*, trans. Caroline Hillier (New York: William Morrow, 1975/
ib), which begins with the fall of Tyre and moves on to earlier
times. Sabatino Moscati's *The World of the Phoenicians*, trans.
Alastair Hamilton (London: Wiedenfeld & Nicolson, 1968/ib),
and John Gray's *The Canaanites* (London: Thames and Hudson,
1964/ib) are both books by experts, the latter one focused more
heavily on the Ugaritic material than the former is. Donald Harden's
The Phoenicians (London: Thames and Hudson, 1962/ib) is the
most visually appealing of the four books, but it is not textually
as good as the others. D. Barameki's *Phoenicia and the Phoenicians*
(Beirut: Khayats, 1969) is brief but useful, as is Aldo Massa's *The
Phoenicians*, trans. David Macrae (Geneva: Minerva Editions,
1977/i), a popularized, largely pictorial volume.

   Chapter five in Sabatino Moscati's *Ancient Semitic Civilizations*
(New York: Capricorn, 1960/bp) is a nicely done, broad overview
of Canaanite culture. In D.J. Wiseman's *People of the Old Testament* (Oxford: The Clarendon Press, 1973) a chapter each is
devoted to the Canaanites (by A.R. Millard) and the Phoenicians
(by D.R. Ap-Thomas). Articles in periodicals abound, of course,
but one of the very best I've seen is Samuel Matthews' "The
Phoenicians: Sea Lords of Antiquity" in *National Geographic*,
146 (August 1974/i), pp. 149-89, a visual and textual delight.

   Don't overlook, by the way, the books and articles dealing
with important Phoenician cities such as Tyre and Byblos. In
L. Sprague de Camp's *Great Cities of the Ancient World* (Garden
City, N.Y.: Doubleday, 1972/i), for instance, there's a good
chapter on Tyre (among a great many other ancient cities). There
are plenty of books on Tyre, such as Wallace B. Fleming's *History
of Tyre* (New York: Columbia University Press, 1915) or, more
recently, H. Jacob Katzenstein's *The History of Tyre* (Jerusalem:
Schocken Institute, 1973) and Nina Jidejian's *Tyre Through the
Ages* (Beirut: Mashreq Publishers, 1969). Jidejian also wrote
Byblos Through the Ages (Beirut: Mashreq, 1968).

Works on Archaeology, Language, and Art

The best sources for information on the archaeological work done on the Phoenicians/Canaanites is actually what will be found in many of the background historical works above or in encyclopedias and atlases of archaeology. However, for works that deal predominantly with the philologist's role in bringing to light what we now know about Ugarit, and therefore, the Phoenicians, there are several good sources to look into. Maurice Pope's *The Story of Archaeological Decipherment* (New York: Charles Scribner's Sons, 1975/i) and Ernst Doblhofer's *Voices in Stone* (New York: The Viking Press, 1961) both have good chapters on the deciphering of Ugaritic. C.F.A. Schaeffer, the excavator and original translator of many of the texts found at Ras Shamra tells of his own experiences in deciphering and then translating that language in *The Cuneiform Texts of Ras Shamra-Ugarit* (London: Oxford University Press, 1939) and tells of "the discovery of Ugarit" on pp. 301–06 of *Hands on the Past* (New York: Alfred A. Knopf, 1966/p), ed. C.W. Ceram. And, should you ever go so far as to need good examples of Ugaritic cuneiform, or be interested in Phoenician grammar, there's Cyrus H. Gordon's *Ugaritic Manual* (Rome: Pontificium Institutum Biblicum, 1955).

The pictures in many of the articles and books mentioned earlier in this section will serve as sources for Phoenician art, but Guitty Azarpay's *Ugaritian Art and Artifacts* (Berkeley: University of California Press, n.d./i) is a fine book for description of the artistic modes, styles, and the like. O. Negbi's *Canaanite Gods in Metal: An Archaeological Study of Ancient Syro-Palestinian Figurines* (Tel-Aviv: Publication of the Archaeological Institute no. 5, 1976/i) can be of use for its many illustrations. There are also many fine black and white pictures of Ugaritian art in James B. Pritchard's *The Ancient Near East in Pictures* (Princeton: Princeton University Press, 1969/i; abridged, paperbound version entitled *The Ancient Near East: An Anthology of Texts and Pictures*).

Persian Mythologies

Bordered on the west by present-day Turkey and Iraq, on the southeast and south by the Persian Gulf and Gulf of Oman, on the east by Pakistan and Afghanistan, and on the north by the

Soviet Union, Persia (Iran) has apparently contributed much to the religious beliefs of the western world. Isma'il R. al Faruqi has said, for example, that "It is safe to say that the whole of Jewish eschatology, angelogy, Day of Judgment and Paradise and Hell, resurrection of the flesh, and Messianism, both exilic and postexilic, came from Persia. In turn, these ideas, have become Jewish, exercised enormous influence on Christianity." (*Historical Atlas of the Religions of the World*, New York: Macmillan, 1974, p. 137.)

At one time, presumably as early as 1800 B.C., the two cultures representing the scriptural traditions of the Indian *Rig-Veda* and Iranian *Avesta* were unified. Just when this unity ended is hard to pinpoint, but 1500 B.C. may be a reasonable guess as to the time when the Iranian plateau region was settled by those who brought with them the traditions that were to evolve, over a thousand-year period, into Zarathustrianism or Zoroastrianism, Mazdakism, Manichaeism, and Mithraism. The tenets and myths of these interrelated Persian religions and cults have migrated, as already suggested, well beyond the western and northern boundaries of Persia and have shown up in many forms of western worship and mythology since about 600 B.C.—a period that begins with Persian military and political influence throughout the eastern and northeastern Mediterranean.

Collections of the Myths

Because Persia's religions and mythology (or, more appropriately, mytholog*ies* due to those changes over time and cult differences at various times) have been influential, it goes without saying that Persian mythology is an important one to study. A good place to start is with John R. Hinnells' *Persian Mythology* (London: Paul Hamlyn, 1973/ib). It covers each historical unit of the mythology separately rather than as though there were a single myth system involved, provides excellent historical background at the start, and the book is both colorful and as complete as any I know of. The *Larousse Encyclopedia of Mythology*, trans. Richard Aldington and Delano Ames (London: Paul Hamlyn, 1959/ip), ed. Felix Guirand, has far less space devoted to the subject of Persian mythology, but in lieu of any source more complete, what P. Masson-Oursel and Louise Morin have to say about it is helpful, with many important myths included. The same holds for J. de Menasce's "Persia: Cosmic Dualism" in the *Larousse World Mythology*, trans. Patricia Beardsworth (New York: Putnam,

1965/i). Here the breakdown into separate historical and religious units is like that offered by Hinnells, but on a smaller scale. There's a section on Persian mythology by Clement Huart in *Asiastic Mythology* (New York: Thomas Y. Crowell, 1963/i), by J. Hackin *et al*, which has somewhat different, but effective, historical organization. It could prove helpful enough, as could M.J. Dresden's "Mythology of Ancient Iran," in *Mythologies of the Ancient World* (Garden City, N.Y.: Anchor, 1969/ip). The section devoted to "Ancient Iran" in Volume III of the *Pears Encyclopedia of Myths and Legends* (London: Pelham Books, 1977/i) is pretty brief compared even to the relatively small sections just discussed. Albert J. Carnoy's discussion and the number of myths included makes Volume VI in *The Mythology of All Races* (Boston: Marshall Jones Company, 1916–32) surprisingly useful for Persian mythology still, despite the fact that the book is an older one.

Works on the Myths and Religion

Joseph Campbell's *Occidental Mythology* (New York: Viking Press, 1964/p) will be usefully consulted for relevant background to Persian mythology. From chapter five onward, there are good discussions of the myths and religions of Zoroastrianism and Mithraism to be found. Three short chapters on Mithraism, Manichaeism, and Mazdakism by Irach J.S. Taraporewala are included in Vergilius Ferm's *Ancient Religions* (New York: Citadel Press, 1965/p; originally published as *Forgotten Religions* in 1950). These will have utility as background, as will the discussions of Zoroastrianism that are included in a great many general, descriptive works on religion. Some of the more pertinent ones are Hans-Joachim Schoeps' *The Religions of Mankind*, trans. Richard and Clara Winston (Garden City, N.Y.: Anchor Books, 1968/p); Jack Finegan's *The Archaeology of World Religions*, Volume I (Princeton: Princeton University Press, 1952); John A. Hardon's *Religions of the World*, Volume I (Garden City, N.Y.: Doubleday Image Book, 1968/p); and *Historical Atlas of the Religions of the World* (New York: Macmillan, 1974), ed. Isma'il Ragi al Faruqi.

Louis H. Gray's *The Foundations of the Iranian Religions* (Bombay: D.B. Taraporevala Sons, 1925), though fairly old now, is a good longer introduction to the Persian religions that includes lists of divinities and discussion of the diffusion of the religions elsewhere. E. Benveniste's *The Persian Religion According to the Chief Greek Texts* (Paris, 1929) is worth looking into for information that does not always show up in other sources; although there was no love lost between the Persians and Greeks when most of the texts referred to by Benveniste were written, the Greeks did, as a rule, record with reasonable attention to detail. E.O. James' interest in *The Ancient Gods* (New York: Capricorn Books, 1964/p) is intended principally to provide a sweeping history of the religious ideas of deity in the ancient world and of the diffusion of those ideas from culture to culture; still, there's plenty that will prove of value as background to Persian myth study in it, too.

Zoroastrianism has been well covered in books devoted to its history, doctrine, founder, and the like. Maneckji N. Dhalla's *History of Zoroastrianism* (New York: AMS Press, 1972; reprint of the 1928 edition) remains an excellent work of its type and *very* informative for the myth student. R.C. Zaehner's *The Dawn and Twilight of Zoroastrianism* (London: Weidenfeld and Nicolson, 1961), A.V.W. Jackson's *Zoroastrian Studies* (New York: Columbia University Press, 1928), and R.P. Masani's *The Religion of the Good Life* (New York: Collier Books, 1962/p) are all useful in much the same way as Dhalla's book. A.V.W. Jackson's *Zoroaster: The Prophet of Ancient Iran* (London: Macmillan, 1899) is a biography of Zoroaster as well as a history of the early days of Zoroastrianism. J.H. Moulton's *Early Zoroastrianism* (London: Williams and Norgate, 1913) covers those early days, too, and R.C. Zaehner's *The Teachings of the Magi* (London: George Allen & Unwin, 1956) takes on the later Sassanian (Pahlavi) period.

More specialized studies than these are also available for any extensive research you might undertake. W.B. Henning's *Zoroaster: Politician or Witch Doctor?* (London: Oxford University Press, 1951) is an appraisal of Zoroaster's teachings and activities. Manickji N. Dhalla's *Zoroastrian Theology* (New York: AMS Press, 1972; reprint of the 1914 edition) is a comprehensive history of the theology of Zoroastrianism covering the pre-Gathic, Avestan, Pahlavi, decadent, and revival "periods". J.J. Modi's *A Catechism of the Zoroastrian Religion* (Bombay, 1962) is a good run-through on Zoroastrian doctrine and beliefs. Symbols, rituals, and emblems are the focus of J. Duchesne-Guillemin's *Symbols and Values of Zoroastrianism* (New York: Harper & Row, 1970). Its eschatology is Jal Dastur Cursetji Pavry's concern in *The Zoroastrian Doctrine of a Future Life*, 2nd edition (New York: AMS Press, 1965; originally 1926). "Zarathustra and the Dualism of Iran" in *Religion in Ancient History* (New York: Charles Scribner's Sons, 1969), by S.G.F. Brandon, is excellent on the origins, in Zoroastrianism, of good and evil as opposing forces. George Boas' "Warfare in the Cosmos" in *Diogenes*, 78 (Summer 1972), pp. 38–51, carries that sort of discussion on from Zoroastrianism through the Christian applications.

Mithraism has also received a reasonable amount of attention. Since Mithras was a Persian deity, mention of some works is thus in order. M.J. Vermaseren's *Mithras, The Secret God* (London: Chatto & Windus, 1963) and Esmé Wynne-Tyson's *Mithras: The Fellow in the Cap* (New York: Barnes & Noble, 1972; originally published in 1958) are both superb examinations of what is known about Mithras, Mithraism, and its spread into such other religions as Christianity. Franz V. Cumont's *The Mysteries of Mithra*, trans. Thomas J. McCormack (New York: Dover Publications, 1956/p; reprint of the 1903 edition) does much the same thing, but its focus is the doctrine, liturgy, and ritual of Mithraism. Elmer G. Suhr's "Krishna and Mithra as Messiahs," an article in *Folklore*, 77 (Autumn 1966), pp. 205–21, is quite an important comparative study of the Indian and Persian deities, and Raffaele Pettazzoni's "The Monstrous Figure of Time" in his *Essays on the History of Religion*, trans. H.J. Rose (Leiden: E.J. Brill, 1954), goes into a significant aspect of Mithraic symbolism.

Works on Historical/Cultural Background

Historical and cultural background study is most worthwhile. Jim Hicks and the editors of Time-Life Books have put together a colorful, informative work entitled *The Persians* (New York: Time-Life Books, 1975/ib) which among other things, includes a helpful overview chapter called "The Voice of Zoroaster." Meant for younger readers is Robert Collins' *The Medes and the Persians: Conquerors and Diplomats* (New York: McGraw-Hill, 1975/i), also a colorful and brisk survey. J.A. de Gobineau's *The World of the Persians* (Geneva: Minerva Editions, 1971/i) is a quick but color-filled once-over of ancient Persia that can be read by anyone from junior high on up. Richard N. Frye's *The Heritage of Persia* (Cleveland: World Publishing Co., 1963) is a well illustrated history of Iran that includes some useful chapters on Zoroaster and Zoroastrianism. Ernst Herzfeld's *Zoroaster and His World* (Princeton: Princeton University Press, 1947) is a mammoth two-volume work that incorporates history in the times of Zoroaster *and* a comprehensive biography of the prophet. Both older works by well known scholars, *Persia, Past and Present* (New York:

Macmillan, 1906), by A.V.W. Jackson, and *Zoroastrian Civiliza-tion* (New York: Oxford University Press, 1922), by Maneckji N. Dhalla, still offer reliable historical and cultural information about ancient Persia. For Persia prior to Zoroaster, try "The Persians" by George Widengren in *Peoples of the Old Testament* (Oxford: Clarendon Press, 1973), ed. D.J. Wiseman, or G.G. Cameron's *History of Early Iran* (Chicago: University of Chicago Press, 1936) among some other works that could be mentioned. For the best overall history of Iran, though, the *Cambridge History of Iran* (from 1968), particularly the first few volumes, must be looked into; it's published by Cambridge University Press.

Because of the great importance of ancient Persia, its myths and religions, in the western world, the concern of many scholars for diffusion of ideas both into and out of Persia might be expected. A.J. Arberry's *Legacy of Persia* (Oxford: Clarendon Press, 1953) is an examination of the "out" part principally. So, too, is J. Duchesne-Guillemin's *The Western Response to Zoroaster* (Oxford: Clarendon Press, 1958). Ruhi Muhsen Afnan localizes this diffusion from Persia to what the Greek philosophers picked up in *Zoroaster's Influence on Greek Thought* (New York: Philoso-phical Library, 1965). John R. Hinnells' "Zoroastrian Saviour Imagery and Its Influence on the New Testament," which you'll find in *Numen*, 16 (December 1969), pp. 161–85, obviously localizes it in another way.

Concern for the influence on or diffusion into ancient Persia of ideas may be found in other works. George Widengren's *Meso-potamian Elements in Manichaeism* (Uppsala: Uppsala Universitet Arsskrift, 1946), which is Volume II in the six-volume *King and Saviour* series, is one such work. Roughly half of Jehangie Cooveiju Coyajee's *Cults of Ancient Iran and China* (Fort Bom-bay: J.B. Karani's Sons, 1936) deals with the parallels in the "exchange and transmission of legends" between those two countries. Georges Dumézil's *The Destiny of a King*, trans. Alf Hiltebeitel (Chicago: University of Chicago Press, 1973) is a comparative Indian-Iranian study in which epic material is seen as deriving from a common source for both ancient cultures. It is difficult reading for the nonphilologist, though.

Translations

The principal sources of Persian myths are the sacred *Avesta*, as you may already have gathered, and Firdausi's *Shah-nameh*, an epic poem. Relevant translations of the *Avesta* as well as other

Zoroastrian texts may be found in the long-time standard source for such translations, *The Sacred Books of the East* (New York: Parke, Austin and Lipscomb, 1917), a series comprised of fifty-odd volumes found in most better libraries either in the original edition or later reprints. J. Duchesne-Guillemin's *The Hymns of Zarathustra*, trans. Mrs. M. Henning (London: J. Murray, 1952) and D.J. Irani's *The Divine Songs of Zarathustra* (London: George Allen and Unwin, 1924) are two of many books which have translations of some of the "Gathas" or "divine songs" in which tenets and some myth material of Zarathustrianism are preserved. The Persian creation myth is translated in *Origins: Creation Texts from the Ancient Mediterranean* (Garden City, N.Y.: Anchor Books, 1976/p), ed. Charles Doria and Harris Lenowitz, and in S.G.F. Brandon's *Creation Legends of the Ancient Near East* (London: Hodder and Stoughton, 1963). The latter work also has extensive commentary and interpretation. Finally, the *Shahnameh* is available in several English editions.

Works on Archaeology and Art

Unfortunately, there are in English few nontechnical sources that dwell on the archaeology of ancient Iran at any length. M.E.L. Mallowan surveys the archaeological information in *Early Mesopotamia and Iran* (London: Thames and Hudson, 1965). Carl Nylander also spends some time on it in *The Deep Well*, trans. Joan Tate (New York: St. Martin's Press, 1970). Then too, in many of the cultural and historical background sources listed above, as well as in most atlases and encyclopedias of archaeology, there are useful sections. For the deciphering of old Persian cuneiform *and* some information on the archaeology involved, see the relevant sections in Maurice Pope's *The Story of Archaeological Decipherment* (New York: Charles Scribner's Sons, 1975) or Ernst Doblhofer's *Voices in Stone* (New York: Viking Press, 1961). And should you at some time find yourself so far along as to need more on the old Persian, see Roland G. Kent's *Old Persian* (New Haven: American Oriental Society, 1953).

Art in "old" Persia is well surveyed, and many archaeological sites pictured, in Roman Ghirshman's *The Arts of Ancient Iran*, trans. Stuart Gilbert and James Emmons (New York: Golden Press, 1964/i). The book has almost 600 illustrations all told, including numerous maps, and has much myth-related material in texts and pictures. Not quite as splendorous as volumes, but nonetheless textually and pictorially worthwhile, are André

Godard's *The Art of Iran,* trans. Michael Heron and ed. Michael
Rogers (London: George Allen and Unwin, 1965/i), and Edith
Porada's *The Art of Ancient Iran* (New York: Crown Publishers,
1965/i). Lloyd Seton's *The Art of the Ancient Near East* (New
York: Praeger, 1969/i) also has a good section on Persia.

Biblical Mythologies

As is well known in the western world, where Judeo-Christian
tradition is strongest, the land of the Hebrews of the Old and
New Testaments was principally the eastern end of the Mediterranean (now Israel and Jordan), with the range of wanderings,
in the Old Testament, to or from Egypt in the southwest, Canaan
and the land of the Hittites (now Syria and Turkey) in the north,
and Mesopotamia (now Iraq) in the east. The beginnings of the
history of biblical Israel occurred roughly in the middle of the
eighteenth century B.C. with the settlement of Hebron (south
of Jerusalem) by Abraham and those whom he led from Ur
(southern Mesopotamia), with the later settlement near Shechem
of Aramaeans led by Jacob, and with still a third settlement by
those who entered Canaan from the south and east at the end of
the thirteenth century B.C. The first books of the Old Testament
were written, it is believed, in the old Semitic script soon after;
those of the New Testament were composed largely during the
century after the death of Jesus.

   The study of biblical mythology has long been hampered by
those, on the one hand, who are defensive and see the *Bible* as
literal truth and by those, on the other, who are principally
"de-mythologists" out to debunk the myths of the *Bible.* The
division between the two camps is unfortunate, of course, and
has resulted in a body of works in English rivaled in size only by
that associated with Greco-Roman mythology but so uneven in
quality as to be rivaled by virtually no other subjects. The problem
is one of definitions for the most part, the word "myth," as
always, the culprit. The one side feels threatened by a word which
has so long a history of "fabrication" and "falsehood" associated
with it, and the other is too often not averse to using the word
offensively in just that way. It would take too much space to
unravel the complications involved, so suffice it to say that serious
myth students do not concern themselves with the true-false
arguments surrounding the word "myth" in popular usage. Rather,
they use it simply to mean "traditional stories," knowing full well

that any such stories or "myths"—whether among the Azande in Africa or among present-day Chicagoans—will be believed or not depending on the believer's or nonbeliever's affiliations and experiences. Having one's sacred beliefs lumped together as "mythology" with beliefs regarded to be those of "pagans" must be a discomforting experience to anyone who has never really studied mythology. But mythology can be studied conscientiously and objectively with the end in mind of learning something instead merely of defending scholastically or rejecting haphazardly.

Collections of the Myths

For some reason, possibly because the *Bible* itself is so accessible in English-speaking countries, there haven't been very many English-language anthologies of biblical myths. After all, from the first few lines of Genesis, where we get into the Hebrew cosmogony, through the last book of the New Testament, where we encounter the apocalypse of John, the authoritative collection is at hand. The only worldwide mythography that does anything much with biblical myths is, in fact, the *International Mythology* series published by Paul Hamlyn Publishers of London. In that series, John Gray's *Near Eastern Mythology* (London: Paul Hamlyn, 1969/i) has a good section on Hebrew myths, and George Every's *Christian Mythology* (London: Paul Hamlyn, 1970/ib) is as extensive a collection of Christian myths as will be found. Both have good historical background information in them as well and are beautifully illustrated in color and black and white. Also a pretty book, but with flimsy text by comparison, is Gilbert Thurlow's *All Color Book of Biblical Myths and Mysteries* (London: Octopus, 1974/i). Despite its coverage of both Old and New Testaments, it is just about half as long as Every's *Christian Mythology*. Veronica Ions' *The World's Mythology in Colour* (London: Paul Hamlyn, 1974/i) has just a few pages devoted to biblical mythology and is mainly useful for its pictures. Four chapters in S.H. Hooke's *Middle Eastern Mythology* (Harmondsworth, G.B.: Penguin, 1963/ip) are devoted to biblical mythology and ritual, but the purpose is not presentation of all of the myths as much as to locate and interpret many of them in Middle Eastern context. Because the flow into western civilization of the ancient myths of Western Asia is largely through biblical myth, Gerald A. Larue states, in his *Ancient Myth and Modern Man* (Englewood Cliffs, N.J.: Prentice Hall, 1975/ip), that his book seems "to emphasize biblical mythology disproportionately." True, but for anyone looking to see that "flow" from most ancient to very modern, *Ancient Myth and Modern Man* is as good a place to do so as will be found, and there are plenty of biblical myths dealt with in its thematically organized contents.

Among collections of related myths and legends, Louis Ginzberg's seven-volume *Legends of the Jews,* trans. Henrietta Szold (Philadelphia: Jewish Publication Society, 1909-46) is a marvelous resource for myths and legends involving well known personages from the *Bible.* Angelo Rappaport's three-volume *Myth and Legend of Ancient Israel* (New York: Katz Publishing House, 1966; originally 1928) is also a fine collection despite the many outdated conclusions and observations it contains. It includes trips to Hell, creation stories, stories of the death of Moses and the prophet Elijah, and the like. Zev Vilnay's *Legends of Judea and Samaria,* two volumes (Philadelphia: The Jewish Publication Society of America, 1975), has some good biblical myth and folklore material, but it is mainly devoted to stories and local legends that have arisen about places in the Old Testament. Also, John D. Yohannan has edited a useful collection called *Joseph and Potiphar's Wife in World Literature* (New York: New Directions, 1969). In it are tales of the chaste youth—lustful stepmother—punishing father, including the lead tale from the *Bible* (Genesis 39), the Greek Hippolytus-Phaedra-Theseus story, Fardausi's (Persian) Siyawush-Sudaba-Kaikaus, the *Koran's* Yusuf-prince's wife–prince, and many others.

Studies of Old Testament Myth

Now we come to a very large category—works which are mainly interpretive and/or comparative in nature, some of them covering both Old and New Testaments, others just one or the other, still others only individual myths.

One of the older works still of value is Thomas W. Doane's *Bible Myths and Their Parallels in Other Religions* (New York: The Truth Seeker Company, 1883; later reprinted by University Books of New Hyde Park, N.Y.). It is old enough to be filled with errors of the most conspicuous sort, biblical and other mythological scholarship having progressed much since Doane's day, but it is a fine attempt at "comparison of the Old and New Testament Myths and Miracles with those of Heathen nations of antiquity." Doane was a solar naturalist disciple of Max Müller, so the interpretive part is not as valuable as the examples and parallels used.

J.E.T. Rogers' *Bible Folk-Lore: A Study in Comparative Mythology* (New York: J.W. Bouton, 1884) is one of many overly excited nineteenth-century attempts at demonstrating that quite a few of the stories in the *Bible* are part of a long tradition of such stories, but it is still useful as background. Rogers was also in the tradition of the natural theorists and saw the growth and spread of myths as "the imperfect language and imperfect thought of mankind while yet in the infancy of intellectual growth." Sir James George Frazer's later three-volume *Folklore in the Old Testament: Studies in Comparative Religion, Legend and Law* (London: Macmillan and Company, 1918; reprinted in one volume by Hart Publishing Company of New York in 1975) is a somewhat more temperate, and certainly more scholarly, handling of the same general material. It has as its main asset the inclusion of extensive parallel myths to those from the *Bible* with which it deals. Theodor H. Gaster revised, updated, and extensively added to Frazer's book in his two-volume *Myth, Legend, and Custom in the Old Testament* (New York: Harper & Row, 1969; Torchbook edition 1975/ip). Warren W. Jackson's *Legend, Myth and History in the Old Testament* (Wellesley, Mass.: Independent School Press, 1970) is better suited for high school students, but it does have useful information in it. Lloyd Graham's *Deceptions and Myths of the Bible* (Secaucus, N.J.: University Books, 1975) is by a man who knows a great deal but whose interest in debunking both parts of the *Bible* is so strong that a great many people will be put off by the book. It *should* be read by the serious student of myth but *only* after enough other background in myth study and the *Bible* to allow for objective reading. *The Ignorance of Certainty* (New York: Harper & Row, 1970), by Ashley Montagu and Edward Darling, has the purpose of investigating popular "myths," some of them biblical, most of them modern, toward the end of clarifying how certainty—whether of the truth of an unproven biblical incident or of a common modern belief—is a kind of nonsense that the thoughtful will eschew. Because "myth" is here defined as "misconception" or "erroneous belief," like Graham's book it should be read only after adequate training in myth study. The same holds for chapter three in *Occidental Mythology* (New York: Viking Press, 1964/p) by Joseph Campbell. It is an excellent interpretive background to Hebrew myth, but will startle some people with its abruptness.

There are additionally quite a few works which can be read best as a way of coming to grips with the differing definitions of "myth" that have guided discussion of Old Testament stories. While each of the works does deal with some facet of the mythology involved, their use just in clarifying terms and issues is great. James Barr's "The Meaning of 'Mythology' in Relation to the Old Testament" in *Vetus Testamentum*, 9 (1959), pp. 1-10, is one such work. John L. McKenzie's "Myth and the Old Testament" in *The Catholic Biblical Quarterly*, 21 (1959), pp. 265-82, would go well with Barr's article, as would G.H. Davies' "An Approach to the Problem of Old Testament Mythology" in the *Palestine Exploration Quarterly* (1956), pp. 83-91. John L. McKenzie, a Jesuit priest, also offers some sound scholarship in defense of orthodoxy in *Myths and Realities: Studies in Biblical Theology* (Milwaukee: Bruce Publishing Company, 1963), the chapters entitled "Myth and the Old Testament" and "The Hebrew Attitude toward Mythological Polytheism" being good examples of the kinds of content the book has. Brevard S. Childs' *Myth and Reality in the Old Testament*, 2nd edition (London: SCM Press, 1962) is a work in biblical theology which can be looked into to see what can be done to reconcile the demythologizing and dogmatic approaches to Old Testament myth. J.W. Rogerson's *Myth in Old Testament Interpretation* (New York: Walter de Gruyter, 1974/i) is a fine survey of the interpretative approaches to myth and their application to the Old Testament. H.G. May's "Pattern and Myth in the Old Testament" in *The Journal of Religion*, 21 (1938), pp. 258-99, and Lawrence E. Toombs' "The Formation of Myth Patterns in the Old Testament" in *The Journal of Bible and Religion*, 29 (1961), pp. 108-12, are both useful for their excellent handling of mythic patterns that prevail in the Old Testament; and Raphael Patai asks and answers perhaps the most important question of all in "What is Hebrew Mythology?" in *Transactions of the New York Academy of Sciences* (November 1964), pp. 73-81.

Chapters eight and nine in *The Intellectual Adventure of Ancient Man* (Chicago: University of Chicago Press, 1946), ed. the Frankforts *et al*, are William A. Irwin's "The Hebrews," a fine discussion of God, man, and nation in Hebrew thought and myth. George Widengren's "Myth and History in Israelite-Jewish Thought" in *Culture in History* (New York: Columbia University Press, 1960), ed. Stanley Diamond, is another work that will provide excellent background, as will the more expansive *Man and Earth in Hebrew Custom, Belief, and Legend*, two-volumes (Jerusalem: Hebrew University Press, 1942-43), by Raphael Patai.

Like his *The Hebrew Goddess* (New York: Ktav Publishing House, 1967/i), a good work for prebiblical matter, the two volumes are an example of the thoroughgoing research typical of Raphael Patai.

Works having to do with single books or individual myths in the Old Testament are worth looking into also. *Hebrew Myths: The Book of Genesis* (Garden City, N.Y.: Doubleday, 1963/b), by Robert Graves and Raphael Patai, is a first-rate source for the serious myth student. Here, in somewhat "heavy" packaging, the two well known scholars sort out the myths in Genesis, drawing upon comparative evidence from other Hebrew and worldwide sources. In 1901 Hermann Gunkel's *The Legends of Genesis* (New York: Schocken Books, 1964/p) first appeared and still may be used by myth students for its excellent speculation on the historicity of the patriarchs. There's a fine explanatory chapter on the Hebrew creation myth in *Creation Legends of the Ancient Near East* (London: Hodder and Stoughton, 1963/b), by S.G.F. Brandon. In Edmund Leach's "Genesis as Myth," there's an informative structural analysis of the biblical story of the Creation (including the Garden of Eden and Cain-Abel). The essay has often been anthologized, as in John Middleton's *Myth and Cosmos* (Garden City, N.Y.: The Natural History Press, 1967/p). If you can locate Edmund Leach's *Genesis as Myth and Other Essays* (London: Jonathan Cape, 1969), you'll also find two other fine analyses—"The Legitimacy of Solomon," in which Leach looks into the myth of Solomon's ascendancy to the Throne of Israel, and "Virgin Birth," in which he juxtaposes primitive (Oceanic primarily) versions of virgin birth with more sophisticated ones (notably biblical). The story of the visit of a Queen of Sheba to Solomon, found in the First Book of Kings (10:1–13), is the subject of an anthology of essays edited by James B. Pritchard, *Solomon and Sheba* (London: Phaidon Press, 1974/ib). It includes chapters on "The Legend and Its Diffusion" and "The Age of Solomon," and four chapters are devoted to the legend in Judaic, Islamic, Ethiopian, and Christian tradition. *The David Myth in Western Literature* (West Lafayette, Ind.: Purdue Univeristy Press, 1979), ed. Raymond-Jean Frontain and Jan Wojcik, is a collection of eleven essays, only some of which will have use in myth study, but it is worth considering. *The Stories of Elijah and Elisha as Polemics Against Baal Worship* (Leiden: E.J. Brill, 1968), by L. Bronner, also has value to myth students if only peripherally. Robert R. Wilson concludes that the biblical scholar must understand the possible functions of genealogies

anywhere before assuming a point about the biblical ones in his
"The Old Testament Genealogies in Recent Research," an article
in *Journal of Biblical Literature*, 94 (June 1975), pp. 170-89.
Karin R. Andriolo's "A Structural Analysis of Genealogy and
Worldview in the Old Testament," *American Anthropologist*,
75 (October 1973), pp. 1657-59, has the purpose of showing
that genealogies in the Old Testament function "as a model
for the resolution of certain conflicts within the worldview"
and to reveal the cultural meanings structurally embedded in the
genealogies. Andrew M. Greeley's *The Sinai Myth: A New Interpretation of the Ten Commandments* (Garden City, N.Y.: Image
Books, 1975/p) focuses on the nineteenth and twentieth chapters
of Exodus in attempting to interpret what a given set of symbols
means. The work is not one in mythological interpretation in the
same way others that have been mentioned are, but the fact
that Greeley considers "The Sinai event" as neither true nor
false—neither as a real occurrence nor as a fiction—shows that his
thinking is attuned to the mythologist's objectivity in the absence
of solid proof and makes it worthwhile as a source in biblical
myth study. Nahum Sarna's *Understanding Genesis* (New York:
Schocken Books, 1970/p) is another work not clearly in the
category of myth study, but because its author takes us through
Genesis, using biblical and extra-biblical sources (archaeological,
comparative, mythological, historical, philological), it is useful in
myth study. *Genesis and Geology* (Cambridge: Harvard University
Press, 1951; Harper Torchbook, 1959/p), by Charles C. Gillespie,
is still another one only peripherally involved in myth study as
such that could prove useful. Then there's Irwin Ginsburg's
First Man, Then Adam (New York: Simon and Schuster, 1977).
Ginsburg, a Ph.D. in physics, postulates—as more or less have
others in the Erich von Daniken "school before him—that Adam
and Eve were actually space travellers who landed on earth. Like
all theories of origins, it has its place in myth study as long as one
is aware of the other ways of looking at the same phenomenon.
And finally, although it comes less under the head of myth than
doctrine, F.R. Tennant's *The Sources of the Doctrine of the Fall
and Original Sin* (New York: Schocken Books, 1946/p) will be
usefully looked into as an analysis of one of the primary Judeo-
Christian myths in the Old Testament.

Studies of New Testament Myth

That certainly does not exhaust the possibilities for use in the
study of Old Testament myth, but it will serve as a fair start.

Needless to say, there are also a great many works useful in the study of New Testament myth.

Thomas James Thorburn's *The Mythical Interpretation of the Gospels* (New York: Charles Scribner's Sons, 1916/b) is an interesting place to begin, for Thorburn's aim is to puncture earlier interpretations given of the four New Testament Gospels as "myth" and "demonstrate the divine origin and authority of the Christian scriptures." By starting with this work, the myth student is provided with an excellent bibliography of prior works which Thorburn presents in his preface and works with thereafter. Thorburn provides good perspective on the subject matter and the controversy involved in the study of New Testament myth. Arthur Weigall's *The Paganism in Our Christianity* (New York: G.P. Putnam's Sons, 1928) is perhaps the perfect example of the *kind* of work, if later in date, which Thorburn seeks to defuse, for it is a solid representative of what in myth study is called "demythologizing"—or even "mythoclasm"—in which an author deals with traditional Christian stories that are not susceptible to ordinary proof in order to show that they didn't happen in the way the stories purport. Weigall attempts to demythologize everything in Christianity that he regards as fabulous. Such attempts have been at various times undertaken ever since the discoveries of Galileo during the Age of Reason (seventeenth and eighteenth centuries), for example, in such works as David Hume's "Of Miracles" and Thomas Paine's *The Age of Reason.* The word "demythologize," however, became popular much later through the Protestant theologian Rudolf Bultmann and his *entmythologisierung*, an approach to Christian myth and ritual that has precipitated a long list of works since the 1940s. The works in this list employ many techniques of modern-day comparative mythology at the same time as they represent aspects of a theological hassle.

First, Hans Werner edited a work called *Kerygma and Myth: A Theological Debate*, 2 volumes, trans. Reginald H. Fuller (London: S.P.C.K., 1953 and 1962) which embraces Bultmannian demythologizing as the center of a "debate." In the two volumes are Bultmann's "New Testament and Mythology," the lead essay, Friedrich Schumann's "Can the Event of Jesus Christ Be Demythologized?," Karl Jaspers' "Myth and Religion," and Bultmann's "The Case for Demythologizing" among others. In 1958, Noonday Press of New York released *Myth and Christianity* (p), trans. Norman Guterman, which includes the last two essays noted above and some further exchanges between Bultmann and Jaspers.

Bultmann's *Jesus Christ and Mythology* (New York: Charles
Scribner's Sons, 1958) is also well worth reading. Ernest William
Barnes, Bishop of Birmingham, wrote *The Rise of Christianity*
(London: Longman's Green and Co., 1947) as an attempt to
bring order and clarity to the controversies besetting the myth
and dogma of Christianity. By placing the New Testament and
Jesus in their time, dealing with the origins of the New Testament
and the traditions around it in the ancient world, Barnes himself
demythologizes miracles and the supernatural. Richard W. Boynton,
likewise trained for the ministry, wrote *Beyond Mythology*
(Garden City, N.Y.: Doubleday, 1951) as a rather aggressive
argument in favor of the demythologization of religion; the
supernatural element is his emphasis. Roger A. Johnson's *The
Origins of Demythologizing* (Leiden: E.J. Brill, 1974) is a fine,
fairly up-to-date discussion of Bultmann's thinking about demythologizing and related matters. Eugene Thomas Long, author of
*Jaspers and Bultmann: A Dialogue between Philosophy and
Theology in the Existentialist Tradition* (Durham, N.C.: Duke
University Press, 1968), states his purpose in the book as being
"to make a contribution toward an understanding of some issues
raised in the contemporary dialogue between philosophy and
theology." Along the way, he offers a good summary of Bultmann's and Jaspers' thinking on New Testament myth and engages
in some useful discussion of faith and revelation. Schubert M.
Ogden, a Protestant like Bultmann, took a moderate stand in
*Christ Without Myth: A Study Based on the Theology of Rudolf
Bultmann* (London: Collins, 1962); his position is that demythologizing of the New Testament is inevitable, but retention of
the essential message of Jesus is a *sine qua non*. Along the same
lines, Friedrich Gogarten suggests that the truth must be arrived
at, that demythologizing is a possibility, and that God's word
will prevail in the end—this in his *Demythologizing and History*,
trans. Neville Horton Smith (New York: Charles Scribner's Sons,
1955). Robin Attfield's "On Translating Myth" in the *International Journal for Philosophy of Religion*, 2 (Winter 1971),
pp. 228–45, is a helpful article which calls for demythologizing
"when myth involves *notions once symbolic but now obsolete.*"
His examples are drawn from Bultmann's writings and the New
Testament. Geraint Vaughan Jones, in his *Christology and Myth in
the New Testament* (New York: Harper & Brothers, 1956), concludes that the New Testament "should be understood poetically
and metaphorically rather than as consisting of objective state-

ments about Jesus and his place in creation." The book has some excellent discussions of myth and the mythological throughout it. J. Macquarrie's *An Existentialist Theology: A Comparison of Heidegger and Bultmann* (New York: Macmillan, 1955) is a thoughtful critique of two positions in the demythologizing discussion. An offshoot of the discussion is found in the "God is Dead" controversy which was current in Protestant circles in the 1960s especially. Look into Thomas J. J. Altizer's and William Hamilton's *Radical Theology and the Death of God* (Indianapolis: Bobbs-Merrill, 1966; Harmondsworth, G.B.: Penguin, 1968/bp) as the primary source, with a superior bibliography on the subject, and into Thomas W. Ogletree's *The Death of God Controversy* (Nashville: Abingdon Press, 1966/p), a "constructive explanation" of the writing of Altizer, Hamilton, and a third person prominent in the controversy, Paul Van Buren.

Ian Henderson's little booklet *Myth in the New Testament* (Chicago: Henry Regnery, 1952) very nicely elaborates on the positions of Bultmann and Heidegger in the process of making clear the theologian's feeling for the necessity of myth in Christian circles. It is, in fact, one of the most satisfying reconciliations of faith and myth that I've come across, avoiding as it does the scholastic logic so common in such attempts. L. Malavez's *The Christian Message and Myth* (London: S.C.M., 1958) is a bit more defensive and, therefore, not quite as effective a reconciliation, but it can be read profitably by myth students. Paul Bauer's *Christianity or Superstition* (London: Marshall Morgan and Scott, 1966) and J. Schonberg Setzer's *What's Left to Believe?* (Nashville: Abingdon Press, 1968) are both even more defensive than Malavez's book. They exhibit the kinds of commitment to a belief and a doctrine which eliminates all possibilities for objectivity, thus making them of questionable value in serious myth study. They are representative of a great many essentially dogmatic religious works.

Works about Jesus comprise another group showing wide range from unquestioning reverence to wildly mythoclastic. Examples of works closest to the former while still useful in myth study are Heinz Zahrnt's *The Historical Jesus*, trans. J.S. Bowden (New York: Harper & Row, 1963) and Andrew W. Greeley's *The Jesus Myth* (Garden City, N.Y.: Image Books, 1971/p). Zahrnt, for instance, takes the opposite track from the mythoclast's in arriving at the conclusion that Jesus was historical and was the son of God, but he is insistent that there is

no way of *knowing* the divinity of Jesus or if the New Testament
was divinely inspired. Greeley, as in his other fine book *The Sinai
Myth*, is highly conscious of the symbolic and the metaphorical
quality of religious experience; he therefore neither broaches the
issue of Jesus' divinity as such nor works to expose the potentially
mythical. Examples of works at the other extreme are, as a rule,
heavily speculative and given to loose use of comparative mythological information. For instance, Gerhard Steinhauser's *Jesus
Christ—Heir to the Astronauts* (N.Y.: Abelard-Schuman Ltd.,
1975) uses the latter-day euhemerist interpretation of Erich
von Daniken to suggest that Jesus was an astronaut who visited
Earth and that the Christian faith is the superstitious vestige
of a primitive encounter. G.A. Wells' *Did Jesus Exist?* (London:
Elek/Pemberton, 1975/b) offers the view that Jesus did not
in fact even exist, that his whole life as revealed in the gospels
was prefabricated from extant scriptural and mythological ideas.
Albert Schweitzer's *The Quest of the Historical Jesus* (New
York: Macmillan, 1948; originally published in English in 1910)
has a like thesis. Said Schweitzer (p. 398), "The Jesus of Nazareth
who came forward publicly as the Messiah, who preached the ethic
of the Kingdom of God, who founded the Kingdom of Heaven
upon Earth, and died to give His work its final consecration,
never had any existence. He is a figure designed by rationalism,
endowed with life by liberalism, and clothed by modern theology
in historical garb." (See also Schweitzer's *The Mystery of the
Kingdom of God*—originally published in 1914; New York:
Schocken Books, 1964/p). These several books are, though,
useful in myth study as long as kept in perspective.

Kersey Graves' *The World's Sixteen Crucified Saviors: or
Christianity Before Christ*, 6th edition (New Hyde Park, N.Y.:
University Books, 1971; originally published in 1875) is a metic-
ulous comparison of Jesus' life with the lives of other "crucified"
saviors; it proffers "useful popular criticism of the orthodox
Christian claim to exclusive revelation." Graves' investigation
is one of the earlier ones in which what are essentially heroic
attributes are isolated as being descriptive of any number of
culture heroes throughout history, Jesus included. S.G.F. Brandon,
a fine biblical scholar, investigates "The Jesus of History" briefly
in his *Religion in Ancient History* (New York: Charles Scribner's
Sons, 1969/b) as does Meyrick H. Carre in "A View of Jesus"
in *The Humanist*, 85 (June 1970), pp. 170-72. Both demythologize, Carre more than Brandon, in a manner not unlike that in

a work written eighty years earlier, George Solomon's *The Jesus of History and the Jesus of Tradition Identified*, which its London publisher declared to be "the first attempt . . . made to introduce the Christian world to Jesus, as known to history before his figure was distorted by popular belief." Charles Guignebert's *The Christ*, trans. Peter Ouzts and Phyllis Cooperman (New Hyde Park, N.Y.: University Books, 1968), the third volume in what amounts to a trilogy that includes the earlier *The Jewish World in the Time of Jesus* and *Jesus*, is a fine, objective look at how Jesus, a rebel leader in the holy land, later came to be a God. Each step is carefully investigated by Guignebert, using all of the known scriptural and extrascriptural sources (comparative mythological included). The biblical scholar Hugh J. Schonfield has been accused of some slovenly scholarship in his *The Passover Plot: New Light on the History of Jesus* (New York: Bernand Geis Associates, 1965/p), but it is in the vein of Guignebert's work—in this case, though, focusing only on Jesus' route to the cross. Morton Scott Enslin's *The Prophet from Nazareth* (New York: Schocken Books, 1968/p) tackles the problem of what kind of man Jesus was, disregarding generally the polar opposites, demythologized version and unquestioned son of God. Marcello Craveri's *The Life of Jesus* (New York: Grove Press, 1967/p) does much the same thing. However, opposite these we can see the obvious use in myth study of Charles Edgar Pratt's *Paganism in Christianity* (New York: Exposition Press, 1969), which is meant "for only those who never have been able to believe in the miracles and supernatural life of Jesus Christ." Pratt knows his sources well, as do the seven British Protestant theologians-scholars whose essays are collected in John Hicks' *The Myth of God Incarnate* (Philadelphia: Westminster Press, 1977/p). While the collection is clearly in the long tradition of works that demythologize, the fact that several ordained ministers are here involved makes it rather a unique work. Charles Francis Potter's *The Lost Years of Jesus Revealed* (New York: Fawcett Publications, 1958/p) proposes that the Dead Sea scrolls and our new knowledge of the Essenes must change our thinking about Jesus' mission since what the Essenes knew was what Jesus in some ways preached (a highly controversial position, however).

Slightly different in their approach are another group of works. S.G.F. Brandon's excellent *Jesus and the Zealots* (New York: Charles Scribner's Sons, 1967) investigates Jesus' relation to the zealots of his time and reassesses the reasons for his crucifixion.

Adolf Holl's *Jesus in Bad Company* (New York: Avon Books, 1970/p) perhaps extends Brandon's approach since it views Jesus as a radical who kept company with what in Holl's view was a criminal element. Joseph Jacobs' *Jesus as Others Saw Him: A Retrospect A.D. 54* (New York: Arno Press, 1973; reprint of the 1925 edition) is an old work in recreating what the Jewish people in Jesus' time thought of him. The title essay in Erich Fromm's *The Dogma of Christ and Other Essays* (Garden City, N.Y.: Anchor Press, 1966/p) is worth looking to for its exploration of the dogma surrounding Jesus' ministry. Charles Talbert's "The Concept of Immortals in Mediterranean Antiquity" in *Journal of Biblical Literature*, 94 (September 1975), pp. 419-36, concludes that the early Christians knew well the tradition of immortals in the Mediterranean area and drew on it in their "proclamation of Jesus." H. van der Loos' *The Miracles of Jesus* (Leiden: E.J. Brill, 1965) and Hermann Samuel Reimarus' *The Goal of Jesus and His Disciples* (Leiden: E.J. Brill, 1970) are both useful works. Finally, for novels which demythologize the life of Jesus, try Robert Graves' *King Jesus* or Nikos Kazantzakis' *The Last Temptation of Christ*, both of which have been available in hardbound and paper. Theodore Ziolkowski's fine literary study called *Fictional Transfigurations of Jesus* (Princeton: Princeton University Press, 1976/bp) will provide you with background and further works.

There's also a broad group of other kinds of works that may be useful to you in studying Christian myth. First of all, studies of messianism. Wilson D. Wallis' *Messiahs: Christian and Pagan* (Boston: The Gorham Press, 1918) is an old source but still a good one for investigation of messianism. Wallis was one of the first to note the important conditions which give rise to it— attempts made "to revive a decadent religion," the "need for salvation," and "crisis" situations—and include Jesus among many other "messiahs" as examples. On pages 155-203 in his *Cows, Pigs, Wars & Witches: The Riddles of Culture* (New York: Random House, 1974), Marvin Harris discusses messiahs, too; and there's a good deal of information on them in Weston LaBarre's *The Ghost Dance: The Origins of Religion* (New York: Dell, 1972/p), particularly in appendix one. Another subject of special interest is the virgin birth. Geoffrey Ashe's *The Virgin* (London: Routledge & Kegan Paul, 1976/b) is concerned with the cult of Mary and with the general mythmaking process that yielded the myths of the virgin birth, the assumption, and marian devotion. It is far and away the best source of its kind; but Thomas Boslooper's *The Virgin Birth* (Philadelphia: Westminster Press, 1962) can also be read profitably. His is essentially a theological argument which accepts that "the virgin birth is 'myth' in the highest sense," and which develops an "interpretation of the story of the origin of our Lord." Although Edmund Leach uses Oceanic myth predominantly in his "Virgin Birth," in *Genesis as Myth and Other Essays* (London: Jonathan Cape, 1969), the implications for understanding the biblical myth are there that make the essay worth reading. Finally, legends of the cross, though medieval largely, may prove helpful in Christian myth study. W.C. Prime's *Holy Cross, A History of the Invention, Preservation, and Disappearance of the Wood Known as the True Cross* (New York: A.D.F. Randolph & Co., 1877) and John Ashton's *The Legendary History of the Cross* (London: Fisher Unwin, 1887) are old but excellent on the subject.

Specialized Studies of Old and New Testament Myths

The myth-ritual-kingship school went to work on Hebrew-Christian myth much to our profit. In the seminal volume edited by S.H. Hooke, *Myth and Ritual* (London: Oxford University Press, 1933), four chapters are devoted more or less exclusively to the Hebrews. The sequel volume, also edited by Hooke, *The Labyrinth: Further Studies in the Relation between Myth and Ritual in the Ancient World* (London: Macmillan, 1935), is focused on "dramatic ritual representing the death and resurrection of the king, who was also a god"; chapters three through eight are devoted to Judeo-Christian studies. S.H. Hooke also edited *Myth, Ritual and Kingship* (Oxford: Clarendon Press, 1958/b), a good survey of the subject in the ancient Near East; the opening and closing chapters are excellent summaries of the myth-ritual-kingship position as it developed over twenty-five years. Three other chapters are of use directly in biblical myth study: G.E. Widengren's "Early Hebrew Myths and Their Interpretation," Aubrey R. Johnson's "Hebrew Conceptions of Kingship," and H.H. Rowley's "Ritual and the Hebrew Prophets." Henri Frankfort's *Kingship and the Gods* (Chicago: University of Chicago Press, 1948) includes an epilogue on the Hebrews. Aubrey Johnson's *Sacral Kingship in Ancient Israel* (Cardiff: University of Wales Press, 1955) focuses on two groups of psalms for source material, in the process uncovering ritual patterns and cult worship schemes. E.O. James, an active myth-ritualist, published four volumes all of which have some chapters at least that will be helpful in biblical myth study: *Myth and Ritual in the Ancient Near East* (New York: Praeger, 1958), *Christian Myth and Ritual* (London: J. Murray, 1937), *Seasonal Feasts and Festivals* (New York: Barnes and Noble, 1963/bp), and *Origins of Sacrifice* (Port Washington, N.Y.: Kennikat Press, 1971; reprint of 1933 edition). Alan W. Watts' *Myth and Ritual in Christianity* (Boston: Beacon Press, 1968/p) is a significant book in the broad area of Christian myth despite its approach through Catholic doctrine and ritual. The remains of seasonal drama-ritual are explored in Theodor H. Gaster's *Thespis: Ritual, Myth and Drama in the Ancient Near East* (Garden City, N.Y.: Doubleday, 1961; New York: W.W. Norton, 1977/p). Raphael Patai's *Man and Temple in Ancient Jewish Myth and Ritual* (London: Thomas Nelson, 1947) is concerned with "the principle of sympathy in nature as revealed in such diverse forms as rituals performed in the Second Temple of Jerusalem, myths centering around the temple, and beliefs concerning the conduct and actions of the people in general and of the children, the rulers, and the pious and righteous men in particular." The origins, functions and activities of the priesthood in the Asian and European world are studied in Leopold Sabourin's *Priesthood: A Comparative Study* (Leiden: E.J. Brill, 1973); some attention is given to the Hebrew-Christian in it.

Symbolism and symbolic interpretation of biblical myth and ritual have been the preoccupation of many over the years. One volume which ought first to be consulted for symbolic meanings, however limited and limiting the author's choices, is G.A. Gaskell's *Dictionary of All Scriptures and Myths* (New York: Julian Press, 1960). Look up Jesus, Job, and John the Baptist just for starters— and for good indication of the book's uses. Thomas Inman is one of the earlier authors whose work on symbolism related to the biblical is available in English. In *Ancient Pagan and Modern Christian Symbolism* (London: printed for the author, 1869), he tries to trace the ideas underlying symbols in Christianity back to their pagan sources. For instance, Inman works with symbolic relationships between Asshur and Jehovah, or between Baal and the New Testament God—sometimes with surprising effectiveness considering that archaeology had in his time not provided him with the evidence we now possess! Edwyn Bevan's *Symbolism and Belief* (Port Washington, N.Y.: Kennikat Press, 1968; reprint of the 1938 edition) is a good survey of symbolism in Christian myth, ritual, and worship covering height, time, light, spirit, the wrath of God, among other things. Discovering the fundamental order of the Christian world, through focus on some ways the pair of opposites, male and female, functioned in several early Christian groups, is Wayne A. Meeks' aim in "The Image of the Androgyne: Some Uses of a Symbol in Earliest Christianity," *History of Religions*, 13 (February 1974), pp. 165-208. Other opposites, good and evil, are discussed from their Zoroastrian origins through Christian applications in George Boas' "Warfare in the Cosmos," *Diogenes*, no. 78 (Summer 1972), pp. 38-51. Chapters four through six on the fall of man are especially relevant to biblical myth study in Theodore Reik's *Myth and Guilt* (New York: George Braziller, 1957). The book as a whole is a psychoanalysis of "The Crime and Punishment of Mankind"—original sin and redemption, the matter of guilt, etc.— an excellent work in symbolism, in other words. *Myth and Symbol* (London: S.P.C.K., 1966/p), ed. Frederick W. Dillistone, is a good collection of essays on religious symbolism overall, much of it related to Hebrew-Christian myth and practice. Bruno Bettelheim's *Symbolic Wounds: Puberty Rites and the Envious Male* (Glencoe, Ill.: The Free Press, 1954) relies heavily on myth for source material, and in it you'll find varied information related to biblical mythology, such as in the section called "Monotheism and the Castrating Father," in which biblical myth and the rite of circumcision are dealt with. James S. Forrester-Brown's *The Two Creation Stories in Genesis: A Study in Their Symbolism* (New York: Shambhala Publications, 1974/p) is an interesting and useful little book, too. Abraham Palmer Smythe's *The Samson Saga and Its Place in Comparative Religion* (New York: Arno Press, 1977; reprint of the earlier edition) deals with Samson, postulating that he symbolized the sun and was in fact a part of an ancient drama dealing with the sunset. Solar naturalism is a bit far-fetched for our tastes today, but the book is surely one of the fine examples of what strange avenues symbolic interpretation may take us down. So, too, with two books by Heline Corrine, *The Twelve Labors of Hercules*, 3rd edition (La Canada, Calif.: New Age Press, 1974/p) and *Mythology and the Bible*, 4th edition (La Canada, Calif.: New Age Press, 1972/p), both of which handle Greek and Christian myth in symbolic terms, the Greek being glossed by the Christian.

Eschatology: The Doctrine of a Future Life in Israel, Judaism and Christianity (New York: Schocken Books, 1970/p; originally published in 1899) remains the standard work on biblical escha-

tology, covering the full historical development of the doctrine
from earliest Old Testament through New Testament times.
Edmund B. Keller's "Hebrew Thoughts on Immortality and
Resurrection" in the *International Journal for Philosophy of
Religion*, 5 (Spring 1974), pp. 16-44, covers the development of
the belief in immortality and resurrection from its Near Eastern
backgrounds to Hebraic thought through New Testament times.
Paul Badham's *Christian Beliefs in Life After Death* (New York:
Harper & Row, 1976) is fuller development of the same general
area and is excellent as background to biblical myth study. Hywel
D. Lewis is more inclined toward philosphically discussing whether
or not there will be life after death than anything else in his *The
Self and Immortality* (London: Macmillan, 1973), but there's
lots in the book on Christian eschatological mythology, too.
S.G.F. Brandon's *History, Time and Deity* (New York: Barnes and
Noble, 1965) is a good eschatological study as well as primarily
an investigation of the Christian concept of time. Brandon sees
death as the main thrust of the concept of time in Christianity.

In biblical myth study symbolism and eschatology both involve
the devil and Hell. Although mainly developed in Christianity
during the Middle Ages, the devil does have a long history in
various guises in ancient Egyptian, Mesopotamian, Persian, and
Indian cultures. Paul Carus considers the devil's antecedents
in his *The History of the Devil and the Idea of Evil* (New York:
Bell Publishing Co., 1969/i; reprint of an earlier edition). The
book is a main source still, but don't overlook Jeffery Burton
Russell's *The Devil: Perceptions of Evil from Antiquity to Primitive
Christianity* (Ithaca, N.Y.: Cornell University Press, 1977/ibp)
as a good study of the devil as personification of evil, or William
Woods' *A History of the Devil* (New York: Berkeley Publishing
Corp., 1975/ip). Dennis Wheatley's *The Devil and All His Works*
(London, 1976/i) is pictorially the best of the volumes, with 167
illustrations, 48 in color, but for equally well reproduced pictures
and large format, Richard Cavendish's *Visions of Heaven and
Hell* (New York: Harmony Books, 1977/ip) is also excellent.
Such chapters as these in Cavendish will reveal his broader plan:
"Life After Death," "Paradise and Heaven," "The Underworld,"
and "The Abyss of Hell." Maximilian Rudwin's *The Devil in
Legend and Literature* (LaSalle, Ill.: Open Court, 1973/p; reprint of the 1931 edition) contains a good deal of comparative
demonology as well as a thoroughgoing investigation of various
legends of Lucifer, Lilith, and journeys to Hell. Lauran Paine's

The Hierarchy of Hell (New York: Hippocrene Books, 1972) is a full-blown study of the concept of Hell, from most ancient to modern, which deals with parallels in other cultures, possible diffusion, and borrowing. James W. Boyd's *Satan and Mara: Christian and Buddhist Symbols of Evil* (Leiden: E.J. Brill, 1975) includes all the author could find on the two religions' embodiments of evil, Satan and Mara. It's a good comparative study. If you're curious about *Evidence of Satan in the Modern World*, see the book with that title written by Leon Cristiani (New York: Avon, 1973/p); it is as good as any (and there are many) like it in dealing with possession and exorcism.

Reference Works

Reference works on the *Bible* exist in such large numbers and can indeed be handy in myth study. Perhaps the best of the lot is the *Dictionary of the Bible* (New York: Charles Scribner's Sons, 1963), ed. James Hastings and revised by Frederick C. Grant and H.H. Rowley. Look up anything relevant to the *Bible*, ancient cultures coexistent with the biblical, and even some of the terminology shared by religious and myth study, and you'll very probably find it. Also, there are great maps, and a fine cross-referencing system employed. Henry Snyder Gehman's *The New Westminster Dictionary of the Bible* (Philadelphia: Westminster Press, 1970) and Madeleine S. Miller's and J. Lane's *Harper's Bible Dictionary*, 8th edition (New York: Harper & Row, 1973) are very close in content to the Scribner's volume, including the good maps. *A New Standard Bible Dictionary*, 3rd edition revised (New York: Funk and Wagnalls, 1971), ed. Jacobus, Lane and Zenos, can also serve a useful purpose in myth study, but I cannot recommend it quite as highly as the preceding three.

More specialized in content than the preceding dictionaries are a number of other works which have their places in myth study. *The Interpreter's Dictionary of the Bible*, four volumes (Nashville: Abingdon Press, 1976) is one such work. *Peake's Commentary on the Bible*, ed. Matthew Black (London: Thomas Nelson, 1962) is another; A. Richardson's *Dictionary of Christian Theology* (London: SCM, 1969) and *A Theological Word Book of the Bible* (London: SCM, 1954/bp) still others. *Teaching the Old Testament in English Classes* (Bloomington: Indiana University Press, 1973) has some good, useful information for myth students—especially on historical background—and its extensive, annotated bibliography will carry you well beyond the sources I am able to describe here. A pair of volumes of interest and value because their author is so scientifically inclined are *Asimov's Guide to the Bible: New Testament* and *Old Testament*, 2 volumes (New York: Avon Books, 1969/p). Erich Fromm's *You Shall Be As Gods* (Greenwich, Conn.: Fawcett Publications, 1966/p) is a "radical humanist" approach to the Old Testament that falls well within the bounds of myth study. Finally, if it's biblical names you're curious about, a good, inexpensive source is *The Mentor Dictionary of Mythology and the Bible* (New York: NAL Mentor, 1973/p) by Richard J. Daigle and Frederick R. Lapides; it covers classical and biblical mythology only.

Works on Religion and Related Matters

Many of the reference tools just mentioned will provide background to biblical religions, but books that deal with religions generally will, as a rule, have excellent brief summaries of Judaism, Christianity, and related sects. For instance, the discussions of the varieties of Judaism and Christianity are excellent and up to date in Robert S. Ellwood, Jr.'s *Many Peoples, Many Faiths* (Englewood Cliffs, N.J.: Prentice-Hall, 1976/b) and in the *Historical Atlas of the Religions of the World* (New York: Macmillan, 1974/b), ed. Isma'il Ragi al Faruqi. Both have fine bibliographies for further study, and the Macmillan *Atlas* is loaded with maps and charts.

For Judaism alone, try Arthur Hertzberg's *Judaism* (New York: George Braziller, 1961), a nicely written introduction to the subject. Bernard J. Bamberger's *The Story of Judaism* (New York: Schocken Books, 1970/p) is also a good introduction, as is Jacob Neusner's *The Way of Torah: An Introduction to Judaism*, 2nd edition (Encino, Calif.: Dickensen Publishing, 1974). Gershom G. Scholem's *Major Trends in Jewish Mysticism* (New York: Schocken Books, 1961) covers mysticism well, and Adolphe Franck's definitive study of *The Kabbalah* (New York: Bell Publishing, 1940; originally 1843 in French) remains excellent for deep background study of that religious belief. You might also find benefit in checking on Julius Gutmann's *Philosophies of Judaism*, trans. D.W. Silverman (New York: Holt, Rinehart and Winston, 1964) and Yehezkel Kaufman's *The Religion of Israel*, trans. Moshe Greenberg (Chicago: University of Chicago Press, 1960).

For Christianity alone, Kenneth S. Latourette's *A History of Christianity* (New York: Harper & Row, 1953/bp) is a mammoth 1500-page "standard," but if that's short on what you're looking for, try his seven-volume *A History of the Expansion of Christianity* (New York: Harper & Row, 1937–45) and five-volume *Christianity in a Revolutionary Age* (New York: Harper & Row, 1958–62). Charles Guignebert, a man who for thirty-one years taught the history of Christianity at the Sorbonne, also has written a provocative and well researched history called *Ancient, Medieval and Modern Christianity: The Evolution of a Religion* (New Hyde Park, N.Y.: University Books, 1961; reprint of the 1927 edition) that I have found to be most helpful. One of the more recent histories, Paul Johnson's *A History of Christianity* (New York: Atheneum, 1979/bp; originally in hardback in 1976), may well, if reviews can be trusted, be "the best one-volume history of Christianity ever done" (Richard Marius in *The Christian Century*). Roland H. Bainton's *The History of Christianity* (London: Nelson, 1964) is useful not so much for its text as for the hundreds of illustrations it has, some in color. Specifically on earlier Christianity, several additional works are worth considering: Philip Carrington's *The Early Christian Church*, two volumes (Cambridge: Cambridge University Press, 1957); Rudolf Bultmann's *Primitive Christianity in Its Contemporary Setting*, trans. R.H. Fuller (New York: Meridian Books, 1956); Robert M. Grant's *A Historical Introduction to the New Testament* (New York: Harper & Row, 1963/bp); and Robert L. Wilken's *The Myth of Christian Beginnings* (Garden City, N.Y.: Doubleday Anchor, 1972/p). Don't, by the way, overlook J. Morgenstern's *Some Significant Antecedents of Christianity* (Leiden: E.J. Brill, 1966), a little but useful book that will give you broad background in the possible antecedents of Christianity and in earlier similar worship forms.

Two other groups within the broad framework called "Judaism" (even Christianity might be construed a part of it) are important for their relationship to (and possible influence on) early Christianity, so some mention should here be made of relevant works. First are the Essenes and the famous Dead Sea scrolls found at Qumran. Geza Vermes' "The Impact of the Dead Sea Scrolls on the Study of the New Testament," in *Journal of Jewish Studies*, 27 (Autumn 1976), pp. 107–16, is a recent brief introduction to the subject. A. Dupont-Sommer's "Problems Regarding the Dead Sea Scrolls," trans. Elaine P. Halperin, in *Diogenes*, 22

(Summer 1958), pp. 75–102, is also a most useful introductory discussion of the meaning for Christian origins of the discovery of the scrolls. Longer works include Arthur Powell Davies' *The Meaning of the Dead Sea Scrolls* (New York: NAL Mentor, 1956/ ip); J. Allegro's *The Dead Sea Scrolls: A Reappraisal* (Harmondsworth, G.B.: Penguin, 1976/ibp), and C.F. Pfeiffer's *The Dead Sea Scrolls and the Bible* (Grand Rapids, Mich.: Baker Book House, 1969/ip)—all of them quite satisfactory as sources for background, the first two especially. Millar Burrows' *The Dead Sea Scrolls* (New York: Viking Press, 1961/i) includes descriptions of the finds at Qumran, appraises their value, discusses their content, and even includes translations, by Burrows, of principal texts. Theodor H. Gaster's *The Scriptures of the Dead Sea Scrolls* (London: Secker and Warburg, 1957) and Geza Vermes' *The Dead Sea Scrolls in English* (Harmondsworth, G.B.: Penguin, 1962/p) both also provide good translations of scrolls if you're looking for primary source material. A difficult collection of essays dealing with the philological/textual problems in the scrolls is *Qumran and the History of the Biblical Text* (Cambridge: Harvard University Press, 1975), ed. Frank Moore Cross.

The Gnostics are a second significant group, but it is only relatively recently that important primary material could be studied, that is, since the discovery, in the mid 1940s, at Nag Hammadi in Egypt, of over forty Gnostic documents. These have been translated and are now available in *The Nag Hammadi Library* (N.Y.: Harper & Row, 1978), ed. James E. Robinson. Elaine Pagels' award-winning study entitled *The Gnostic Gospels* (New York: Random House, 1979/b) assesses the contents of the related writings and their impact on traditional Christian thought. Such earlier works on the Gnostics as C. William King's *The Gnostics and Their Remains* (London: David Nutt, 1887; originally 1864) and even G.R.S. Mead's turn-of-the-century *Fragments of a Faith Forgotten* (New Hyde Park, N.Y.: University Books reprint edition, 1960) are now severely dated by the Nag Hammadi find. Robert M. Grant's *Gnosticism and Early Christianity*, 2nd edition (New York: Columbia University Press, 1966), and Hans Jonas' *The Gnostic Religion* (Boston: Beacon Press, 1963/p) are the best and most useful works of an introductory sort now available, but for a highly impressionistic, interpretive journey through Gnosticism, you might also find Jacques Lacarriere's *The Gnostics*, trans. Nina Rootes (New York: E.P. Dutton, 1977/bp), worthwhile.

Comparative Studies

The interrelationship of the Essenes, Gnostics, and Early Christians brings to mind what S.H. Hooke once said: "It is not an exaggeration to say that some knowledge of Babylonian religion is indispensable for a proper understanding of the Hebrew religion." He could well have expanded that to include a number of other religions and myth systems, as we'll now see in dealing with works having to do with the syncretistic "flow" into and from the biblical religions and mythologies.

As a broad starting point, I highly recommend three works in particular. The first is William Foxwell Albright's *From Stone Age to Christianity: Monotheism and the Historical Process*, 2nd edition (Garden City, N.Y.: Anchor, 1957/p), a fine work which traces the development of monotheism in the ancient world, seeking initially its roots in the Mesopotamian cultures and Egypt and culminating in the Old Testament and Christianity. The second is E.O. James' *The Ancient Gods: The History and Diffusion of Religion in the Ancient Near East and the Eastern Mediterranean* (New York: Capricorn Books, 1964/p), a superb volume for seeing the interrelatedness mentioned earlier. The third, in some ways representative of a great many books on ancient Western Asian history but focused primarily on religion and philosophy in that context, is Cornelius Lowe's *Myth, Sacred History & Philosophy: The Pre-Christian Religious Heritage of the West* (New York: Harcourt, Brace & World, 1967). The three books are general, true, but they provide solid basis for seeing biblical myth in historical context, a most important part of the study of any myth system.

Mesopotamian influences on biblical myth, parallels in the two myth systems, and general relationships between the two cultures are the subject of quite a body of works. Among the more pertinent ones are André Parrot's *Babylon and the Old Testament*, trans. B.E. Hooke (New York: Philosophical Library, 1958/i), a book divided into four parts, the second of which deals with biblical references to Babylon and with the archaeological evidence. Gerald A. Larue's *Babylon and the Bible* (Grand Rapids, Mich.: Baker Book House/p) is a collection of articles covering the several topics mentioned above. C. Leonard Woolley's *The Excavations at Ur and the Hebrew Records* (London: George Allen & Unwin, 1929) is an early effort to relate the Mesopotamian evidence to the biblical stories. Thorkild

Jacobsen's "Ancient Mesopotamian Religion: The Central Concerns" in *Proceedings of the American Philosophical Society*, 107 (December 20, 1963), pp. 473–84, is good on the diffusion of Mesopotamian ideas to the biblical cultures. The third chapter in Alexander Heidel's *The Babylonian Genesis*, 2nd edition (Chicago: University of Chicago Press, 1951), a book which deals with the Babylonian cosmogony, is entitled "Old Testament Parallels." In that chapter, Heidel concludes that the issue of whether or not the Babylonian story influenced the Old Testament cosmogonies must still be "left open." In another work, *The Gilgamesh Epic and Old Testament Parallels* (Chicago: University of Chicago Press, 1949), Heidel covers diffusion possibilities to Old Testament myth as well as parallels (particularly flood myth). Thomas C. Hartman's "Some Thoughts on the Sumerian King List and Genesis 5 and 11 B" in *Journal of Biblical Literature*, 91 (March 1972), pp. 25–32, suggests that biblical writers did not draw upon the Sumerian King list as model for the Old Testament genealogies mentioned in the title. Robert William Rogers provides a general overview of parallels in *Cuneiform Parallels to the Old Testament* (New York: Eaton and Mains, 1912).

Phoenician/Canaanite parallels, influences, and the like have also been extensively discussed. Among the better general works are John Gray's *The Legacy of Canaan: The Ras Shamra Texts and Their Relevance to the Old Testament* (Leiden: E.J. Brill, 1957/b) and Arvid S. Kapelrud's *The Ras Shamra Discoveries and the Old Testament*, trans. G.W. Anderson (Norman: University of Oklahoma Press, 1963). Kapelrud's chapter entitled "The Deities of Ras Shamra: Old Testament Parallels" is particularly helpful. Frank Moore Cross' *Canaanite Myth and Hebrew Epic* (Cambridge: Harvard University Press, 1973) is worth looking into also, as are E.A. Leslie's *Old Testament Religion in the Light of Its Canaanite Backgrounds* (New York, 1936) and J.W. Jack's *The Ras Shamra Tablets: Their Bearing on the Old Testament* (Edinburgh: Clark, 1935). A bit more specialized in approach are William Foxwell Albright's *Yahweh and the Gods of Canaan: A Historical Analysis of Two Contrasting Faiths* (Garden City, N.Y.: Doubleday, 1968), Gunnar Osborn's *Yahweh and Baal* (Lund: Lunds Universitets, 1956), and Norman C. Habel's *Yahweh Versus Baal: A Conflict of Religious Cultures* (New York: Bookman Associates, 1964). Cyrus H. Gordon's three-way comparison/contrast of Biblical, Ugaritic, and Minoan writings in *Ugarit and Minoan Crete* (New York: W.W. Norton, 1966) is worth looking into, too. As Gordon says (on page 152), "Ugaritic literature has bridged the gap between Homer and the *Bible*. Thanks to Minoan texts we know that from about 1800 to about 1400 B.C., Greece was dominated by Northwest Semites (Phoenicians) who linked it linguistically and culturally with the whole Semitic Levant."

Gordon also wrote a work called *Before the Bible: The Common Background of Greek and Hebrew Civilizations* (New York: Harper & Row, 1962; Arno Press, 1972), which describes the influence of Egypt and the Near East on Greece and the Hebrews. The Greeks, according to many, influenced early Christianity rather directly, though. For information on this, see Hugo Rahner's "The Christian Mystery and the Pagan" in *Pagan and Christian Mysteries* (New York: Harper Torchbook, 1963/ip), ed. Joseph Campbell, or Rahner's *Greek Myths and Christian Mystery*, trans. Brian Batteshaw (New York: Biblo and Tannen, 1971). Also, Werner Jaeger's *Early Christianity and Greek Paideia* (Cambridge: Harvard University Press, 1961) provides evidence that early Christianity made extensive use of many Greek ideals, traditions, and the like. Walter Woodburn Hyde's *Greek Religion and Its Survivals* (New York: Cooper Square Publishers, 1963) is an interesting work on much the same subject, its second chapter especially: "The Influence of Greek Religion on Early Christianity: The Greek Gods Turned Saints." For the Orphic influence on Christianity, see Robert Eisler's *Orpheus the Fisher: Comparative Studies in Orphic and Early Christian Cult Symbolism* (London: J.M. Watkins, 1921) and W.K.C. Guthrie's *Orpheus and Greek Religion* (New York: W.W. Norton, 1966/ip; originally published in hardbound in 1935), especially pp. 261-71.

Samuel Angus' *The Mystery Religions and Christianity* (New York: Dover Publications, 1975; originally published in 1925/bp) is the work on mystery religions generally in the Greco-Roman world; the impact on Christianity of Greco-Roman influences is its special focus. Frederick C. Grant's *Roman Hellenism and the New Testament* (New York: Charles Scribner's Sons, 1962/b) is excellent on the run of influences that affected the content and style of the New Testament. John R. Hinnels' "Zoroastrian Saviour Imagery and Its Influence on the New Testament" in *Numen*, 16 (December 1969), pp. 161-85, and Esmé Wynne-Tyson's *Mithras: The Fellow in the Cap* (New York: Barnes and Noble, 1972) are two excellent sources for seeing Persian influences on the New Testament. R.J. Williams' "'A People Come Out of Egypt,'" in *Supplement to Vetus Testamentum: Congress*

Volume: Edinburgh 1974 (Leiden: E.J. Brill, 1975), pp. 231ff., deals with the apparent influences of Egypt on Israel.

A couple of comparative studies by Geoffrey Parrinder, a well known comparative religionist, are also well worthwhile sources: *Upanishads, Gita, and Bible: A Comparative Study of Hindu and Christian Scriptures* (London: Faber, 1962) and *Avatar and Incarnation* (New York: Barnes and Noble, 1970). Although neither deals with "influences" as such, they do afford excellent bases for thinking about the religions involved, hence about the mythologies.

Works on Historical/Cultural Background

There are so many works available in studying the historical and cultural background to biblical myth that only a "sampler" can here be listed. Such study can be started best, I believe, through brief surveys. In his book called *Ancient Semitic Civilizations* (New York: Capricorn, 1960/bp), for instance, Sabatino Moscati has an excellent little chapter, "The Hebrews," which will introduce what is a bulky subject in rather uncomplicated fashion. So, too, will H. Cazelle's "The Hebrews," the first chapter in D.J. Wiseman's *The Peoples of the Old Testament* (Oxford: Clarendon Press, 1973). These are just examples from among a great many possibilities, of course. Histories of the ancient world, although mostly tending to skim the Hebrews in favor of other peoples and countries, could also provide brief introduction of a useful sort. General encyclopedias are excellent sources, as are such specialized encyclopedias as the *Encyclopedia Judaica*, sixteen volumes plus yearbooks (Jerusalem: Keter Publishing House, 1972). *The World History of the Jewish People* (Tel Aviv: Massadah Publishing Company, 1964; also in Rutgers University Press edition), a multi-volume work well illustrated with photographs and drawings, has many useful sections, but it tends toward more comprehensive articles and, thus, fuller treatment. John Bright's *A History of Israel* (Philadelphia: Westminster Press, 1972), which goes from the earliest period through Hellenism in Israel, is a fine example of the many longer histories available, just as A.W.F. Blunt's *Israel: Social and Religious Development* (London: O.U.P., 1924) is an example of the briefer, more specialized kinds of historical-cultural works that have been published. Robert M. Grant's *Augustus to Constantine* (New York: Harper & Row, 1970/i) begins in A.D. 14 and ends in A.D. 337 and deals comprehensively with early Christian history, thus making it a useful volume for heavily focused background to the growth and spread of Christian mythology. Robert Payne's *The Christian Centuries: From Christ to Dante* (New York: W.W. Norton, 1966) extends its historical coverage, to the thirteenth century.

There are several excellent atlases to consider, for example L.H. Grollenberg's *Atlas of the Bible*, trans. and ed. Joyce M.H. Reid (London: Nelson, 1956) and Yohanon Aharoni's and Michael Avi-Yonah's *The Macmillan Bible Atlas*, revised edition (New York: Macmillan, 1977/i), both well illustrated with maps and pictures. R. de Vaux's *The Early History of Israel* (Leiden: E.J. Brill, 1978), is a two-volume work that has much to offer in the way of historical background to biblical myth study. The three-volume *Cambridge History of the Bible* (Cambridge: Cambridge University Press, 1969), though concerned with other matters than the history of Israel and the Christians alone, does have useful parts (particularly in Volume I and the first part of Volume II). Books like *Everyday Life in Bible Times*, revised edition (Washington, D.C.: National Geographic Society, 1977), are valuable in any number of ways—for their pictures, or discussions of customs and social life, for example. Werner Keller's companion volumes *The Bible as History* and *The Bible as History in Pictures*, both trans. William Neil (New York: William Morrow, 1956 and 1964/ib) back Old and New Testament narratives with whatever facts are known, making them a kind of history *and* myth source heavily reliant on archaeological finds. *Adam to Daniel* and *Daniel to Paul* (New York: Macmillan, 1962/b), both edited by Gaalyahu Cornfeld, are two beautiful volumes which trace the historical and religious background to the *Bible* through biblical narratives themselves, as well as through outside sources. The books are beautifully printed and illustrated.

A number of other works more specialized in their approaches also are available for the study of historical/cultural background to biblical myth. Kathleen M. Kenyon's *Amorites and Canaanites* (London: Oxford University Press, 1966/i) is a study of "the history and culture of the peoples that the Israelites found in occupation of the Promised Land." Kenyon also assesses the effect of those peoples and their culture on the Israelites. A book filled with content heavy in myth and religion-related matter is Allen H. Jones' *Bronze Age Civilization: The Philistines and the Danites* (Washington, D.C.: Public Affairs Press, 1975), in which the influence of the Philistines on the Aegean and Hebrew worlds is especially emphasized. W.G. De Burgh's *The Legacy of the Ancient World* (Harmondsworth, G.B.: Penguin, 1961/p; originally published in 1923) traces the contributions of Israel, Greece, and Rome to Christianity and the Christian world. William Foxwell Albright's *History, Archaeology, and Christian Humanism* (New York: McGraw-Hill, 1964) has many useful pages, too, particularly pp. 103-56, where he deals with the syncretistic tendencies and realizations in the ancient Near East, or the first chapter, in which he surveys the history of Near Eastern studies and the refining of the historical method employed. *The Bible and the Ancient Near East* (Garden City, N.Y.: Doubleday, 1961), ed. G. Ernest Wright, is a collection of essays in honor of Albright. Roughly half the volume is devoted to ancient Israel, the essays therein forming a kind of overview of Old Testament scholarship— from the language and textual problems, to a review of the history of biblical studies, to matters of chronology in Old Testament study. It would be an excellent volume to put at either end of your work in background to biblical mythology—at the beginning as a sophisticated introduction, at the end as summation of the state of the knowledge.

Works on Archaeology

Archaeology has played a role in our understanding of the history and life of ancient West Asia generally, so not surprisingly, any archaeological work relevant to events or places in the *Bible* has received much attention in print. The multi-volume *Encyclopedia of Archaeological Excavations in the Holy Land* (Leiden: E.J. Brill, 1973, etc./i) is the major reference source on the archaeological finds which have shed light on the *Bible*. Magnus Magnusson's *Archaeology of the Bible* (New York: Simon and Schuster, 1978/i) is the best single-volume source written as it was by one who knows the territory, arguments, and evidence well. A good short but nicely illustrated work is A. Negev's *Archaeology in the Land of the Bible* (Leiden: E.J. Brill, 1977/i). Joseph P. Free's *Archaeology and Bible History* (Wheaton, Ill.: Victor Books, 1950/ip) is a good general run-through of the relation to biblical history of much archaeological work through the middle of this century. Robert T. Boyd's *A Pictorial Guide to Biblical Archaeology* (New York: Bonanza Books, 1969/i; previously published as *Tells, Tombs and Treasure* by Baker Book House, Grand Rapids, Mich.) does, too, but the great flaw in the work—and it is quite a flaw—is the author's persistent claim that a given archaeological find "proves" the *Bible* when in fact no such claim can be made. It does have the advantage of being a very brief introduction to major finds and their connections to the *Bible*, however. William Foxwell Albright's *Archaeology and the Religion of Israel* (Baltimore: Johns Hopkins Press, 1942) covers much the same territory but involves related regions like Canaan and Mesopotamia, and how they relate to biblical references. Stanley A. Cook's *The Religion of Ancient Palestine in the Light of Archaeology and Inscriptions* (London: Oxford University Press, 1930/i) is a now somewhat dated survey of Old Testament-related archaeology. John Gray's *Archaeology and the Old Testament World* (New York: Harper & Row, 1965/ip) is divided into two parts, one dealing with various regions related by biblical references, the other with the period from Judges through later Old Testament days. *The Biblical Archaeological Reader* (Chicago: Quadrangle Books, 1961), ed. Ernest Wright and David Noel Freedman, is slightly more technical than some will wish or need, but it, too, can be helpful. A little article by Maurice L. Zigmond on the matter of jumping to conclusions before all the archaeological evidence is in would make worthwhile reading for just about anyone who has seen, as I have, preposterous claims made and defended through the fusion of scant archaeological evidence and something in biblical myth. The article is "Archaeology and the 'Patriarchal Age' of the Old Testament," *Explorations in Cultural Anthropology* (New York: McGraw-Hill, 1964), ed. Ward H. Goodenough, pp. 571–98. Two books related to the archaeology of the New Testament are especially worth mentioning. E.M. Blaiklock's *The Archaeology of the New Testament* (Grand Rapids, Mich.: Zondervan Publishing House, 1970/i) and R.K. Harrison's *Archaeology of the New Testament* (New York: Association Press, 1964/ib). The latter work also has an exceptionally useful bibliography for further research. And, needless to say, there are a great many books and multi-volume sets available today which focus on single sites. Two of the more recent ones are Yigael Yadin's *Hazor: The Rediscovery of a Great Citadel of the Bible* (New York: Random House, 1975/i) and the three-volume *Beth She'Arim* (New Brunswick, N.J.: Rutgers University Press, 1973–76), by B. Mazar, Schwabe and Lifshitz, and N. Avigad.

Closely related are volumes which deal with places and/or personalities in the *Bible*. These often present an equal mix of archaeology and still existent places, photographs and text.

Kathleen Kenyon's *Royal Cities of the Old Testament* (London: Barrie & Jenkins, 1971/i) is one of the best of them—an archaeological tour of Jerusalem, Samaria, and other biblical places that includes over a hundred black and white photos, twenty-eight diagrams, and floor plans. Also good is *Historical Sites in Israel* (New York: Vanguard Press, 1964/i) by Moshe Pearlman and Yaacov Yannai. A more specialized focus on Jerusalem is offered in B. Mazar's *The Mountain of the Lord: Excavating in Jerusalem* (Garden City, N.Y.: Doubleday, 1975). Leah Bronner's *Biblical Personalities and Archaeology* (Jerusalem: Keter Publishing House, 1974/ib) is organized around individuals in the *Bible*—Abraham, Moses, Joshua, David, and on to Nehemiah—and combines text and pictures dealing with the archaeological evidence. John Wilkinson's superb *Jerusalem as Jesus Knew It: Archaeology as Evidence* (London: Thames and Hudson, 1978/i) is an interesting approach to the fusion of the biblical and archaeological evidence, just as D. Alexander's *Photo Guide to the New Testament* (Leiden: E.J. Brill, 1973/i) is—although it does not use archaeological evidence as extensively as Wilkinson's book does. *Jesus: History and Culture of the New Testament* (New York: Herder and Herder, 1971/i), by Erich Lessing *et al*, includes some chapters directly relevant to myth study, those that deal with the historicity of New Testament places especially. *In the Footsteps of Jesus: A Pilgrimage to the Scenes of Christ's Life* (Westminster, Md.: Christian Classics, 1975/i), by W.E. Pax, is less archaeologically oriented, but its beautiful illustrations, sixty-eight of them in color, make it a remarkably useful text-and-pictures backdrop to the study of New Testament mythology. Moshe Pearlman's *In the Footsteps of Moses* (New York: Leon Amiel, 1976/i) has about as many illustrations, forty-seven in color, and is as useful a book as Pax's. There's also an article entitled "In Search of Moses," by Harvey Arden, in *National Geographic*, 149 (January 1976/i), pp. 2-37, which has good photography and text in combination. If you want to get into the problems philologists have had with New Testament texts, see book three in Leo Deuel's *Testaments of Time* (New York: Alfred A. Knopf, 1965).

The flood and Noah's Ark have inspired an enormous number of articles, books, and even films that have exploited some archaeological and geological clues. The following articles are useful: "George Smith: The Story of the Flood" in C.W. Ceram's *Gods, Graves, and Scholars* (New York: Alfred A. Knopf, 1951; Bantam, 1972/p); Sir Leonard Woolley's "The Flood" in *Myth or Legend?*

(New York: Capricorn, 1968/p); Fred Warshofsky's "Noah: The Flood, The Facts" in *Reader's Digest*, (September 1977), pp. 129–34; or Gordon Gaskill's "The Mystery of Noah's Ark" in *Reader's Digest*, (September 1975), pp. 150–54. The first three articles focus on the evidence of the flood, the one by Gaskill on the possible existence of remains of Noah's Ark. Then, for more on the flood, try a marvelous set of seven cassette tapes put out in 1977 by the University of California Extension Media Center, Berkeley, Calif. 94720 (Set no. AT335–41). The series is entitled *The Flood Myth: An Inquiry into Causes and Circumstances* and contains an extensive comparative treatment of flood myths, particularly West Asian and Greek, and the evidence in support of or against the occurrence of floods in the regions where the flood myths came into being. For more on the supposed remains of Noah's Ark and work that has been done towards finding them, any of these books will serve nicely: Kelly L. Seagraves' *Search for Noah's Ark* (Chino, Calif.: Beta Book Co., 1975/p), Violet M. Cummings' *Noah's Ark: Fable or Fact?* (Moonachie, N.J.: Pyramid Publications, 1975/p), or John W. Montgomery's *Quest for Noah's Ark* (Minneapolis: Bethany Fellowship, 1972/p).

Translations

If you're looking for translations of texts useful in the study of biblical mythology, you've not too far to look, of course, the *Bible* being the primary source of most importance. While many translations exist, it is recommended that in myth study you use a nicely cross-referenced one, such as *The Jerusalem Bible* (Garden City, N.Y.: Doubleday, 1966). It has good introductions to major books and sections, an excellent chronological chart, maps, an index of biblical themes, etc. as additional aids. Also, don't overlook the fifteen aprocryphal books included between Old and New Testaments in *some* Protestant editions (some of them in some Catholic *Bibles*, too) but missing from many others. *The Jerusalem Bible* includes only a few of them, so an edition of the Apocrypha will be a necessary additional book. *The Lost Books of the Bible* and *The Forgotten Books of Eden* (New York: N.A.L. Meridian Book, 1974/p) is also a valuable source for some pseudepigraphic and other noncanonical writings. (Doubleday plans publication of the *complete* pseudepigrapha in 1980 in a volume similar to *The Jerusalem Bible*.) Also, some of the Nag-Hammadi writings of the Gnostics mentioned earlier should be considered in the primary source category, just as the translations made from the Dead Sea scrolls found at Qumran (covered earlier, too) should certainly be. Even books like E.A. Wallis Budge's translations from Syriac texts called *History of the Blessed Virgin Mary* and *History of the Likeness of Christ* (Luzac, 1899) might eventually have some value to you in the course of your work in biblical mythology—as might such collateral works as Howard Clark Kee's *The Origins of Christianity: Sources and Documents* (Englewood Cliffs, N.J.: Prentice-Hall, 1973/p), W. Beyerlin's *Near Eastern Religious Texts Relating to the Old Testament* (Leiden: E.J. Brill, 1978), D. Winton Thomas' *Documents from Old Testament Times* (New York: Harper Torchbook, 1961/p), and James B. Pritchard's *Ancient Near Eastern Texts Relating to the Old Testament* (Princeton: Princeton University Press, 1969/i), which was also published by the same publisher in an abridged two-volume paperbound edition called *The Ancient Near East: An Anthology of Texts and Pictures.*

Works on Art

For art, the best sources are well illustrated books mentioned earlier, art histories, and varied books exemplified by these few: A. Reifenberg's *Ancient Hebrew Arts* (New York: Schocken Books, 1950/i), which surveys the arts of Palestine during the biblical period and early Jewish Diaspora; René Huyghe's the *Larousse Encyclopedia of Byzantine and Medieval Art*, trans. Dennis Gilbert, Ilse Schreier, and Wendela Schurmann (London: Paul Hamlyn, 1963/i), which has extensive photographs of Christian art; and Ronald Sheridan's and Anne Ross's *Gargoyles and Grotesques: Paganism in the Medieval Church* (Boston: N.Y. Graphic Society, 1975/i), which amply illustrates how imagery was absorbed from "pagan" sources by medieval Christianity. The possibilities here, obviously, are endless, but the sampling of works mentioned should suffice for "starters."

Islamic Mythologies

Just under 800 statute miles southeast of Jerusalem is Mecca, in Saudi Arabia, birthplace of the Islamic prophet Muhammed and traditional center of the Moslem religion he founded. Born in approximately A.D. 570, Muhammed gave the world, through revelation, the book known as *Qur'an* (Koran), in which we

discover Moses and Jesus to be forerunners of Muhammed as con-
veyors of God's will. Moslem religion now is spread widely around
the world—particularly from Pakistan on the east, through the Arab
Middle East, and on throughout North Africa—its membership
presently exceeding a half billion people.

As is the case with biblical mythology, there is controversy
over whether the *Qur'an* and Moslem traditional material convey
a body of myths. Once again, the difficulties of understanding
and properly using the word "myth" must be pointed to as
at least part of the cause of the controversy. There is little doubt
that any religious system has myths and legends, however few in
number or sketchy in form, once the terms are appropriately
handled.

In the case of Islamic "mythology" there is more of a problem
than with most mythologies, however. The kinds of traditional
stories rich in imagery, character, and plot that are characteristic
of most myth systems are not commonly found in Islamic oral
or written traditions. Such stories as are found are as a rule sufficiently undeveloped, almost allusions instead, to precipitate
the comment that "there is no Islamic mythology." Look through
the *Qur'an* and the difficulties are apparent. The "story" of Adam
and Satan in the Garden, for instance, told mainly in Surah VII,
verses 19 and following, is completely undeveloped and in outline
form compared with the story in Genesis. The "story" of Mary
and the birth of Jesus, told at greatest length in Surah XIX,
verses 16–34, is but a shadow of the renderings to be found in
the New Testament. Still, they are traditional stories—as much
stories, that is, as are to be found in a tradition which does not
ordinarily allow for the representation of any living things. The
only exceptions to this occur where the Islamic faith has been
imported outside Arabia and an old tradition of stories allowed
to continue or to grow in connection with the new religion.

Collections of the Myths; Translations

The result of this peculiarity is that there are no mythographies
that deal generally with Islamic mythology—at least in English
there aren't. The Sufis, a mystical Moslem sect, have their legends,
and there is the book called *Legends of the Sufis* (Wheaton, Ill.:
Theosophical Publishing House, 1977/p) by Shemsu-D-Din Ahmed,
El Eflaki. It contains more than 200 stories of Sufis in the Mehlevi
school. Also, in the sections on Persian mythology in J. Hackin's
Asiatic Mythology (New York: Thomas Y. Crowell, 1963/i)

and the *Larousse Encyclopedia of Mythology* (London: Paul
Hamlyn, 1959/ip), ed. Felix Guirand, some space is devoted to
Moslem mythology in Persia. That's it, however. From there,
it's straight to the source of greatest importance, the *Qur'an* and
such myths as the conversion of the tribes of A'ad and Thamud
(Surah VII, verse 65 and following), the creation (in several
Surahs, but see XIII, 2-4), Solomon (Surah XXVII mainly, 16ff.),
and others. Several translations into English of the *Qur'an* have
been done. A.J. Arberry's two-volume *The Koran Interpreted*
(New York: Macmillan, 1955-56) is the best in my estimation.
Not only does it offer the reader the most help in understanding
the *Qur'an*, but it is not as "stiff" as others I've seen. Mohammed
Marmaduke Pickthall's translation called *The Meaning of the
Glorious Koran* (New York: N.A.L. Mentor, 1953/p; originally
published in hardbound in London by George Allen & Unwin)
is usable and does have some editorial apparatus to aid the reader,
but the language is to me pretty difficult when compared with
Arberry's, as it is in N.J. Dawood's translation, *The Koran* (Harmondsworth, G.B.: Penguin, 1968/p). The latter two translations
bring to mind Thomas Carlyle's words, upon trying to read the
Qur'an, that is was "as toilsome reading as I ever undertook."

Works on the Myths and Religion

Background to Islamic religion and myth can be gotten a good
deal more easily than can the myths themselves. I would highly
recommend as a starting point Isma'il Ragi al Faruqi's chapter on
"Islam" in the superb book he edited, *Historical Atlas of the
Religions of the World* (New York: Macmillan, 1974/ib). It is
a brief but lucid overview of the varieties and history of Islamic
religions written by an expert in Islamic studies. It is possible
to find plenty of other short, introductory discussions—John A.
Hardon's, for instance, in Volume II of *Religions of the World*
(Garden City, N.Y.: Doubleday Image Book, 1968/p) or Geoffrey
Parrinder's in *Introduction to Asian Religions* (New York: Oxford
University Press, 1976/p) but al Faruqi's is the finest. Of the
longer works on Islamic religion, John Alden Williams' *Islam*
(New York: George Braziller, 1961) is excellent since, in addition
to providing the overview, it provides numerous excerpts from
Islamic literature. William Montgomery Watt's *What is Islam?*
(London: Longmans, 1968) is also a fine work written by an
expert in Islamic studies. A.M.R. Muhajir's *Lessons from the*

Stories of the Qur'an (Lahore: Ashraf, 1965) is more directly to the myth student's purposes than a longer survey of the religion would be. So, too, are A.J. Arberry's *The Holy Koran: An Introduction* (London: George Allen and Unwin, 1953) and *Revelation and Reason in Islam* (London: George Allen and Unwin, 1957).

Works on Historical/Cultural Background

For cultural and historical background, as well as religious in most cases, books like John B. Christopher's *The Islamic Tradition* (New York: Harper & Row, 1972/p) are recommended—or Mohammed Marmaduke Pickthall's *Cultural Side of Islam* (Madras: Universal Publishers, 1959/b) and A.J. Arberry's *Aspects of Islamic Civilization: As Depicted in the Original Texts* (New York: A.S. Barnes and Co., 1964). Wilfred Blunt's *Splendors of Islam*, new edition (New York: Viking Press, 1976) and Michael Rogers' *The Spread of Islam* (New York: Phaidon, 1975) are both beautifully illustrated surveys of the history, culture, and arts of Islam. F.E. Peters' *Alah's Commonwealth: A History of Islam in the Near East, 600–1000 AD* is an ambitious 800-page history you might also wish to look into for background help. Bernard Lewis' two-volume history of Islam from Muhammed to the year 1453, *Islam* (New York: Harper & Row, 1973) is even more ambitious, but the multi-volume *Cambridge History of Islam* (Cambridge: Cambridge University Press, 1975, etc.) is far and away the most comprehensive historical source available. Another multi-volume work emerging as a major source for just about *anything* Islamic is the new edition of *The Encyclopedia of Islam* (Leiden: E.J. Brill, 1954 and following). *Islam and the Arab World* (New York: Alfred A. Knopf, 1976/i), by Bernard Lewis and others, is a superbly illustrated survey of the culture and history that ought not to be overlooked in any rush to the bigger works, however.

There are also some fine books on Mohammed which will serve well as background. Maxime Rodinson's *Mohammed*, trans. Anne Carter (New York: Pantheon Books, 1971/b) is a fine one. William Montgomery Watt's *Muhammed at Mecca* (Oxford: Clarendon Press, 1953) and *Muhammed at Medina* (Oxford: Clarendon Press, 1956) are also to be considered.

Comparative Studies

Some interesting works in the "comparative" category may also be of use to you. Pandit Sunderlal, as an example, has epitomized the teachings of the Indian *Gita* and Islamic *Qur'an* and then shown their resemblances in philosophy and thought in *The Gita and the Qur'an*, trans. Syed Asadullah (Hyderabad: Institute of Indo-Middle East Cultural Studies, n.d.). In *Solomon and Sheba* (London: Phaidon Press, 1974), ed. James B. Pritchard, William Montgomery Watt's chapter is entitled "The Queen of Sheba in Islamic Tradition," and the book as a whole will be useful. The story from the *Qur'an* of Yusuf, the prince's wife, and the prince is told in John D. Yohannan's *Joseph and Potiphar's Wife in World Literature* (New York: New Directions, 1968) and thus is related to the biblical and other versions around the world of the chaste youth–lustful stepmother–punishing father theme. Geoffrey Parrinder's *Jesus in the Qur'an* (New York: Oxford University Press, 1977) notes the many ties of Islamic religion to Christianity in the course of dealing with the title subject.

Finally, the influence of Egypt on Islam is the subject of an excellent article in J.R. Harris' *The Legacy of Egypt*, 2nd edition (Oxford: Clarendon Press, 1971).

Works on Art

Neither archaeology nor art are categories especially applicable to Islamic mythology and religion. K. Critchlow's *Islamic Patterns: An Analytical and Cosmological Approach* (New York: Schocken Books, 1976/i) could be of some use, though, for it deals with the thematic foundations of Islamic art based on Islamic views of the universe. Some volumes in the *Islamic Architecture Series* published by the Great Eastern Book Company of Boulder, Colorado, might prove useful, too, especially *Iran 1* and *Iran 2* by Anthony Hutt and Leonard Harrow, (1978). The two volumes trace the history of Islamic architecture from earliest times to the present, and both are well illustrated.

South and East Asian Mythologies

The geographical region here referred to is limited to that portion of Asia east of Iran and generally south of the Soviet Union and includes only India, Japan, and China since so very little is available in English on any other myth systems and groups in the area.

It was not very long ago at all that India, China, and Japan were virtually unknown in the western world, and it is only in relatively recent times that their role as contributor to western culture and myth in ancient times has been discovered. The oriental influence in the art of the ancient cultures in West Asia has long been observed, of course, but the connections between that influence and others has been only slowly uncovered and is still to be understood to any significant extent. According to artifacts uncovered in archaeological digs, the strong possibility now exists, though, that the early civilizations of India's Indus Valley were in contact with those of the Mesopotamian part of the fertile crescent. Because we know well that the ancient Mesopotamians contributed heavily to cultures north and west of them, the scope of influences from the east may well eventually be found to be quite extensive. How extensive can only be conjectured at present, though. Also, there are reasons to believe that the ancient Chinese and Japanese may have travelled greater distances than was formerly believed. The Chinese, especially, appear to have ventured as far as the west coast of the Americas— at least according to the archaeological evidence.

These few instances are mentioned only to underscore the potential importance to the western world of mythologies and ancient cultures which earlier were passed by as of little relevance or interest. The indebtedness of west to east could turn out to be very little, of course, and there's even the possibility, now pretty remote, that direction of influence will be found to have been the other way around. In that event, there's still reason to look

---

The following symbols will be found, where applicable, in the bibliographic citation, usually following the date of publication: i = has useful illustrations; b = has a useful bibliography; p = has been published in paperbound edition.

to the mythologies of India, Japan, and China. Linked in tradition
as they are, they become important for their present-day impact
on the western world. Many of the cult movements and so-called
"new religions" in the United States and elsewhere in the western
world have come from the eastern countries. Their roots are deep,
the ancient mythologies of India, Japan, and China their well-
spring. That fact alone—if no other will suffice—makes the ancient
eastern mythologies of importance to the western world. Of how
great an importance, only time will tell.

Collections of the Myths

If you're interested in finding single-volume sources of the myths
of India, Japan, and China, there are a number of books that
can be recommended. First and best—because largest and most
comprehensive—is the book called *Asiatic Mythology* (New York:
Thomas Y. Crowell, 1963/i), ed. J. Hackin. In addition to covering
the variations among the three mythologies mentioned, there
are sections on Persian, Indo-Chinese, and Tibetan, too. There
are very useful sections on Indian, Japanese, and Chinese mythologies in *Mythologies of the Ancient World* (Garden City, N.Y.:
Doubleday Anchor, 1961/p), ed. Samuel Noah Kramer, as well
as in the *Larousse World Mythology* (New York: Putnam, 1965/i),
ed. Pierre Grimal, trans. Patricia Beardsworth, and in the *Larousse
Encyclopedia of Mythology* (London: Paul Hamlyn, 1959/ip),
ed. Felix Guirand, trans. Richard Aldington and Delano Ames.
Volume III of the *Pears Encyclopedia of Myths and Legends*
(London: Pelham Books, 1977/ib) has the three mythologies
plus ancient Iranian and some coverage of Tibetan and Korean.
Although Indian, Japanese, and Chinese mythologies are represented in Veronica Ions' *The World's Mythology in Colour* (London:
Paul Hamlyn, 1974/i) and in the *Encyclopedia of World Mythology* (New York: Galahad Books, 1975/i), the pictures in each
will prove far more useful than the text, which is minimal in both.

Although there's no point in going further than to point out
that topical or thematic anthologies of myths may also prove
useful, a couple of examples are still in order. James George
Frazer's *Myths of the Origin of Fire* (London: Macmillan & Co.,
1930) has chapters eight and sixteen devoted to "Asia" and
"India" respectively, and you'll find all the relevant creation
myths in Maria Leach's *The Beginning: Creation Myths Around
the World* (New York: Funk and Wagnalls, 1956). (For other
possibly useful thematically organized anthologies, see the ap-

propriate part of the section entitled "Worldwide Mythologies" earlier in this guide.)

Works on the Myths and Religion

Two books by Joseph Campbell are excellent for background to the myths of India, Japan, and China. Volume II in *The Masks of God* series, *Oriental Mythology* (New York: Viking Press, 1962/p) includes fine discussions of the religions involved, the history of the mythologies, and ways of interpreting the myths. *Myths to Live By* (New York: Viking Press, 1972/p), which is comprised of a series of talks Campbell gave over the years, is useful only in part, but such chapters as "The Confrontation of East and West" and "Mythologies of War and Peace" contrast the differences between eastern and western mythologies.

Geoffrey Parrinder's *Introduction to Asian Religions* (New York: Oxford University Press, 1976/p; originally published in 1957) is a good, brief introduction to the religions, in this instance including Islamic. Sydney Cave's *An Introduction to the Study of Some Living Religions of the East* (London: Duckworth & Co., 1921) is another that covers Hinduism and Buddhism especially well. Jack Finegan's *The Archaeology of World Religions* (Princeton: Princeton University Press, 1952), a three-volume work, covers Hinduism, Jainism, Buddhism, Confucianism, Taoism, Shintoism, and Sikhism among a number of others. Like Finegan's world survey of religions are many others that will be helpful, Robert S. Ellwood, Jr.'s *Many Peoples, Many Faiths* (Englewood Cliffs, N.J.: Prentice-Hall, 1976/b) and the *Historical Atlas of the Religions of the World* (New York: Macmillan, 1974/b), ed. Isma'il Ragi al Faruqi, to mention just a couple.

Just about all the primary texts can be found in the fifty-volume *Sacred Books of the East* (London: Clarendon Press, 1879; often reprinted since). No other volume or volumes can be recommended quite as highly.

Works on Historical/Cultural Background

For historical background, quite a few sources can be recommended. Will Durant's *Our Oriental Heritage* (New York: Simon and Schuster, 1935), which is Volume I of *The Story of Civilization*, is as interesting a single-volume source as you'll encounter. Not too far behind for interest are Stuart Piggott's *The Dawn of Civilization* (New York: McGraw-Hill, 1969), a mammoth volume, and *Prehistory and the Beginnings of Civilization* (New York:

Harper & Row, 1963), in the UNESCO *History of Mankind*. Volume I of *A History of Asia* (Boston: Allyn and Bacon, 1964) by Bingham, Conroy and Ikle, covers Asia from antiquity to A.D. 1660. Also, don't discount the help that's available in the multi-volume *The Cambridge Ancient History*, 3rd edition (Cambridge: Cambridge University Press, 1971). And especially for what it has to offer about the spread and contact of cultures, see the three-volume *An Ancient Economic History* (Leiden: A.W. Sijthoff's Uitgeversmaatschappij, 1958–70) by Fritz M. Heichelheim. Finally, Keith Branigan's *Atlas of Ancient Civilizations* (New York: John Day, 1976/i) has good sections on the Indus Valley and China.

The only really useful general archaeological survey is the *Larousse Encyclopedia of Archaeology* (London: Paul Hamlyn, 1972/i), ed. Gilbert Charles-Picard, trans. Anne Ward. Most others either focus on a few finds and sites or don't cover all the countries of interest. *Archaeological Atlas of the World* (San Francisco: W.H. Freeman and Co., 1975/b) by David and Ruth Whitehouse, does, though, offer a good series of maps that will be of use even if the text is cursory. Dictionary-style volumes will have brief entries of interest. Two of the volumes worth mentioning are *The Concise Encyclopedia of Archaeology* (New York: Hawthorne Books, 1960), ed. Leonard Cottrell, and *Encyclopedia of Archaeology* (New York: Thomas Y. Crowell, 1977), ed. Glyn Daniel.

Broad surveys of South and East Asia's art are not as a rule too useful, but two volumes in which motifs are pursued will be of some help: Pratapaditya Pal's *The Sensous Immortals* (Cambridge: MIT Press, 1977/i) and Joseph Campbell's *The Mythic Image* (Princeton: Princeton University Press, 1974). Both are works for anyone interested in seeing interrelationships among the South and East Asian countries.

Indian Mythologies

The existence of mature and geographically extensive civilization in the Indus Valley as early as the mid-third millenium B.C., the interrelationship of Sanskrit (the ancient language of Hinduism) with the predominantly western language "family" that has been called "Indo-European," and the prominent coastline and centrality of the South Asian country of India have all contributed heavily to varied speculations concerning India's role in the reception and spread of culture in ancient times. Such contact-diffusionist possibilities, though far from conclusively proven at present, make the myths of India potentially important beyond what is ordinary in myth study. The probability of interconnections among the Hindu-Biblical-Mesopotamian mythologies is particularly strong, but until the written language of the Indus Valley is understood and appropriate documents translated (assuming the ones that exist are appropriate, of course) it is likely no sound case will be developed pro or con.

Something else that makes Indian mythology particularly important is its duration. Unlike most other myth groups, where one system has replaced another in time, a great deal of Hindu mythology has endured relatively intact over a period of more than 4,000 years. The most ancient Hindu myths can be found today in India, not infrequently remolded to fit later conditions and attitudes, but nonetheless intact despite their antiquity.

Aside from traditional Hindu mythology, there are other distinct mythologies extant in India. Most widely known to the western world, of course, is Buddhist. Siddhartha Gautama (or Buddha, "the enlightened one"), who lived c. 563-483 B.C. in the north of India, was a reformer of popular Hinduism around whose life and doctrine a sizeable body of myths has arisen over the years. Buddhism has flourished more in other parts of Asia than in India, but because Buddhist mythology in part draws upon Hindu mythology and because it is so often treated in books with the Hindu, it is for purposes of this guide included under "Indian." The mythologies of the Sikhs and Jains, both reformed varieties of Hinduism, are also sometimes treated in books separately from Hindu mythology, and the Parsees (Parsis), Indian Zoroastrians, of course have a mythology closely related to the parent Zoroastrian mythology of Persia. Of these disparate mythologies only the Buddhist will be treated at all in this section otherwise devoted mainly to Hindu mythology.

Collections of the Myths

There are fine discussions of Hindu and Buddhist mythology in *Asiatic Mythology* (New York: Thomas Y. Crowell, 1963/i), ed. J. Hackin, both written by experts, both covering the main myths and religious ideas. *Myths of the Hindus and Buddhists* (New York: Dover Publications, 1967/ip; originally 1913) by Amanda

K. Coomaraswamy and Sister Nivedita, is excellent, if highly
selective from among the available myths. Veronica Ions' *Indian
Mythology* (London: Paul Hamlyn, 1967), a volume in Hamlyn's
International Mythology Series covers Hindu, Buddhist, and
even devotes some space to the mythology of the Jains. It is a
beautiful volume—probably the most comprehensive Indian
mythography easily available in this country. Hindu, Buddhist, and
Jain mythology are also covered reasonably well in the *Larousse
World Mythology* (New York: Putnam, 1965/i), ed. Pierre Grimal,
trans. Patricia Beardsworth, and in the *Larousse Encyclopedia of
Mythology* (London: Paul Hamlyn, 1959/ip), ed. Felix Guirand,
trans. Richard Aldington and Delano Ames. The section on Indian
mythology written by W. Norman Brown for *Mythologies of the
Ancient World* (Garden City, N.Y.: Anchor, 1969/bp), ed. Samuel
Noah Kramer, makes sure distinction between Hindu and Buddhist
particularly, but is not as useful for seeing the separateness of the
two mythologies as are the other works already mentioned.
Roughly the same judgment holds for the part of chapter five
devoted to Indian mythology in Volume III of the *Pears Ency-
clopedia of Myths and Legends* (London: Pelham Books, 1977/i).
The portions of the *Encyclopedia of World Mythology* (New
York: Galahad Books, 1975/i) and Veronica Ions' *The World's
Mythology in Colour* (London: Paul Hamlyn, 1974/i) allotted to
Indian mythology are too small really to be useful—except that the
pictures in the latter are numerous and unquestionably splendid.

Quite a few books deal solely with Hindu mythology—or very
much so at the expense of, say, Buddhist—and are quite useful in
so doing. One of the more recent is *Hindu Myths: A Sourcebook
Translated from the Sanskrit* (Harmondsworth, G.B.: Penguin
Books, 1975/bp), ed. and trans. by Wendy Doniger O'Flaherty.
It has a helpful introduction, an exceptional bibliography of
primary sources, and includes a total of seventy-five myths translated directly from the primary sources. It is not a complete
mythography as such, but used along with one of the better
ones mentioned above or following, it will be a worthwhile acquisition. Another useful volume of translations is *Classical
Hindu Mythology: A Reader in the Sanskrit Puranas* (Philadelphia:
Temple University Press, 1978/p), ed. and trans. Cornelia Dimmitt
and J.A.B. van Buitenen. The introductions are particularly
worthwhile, and there's a helpful glossary included. The older
group—many of them very old, some of them reprinted in recent
years—is best headed, in my estimation, by Martin E. Osborn's

The Gods of India: Their History Character & Worship (Delhi: Indological Book House, 1972; reprint of the 1913 edition), a good survey of Hindu mythology that includes, in Part I, a helpful discussion of the development of the mythology and the sacred books involved. Volume VI in *The Mythology of All Races* (reprint of the 1916–32 edition, New York: Cooper Square Press, 1964, etc.), ed. Louis H. Gray, has a still reliable section in it on Indian myth by A. Berriedale Keith. Donald A. Mackenzie's *Indian Myth and Legend* (London: Gresham Publishing Co., 1919/i), in Gresham's *Myth and Legend in Literature and Art* series, is also a valuable book—particularly for its attention to art and literature as well as to the Hindu myths. And talking about art, Donald and Jean Johnson leaned heavily on artistic representation for their brief little survey of Hinduism, its deities and myths, called *God and Gods in Hinduism* (New Delhi: Arnold Heinemann, 1972/i). Shakti M. Gupta's *Loves of Hindu Gods and Sages* (Bombay: Allied Publishers, 1973/i) is also brief—a collection of some of the myths of the Hindus only, mainly ones in which the book's author was able to "depict the foibles and weaknesses of the rishis and gods." Paul Thomas's *Epics, Myths and Legends of India* (Bombay: 1958; New York: Tudor Publishing Co., 1963) is a fine much more comprehensive collection of mainly Hindu myths. Despite their age—and all are *at least* eighty years old now—the following books are also useful sources of principally Hindu myths: W.J. Wilkins' *Hindu Mythology: Vedic and Puranic* (London: W. Thacker, 1882; Totowa, N.J.: Rowman and Littlefield, 1973), Charles Coleman's *The Mythology of the Hindus* (London: Parbury, Allen, and Co., 1832), Edward Moor's *The Hindu Pantheon* (Varanasi: Indological Book House, 1968; originally London, 1810), Arthur A. Macdonell's *Vedic Mythology* (New York: Gordon Press Reprint, 1975; originally Strassburg, 1897), John Dowson's *A Classical Dictionary of Hindu Mythology and Religion, Geography, History, and Literature*, 10th edition (London: Kegan Paul, 1961; originally London, 1879). The Dowson book is still an adequate reference work, believe it or not!

There are books which offer more specialized collections of myths from India. Three books by Verrier Elwin, for instance, are excellent should you go as far in your study of Indian mythology as to want regional myths, legends and folktales: *The Myths of Middle India* (New York: Oxford University Press, 1949), *Tribal Myths of Orissa* (New York: Oxford University Press, 1954), and *Myths of the Northeast Frontier of India* (Shillong,

India: North-East Frontier Agency, 1958). All are big books
(from 448 pages to 700) that include plenty of stories, the Orissa
book containing over 1,000 of them plus glossary and keying
to Stith Thompson's *Motif Index*. Michael Viggo Fausboll's *Indian
Mythology in Outline, According to The Mahabharata* (London:
Luzac and Co., 1902) is useful given the limitation the title
describes. J.E.B. Gray's *Indian Tales and Legends* (London:
Oxford University Press, 1969) comprises stories from the Sanskrit
and Pali, with emphasis on folktales involving transmigration
and caste. W. Crooke's *The Popular Religion and Folklore of
Northern India* (London: North Western Provinces, 1894) includes
both myths and religious practices of "the races of Upper India."
Tales of the Mystic East, 2nd edition (Punjab: Radha Soami
Satsang, Blas, 1964), by Huzur Singhji and Maharaj Sawan, is a
volume of myths known as "teachings of the saints"; it includes
a very useful glossary of names and terms.

Studies of the Myths

As might be expected, with so many collections of myths available
and interest in Indian mythology high generally, there are some
excellent sources which go more deeply into the myths, rituals,
and philosophies than most collections of myths do. A prime
example is Joseph Campbell's superb *Oriental Mythology* (New
York: Viking, 1962/p), Volume II in his *The Masks of God* series.
Not only are better than 200 pages (as part two) devoted to Indian
mythology and religion, other chapters will prove useful too.
The findings of archaeology and psychology especially are Campbell's forte. A. Berriedale Keith's *Religion and Philosophy of the
Veda* (Cambridge: Harvard University Press, 1925), which is in
the *Harvard Oriental Thought Series*, includes long discussions of
the various deities and has fairly good background help on Vedic
eschatology, philosophy, and ritual. Alain Danielou's *Hindu
Polytheism* (New York: Pantheon Books, 1964/i) is a remarkable
background source. Because it sticks close to primary sources
of the myths it is useful as a limited sort of mythography, but
because it attempts depth analysis as well, "explaining the significance of the most prominent deities in the way in which they are
envisaged by the Hindus themselves," it really is much more than
just a collection of myths. (The opening chapter, "The Theory
of Polytheism" is highly recommended even if Indian mythology
isn't what you're after!) Also more than a collection of myths
is Govinda Krishna Pillai's *Hindu Gods and Hidden Mysteries*

(Allahabad, India: Kitabmahal, n.d./b). The author takes the position that all gods are creations of men and interprets the origins of such deities as Agni, Indra, Varuna, and others with that perpsective as starting point. N.G. Tavakar studies four groups of semi-divine beings toward understanding their historicity and relationships to one another, in *The Essays Throwing New Light on the Gandharvas, the Apsarases, the Yakshas, and the Kinnaras* (Bombay: Bhatkal Books, 1971). A good study of the Great Goddess in India that includes variant myths is Stella Kramrisch's "The Indian Great Goddess" in *History of Religions*, 14 (May 1975), pp. 235–65. Milton Singer edited the collection of eight essays called *Krishna: Myths, Rites, and Attitudes* (Honolulu: East-West Center Press, 1966/b). The essays address, in various ways, the problems of Krishna as divine child and divine lover. Nigel Frith's *The Legend of Krishna* (New York: Schocken Books, 1976/p) is partially a retelling of the myths and partially an analysis. Frith is not a scholar in the area of Indology, but he has the enthusiasm for his subject that some scholars could use. David Kinsley's *The Sword and the Flute: Kali and Krsna—Dark Visions of the Terrible and the Sublime in Hindu Mythology* (Berkeley: University of California Press, 1975/p) is a fine study of two principal figures from Hindu mythology also written with a vigor and simplicity that will make it pleasureable reading for anyone interested in the background. Not at all as easily read, but superb background nonetheless, are two Dumézilian analyses, Alf Hiltebeitel's *The Ritual of Battle: Krishna in the Mahabharata* (Ithaca, N.Y.: Cornell University Press, 1976) and P. Thieme's *Mitra and Aryaman* (New Haven, Conn.: Academy of Arts and Sciences, 1957).

Wendy Deniger O'Flaherty's *The Origins of Evil in Hindu Mythology* (Berkeley: University of California Press, 1976/p) is a rather unusual study considering that "evil" as such is commonly thought of as being a concept of the western world. It is a myth-filled book in which we see, among other things en route to fulfillment of the title's intention, how the gods in Hindu mythology are disinterested in man. O'Flaherty's book entitled *Asceticism and Eroticism in the Mythology of Siva* (New York: Oxford University Press, 1973) is also well worth looking into. And on the subject of Siva, a god of a thousand names, an old but still helpful book is Hyde Clark's *Serpent and Siva Worship* (London: Trubner and Co., 1876). "Meaningful God Sets from a Chinese Personal Pantheon and a Hindu Personal Pantheon,"

an article by John M. Roberts, Chien Chiao, and Triloki N. Pandey
in *Ethnology*, XIV (April 1975), pp. 121-48, will prove helpful,
too, if you've ever wondered how the ordering of a pantheon may
occur and, in connection with complex polytheistic systems, how
the individual believer may "deal with a system of knowledge. . .
too large for his comprehension." Edward Washburn Hopkins'
Epic Mythology (Strassburg: Verlag-Trubner, 1915; reprinted
in 1968) provides good background to the deities and spirits in the
two epics *Ramayana* and *Mahabharata*. Robert P. Goldman's
Gods, Priests, and Warriors (New York: Columbia University
Press, 1977) is concerned with the myths of the Bhargava as
found in *Mahabharata;* translations of the myths and analyses
are provided.

Treatment of Nature in the Rgveda* (Hoshiarpur, India: Vedic
Sahitya Sadan, 1970) is an informative volume on Hindu mythology (particularly part one, pp. 1-180); the Vedic deities are
especially well treated. W. Norman Brown has analyzed "The
Creation Myth of the Rig Veda" in *Journal of the American
Oriental Society*, 62 (1942), pp. 85-97, and F.B.J. Kuiper uses
that creation myth to assess the concept that lies at a central point
in Vedic religion in his "The Basic Concept of Vedic Religion,"
History of Religions, 15 (November 1975), pp. 107-20. A collection of essays edited by L. Bardwell Smith entitled *Hinduism:
New Essays in the History of Religions* (Leiden: E.J. Brill, 1976)
has some essays myth students might find worthwhile as background to Indian mythology, most notably J. Bruce Long's "Life
Out of Death: A Structural Analysis of the Myth of the 'Churning
of the Ocean of Milk,' " pp. 171-207, and Alf Hiltebeitel's "The
Burning of the Forest Myth," pp. 208-24. David Kinsley's
" 'Through the Looking Glass': Divine Madness in the Hindu
Religious Tradition" in *History of Religions*, 13 (May 1974), pp.
270-305, is an interesting survey of myths in which the gods and
goddesses are either called "mad" or in which they act that way,
the object being to see the role of the theme in the Hindu conception of the divine and vision of salvation. Shastri Suryakanta's
The Flood Legend in Sanskrit Literature (Delhi: S. Chand and Co.,
1950) includes translations of variants of the flood myth in
Sanskrit, as well as translations of the Babylonian and Hebrew
flood myths for comparison, but perhaps its main virtue as a book
is the good introductory section in which theories of flood myths
are gone into concisely and with clarity. Finally, Nancy E. Falk's
"Wilderness and Kingship in Southeast Asia," in *History of Reli-*

gions, 13 (August 1973), pp. 1-15, deals with myth and ritual in one area of Indian mythology.

Works on Religion and Related Matters

Any good book in which the major religions of the world are discussed will make clear that background to Indian myth study becomes pretty complicated where religion is concerned. There are varieties of Hinduism and varieties of Buddhism. An excellent place to be introduced to this fact is the *Historical Atlas of the Religions of the World* (New York: Macmillan, 1974/ib), ed. Isma'il Ragi al Faruqi. The principal varieties are handled well but concisely, thus making the book valuable for starters. The same can be said, perhaps to lesser degree though, of a number of other books, some among them being Robert S. Ellwood, Jr.'s *Many Peoples, Many Faiths* (Englewood Cliffs, N.J.: Prentice-Hall, 1976/b); Jack Finegan's *The Archaeology of World Religions,* three volumes (Princeton: Princeton University Press, 1952/b); Volume I of John A. Hardon's *Religions of the World* (Garden City, N.Y.: Doubleday Image, 1968/p); and Hans-Joachim Schoeps' *The Religions of Mankind,* trans. Richard and Clara Winston (Garden City, N.Y.: Doubleday Anchor, 1968/p). Also, don't overlook the many books which deal with Asian religions, such as Geoffrey Parrinder's *Introduction to Asian Religions* (New York: Oxford University Press, 1976/p; originally 1957) or Sydney Cave's *An Introduction to The Study of Some Living Religions of the East* (London: Duckworth and Co., 1921).

Narrower in scope are such works as Edward Washburn Hopkins' *The Religion of India* (Boston: Ginn and Company, 1895), an older but highly useful introduction that even devotes four chapters to the Hindu divinities. Max Weber wrote a book with that same title (London: Allen & Unwin, 1958; published originally much earlier) which is more helpful as a sociological analysis of the religions of India. P.D. Mehta's *Early Indian Religious Thought* (London: Luzac and Company, 1956) is an excellent work that covers Hinduism and Buddhism well and which has fairly good discussions of Hindu deities, conceptions of good and evil, god, and redemption. Sir Charles Eliot and Amanda K. Coomaraswamy both wrote books entitled *Hinduism and Buddhism* (London: Edward Arnold & Co., 1929 and New York: Philosophical Library, n.d., respectively). Each is relatively brief and includes some discussion of the mythologies involved.

There are a great many books on Hinduism alone, as might be surmised, just about any of them useful as background to myth study. Here are a few, more or less in order of my own preference: Louis Renou's *Hinduism* (New York: George Braziller, 1969/b)— which includes a number of excerpts translated from primary sources along with the introductory discussions; R.C. Zaehner's *Hinduism*, 2nd edition (New York: Oxford Galaxy, 1966/p); K.M. Sen's *Hinduism* (Harmondsworth, G.B.: Penguin, 1962); Herbert Stroup's *Like a Great River: An Introduction to Hinduism* (New York: Harper & Row, 1972); Solange Lemaitre's *Hinduism*, trans. Jean-Francis Brown (New York: Hawthorne Books, 1959); J.N. Farquhar's *A Primer of Hinduism*, 2nd edition (London: Oxford University Press, 1912); K.W. Morgan's *The Religion of the Hindus* (New York: Ronald Press, 1953); and L.S.S. O'Malley's *Popular Hinduism* (Cambridge: The University Press, 1935). Then there's Benjamin Walker's gigantic two-volume *Hindu World: An Encyclopedic Survey of Hinduism* (London: George Allen & Unwin, 1968) for just about all you've ever wanted to know about the subject.

The same abundance of books exists for Buddhism, too. Peter A. Pardue's *Buddhism* (New York: Macmillan, 1968) is a nice introduction to the several national forms Buddhism has taken— in India, China, Japan, Southeast Asia, and Tibet—and does a good job of examining the diverse influences of culture, politics, and local doctrine on the religion. All useful as introductions to Buddhism are the following, more or less in order of my own preferences: Thomas Berry's *Buddhism* (New York: Hawthorne Books, 1967); Richard H. Robinson's *The Buddhist Religion: A Historical Introduction* (Belmont, Calif.: Dickinson Publishing Co., 1970); Richard A. Gard's *Buddhism* (New York: George Braziller, 1962); Kenneth K.S. Chen's *Buddhism The Light of Asia* (Woodbury, N.Y.: Barron's Educational Series, 1968/bp); Mrs. Rhys Davids' *Outlines of Buddhism: A Historical Sketch* (London: Methuen, 1934); and Erik Zurchner's *Buddhism: Its Origin and Spread in Words, Maps and Pictures* (London: Routledge, 1962). If you'd like a useful, brief history of Buddhism, try A.L. Basham's "The Rise of Buddhism in Its Historical Context," an article in *Asian Studies*, 4 (December 1966), pp. 395–411.

Other books on Buddhism and Buddha that might be of interest in your background study are also a very large group from which only selected titles are included here. Nolan Pliny Jacobson's *Buddhism: The Religion of Analysis* (London: George Allen & Unwin, 1966/b) is an interpretation which focuses on central tenets and teachings. Govind Chandra Pande's *Studies in the Origins of Buddhism* (Allahabad, India: Dept. of Ancient History, Culture, and Archaeology, 1957) consists of a series of interconnected essays on the doctrinal history; chapter eight, on nirvana, is especially useful for its eschatological considerations. Jamshed K. Fozdar's *The God of Buddha* (New York: Asia Publishing Co., 1973) is a strange little book which aims at clarification of the doctrine and scriptures of Buddhism. It also has a very useful glossary. And for other glossaries, Christmas Humphreys' *A Popular Dictionary of Buddhism* (New York: Citadel Press, 1963) covers terms and names in brief fashion—as does Nyanatiloka's *Buddhist Dictionary: Manual of Buddhist Terms and Doctrines*, revised edition (Colombo, Ceylon: Frewin & Co., 1956). Brian Brown's *The Story of Buddha and Buddhism* (Philadelphia: David McKay, 1927) is a sound introduction to the life of Buddha as well as to the religion founded in his name. Rene Grousset's *In the Footsteps of Buddha* (London: George Routledge & Sons, 1932) offers a straightforward telling of the life of Buddha and of the Buddhist faith. Thomas J. Edwards attempts to separate history from legend and myth in *The Life of Buddha as Legend and History* (New York: Barnes & Noble, 1952). William MacQuitty's *Buddha* (New York: Viking Press, 1969/i) is a beautiful text-and-pictures volume, some of the pictures in color; but *the* visual book on Buddhism has to be Shri P.M. Lad's *The Way of Buddha* (Delhi, India: Ministry of Information and Broadcasting, n.d./ib). There are hundreds of black and white pictures in it, nicely tied together through excerpts from the sacred texts.

Translations

A great deal of what we have called "Indian" mythology is in fact available in translation from primary sources. Mentioned earlier, Wendy O'Flaherty's *Hindu Myths* (Harmondsworth, G.B.: Penguin Books, 1975/bp) is an excellent one-volume source of translated myths you might find useful, and it has a fine bibliography of available translations into English at the end. Also, don't forget about *Classical Hindu Mythology: A Reader in the Sanskrit Puranas* (Philadelphia: Temple University Press, 1978/p)—another work mentioned earlier. A fifty-volume series of translated texts, quite a few of them of significant help in Indian myth study, is the often reprinted *Sacred Books of the East* (London: The Clarendon Press, 1879/b). *The Hindu Tradition* (New York:

Modern Library, 1966), ed. Ainslee T. Embree, is an inexpensive volume which has many useful translations in it, as is *The Beginnings of Indian Philosophy: Selections from the RigVeda, Artharva Veda, Upanishads, and Mahabharata* (London: George Allen & Unwin, 1965), ed. Franklin Edgerton. John B. Alphonso-Karkala's *An Anthology of Indian Literature* (Harmondsworth, G.B.: Penguin Books, 1971/p) is one of many anthologies of Indian literature which have enough myth-relevant excerpts to be of use. Also, Edward Conze's *Buddhist Texts Through the Ages* (Oxford: Bruno Cassirer, 1954) is a mine of specifically Buddhist myths. In general, translations of the following texts comprising the main primary sources are available in many editions: the *Veddas* (or *Vedas),* the *Ramayana,* the *Mahabharata,* the *Upanishads,* the *Brahmanas,* the *Puranas.*

Works on Historical/Cultural Background

Background to both the religion and mythology of India is a varied category. Certainly a book like Jeanine Miller's *The Vedas: Harmony, Meditation and Fulfillment* (London: Rider & Co., 1974/b), which the author calls a "psycho-philosophical analysis" and interpretation of the *RigVeda,* is a worthwhile starting point, especially section one, "Mythology and the Vedic Myth," and section three, "Vedic Eschatology." K. Satchidananda Murty's "Philosophical Thought in India," in *Diogenes,* no. 24 (Winter 1958), pp. 17-31, while not apparently relevant to Indian myth study, has in fact much to offer concerning philosophies which show up with regularity in the myths. For the eschatological, check on what is said in Clifford Herschel Moore's *Ancient Beliefs in the Immortality of the Soul* (New York: Longmans, Green & Co., 1931) or, for even more that will clarify matters, in Geoffrey Parrinder's *The Indestructible Soul: The Nature of Man and Life After Death in Indian Thought* (New York: Barnes & Noble, 1973/p). The book called *Hindu Theology Reader* (Garden City, N.Y.: Doubleday Image Book, 1976) will put you in touch with some of the finer points of Hindu theology, an excellent way to deepen your background to Indian mythology. Kenneth W. Morgan has edited an anthology of essays by devout Hindus which will serve pretty much the same purpose; it's called *The Religion of the Hindus* (New York: Ronald Press, 1953) and has the added advantage of a good glossary and a section of sacred writings. Wendell C. Beane's "The Cosmological Structure of Mythic Time: Kali-Sakti," in *History of Religions,* 13 (August 1973), pp. 54-83, is a good investigation of the black goddess, Kali, as revealed in the "rubrics of cosmogenesis, devigenesis, and cosmoredemption." The "why" of belief is interestingly dealt with in two articles on the sacred cow: "An Approach to the Sacred Cow of India" by Alan Heston *et al* in *Current Anthropology*, 12 (April 1971), pp. 191-99, and "Mother Cow" in *Cows, Pigs, Wars & Witches: The Riddles of Culture* (New York: Random House, 1974) by Marvin Harris. As should be apparent, there is a great deal to be learned about myth in the process of understanding belief and superstition as concepts. Try reading Clarence Maloney's excellent essay "Don't Say 'Pretty Baby' Lest You Zap It With Your Eye" in *The Evil Eye* (New York: Columbia University Press, 1976), pp. 102-48.

Although P. Spratt discusses Hindu mythology only in chapter six of his *Hindu Culture and Personality: A Psychoanalytic Study* (Bombay: Manartalas, 1966/b), the entire book is worthwhile as a backdrop to Indian myth study. Also a psychological study and good backdrop, G. Morris Carstairs' *The Twice-Born: A Study of a Community of High-Caste Hindus* (Bloomington: Indiana University Press, 1961) has a particularly useful chapter called "Religion and Phantasy." Jean Antoine Dubois' *Hindu Manners, Customs, and Ceremonies*, 3rd edition, trans. Henry K. Beauchamp (Oxford: Clarendon Press, 1897) is good on its topic and has good descriptions of Hindu rituals and religion in parts two and three. On the subject of rituals as such, *The Keys of Power: A Study of Indian Ritual and Belief* (Secaucus, N.J.: University Books, 1974; originally published in 1932) offers extensive discussion, in its 560 pages, on the power of various customs and practices in Indian life. Sarvepalli Rhadhakrishnan's *The Hindu View of Life* (London: Unwin Books, 1927) is also fine for background despite its age.

Gaining historical background will be no problem—at least where availability of good books is concerned. Start with the mammoth, multi-volume *Cambridge History of India* (Cambridge: University Press, 1953/p) by various authors. A.L. Basham's *The Wonder That Was India*, 3rd edition (New York: Taplinger, 1968/b; many times reprinted, including as an Evergreen paperback by Grove Press) is a "standard" history of India before the Moslems that should prove useful, as should Volume I of Romila Thapar's *A History of India* (Harmondsworth, G.B.: Penguin Books, 1966/ p), Vincent A. Smith's *The Oxford History of India* (Oxford: Clarendon Press, 1958), or Stanley Wolpert's recent *A New History of India* (New York: Oxford University Press, 1977/ib).

Percival Spear's *India: A Modern History* (Ann Arbor: University
of Michigan Press, 1961) also has usefulness, particularly part one,
but for sheer visual beauty in combination with adequate text,
try *Historic India* (New York: Time-Life Books, 1969/ib), a
volume in Time-Life's *Great Ages of Man Series,* or Gustav Le
Bon's *The World of Indian Civilization,* trans. David Macrae
(New York: Tudor Publishing Co., 1974/i). Both focus on early
India, as do Mortimer Wheeler's *Early India and Pakistan to
Ashoka,* revised edition (New York: Frederick A. Praeger, 1959)
and D.D. Kosambi's *The Culture and Civilization of Ancient
India* (London: Routledge and Kegan Paul, 1965/i). More con-
cerned with the most ancient times in India are Stuart Piggott's
Prehistoric India to 1000 B.C. (Harmondsworth, G.B.: Penguin
Books, 1950/p); P.H. Gordon's *The Prehistoric Background of
Indian Culture* (Bombay, India, 1938); and Ernest Mackay's
The Indus Civilization, 2nd edition (London: Luzac and Co.,
1948/i), which has excellent chapters on religion and on possible
prehistoric connections with other countries. Also, in the course
of your work, you'll no doubt find good use for Collin C. Davies'
An Historical Atlas of the Indian Peninsula, 2nd edition (London:
Oxford University Press, 1959/i); it is filled with maps and illustra-
tions. Another useful atlas is J.E. Schwartzberg's *A Historical
Atlas of South Asia* (Leiden: E.J. Brill, 1978/i).

There are additionally many broader works which include
good sections or chapters on Indian history. My own favorites
are as follows. In Jacquetta Hawkes' *The First Great Civilizations*
(New York: Alfred A. Knopf, 1973/i), there's a fine section on
the Indus Valley civilizations. Also, in Volume I of UNESCO's
History of Mankind called *Prehistory and the Beginnings of
Civilization* (New York: Harper & Row, 1963), which was written
by Hawkes and Leonard Woolley, there's quite a bit that will be
of use as background to Indian mythology. There is, too, in *The
Dawn of Civilization* (New York: McGraw-Hill, 1961/i), ed. Stuart
Piggott, and in Volume I of Will Durant's *The Story of Civilization,
Our Oriental Heritage* (New York: Simon and Schuster, 1935).
The Cambridge Ancient History (Cambridge: Cambridge University
Press, 1971, etc.) will be helpful, as will Volume I of *A History of
Asia* (Boston: Allyn and Bacon, 1964) by Bingham, Conroy,
and Ikle. Particularly useful for diffusionist possibilities is Fritz M.
Heichelheim's *An Ancient Economic History,* three volumes
(Leiden: A.W. Sijthoff's Uitgeversmaalschappij, 1958/70), and
for discussions of the problems in studying early India's history,

see Volume XVII in the transactions of the Indian Institute of Advanced Study, *Indian Civilization: The First Phase* (Simla, India, 1979), ed. S.C. Malik.

Works on Archaeology

Archaeology has played an important role in establishing India's early history, and its results are therefore important as background to Indian myth study. A good review of what has been done and found is contained in O. Viennot's article entitled "India, Pakistan and Afghanistan" in the *Larousse Encyclopedia of Archaeology* (London: Paul Hamlyn, 1972/i), ed. Gilbert Charles-Picard, trans. Anne Ward. Glyn Daniel's *The First Civilizations: The Archaeology of Their Origins* (New York: Apollo Editions, 1970/p) has a good chapter on the Indus Valley. The official account of the excavations at the Indus Valley site of Mohenjo-daro from 1922–27 is John Herbert Marshall's *Mohenjo-daro and the Indus Civilization*, three volumes (London: A. Probsthain, 1931/i). R.E. Mortimer Wheeler's *Civilizations of the Indus Valley and Beyond* (New York: McGraw-Hill, 1966) is also a good first-hand account of archaeological work done in the Indus Valley primarily. Geoffrey Bibby's *Looking for Dilmun* (New York: Alfred A. Knopf, 1969; N.A.L. paperback, too) is about archaeology in the Persian Gulf, but because the cultures there probably had contact with ancient civilizations in India, it has some interesting information to offer. Robert W. Erich's *Chronologies in Old World Archaeology* (Chicago: University of Chicago Press, 1965), now dated by new findings in radio-carbon and other dating techniques, is still useful for seeing what was done to arrive at chronologies in ancient Europe and Asia, India included. The same problem in oral tradition, so important in myth study, is handled by David P. Herrige in *The Chronology of Oral Tradition* (Oxford: Clarendon Press, 1974). The author is primarily concerned with African materials, but there is an appendix on the Jodhpur Chronicles, and much of what he says elsewhere may be "translated" to Indian materials.

Comparative Studies

Works in which comparisons of Indian myths and texts are made with those of other countries and regions, or in which the parallels between Indian myths and others are investigated, have been fairly commonplace. India's linguistic ties with the Indo-European family of languages is a principal reason, of course, but not the

only one. In two books by Georges Dumézil—*The Destiny of
the Warrior*, trans. Alf Hiltebeitel (Chicago: University of Chicago
Press, 1970), and *The Destiny of a King*, trans. Alf Hiltebeitel
(Chicago: University of Chicago Press, 1973), the linguistic connections are clearly used. Roman and Scandinavian materials are
placed alongside the Indian in the former work, and, in order to
test the hypothesis that the "last of the 'universal' kings in the
Indian and Iranian lists, Yayati and Yima-Jamsid, *may* both have
inherited epic material deriving in part from a common source,"
Iranian and Indian materials are compared and contrasted. Both
are difficult to read, but there's no question they're of interest
for seeing what may well be important possibilities regarding
India's role in the spread and reception of myth. Colonel Vans
Kennedy's *Researches into the Nature and Affinity of Ancient
and Hindu Mythology* (London: Longman, Rees, Orme, Brown,
and Green, 1831) is an early attempt at evaluating parallel elements in Indian and classical mythology; it is still worth looking
into despite its highly tentative conclusions. An interesting article
dealing with parallels in Norse and Indian mythology is Stefán
Einarsson's "Some Parallels in Norse and Indian Mythology,"
pp. 21-26 in *Scandinavian Studies: Essays Presented to Dr.
Henry Goddard Leach* (Seattle: University of Washington Press,
1965), ed. Carl F. Bayerschmidt and Erik J. Friis. Dorothea
Chaplin's *Matter, Myth, and Spirit or Keltic and Hindu Links*
(London: Rider & Co., 1935) is a clearly diffusionist work which
seeks to link Hindu and Celtic cultures while inferring many other
such possibilities; it's a good example of the use of mythology
to illuminate archaeological findings and is, to say the least,
tentative. Elmer G. Suhr compares and contrasts, providing
speculative links to solar myth origins as he does, in his "Krishna
and Mithra as Messiahs," an article in *Folklore*, 77 (Autumn
1966), pp. 205-21.

H.S. Spencer wrote a highly speculative book you may also
find worth looking through, *The Aryan Ecliptic Cycle: Glimpses
into Ancient Indo-Iranian Religious History from 25628 B.C. to
292 A.D.* (Poona, India: H.P. Vaswan, 1965). Any mythophile
would delight in reading this volume in which India, Persia,
the Orient, and Christianity are yoked together in one great
origin! Far more restrained and unquestionably scholarly are
two books by Geoffrey Parrinder, a well known comparative
religionist, *Upanishads, Gita, and Bible: A Comparative Study
of Hindu and Christian Scriptures* (London: Faber, 1962) and

Avatar and Incarnation (New York: Barnes and Noble, 1970). The latter work deals extensively with myth in Hinduism and Christianity and is highly recommended. John Clark Archer's *The Sikhs: In Relation to Hindus, Moslems, Christians, and Ahmadiyyas* (Princeton: Princeton University Press, 1946) is really an elaboration of Sikhism, but the comparisons along the way make it well worthwhile as background for the myth student.

Works on Art

As with just about everything else to do with India, there are plenty of art books that will prove useful as background to the study of its mythology. Heinrich Zimmer's *The Art of Indian Asia*, two volumes, 2nd edition (New York: Pantheon Books, 1960/i), in addition to having over 600 black and white pictures, many of which relate directly to the myth student's main concerns in art books, also has chapters relating to the Mesopotamian influence on Indian art, for example, lotus symbolism. A fair percentage of the mainly black and white pictures in Stella Kramrisch's *The Art of India*, 3rd edition (New York: Phaidon Press, 1954/i) have to do with myth, but the text is minimal. Just about the same evaluation pertains to Ajit Mookerjee's *The Arts of India: From Prehistoric to Modern Times*, revised edition (Rutland, Vt.: Charles E. Tuttle, 1966/i). Hermann Goetz's *India: Five Thousand Years of Indian Art* (New York: McGraw-Hill, 1959/i) is a good history of Indian art and will be helpful as background. Frederic Louis' *The Art of India, Temples and Sculpture* (New York: Harry N. Abrams, 1959/i) and Douglas Barrett's and Basil Gray's *Painting of India* (Skira, World Publishing Co., 1963/i) both have pictures in them that will help the myth student. W.G. Archer's *The Loves of Krishna in Indian Painting and Poetry* (London: George Allen & Unwin, 1957/b) has only one picture in it, but it will be helpful nonetheless since its text is centered on an important deity in Indian mythology. Thoroughly well illustrated, though, is Pal Pratapaditya's *The Sensuous Immortals* (Cambridge: M.I.T. Press, 1977/i), an investigation of how and where the Indian deities were adapted in the art of other Asian nations. Also a beautiful volume is Alfred Nawrath's *Eternal India* (New York: Crown Publishers, 1956/i), with many pictures of deities and temples. V.G. Vitsaxis' *Hindu Epics, Myths and Symbols in Popular Illustrations* (Leiden: E.J. Brill, 1978/i) also has lots of pictures that will be of use.

Heinrich Zimmer's *Myths and Symbols in Indian Art and Civilization*, ed. Joseph Campbell (New York: Pantheon Books, 1946/ip) offers many myths retold, pictures of related art, and symbols explained. Frederick D.K. Bosch's *The Golden Germ: An Introduction to Indian Symbolism* (New York: Humanities Press, 1960/i) is a fine introduction to the hidden language of myth; it has plenty of illustrations and highly useful text. Chapter two in Mircea Eliade's *Images and Symbols*, trans. Philip Mairet (New York: Sheed and Ward, 1961) is also on Indian symbolism and can be used as a brief introduction. *Tree Symbol Worship in India* (Calcutta: Indian Publications, 1965), ed. Sankar Sen Gupta, covers its subject beautifully, but without photographs. And finally, Joseph Campbell's massive *The Mythic Image* (Princeton: Princeton University Press, 1974/i) is devoted to elaboration of the premise that "Imagery, especially the imagery of dreams, is the basis of mythology." While it covers a good deal more than Indian art and myths in the process, it does have much that will be useful concerning them.

Chinese Mythologies

It is now generally acknowledged by scholars that China was still in the Stone Age well after it had ended in the Tigris-Euphrates Valley and in Egypt. But that does not mean at all what it would seem to, that the Chinese were behind the eastern half of the Mediterranean—Northern Africa, Southern Europe, and the ancient Near and Middle East included—for very long. With the emergence of the Bronze Age sometime in the nineteenth century B.C. in the lowlands drained by the Yellow River, "civilized" development in China happened rapidly enough to make unclear the answer to a major question asked by many but best summarized in the title of an article by Lionel Casson, "China and the West: Which Was First?" The article is included in *Mysteries of the Past* (New York: American Heritage Publishing Company, 1977/i), ed. Joseph J. Thorndike, Jr., a book devoted to the kinds of puzzles the partial excavation of the past around the world has left unsolved.

The excavation of Shang sites around the town of Anyang in northern Honan—excavations begun in the 1920s—brought to light for the first time the true extent of the achievement of the Chinese of the Shang dynasty (c. 1523–1027 B.C.). Beautiful bronzes, carvings in jade, writing that much resembles the modern Chinese, well developed town sites, chariots, ceramics, shaft graves, and the like all indicate a civilization sufficiently well developed to make Casson's question and those like it pretty exciting.

For the myth student, other questions will seem at least as important. Whom did the Chinese know that far back in time? Was their development independent or did contacts with peoples to their west influence that development? Diffusionists, of course, see contact as the answer, but polygenesists would dispute that claim. What can the earliest myths tell us of the possibilities for either argument? The available myths, unfortunately, do not date further back in time than the Chou dynasty (c. 1027-221 B.C.), and even there the myths are not as many in number as those from the later Han dynasty (206 B.C.-220 A.D.). Written records are not the only source of myth, though. In the absence of all else, the examination of burial customs, religious/divination activities, and artifacts has been a way of reconstructing, in however fragmentary and inconclusive a fashion, the "mythology" of a people. Is it possible, therefore, to learn something of value from an archaeological record which includes such fascinating finds as an entire company of soldiers, several charioteers, their chariots, horses and companions buried—apparently as sacrifice— in the central space of a Shang dynasty site? Compare that with the recent, spectacular find at Sian which is detailed in Audrey Topping's article "China's Incredible Find: The First Emperor's Army," *National Geographic*, 153 (April 1978/i), pp. 440-59. The grave vault of the Ch'in dynasty emperor Shih Huang Ti, which dates from about 210 B.C., has been excavated and, at the time of the article, was in the process of yielding a buried army comprised of 6,000 *life-size* pottery figures of men and horses! Why, between those two finds, the myth student has a potential "field day" at his disposal—especially if equipped with parallel information about burials elsewhere, say in Egypt and Middle America. The field day will be one of speculation, true, but not without its rewards since making some sense out of the mythologies of the world is at stake.

Collections of the Myths

Happily for those who would study Chinese mythology, there are plenty of books with the known myths in them—so that not *all* need be speculation. One of the most colorful and comprehensive volumes is Anthony Christie's *Chinese Mythology* (London: Paul Hamlyn, 1968/ib). It has all the myths that are popularly known and includes excellent historical background, a helpful chronology, and a good array of pictures, many of them in color. John C. Ferguson's *Chinese Mythology* (New York: Archaeological Institute of America, 1928) is not quite as pretty a book, but it has just about all the myths you'll want. E.T.C. Werner's *Myths and Legends of China* (London: George Harrap, 1922; reprinted in 1971/i by Benjamin Blom of New York) focuses on the myths deriving from China's middle ages and has thirty-two illustrations in color. Cyril Birch's *Chinese Myths and Fantasies* (London: Oxford University Press, 1962) is something of a mixed bag meant primarily for younger readers. Harry T. Morgan's *Chinese Symbols and Superstitions* (South Pasadena, Calif.: Perkins and Perkins, 1942) is also a mixed bag, but it does cover creation myth, gods, and idols, as well as superstitions, feasts, and festivals. E.T.C. Werner's *A Dictionary of Chinese Mythology* (New York: Julian Press, reprint, 1961; originally Shanghai, 1932) is an excellent reference work which lists virtually all the names in Chinese mythology and, in the process, includes summaries of the major myths.

Henri Maspero's "The Mythology of Modern China" is a long and useful chapter on Chinese myths in J. Hackin's *Asiatic Mythology* (New York: Thomas Y. Crowell, 1963/i). Two older volumes devoted to Chinese *and* Japanese myths are also good sources still—Donald A. Mackenzie's *Myths of China and Japan* (London: Gresham Publishing Co., 1920), which is in Gresham's *Myth and Legend in Literature and Art Series*, and U. Hattori's "Chinese Mythology" in Volume VIII of *The Mythology of All Races* (Boston: Marshall Jones Co., 1916–32; reprinted several times since). Derk Bodde's "Myths of Ancient China" in *Mythologies of the Ancient World* (Garden City, N.Y.: Doubleday Anchor, 1969/bp) is a fairly brief but informative introduction to ancient Chinese mythology—as are the sections on Chinese mythology in the *Larousse Encyclopedia of Mythology* (London: Paul Hamlyn, 1959/ip), ed. Felix Guirand, trans. Richard Aldington and Delano Ames, and the *Larousse World Mythology* (New York: Putnam, 1965/i), ed. Pierre Grimal, trans. Patricia Beardsworth. The latter book really has too little space devoted to Chinese mythology to make it valuable as a one-and-only source, something that can as well be said about the *Pears Encyclopedia of Myths and Legends*, Volume III (London: Pelham Books, 1977/i); the *Ency-*

clopedia of World Mythology (New York: Galahad Books, 1975/
i); and Veronica Ions' *The World's Mythology in Colour* (London:
Paul Hamlyn, 1974/i). The Ions book has by far the better collection of pictures, though.

While Wolfram Eberhard's *Folktales of China* (Chicago:
University of Chicago Press, 1965) has no sacral myths or legends,
the kinds of folktales it does have will often provide excellent
background for myth study. Raymond Van Over's *Taoist Tales*
(New York: N.A.L. Mentor Books, 1973/bp) contains over three
dozen Taoist tales, parables, and poems. Nancy Wood's *The Man
Who Gave Thunder to the Earth* (Garden City, N.Y.: Doubleday,
n.d.) is also a collection of Taoist tales and myths you might
wish to make use of.

Studies of the Myths

Chapter seven of Joseph Campbell's *Oriental Mythology* (New
York: Viking Press, 1962/p), a volume in *The Masks of God* series,
is on Chinese mythology; it is more an analysis and interpretation
than a grouping of myths, however, so should be regarded as
background. His *Myths to Live By* (New York: Viking Press,
1972) will also serve, to some extent, as background since he
deals at times with eastern versus western myth, thought, and
religion, Chinese Buddhism playing some part in that. Bernhard
Karlgren's "Legends and Cults in Ancient China" in the *Bulletin
of the Museum of Far Eastern Antiquities*, no. 18 (1946), pp.
199–365, is not easy to locate, but it has a long and valuable
discussion of ancient Chinese religion and mythology. "Meaningful God Sets From a Chinese Personal Pantheon and a Hindu
Personal Pantheon," by John M. Roberts, Chien Chiao, and
Triloki N. Pandey, in *Ethnology*, 14 (April 1975), pp. 121–48,
uses some Chinese mythology in the process of dealing with *how*
sets of gods can be ordered and recalled, with functions, by
individuals when the "system of knowledge" they embody may
be too large for the individual to comprehend. N.J. Girardot's
"The Problem of Creation Mythology in the Study of Chinese
Religion," in *History of Religions*, 15 (May 1976), pp. 289–318,
deals with the interrelationship of myth and religion in quite an
informative way. Pei-yi Wu's *The White Snake: Evolution of a
Myth in China* (Ann Arbor, Mich.: University Microfilms, 1969)
examines the changes the myth of the white snake underwent in
the 250 years after the mid-sixteenth century, demonstrating

"the archetypal significance of the white snake" in the process. Henry Doré's *Researches into Chinese Superstitions*, trans. M. Kennelly (Shanghai: Tusewei Printing, 1917/i), is a beautifully illustrated multi-volume set in which the gamut of Chinese superstitions is covered, the associations with myth obvious almost all the way through. E.R. Hughes' *Chinese Philosophy in Classical Times* (London: J.M. Dent & Sons, 1942) is an ideal background work for deepening your understanding of the Chinese mind as it was during the periods of myth making and philosophical development.

Works on Religion and Related Matters

A sketchy but certainly useful first look at Chinese religions can be gained from Herbert A. Giles' seventy-page *Religions of Ancient China* (Chicago: Open Court; originally 1905) and Laurence G. Thompson's somewhat longer *Chinese Religion: An Introduction* (Belmont, Calif.: Dickinson Publishing Co., 1969). Similarly sketchy introductions which will prove useful for anyone not yet "into" Chinese religions can be found in most of the books which deal with religions either regionally or around the world. For instance, the thirty-or-so-pages that Geoffrey Parrinder devotes to Chinese religion in his *Introduction to Asian Religions* (New York: Oxford University Press, 1976/p; originally hardbound 1957) are packed with useful information of a basic sort. The same is true of the sections on Chinese religion in Hans-Joachim Schoeps' *The Religions of Mankind*, trans. Richard and Clara Winston (Garden City, N.Y.: Doubleday Anchor, 1968/p); Robert S. Ellwood, Jr.'s fine *Many Peoples, Many Faiths* (Englewood Cliffs, N.J.: Prentice-Hall, 1976/b); and many other works that could be mentioned from the worldwide category.

More substantial coverage of Chinese religion is given in a work such as D. Howard Smith's useful historical survey called *Chinese Religions* (New York: Holt, Rinehart and Winston, 1968) and in older but still helpful works like Marcel Granet's *The Religion of the Chinese People*, trans. Maurice Freedman (New York: Harper Torchbook, 1975/p; reprint of the 1922 edition); W.J. Clennell's *The Historical Development of Religion in China* (New York: E.P. Dutton, 1917); Max Weber's *The Religion of China* (Glencoe, Ill.: The Free Press, 1951; reprint of an earlier edition); and J.J.M. de Groot's monumental, multi-volume study called *The Religious System of China* (Leiden: E.J. Brill, 1901).

Individual works on Taoism, Confucianism, and Buddhism in China can also be found in fair abundance. As examples, John Blofeld's *The Secret and Sublime* (London: George Allen and Unwin, 1973/p) is a good introduction to the 2,000-year-old Taoist religion, its beliefs, tenets, and practices, by a man who lived with and travelled among the people of China for years. *Confucianism* (Woodbury, N.Y.: Barron's, 1973/p), by Chai Ch'u and Winberg Chai introduces its subject in a readable and informative way, and Kenneth Ch'en's *Buddhism in China* (Princeton: Princeton University Press, 1964/p) is excellent as an introduction to the Chinese variety of Buddhism. For those interested in Chinese mythology, though, such works as these will prove useful only as deepest background. (For Buddhism generally, see the section on Indian mythology earlier in this guide.)

Joseph Shih's "The Notions of God in the Ancient Chinese Religion," *Numen*, 16 (September 1969), pp. 99–138, is an excellent article on Chinese mytho-religious conceptions involving deity. Perhaps it will be useful to you at some time, as H.H. Rowley's *Prophecy and Religion in Ancient China and Israel* (New York: Harper and Brothers, 1956) might someday be. Rowley's book demonstrates the parallels between two cultures quite nicely, in the process clarifying the nature of the prophetic codes and prophets in ancient China. C.K. Yang's "The Functional Relationship Between Confucian Thought and Chinese Religion," on pp. 269–90 in *Chinese Thought and Institutions* (Chicago: University of Chicago Press, 1957), ed. John K. Fairbank, is also superb as deeper background to Chinese myth study. And ultimately, those who are serious about that myth study will surely want to come in contact with Herrlee Glessner Creel's *Chinese Thought From Confucius to Mao Tse-tung* (Chicago: University of Chicago Press, 1953), which clarifies why the mythology of the Chinese is the way it is.

Works on Historical/Cultural Background

There are plenty of books on the history of China—something that might be expected with that history having been popular in the western world ever since the thirteenth century voyages of Marco Polo. The standard multi-volume history is *The Cambridge History of China* (Cambridge: Cambridge University Press). All ten volumes of it can usually be found in better libraries. The noted Chinese scholar Kenneth Scott Latourette's *The Chinese: Their History and Culture* (New York: Macmillan, 1964; originally 1934) remains a standard one-volume history that will be of much use to the interested myth student. The first part treats the history chronologically from the beginnings through the first half of the twentieth century, and the second treats aspects of Chinese culture. Chapter seventeen, for instance, is devoted to religion— and most usefully so. Marcel Granet's *Chinese Civilization* (New York: Alfred A. Knopf, 1930) is a valuable cultural history, as is René Grousset's *Chinese Art and Culture*, trans. Haakon Chevalier (New York: Orion, 1959; Grove Press, 1961/p). *Ancient China* (New York: Time-Life Books, 1967/ib), by Edward H. Schafer and the editors of Time-Life Books, is a lovely volume in the *Great Ages of Man* series. Loaded with pictures, charts, maps, and well researched and written, it is an ideal background source to Chinese myth study. Also concerned with earlier China are Herrlee Glessner Creel's *The Birth of China: A Study of the Formative Period of Chinese Civilization* (New York: John Day, 1937); Yong Yap's and Arthur Cotterell's *The Early Civilization of China* (London: Widenfeld and Nicolson, 1975/ib); Leonard Cottrell's *The Tiger of Ch'in* (New York: Holt, Rinehart, and Winston, 1962); and W. Watson's *Early Civilization in China* (London: Thames and Hudson, 1966/i). All are adequate, but *The Early Civilization of China* is the better of the group for its fine pictures, bibliography, and overall readability. Johan Gunnar Andersson's *Children of the Yellow Earth: Studies in Prehistoric China*, trans. E. Classen (Cambridge: M.I.T. Press, 1973/p; originally published 1934) deals extensively with China's earliest times. Also don't overlook *An Historic Atlas of China* (Edinburgh, 1972/i) by A. Hermann. It's a very helpful volume.

A number of volumes dealing with the history of broader areas than just China may also be worth considering: *East Asia: Tradition and Transformation* (Boston: Houghton Mifflin Co., 1973) by John K. Fairbank, Edwin O. Reischauer, and Albert M. Craig; *A History of Asia: Formation of Civilizations from Antiquity to 1600* (Boston: Allyn and Bacon, 1964), by Woodbridge Bingham, Hilary Conroy, and Frank W. Ikle; Will Durant's *Our Oriental Heritage* (New York: Simon and Schuster, 1935); Stuart Piggott's *The Dawn of Civilization* (New York: McGraw-Hill, 1961); and *Prehistory and the Beginnings of Civilization* (New York: Harper & Row, 1963) by Jacquetta Hawkes and Leonard Woolley.

As mentioned earlier, speculation concerning China's ancient contacts elsewhere runs high still. An excellent introduction to the matter can be gotten in Stan Steiner's "China's Ancient Mariners," *Natural History*, 86 (December 1977/ib), pp. 48–63. A fine book with maps, photographs, and text that focuses on the southward wanderings of the Chinese on land and sea in ancient times is C.G. Simkin's *The Traditional Trade of Asia* (London: Oxford University Press, 1968/i). C.P. Fitzgerald's *The Southern Expansion of the Chinese People* (New York: Praeger, 1972) is another useful book for those interested in the diffusion/contact possibilities of the ancient Chinese. Contacts in Middle America made by ancient Chinese are speculated on in *Handbook of Middle American Indians*, Volume IV (Austin: University of Texas Press, 1966), edited by Gordon F. Ekholm and Gordon R. Willey. The articles on pp. 277–315 are especially interesting. A genuine diffusionist work is R.A. Jairazbhoy's *Ancient Egyptians and Chinese in America* (London: George Prior Associates, 1974); while it's the most unabashedly speculative of all the works mentioned, it's fascinating.

Works on Archaeology and Art

Li Chi's *The Beginnings of Chinese Civilization* (Seattle: University of Washington Press, 1957) is a good overview of what archaeology has revealed to us of the most ancient Chinese. So, too, are Judith Treistman's *The Prehistory of China: An Archaeological Exploration* (Garden City, N.Y.: Natural History Press, 1972/ip) and Kwang-Chih Chang's *The Archaeology of Ancient China* (New Haven: Yale University Press, 1963/ibp), the latter work a particularly comprehensive one. Glyn Daniel has included a brief introduction to the archaeological history of ancient China in his *The First Civilizations: The Archaeology of Their Origins* (New York: Apollo Editions, 1970/p). *Archaeology in China* (Toronto: University of Toronto Press, 1959–62/i), a four-volume set by Te-Kun Cheng, is the authoritative work on archaeology in China, but for those interested only in bits and pieces, encyclopedias and dictionaries of archaeology usually have useful entries and articles.

Numerous books will be readily available to anyone looking for Chinese art as background to Chinese mythology. *Arts of China* (Tokyo: Kodansha International, 1968/i), coordinated by Mary Tregear, is a fine two-volume set loaded with pictures.

Chinese Art (New York: Universe Books, 1966/i), by Daisy Lion-Goldschmidt and Jean-Claude Moreau-Gobard, is also well illustrated—as is *China: A History in Art* (New York: Harper & Row, 1972/ib) by Bradley Smith and Wan-yo Weng. *The Art and Architecture of China* (Harmondsworth, G.B.: Penguin Books, 1956/ip), by Lawrence Sickman and Alexander Soper, though smaller in overall size, is a helpful volume too. Michael Sullivan's *The Arts of China* (Berkeley: University of California Press, 1973/ip) is an art history and doesn't have as many illustrations as the larger volumes do, but it is a fine book. James Cahill's *Chinese Painting* (Cleveland: World Publishing Co., 1960/ib) is narrower in focus but does have lovely color illustrations and excellent text. Edmund Capon's *Art and Archaeology in China* (Cambridge: M.I.T. Press, 1977/i) is a marvelous tour of the artwork that has been excavated in China—art from remotest times to the end of the Yuan dynasty, (fourteenth century A.D.).

Japanese Mythologies

Probably because it was not until the middle of the sixteenth century that Japan was "discovered" by Europe—more specifically by the Portuguese—and because it remained outside European trade circles until the middle of the nineteenth century, it is only in the past hundred years that the aura of mystery associated with all that is "Japanese" has begun evaporating. In the nineteenth century especially, theories about the Japanese, their origins and their culture were in abundance, one of the most interesting of them that the Japanese were descended from a lost tribe of Israel, that of Benjamin.

Just where and when the Japanese became a distinct people is, to be sure, a mystery. Tradition has it that the Japanese empire was started by one Emperor Jimmu, a direct descendent of the sun goddess, in 660 B.C., a date sometimes corrected to one closer to the time of Jesus. It was not until much later, though, that the historical period in Japan began with the laying of the foundations of the Japanese state in the fifth century A.D. During that period, Chinese writing was introduced in Japan by way of Korea, and for a period of two hundred or so years the influence of China and Korea on Japan was quite strong. In 552 Buddhism spread into Japan, again through China and Korea, and with the native Shintoism it has remained a strong religion there ever since.

Collections of Myths

Japanese mythology is less myth "system" than assemblage. Two early eighth century books are the main sources of the myths as we know them—the *Kojiki* (A.D. 712) and *Nihongi* (A.D. 720). An excellent collection of myths, legends, and folklore drawn from these two sources is F. Hadland Davis' *Myths and Legends of Japan* (London: Harrap, 1913/i); despite its age, it is still a colorful and useful volume. Juliet Piggott's *Japanese Mythology* (London: Paul Hamlyn, 1969/ib), in Hamlyn's *International Mythology* series is a beautifully illustrated and probably the best single-volume source available commonly for the myths. There's also an excellent section on Japanese mythology by Serge Eliséev in *Asiatic Mythology* (New York: Thomas Y. Crowell, 1963/i), ed. J. Hackin. Two older volumes devoted to the myths of China and Japan are still quite helpful: *Myths of China and Japan* (London: Gresham Publishing Co., 1923) by Donald A. Mackenzie, and Volume VIII in the *Mythology of All Races: Chinese, Japanese* (Boston: Marshall Jones Co., 1916–32 and later reprint editions) by U. Hattori and Masaharu Anesaki. E. Dale Saunders' chapter on Japanese mythology in *Mythologies of the Ancient World* (Garden City, N.Y.: Doubleday Anchor, 1961/bp), ed. Samuel Noah Kramer, is a good, if somewhat brief, introduction, as are the sections devoted to it in the *Larousse World Mythology* (New York: Putnam, 1965/i), ed. Pierre Grimal, trans. Patricia Beardsworth, and the *Larousse Encyclopedia of Mythology* (London: Paul Hamlyn, 1959/ip), ed. Felix Guirand, trans. Richard Aldington and Delano Ames. The *Pears Encyclopedia of Myths and Legends*, Volume III (London: Pelham Books, 1977/i) has a fairly good section on Japanese mythology, but it is too brief to be alone relied upon to any extent. The *Encyclopedia of World Mythology* (New York: Galahad Books, 1975) and Veronica Ions' *The World's Mythology in Colour* (London: Paul Hamlyn, 1974/i) have too little in them on Japanese mythology to be of value—although the Ions book does have a fine run of pictures in it.

A few other anthologies you may find useful should also be mentioned. Helen and William McAlpine's *Japanese Tales and Legends* (London: Oxford University Press, 1958), R.G. Smith's *Ancient Tales and Folklore of Japan* (London: A. & C. Black, 1908), Lord Redesdale's (A.B. Mitford's) *Tales of Old Japan* (London: Macmillan, 1876), and Richard M. Dorson's *Folk Legends of Japan* (Rutland, Vt.: Charles Tuttle, 1962/i) are all volumes devoted mainly to folktales, but in each there are myths. The Dorson volume will possibly prove of most value to myth students.

Works on Religion and Related Matters

A number of excellent histories of Japanese religion are available for background study. Masaharu Anesaki's *History of Japanese Religion* (Rutland, Vt.: Charles E. Tuttle, 1963—reprint of an earlier edition) is a fine survey that has lots in it on myth as well. William K. Bunce's *Religions in Japan: Buddhism, Shinto, Christianity* (Tokyo: Charles E. Tuttle, 1955/b) is also adequate as is the survey by the Japanese Agency for Cultural Affairs, *Japanese Religion* (Tokyo: Kodansha International, 1972/b). Joseph M. Kitagawa's *Religion in Japanese History* (New York: Columbia University Press, 1966) has much to offer, including a superb glossary of terms. Floyd Hiatt Ross' *Shinto: The Way of Japan* (Boston: Beacon Press, 1965) should be of particular interest since the bulk of purely Japanese mythology derives from Shinto tradition and since Ross inspects that tradition thoroughly. Two chapters of special importance are "The Japanese Myth" and "Shinto Ideas of Karni." Also, don't overlook the general books on religions of the world. John A. Hardon's discussion of Shinto in Volume I of his *Religions of the World* (Garden City, N.Y.: Doubleday Image, 1963), for instance, is brief but fine as an introduction. (Books on Buddhism are included in the section of this guide on Indian mythology.)

If you're interested in Japanese shamanism, see the good discussion of it in Emiko Ohnuki-Tierney's "The Shamanism of the Ainu of the Northwest Coast of Southern Sakhalin," *Ethnology*, 12 (January 1973), pp. 15–29. Michael Czaja's *Gods of Myth and Stone: Phallicism in Japanese Folk Religion* (New York: Weatherhill, 1974/i) is another more specialized study. In this case, the focus is the worship of fertility in Japan through roadside and other local sculpture. Part four has a good discussion of Japanese mythology, and part three covers folk worship, including shamanism in Japan. A good look, through artifacts, at the prehistoric religion of Japan is contained in Johannes Maringer's article entitled "Clay Figurines of the Jomon Period: A Contribution to the History of Ancient Religion in Japan" in *History of Religions*, 14 (November 1974), pp. 128–39.

Chapter eight of Joseph Campbell's *Oriental Mythology* (New York: Viking Press, 1962/p), the second volume in his *The Masks of*

God series, is on Japanese mythology—an excellent background discussion. Other parts of that volume will also prove useful, as will parts of his *Myths to Live By* (New York: Viking Press, 1972/p). Susan Matisoff's *The Legend of Semimaru, Blind Musician of Japan* (New York: Columbia University Press, 1977), although not clearly "mythology"-related, may prove of value since the history of a legend is here traced rigorously, indirectly throwing light on the process on myth growth and transmission in Japan. Joseph M. Kitagawa's "The Japanese *Kokutai* (National Community) History and Myth," in *History of Religions*, 13 (February 1974), pp. 209-26, also has what may be indirectly useful discussions of the "historicization of myth and mythologization of history" among other things. Takakuni Hirano's "On the Truth: A Study Considering the Religious Behavior Concerning Mt. Fuji," in *Diogenes*, no. 79 (Fall 1972), pp. 109-27, covers the myth and folklore centered on Mt. Fuji in Japan but is more useful on the true-false spectrum in relation to Japanese myth. Additionally, Joseph M. Kitagawa's "Ainu Myth," on pp. 309-23 in *Myths and Symbols: Studies in Honor of Mircea Eliade* (Chicago: University of Chicago Press, 1969), ed. Joseph M. Kitagawa and Charles H. Long, is quite valuable on ancient Japanese mythology.

Works on Historical/Cultural Background

There's no paucity of histories of Japan for use as background. R.A. Brinkley's *A History of the Japanese People* (New York: Encyclopedia Britannica Co., 1914) is an old work that still has value—particularly because of the two chapters devoted to Japanese mythology but also for the historical survey as well. Another old book which has both history and a couple of chapters devoted more or less to mythology is Herbert H. Gowen's *An Outline History of Japan* (New York: D. Appleton and Co., 1927). Two comprehensive histories, each three volumes, are George B. Sansom's *History of Japan* (Palo Alto, Calif.: Stanford University Press, 1958-63) and James Murdock's *History of Japan* (New York: Frederick Ungar, 1964). *Early Japan* (New York: Time-Life Books, 1968/ib), a volume in the *Great Ages of Man* series, is fairly brief, but it is well written and researched, and it has the advantage of lots of pictures, an excellent chronology, and several maps. Edwin O. Reischauer's *Japan: Past and Present*, 3rd edition (New York: Alfred A. Knopf, 1965), also has a good chronology at the end, but only the first half of the book will otherwise be useful to myth students. K.S. Latourette's *The History of Japan*

(New York: Macmillan, 1957) and R.G. Webster's *Japan: From the Old to the New* (London: S.W. Partridge & Co., 1905) are both of limited value for the myth student's purpose of background for his study.

Broader in coverage than just Japan describes a number of other histories that are valuable for what they do have of Japanese history in them. *East Asia: Tradition and Transformation* (Boston: Houghton Mifflin Co., 1973), by John K. Fairbank, Edwin O. Reischauer, and Albert M. Craig, is a history of East Asia "through the histories of its four major national units—China, Japan, Korea, and Vietnam." *A History of Asia*, Volume I (Boston: Allyn and Bacon, 1964), by Woodbridge Bingham, Hilary Conroy and Frank W. Ikle, offers even slighter coverage of Japanese history than *East Asia* does, but as an introduction it can be of use. Just about the same evaluation can be made of several other fine books: Will Durant's *Our Oriental Heritage* (New York: Simon and Schuster, 1935), which is Volume I of the Durants' *The Story of Civilization*; Stuart Piggott's *The Dawn of Civilization* (New York: McGraw-Hill, 1961); and Jacquetta Hawkes' and Leonard Woolley's *Prehistory and the Beginnings of Civilization* (New York: Harper & Row, 1963), Volume I of UNESCO's *History of Mankind*.

Of special interest to those who have diffusionist leanings, "A Transpacific Contact in 3000 B.C.," by Betty J. Meggers and Clifford Evans, in *Scientific American*, 214 (January 1966), pp. 28–35, deals with pottery discoveries in Ecuador which match Japanese designs and types from approximately the same time period.

While archaeological work has been carried out in Japan just as it has anywhere culture dates back a few thousand years, not much on that archaeological activity is available in English. J. Edward Kidder, Jr.'s *Japan Before Buddhism* (London: Thames and Hudson, 1959; revised New York: F.A. Praeger, 1966) remains the usually referred to source. Good encyclopedias and atlases of archaeology will be of some use if the Kidder volume is not available.

Translations, Works on Art

Port Wheeler's *The Sacred Scriptures of the Japanese* (New York: Henry Schuman, 1952) is an excellent source for myths of the Japanese in translation. *Nihongi: Chronicles of Japan from the*

Earliest Times to A.D. 697, trans. W.G. Aston (London: George Allen and Unwin, 1956; first published in 1896), is, with the *Kojiki*, a primary source for Japanese myths; parts one and two will be especially helpful in this particular translation. Donald L. Philippi's translation of the *Kojiki* (Tokyo: University of Tokyo Press, 1968) is commonly found in better libraries.

Interest in Japanese art and architecture has been sufficiently high in the western world to make books that deal with it popular. Bradley Smith's *Japan: A History in Art* (New York: Simon and Schuster, 1964/i) is a combination history and arts volume that will no doubt be of use as background, as will Louis Frederic's *Japan: Art and Civilization* (London: Thames and Hudson, 1971/i), a lovely little volume. H. Patterson Boger's *The Traditional Arts of Japan* (Garden City, N.Y.: Doubleday, 1964/i) is a fine book for its pictures and text. So, too, is *Japan, Art and Culture* (Tokyo: Government of Japan, 1964/i) by Tatsuo Shibata *et al. The Art and Architecture of Japan*, revised edition (Harmondsworth, G.B.: Penguin Books, 1960/ibp), by Robert Treat Paine and Alexander Soper, has a limited number of pictures but does have good textual matter of interest to myth students. Seiroku Noma's *The Arts of Japan*, two volumes, trans. John Rosenfield (Tokyo: Kodansha International, 1966/i) and Yahino Yukio's *Art Treasures of Japan*, two volumes (Tokyo: Kokusai Bunka Shinkokai, 1960/i) are both superb pictures-and-text volumes. Akiyama Terukazu's *Japanese Painting* (New York: Rizzoli International, 1978/i) and J. Edward Kidder, Jr.'s *Masterpieces of Japanese Sculpture* (Tokyo: Charles E. Tuttle, 1961/i) are also beautiful. Perhaps the most useful volume of all—to myth students, at least—is *Mythological Japan* (Philadelphia: Drexel Biddle, 1902/i) by Alexander Francis Otto and Theodore S. Holbrook. It deals with the symbolism in Japanese art which has myth as its focus. Here are Hotri, god of good things; Urashima, the Japanese Rip van Winkle; Ebisu, god of plenty and daily food; and many others. The illustrations are beautiful, too.

European Mythologies

To those of us sufficiently imbued with the great cultural tradition of the western world, a tradition we've usually thought of as rooted in ancient Greece and Rome but very nearly dormant for more than a thousand years before regaining its forward thrust in fifteenth century Italy, it must come as a shock how far antecedent to eighth century B.C. Greece our human and cultural roots in time have been traced and how far afield of Europe some of our cultural roots have been shown to reach. Archaeologists, ever digging, ever surprising, tell us that Europe was convincingly inhabited long before Greece or Rome and long before even the civilized centers of ancient Western Asia and Egypt. Hunters occupied sites throughout Europe as far back, possibly, as a million years ago. Le Vallonet cave, near Menton in France, is the oldest such site in Europe, but there are others in France alone dating back beyond 70,000 B.C. In Germany, the discovery of the lower jawbone of a pithecanthropine hominid dating from mid-Pleistocene times—perhaps also a million years ago—corroborates the incredibly early habitation of Europe, as do other finds in other European places. Even in the northern outposts of Europe, the British Isles and Scandinavia, evidence of early habitation has been turned up by the archaeologist's spade. Creswell Crags and Cheddar Gorge are the earliest known habitation sites of prehistoric man in England—15,000 years ago at least—and the remains of early hunting communities in southern Scandinavia have been dated to at least 8,000 years ago.

The conjecture is that the spread of farming in Europe came as the result of migrations from the ancient birthplace of farming, western Asia. The first farmers in southeastern Europe worked the soil around 6,000 B.C., according to carbon-14 dating, and farming spread during the next 2,000 years as far north as the southern portions of the British Isles and Scandinavia. It was

The following symbols will be found, where applicable, in the bibliographic citation, usually following the date of publication: i = has useful illustrations; b = has a useful bibliography; p = has been published in paperbound edition.

almost simultaneous with the spread of farming that the art of
metal-working also spread throughout Europe according to the
archaeological evidence.

This long-winded excursion into the prehistory of Europe
is not without purpose. As will be seen in the sections on the
individual European mythologies, prior to the Romanization
and Christianization of Europe there were independent traditions
in Europe further along than we are inclined to acknowledge.
It matters, for instance, that the Celts were a powerful and influential, if somewhat widespread and politically disorganized,
people even before the Romans and Christianity made inroads
north of the Mediterranean. It matters also that the Finno-Ugric
race was widespread throughout eastern Europe and much of
Russia well before a Roman footstep was heard north of the
Italian Alps and that the Teutons were settled and solid in Europe
at almost as early a time. It matters most of all to myth students
that the mythologies of these peoples and others were very probably fully developed by the time Christianity advanced northward
in Europe. The cultural roots of Europeans were strong enough
for vestiges of the earlier-than-Christian mythologies, rituals, and
religions to persist on into Christian Europe and to remain visible,
in whatever minor ways, even today. However pervasive the
influence of Roman Hellenism and Christianity have been in
European life, in other words, the roots of the mythologies of
old and medieval Europe go deeper into the past than they do.
The philologist insists that Indo-European languages are rooted
in the Orient, and the archaeologist continues to put physical
evidence of the earlier heritage at our disposal. Maybe the myth
student can be the one to make real sense of it all.

Works on Archaeology, Historical/Cultural Background

Since the archaeological and historical evidence is so important,
appropriate works concerned broadly with the archaeology
and history of Europe will be first in our compact survey of
relevant sources. There are excellent, if brief, introductions
to the archaeology to be found in the following works: *The
Larousse Encyclopedia of Archaeology* (London: Hamlyn, 1972/i),
ed. Gilbert Charles-Picard, trans. Anne Ward; *Atlas of Ancient
Archaeology* (New York: McGraw-Hill, 1974/ib), ed. Jacquetta
Hawkes; *Archaeological Atlas of the World* (San Francisco:
W.H. Freeman, 1975/ibp), by David and Ruth Whitehouse. More

in certain prehistoric artifacts and religious practices archaeologists have uncovered and in the linguistic connections that link the older Germanic tongues to the Indo-European family of languages.

Just how far the Teutonic culture spread beyond the geographic area I've described is still very much a mystery. It is known that the Vikings sailed north to Iceland and Greenland and west to North America. What are we to make of the notion popular with some middle Americans, though, that Quetzalcoatl, the ancient Toltec god, was Norse? According to one version of his myth, he was blonde. It is known also that the Vikings travelled east far into what is now Russia and south to the Mediterranean. What are we to make of the genealogy attaching the Norse to ancient Troy which was given us by Snorri Sturluson, the thirteenth century Icelandic historian and mythographer? Such questions as these are easily dismissed as being the "stuff" of mythology and, there-fore, not to be taken seriously. Anyone who seriously has studied mythology ends up dismissing nothing, however, and, more importantly perhaps, is prone to ask further questions like what influence did the Norse have, in all these travels, on those with whom they came in contact? What is the residue—if any—of contact with the Norse that may be found in the traditions, mythologies, and cultures of those whom the Norse discovered in their wanderings? Time only will tell, of course—maybe.

Collections of the Myths

With the Norse so prominent a branch of the Teutons, Norse mythology (Scandinavian) has been well preserved for us as the representative variety of Teutonic mythology. Brian Branston's *Gods of the North* (London: Thames and Hudson, 1955/ib) is an excellent collection of the myths in which the sources are continually mentioned. It also includes a helpful concluding chapter on the interpretation of those myths. H.R. Ellis Davidson, a past president of the prestigious Folk-Lore Society of England, has written two excellent Norse mythographies. Her *Gods and Myths of Northern Europe* (Harmondsworth, G.B.: Penguin, 1964/p) is a first-rate source on Norse myth and religion. There's a useful glossary of names and myth sources included, and her introduction to the study of Norse myth is doubtless the best of its kind. Her *Scandinavian Mythology* (London: Paul Hamlyn, 1969/ip) is equally good as a source of the myths and information about Scandinavian religion, and it has the added advantage of beautiful illustrations—over one hundred of them. Axel Olrik's

Teutonic Mythology (New York: Cooper Square Publishers, 1964 reprint of the 1917 edition) is one of many Norse/Teutonic mythographies that is older but still very reliable. It is in *The Mythology of All Races* series originally published in Boston by Marshall Jones Company. John A. MacCulloch's *Eddic Mythology* (New York: Cooper Square Publishers, reprint of the 1932 edition) is also an excellent older volume, but it focuses on Norse myth rather than on both Norse and Teutonic. Donald A. Mackenzie's *Teutonic Myth and Legend* (London: Gresham Publishing Co., 1912; reprinted Boston: Longwood Press, 1978/i) is still pretty good coverage of the Norse/Teutonic group of myths (including Beowulf and the Nibelungen cycle). A classic of comprehensive German scholarship is the four-volume *Teutonic Mythology* (New York: Dover Publications, 1966/p; originally London: George Bell & Sons, 1883) done by Jacob Grimm and translated by James S. Stallybrass. It covers not only the myths but accompanying lore and superstitions—almost as thorough a job with its subject as Robert Graves' *Greek Myths* is with its, and, in enough instances to mention it, just as unreliable in its idiosyncratic analyses and conjecturings. Viktor Rydberg's *Teutonic Mythology*, trans. Rasmus B. Anderson (London, 1907) is also old, but it is a pretty comprehensive and useful collection should you come upon it. Benjamin Thorpe's *Northern Mythology: Comprising the Principal Popular Traditions and Superstitions of Scandinavia, North Germany, and Netherlands* (London: Edward Lumley, 1851) is a remarkable three-volume work, which, like the Grimm volumes, includes "everything but the kitchen sink." It is, needless to say, useful today as a result. H.A. Guerber's *Myths of Northern Lands* (Cincinnati: American Book Co., 1895; reprinted by Singing Tree Press of Detroit, 1970/i) is a nicely illustrated collection of Norse myths "with special reference to literature and art." Her *Myths of the Norsemen* (London: George C. Harrap, 1908/i) is an adaptation of the earlier work, it too is loaded with photographs of paintings of scenes from Norse mythology and landscapes of related interest. R.B. Anderson's *Norse Mythology or, the Religion of Our Forefathers* (London: Trubner & Co., 1879) has a *good* glossary of names and is respectably comprehensive, utilizing the Eddic sources well. A two-volume set that is also highly useful still is Lucy W. Faraday's *Edda: The Divine Mythology of the North* and *The Heroic Mythology of the North* (New York: A.M.S. reprint of the 1902 edition). Peter A. Munch's *Norse Mythology: Legends of Gods and Heroes*, trans. Sigurd B. Hustvedt

(New York: A.M.S. 1970 reprint of the 1926 edition—and other reprints) was a popular book in its own day and is still a good source of the myths. W. Wagner's *Asgard and the Gods: Tales and Traditions of Our Northern Ancestors* (Norwood Editions reprint of the 1882 edition/i) is a beautiful old book that can be resorted to safely. Karl Mortensen's *A Handbook of Norse Mythology*, trans. A. Clinton Crowell (New York: Thomas Y. Crowell, 1913) is something like the counterpart, for Norse myths, to H.J. Rose's *Handbook of Greek Mythology*; both include discussion *and* the myths, making them valuable reference sources.

A group of additional books of Norse myths is made up of those that are, for whatever reasons, not as comprehensive or expansive. Frederick D. Kauffmann's *Northern Mythology*, trans. M. Steele Smith (London: J.M. Dent, 1903) is a very brief survey (106 pages), but its opening chapter, "The Decline of Teutonic Paganism," is a fine discussion of causes and details. Harold Hueberg's *Of Gods and Giants: Norse Mythology*, 4th edition (New York: International Publications, 1969/p) is a little volume in the *Norwegian Guides Series*. All for younger readers are J.H. Walsh's *Norse Legends and Myths* (London: Longman's, 1957), a brief, well managed sequence of *some* Norse myths from the Eddas meant for ages twelve and up; Katharine F. Boult's *Asgard and the Norse Heroes* (London: J.M. Dent, n.d.), a selection of thirty-four myths plus a glossary of names meant for junior high readers; and Dorothy G. Hosford's *Thunder of the Gods* (New York: Holt, Rinehart and Winston, 1952/i), a cute little book meant for nine-to-twelve year olds. *Hammer of the North* (New York: G.P. Putnam's Sons, 1977/i) has the myths retold plus beautiful illustrations.

There's also a group of works which include Norse mythology among others. The best of these is the *Larousse Encyclopedia of Mythology* (London: Paul Hamlyn, 1959/ip), ed. Felix Guirand, trans. Richard Aldington and Delano Ames. The section on Norse myths is really excellent given the limitations of space. The section in the *Larousse World Mythology* (New York: Putnam, 1965/i), ed. Pierre Grimal, trans. Patricia Beardsworth, is perhaps not *quite* as thorough, but it is nonetheless commendable *and* useful. There's also a good section on the Norse/Teutonic myths in Volume II of *The Pears Encyclopedia of Myths and Legends* (London: Pelham Books, 1977/i). The space devoted to Norse myths in the *Encyclopedia of World Mythology* (New York: Galahad Books, 1975/i) is not quite as complete as any of the preceding ones, but it is illustrated nicely and *does* have the main myths. Veronica Ions' *The World's Mythology in Colour* (London: Paul Hamlyn, 1974/i) should be reserved for pictures only; it has a lovely run of them, but the text is quite abbreviated. "The Age of Fable" section of Thomas Bulfinch's *Mythology* (New York: Modern Library, n.d., and other editions) has fair coverage of the Norse myths along with Greco-Roman and Druidic. Edith Hamilton does no more than introduce very briefly some of the Norse myths at the end of her *Mythology* (New York: N.A.L. Signet, 1940/p) as does Charles Gayley in his *The Classic Myths in English Literature and in Art* (New York: Ginn & Co., 1911). Gayley's tellings of the myths are based on Bulfinch's, by the way.

Don't overlook the dictionary and encyclopedias either. Works like Bergen Evans' *Dictionary of Mythology: Mainly Classical* (New York: Dell Laurel, 1972/p) and Herbert Spencer Robinson's and Knox Wilson's *Myths and Legends of All Nations* (Totowa, N.J.: Littlefield, Adams and Co., 1976/p; earlier Bantam edition) can be used as quick reference sources. (There are many of these sources, of course, and for fuller listing see "Worldwide Mythologies" above in this guide.)

Then, there are the works at the periphery. Brian Branston's excellent, beautifully illustrated *The Lost Gods of England* (New York: Oxford University Press, 1974/i) is about the Anglo-Saxon gods of England, but that means there's plenty related to Norse myth as a result. Chapter eleven, "Old Norse and Old English Myth," and the concluding chapter, "Balder into Christ," are especially helpful. C.H. Herford's *Norse Myth in English Poetry* (1918; Folcroft, Pa.: Folcroft Library Editions) is a good work for observing how Norse myth has come to be used in English poetry (and why, in many instances). Axel Olrik's *The Heroic Legends of Denmark*, trans. L.M. Hollander (New York: American Scandinavian Foundation, 1919) is great if you don't know about Helgi and Yrsa, Hroar, Biarki and Agnar, and other heroes. There's also some help with Beowulf—particularly genealogical—in the book. Jacqueline Simpson's *Icelandic Folktales and Legends* (Berkeley: University of California Press, 1972) is just about *all* folktales, but the connections with Norse mythology are pretty close and at times hardly separable. George Webbe Dasent's *East O' the Sun and West O' the Moon* (New York: Dover Publications, 1970/ip; originally published in 1858) also shows that close connection with Norwegian folktales.

Works on Religion and Related Matters

There are several fine works which can be recommended for learning about Norse/Teutonic religion. E.O.G. Turville-Petre's *Myth and Religion of the North: The Religion of Ancient Scandinavia* (New York: Holt, Rinehart and Winston, 1964/i; reprinted in 1975 by Greenwood) is a superb, comprehensive volume on Norse religion (and myth) that must be considered far and away the better choice in a narrow range. William A. Craigie's *The Religion of Ancient Scandinavia* (London: Archibald Constable and Co., 1906; Arno Press Reprint, 1974) is an old but still helpful little book (72 pages compared to 340 in Turville-Petre's). Hector Munro Chadwick's *The Cult of Othin: An Essay in the Ancient Religion of the North* (London: C.J. Clay & Sons, 1899), also a little book, deals with the cults of Odin and their rituals. H.R. Ellis Davidson's monograph entitled *The Battle God of the Vikings* (York: University of York Monograph Series no. 1, 1972) also deals with the cult of Odin in the course of inspecting cult and worship in Norse religion. Her *Pagan Scandinavia* (London: Thames and Hudson, 1967/i) is a very nicely done book which traces "the history of religious cults and symbols in Scandinavia from the earliest archaegological records until the close of the heathen period." Bronze Age, Migration Period, and Viking Age are covered, making it a first-rate background source to the study of Norse myth. Jan de Vries' "Celtic and Germanic Religion," *Saga Book*, 16 (1963-64), pp. 109-23, is a useful, if brief, comparative study.

Very brief surveys of the religions can often be found in historical surveys of the religions of the world. For instance, the section entitled "The Religion of the Germanic Peoples," pp. 242-47 in Robert S. Ellwood, Jr.'s *Many Peoples, Many Faiths* (Englewood Cliffs, N.J.: Prentice-Hall, 1976), is really pretty helpful considering its brevity. The same holds true for Murray Fowler's "Old Norse Religion" in *Ancient Religions* (New York: Citadel Press, 1965/p; originally published as *Forgotten Religions* in 1950).

Studies of the Myths and Religion

Analyses and interpretations of Norse/Teutonic myth and religion comprise another category of work. Hilda R. Ellis (H.R. Ellis Davidson) wrote a fine work on Norse eschatology: *The Road to Hel: A Study of the Conception of the Dead in Old Norse Literature* (1968 Greenwood reprint of the 1943 edition). *Old*

Norse Literature and Mythology (Austin: University of Texas Press, 1969), ed. Edgar C. Palome, sounds quite a bit more promising for myth study than it actually is, but such articles as Erik Wahlgren's "Fact and Fancy in the Vinland Sagas" and A. Margaret Arents' "The Heroic Patterns: Old Germanic Helmets, Beowulf, and Grettis Saga" do have some help in them for students of Norse and Teutonic myth. Ursale Dronke's "Beowulf and Ragnarok," an article in *Saga Book*, 17 (1963-64), pp. 302-25, is more on Norse myth than on Beowulf; it attempts to clarify the issue of whether or not the Beowulf poet knew Norse myth. M.I. Steblin-Kamenskij's *The Saga Mind*, trans. Kenneth H. Ober (Odense, Denmark, 1973), while concerned with the saga, has lots in it that will be useful in the course of Norse study. Although Joseph Campbell doesn't devote a lot of space in his *Occidental Mythology* (New York: Viking Press, 1964/p) to Norse/Teutonic mythology, there's enough in chapter nine to make looking into it worthwhile. Stephen Paul Schwartz's *Poetry and Law in Germanic Myth* (Berkeley: University of California Press, 1973/b) is a good analytic work on some aspects of Teutonic myth, including the myths of Odin and Thor. Hagan is the principal focus in a most interesting chapter on the transformation of gods into heroes. Stefan Einarsson's "Some Parallels in Norse and Indian Mythology," pp. 21-26 in *Scandinavian Studies: Essays Presented to Dr. Henry Goddard Leach* (Seattle: University of Washington Press, 1965), ed. Carl F. Bayerschmidt and Erik J. Friis, is good if you've any inclination toward diffusionist theory *or* just for use as a comparative exercise. W.C. Sawyer's *Teutonic Legends in the Nibelungen Lied and the Nibelungen Ring* (Gordon Press reprint, 1976) is a *very* useful study since it isolates and examines the purposes of Teutonic legend in a major German epic. Grenville Pigott's *A Manual of Scandinavian Mythology* (New York: Arno Press Reprint of the 1839 edition, 1977) is an old but nonetheless helpful work that deals with the cult of Odin and the surrounding mythology as seen in two Eddic sources. John L. Greenway's *The Golden Horns: Mythic Imagination and the Nordic Past* (Athens: University of Georgia Press, 1977) is a book of varied applicability. It focuses on the reuses of Nordic myth for new purposes, but in so doing offers some excellent insights as to various myths, meanings, purposes, and even origins.

The "New Comparative Mythology" of Georges Dumézil—a philological, tripartite analytic/interpretative system—is responsible for much of the recent work done on Norse myth. A collection of essays by Dumézil himself is available—principally a god or more per essay framed by a single problem—*Gods of the Ancient Northmen*, ed. Einar Haugen (Berkeley: University of California Press, 1973/p). Scott Littleton's introduction sketches the techniques of Dumézilian analysis adequately to make clear its fundamentals and make the reading worth the effort. Dumézil's *From Myth to Fiction: The Saga of Hadingus*, trans. Derek Coltman (Chicago: University of Chicago Press, 1973) is a *very* complicated analysis of Saxo's saga to demonstrate how the author gives "content" to the reign of Hadingus by reworking "a Scandinavian account of the career of the god Njordr." Einar Haugen's "The Mythological Structure of the Ancient Scandinavians: Some Thoughts on Reading Dumézil," pp. 855-68 in *To Honor Roman Jakobsen: Essays on the Occasion of His Seventieth Birthday* (The Hague: Mouton, 1967) is well worth looking into once you've done some reading of Dumézil's work. *Myth in Indo-European Antiquity* (Berkeley: University of California Press, 1974), ed. Gerald James Larson, *et al*, offers some excellent help of the Dumézilian sort, too: Udo Strutynski's "History and Structure in Germanic Mythology: Some Thoughts on Einar Haugen's Critique of Dumézil" and Edgar Polome's "Approaches to Germanic Mythology." *Myth and Law Among the Indo-Europeans* (Berkeley: University of California Press, 1970), ed. Jan Puhvel, also has some, if not quite as much, help of the Dumézilian sort in it. "Aspects of Human Sacrifice in Viking Scandinavia and Vedic India" is certainly one of the more interesting of the essays.

As you look for background to Norse/Teutonic myth, don't overlook histories of literature—German, Norwegian, English, medieval especially. While there are plenty of blind alleys to be encountered in seeking help concerning mythology in works that deal with literature as such, you'll be surprised at the number of things you'll turn up that will be helpful—particularly as concerns medieval myths and legends, Norse/Teutonic included. The section entitled "Early Germanic Literature" in W.T.H. Jackson's *Medieval Literature: A History and a Guide* (New York: Collier Books, 1966/p), for example, is really *quite* useful, as is chapter four of W.P. Ker's *The Dark Ages* (New York: N.A.L. Mentor, 1958/p). The early part of Harald Beyer's *A History of Norwegian Literature*, trans. Einar Haugen (New York: New York University Press, 1956/p) is very useful, too, as is Ernst Rose's *A History of German Literature* (New York: New York University Press, 1960), particularly the first two chapters. I mention these few works as examples of others like them.

Works on Historical/Cultural Background

Historical/cultural background to the study of Norse and Teutonic mythology can be gotten easily enough since there are plenty of fine books available. Gwyn Jones' *A History of the Vikings* (New York: Oxford University Press, 1968/ib) is a simply exquisite history of the Vikings, and it includes a good deal on Norse religion scattered through its 504 pages. T.D. Kendrick's *A History of the Vikings* (London: Methuen, 1930) is split into two parts, part one dealing with "The Lands of the Vikings" and part two with the Vikings abroad. E.O.G. Turville-Petre's *The Heroic Age of Scandinavia* (London: Hutchinson's University Library, 1951) is a history of the Norsemen before the death of S. Olaf in 1030 A.D. Chapters three through five deal with heroes. A large and beautiful book filled with illustrations is *The Viking* (New York: Crescent Books, 1975/i), ed. Bertil Almgren *et al.* It's also well written by experts and includes a few chapters on gods, sagas, and magic. Peter G. Foote and David M. Wilson have put together a marvelous "survey of the society and culture of early medieval Scandinavia" in *The Viking Achievement* (New York: Praeger Publishers, 1970/ib). The last chapter, "Religion and Conduct" is made to order as a quick introduction to those areas for myth students. Peter Breut's *The Viking Saga* (New York: G.P. Putnam's Sons, 1975/ib) is a popular history that can be relied on for sound research and really beautiful layout. The chapter entitled "Valhalla and After" will be *most* useful. Holger Arbman's *The Vikings*, trans. Alan Binns (New York: Frederick A. Praeger, 1961/i); Johannes Bronsted's *The Vikings*, trans. Kalbe Skov (Harmondsworth, G.B.: Penguin Books, 1965/ip); and Rudolf Poertner's *The Vikings*, trans. Sophie Wilkins (New York: St. Martin's, 1971/i) are all books with the same title, similar purposes, and good runs of pictures. Part six of the Poertner book is a *particularly* good discussion of myth in Scandinavia, but all three books do have chapters devoted to religion and myth. Jacqueline Simpson's *Everday Life in the Viking Age* (London: Batsford Books, 1967/i) is an attempt at relating what is known of the Vikings' activities to what is known of their natural backgrounds and lives. As such, it is less a history than a cultural investigation. Chapter nine, "Religious Practices and Funerary Rites," is excellent, by the way. Eric Carl Oxenstierna's *The Norsemen*, trans. Catherine Hutter (Greenwich, Conn.: N.Y. Graphic Society, 1965/ib) is a dazzling, up-to-date survey of Viking culture and influence—and, Oxenstierna is an expert on the subject. Also by Oxenstierna, *The World of the Norsemen*, trans. Janet Sondheimer (London: Weidenfeld & Nicholson, 1967/i) is a well-illustrated work which deals with the history of the Vikings as the archaeological record has revealed it to be. In "The Vikings," in *Scientific American*, 216 (May 1967), pp. 67–78, Oxenstierna describes the nomadic spread and contacts of the Vikings starting in the year A.D. 800. Viking expansion is P.H. Sawyer's subject in *The Age of the Vikings*, 2nd edition (London: Edward Arnold, 1971/ib)—although he also engages in some "reinterpretation" of the Viking period. Magnus Magnusson's *Viking Expansion Westwards* (New York: Henry Z. Walck, 1973/ibp) is now the authoritative treatment of westward-directed expansion; and, speaking of Viking expansion. H.R. Loyn's *The Vikings in Britain* (New York: St. Martin's Press, 1977/ib) is excellent on its subject and may be especially useful as you use Brian Branston's *The Lost Gods of England* and other such works.

Some brief surveys of Viking history and achievement may also be of use. David M. Wilson's *The Vikings and Their Origins: Scandinavia in the First Millenium* (New York: McGraw-Hill, 1970/ip) is one such volume—as are Howard La Fay's *The Vikings* (Washington, D.C.: National Geographic Society, 1972/i) and O. Madsen's *The Vikings*, trans. David Macrae (Geneva: Minerva Editions, 1976/i). Each is a beautifully illustrated book that covers the historical/cultural aspects of the Norse in easy-to-read fashion. *Barbarian Europe* (New York: Time-Life Books, 1968/i), by Gerald Simons and the editors of Time-Life, a volume in *The Great Ages of Man* series has much in it on the Norse and the mainland Teutons and would no doubt serve as a useful, quick introduction.

There are several works that can be helpful as historical/cultural background to Teutonic myth study. William Stubbs' *Germany in the Middle Ages: 476–1250*, ed. Arthur Hassall (New York: Howard Fertig, 1969), is excellent, particularly as you get into such medieval primary sources as the *Nibelungenlied*. V. Gronbech's *The Culture of the Teutons* (London: Humphrey Milford and Oxford University Press, 1926) and E.A. Thompson's *The Early Germans* (Oxford: Clarendon Press, 1965) will both be of some help, too. The latter work is meant to be read along with relevant portions of Caesar and Tacitus, by the way—which points up the importance of Roman sources for information on the early Teutons.

Translations

The Poetic and Prose *Edda* comprise the two major primary sources for Norse myth. Many editions of each may readily be found, but for some leads, try these: *The Poetic Edda*, trans. Henry Adams Bellows (Oxford: Clarendon Press, 1969); Eric Carl Oxenstierna's edition of the *Poems of the Elder Edda*, trans. L. Hollander (Austin: University of Texas Press, 1962); *The Prose Edda*, trans. Arthur Gilchrist Brodeur (London: Oxford University Press, 1929); *The Prose Edda of Snorri Sturluson: Tales from Norse Mythology*, selected and translated by Jean I. Young (Berkeley: University of California Press, 1966/p; other earlier editions published in Cambridge and London).

Sagas and epics are another category of primary sources for Norse and Teutonic myth. William Morris' translation called *Volsunga Saga: The Story of the Volsungs and Niblungs* (New York: Collier Books, 1962/p) is an important work as is the epic called *Nibelungenlied* (Penguin paperback edition among others). Ekkehard's *Waltharius Mannfortis* (Walter of the Strong Hand) and *The Lay of Hildebrand* are two other works in the epic tradition which will be important primary sources of Teutonic legend. While Icelandic sagas are not necessarily to be considered "primary" sources for Norse myth, the myth so often plays a role that they are, nonetheless, valuable sources to consider. There are many such sagas; some of the best and most useful are *The Saga of Hrafnkell, Priest of Frey; Njal's Saga; Gautrek's Saga; The Saga of Jomsvikings; Gisla Saga; Vinland Saga*. Penguin Books has editions of a number of the sagas, and Gwyn Jones' *The North Atlantic Saga: Being the Norse Voyages of Discovery and Settlement to Iceland, Greenland, America* (London: Oxford University Press, 1964) has six sagas and chronicles. See Peter Hallberg's *The Icelandic Saga*, trans. Paul Schach (Lincoln: University of Nebraska Press, 1962/p) for a good introduction to and interpretation of the main works.

Because it is usually considered as Teutonic in myth study (rather than, say, medieval English alone), the Old English poem *Beowulf* should be considered a primary source. It exists in many fine paperback editions, Burton Raffel's translation (New York: N.A.L. Mentor, 1963/p) perhaps the best one.

Works on Archaeology and Art

Relevant English language sources on archaeological work done in Northern Europe and Scandinavia are not especially abundant, but there are a few that are excellent. Geoffrey Bibby's *The Testimony of the Spade* (New York: Alfred A. Knopf, 1956/ip) is one of the better ones. It deals with the ice age through the Vikings, but there's plenty in it that will be useful to students of Norse/Teutonic myth. *Scandinavian Archaeology* (Oxford: Clarendon Press, 1937), by Haakan Shetelig and Hjalman Falk, trans. E.V. Gordon, covers all periods in Scandinavia, but there are some excellent chapters relevant to Norse myth study, including one called "Religion." The book is a collaborative effort by an archaeologist and a philologist, incidentally. Shetelig also edited four volumes called *Viking Antiquities in Great Britain and Ireland* (Oslo: H. Aschehoug, 1940–54/i) which have much of value for background purposes. H.R. Ellis Davidson's essay "Gods and Heroes in Stone" in *The Early Cultures of North-west Europe* (Cambridge: Cambridge University Press, 1950), ed. Cyril Fred Fox, is interesting on the problem of interpreting or "reading" what is portrayed in Norse stone sculpture when there is no accompanying text or inscription. Finally, articles appear from time to time in the popular press and magazines that will prove of interest. Maurice Shadbolt's "Who Killed the Bog Men of Denmark? And Why?" condensed in *Reader's Digest*, (June 1977), pp. 197–200, 203–04, is a good example, for it relates directly to the religious practices of the peoples of Norse/Teutonic northern Europe.

By far the best single source on Viking art that I am aware of is David M. Wilson's and Ole Klindt-Jensen's *Viking Art* (London: George Allen & Unwin, 1966). Francoise Henry's *Irish Art During the Viking Invasions (800–1020 A.D.)* (Ithaca: Cornell University Press, 1967) is excellent for seeing the influence of the Norse on others' art, here the art of the Christian Irish. Otherwise, the best sources for Norse/Teutonic art would have to be encyclopedias and histories of art—or, and these are often excellent sources, the collections of myths and the histories covered earlier and noted as having good illustrations.

Arthurian Mythology

"Ask every person if he's heard the story,/And tell it strong and clear if he has not,/That once there was a fleeting wisp of glory,/Called Camelot. . . ." The words, familiar ones by Alan Jay Lerner from the musical *Camelot*, capture well the feeling so many in the English-speaking world have come to associate with the medieval legends of Arthur and his celebrated "Knights of the Round Table." Like all medieval legends—and there are indeed a considerable number of them—they are lost somewhere between the reality of history and the polished inventions of the creative writer, so much so, in fact, that there is precious little evidence at all, aside from local legend and the writings of people like Sir Thomas Malory and Chrétien de Troyes, that Arthur's realm ever existed.

If it did exist, we can estimate its time as between Arthur's birth around A.D. 460, the year Ambrosius became leader of the British, and his death around A.D. 520. The *Annales Cambriae* identify the battle of Mount Badon, which Arthur supposedly fought in, as having occurred in 518 and the battle of Camlan, in which Arthur "fell," as having been fought in 539. These are a few early dates we can affix to Arthur and they, like other such dates, are suspect—hence the discrepancy you've no doubt observed. Only a few other early references to Arthur and others in his realm exist—in poems of the ancient *Black Book of Carmarthen* and in *Kilhwch and Olwen*, a Welsh romance. In the twelfth century *Historia Regnum Britanniae* of Geoffrey of Monmouth, the romantic tradition of Arthur and company is seen clearly; Geoffrey's inventiveness plays a distinct role in the "history" overall, Arthur's life and exploits included. It is in the *Roman de Brut* of Wace of Jersey (c. 1165) that the first extant mention of the Round Table occurs.

This sketchy—and "iffy"—outline of early sources reflects the bases upon which any investigation of the historicity of Arthur and Camelot must be built—and many have been. The questions that remain, therefore, are numerous. Where was Camelot? (In England, of course, but *where?*) Was Arthur Celtic? Was Arthur Christian? Why are the legends so conspicuously Romanized *and* Christianized? Answers to all of these questions and the many more like them have been ventured, but only the question of Arthur's existence can easily be answered with a heavily qualified "probably." The mythic acretions around the kernals of reality that are so often the case in myths elsewhere may well account for the strong tradition of Arthur—a historical person and even chieftain who became the stuff of legend. (On this kind of approach, I should mention that some have even seen the parallel between figures in the Celtic pantheon and Arthur and his knights. A few have reasoned that god and human merged; the earlier mentioned Ambrosius may have been that human prototype.)

Collections of the Myths

Arthurian legends are often covered (usually too briefly) in works dealing with Celtic mythology. Many of the collections of myths included in the section on Celtic myths in this guide contain some Arthurian legends and/or discussion of them. That includes even general mythographies like the two Larousse volumes. By far the best source for the legends retold in a pleasant way, though, is Thomas Bulfinch's *Mythology* (many editions)—in "The Age of Chivalry" section specifically (published separately in New York by New American Library, 1962). Over 150 pages are devoted to the legends. Several of the legends are included in Helen A. Guerber's *Legends of the Middle Ages* (New York: American Book Co., 1909; 1977 reprint edition by Comer House) and a good run of them can be found in *Folklore, Myths, and Legends of Britain* (Pleasantville, N.Y.: Reader's Digest, 1973/i). The beginning of the section called "The Celtic Realms" in *Encyclopedia of World Mythology* (New York: Galahad Books, 1975/i) is surprisingly strong on "King Arthur and His Knights of the Round Table" (pp. 188-99). So, too, is the section on "Arthurian Legends" in *Mythology for the Modern Reader* (Lincoln, Nebr.: Centennial Press, 1974/i; also published as Cliff's Notes *Mythology*), by James Weigel, Jr., pp. 223-47.

Also, don't overlook mythological dictionaries for their reference value where Arthurian legends are concerned. These are listed under "Worldwide Mythologies" earlier in this guide.

Studies of the Myths, Including Literary

Because the Arthurian legends are, in primary source, literary, one of the first places to look for some help of the analytical sort is *The Oxford Companion to English Literature*, 4th edition (London: Oxford University Press, 1967). German, French, and English literature are all involved, so literary histories of these countries will prove of some use, as will histories of medieval literature as such like W.T.H. Jackson's *Medieval Literature: A History and a Guide* (New York: Collier Books, 1966/p).

More specialized sources exist in fair abundance, too. A classic work is John Rhys' *Studies in the Arthurian Legend* (Oxford: Clarendon Press, 1891); it covers a number of angles, making it broadly valuable. Charles Bertram Lewis' *Classical Mythology and Arthurian Romance* (London: Oxford University Press, 1932) is a study of the influences of classical mythology on Chrétien de Troyes' *Yvain*. The large question of how much influence the myths of Greece and Rome might have had on the whole body of Arthurian literature is raised by Lewis, as is, ultimately, the question of the reality of Arthur and his Kingdom generally. It's a most provocative book. Roger S. Loomis edited a collection of forty-one essays *Arthurian Literature in the Middle Ages* (Oxford: Clarendon Press, 1959). It includes Helaine Newstead's "The Origin and Growth of the Tristan Legend," and Loomis' own "The Legends of Arthur's Survival" and "The Origin of the Grail Legends." A thoroughgoing analysis of Geoffrey of Monmouth's *Historia Regnum Britanniae*, J.S.P. Tatlock's *The Legendary History of Britain* (Berkeley: University of California Press, 1950) is excellent, in part, as an analysis of the mythmaking that may well have played a role in Geoffrey's history. One of the most influential pieces of scholarship ever written, Jessie L. Weston's *From Ritual to Romance* (Garden City, N.Y.: Doubleday Anchor, 1957/p; originally 1920) traces the legends of the grail back to archetypal nature-rituals. Weston's *The Quest of the Holy Grail* (New York: Barnes and Noble, 1964; originally 1913), also a ritualist work, is a useful survey and interpretation of the literature of the grail quest. Arthur Edward Waite's *The Holy Grail: The Galahad Quest in the Arthurian Literature* (New York: University Books, 1961) is the most complete and, probably, authoritative discussion of the subject, though, since Waite covers the subject from *all* angles, ritualist included. Alan Dundes' essay "The Father, the Son, and the Holy Grail," pp. 151-62 in his *Analytic Essays in Folklore* (The Hague: Mouton, 1975) is an interesting psychoanalytic interpretation. A good study of the grail from initial phases to later uses in medieval romance is Roger S. Loomis' *The Grail: From Celtic Myth to a Christian Symbol* (New York: Columbia University Press, 1963). His *Celtic Myth and Arthurian Romance* (New York: Haskell, 1969 reprint of the 1927 edition) is still the best overall comparative analysis of Celtic and Arthurian myth. Sigmund Eisner's *The Tristan Legend:*

A Study in Sources (Evanston, Ill.: Northwestern University Press, 1969/i) updates the information on sources of the Tristan legend and more. *The Legend of Sir Gawain: Studies Upon Its Original Scope and Significance* (London: David Nutt, 1897), by Jessie L. Weston, is an attempt to bring together all the known facts about the Gawain Legend; such disparate sources as William of Malmesbury and Italian records are brought into play. Raymond H. Thompson's "Gawain Against Arthur: The Impact of a Mythological Pattern Upon the Arthurian Tradition in Accounts of the Birth of Gawain," in *Folklore*, 85 (Summer 1974), pp. 113-21, is an excellent little article which touches on hero as such. So, too, does "The Arthurian Legend" in Charles Moorman's *Kings and Captains: Variations on a Heroic Theme* (Lexington: University Press of Kentucky, 1971), pp. 148-72; in it, the nature of the hero, Arthurian style, is dealt with.

Works on Historical/Cultural Background

Quite a bit is available on the Arthurian legends that may be called historical/cultural background—perhaps, more accurately, *investigative* historical/cultural background since so little is known about the actual history and culture except what is included in the romances and chronicles. The most ambitious history as such is John Morris' *The Age of Arthur: A History of the British Isles from 350 to 650* (New York: Charles Scribner's Sons, 1973/i). It is broader in scope than *just* the Arthurian, but it embraces it so thoroughly and puts it in context with the general history of early England, Wales, Scotland, and Ireland that it cannot be overlooked as a principal stop enroute to solid background to Arthurian legend. Richard Barber's *Arthur of Britain: An Introduction to the Arthurian Literature and Legends of England* (London: Barrie and Rockliff, 1961/i), 218 pages, like many books on Arthur deals extensively with the legends themselves. Helen Hill Miller's *The Realms of Arthur* (New York: Charles Scribner's Sons, 1969/ib) brings together all sides of the Arthurian—the legends, the archaeology, the history, the culture, the facts, the fiction. Geoffrey Ashe *et al* have also put together a beautiful, all-embracing volume in *The Quest for Arthur's Britain* (London: Pall Mall Press, 1968/i) as has Elizabeth Jenkins in *The Mystery of King Arthur* (New York: Coward, McCann, and Geoghegan, 1975/i), a big expensive volume. Richard Barber's *The Figure of Arthur* (London: Longman, 1972/b) is a most interesting work in which the overall Arthurian controversy (fact? fiction?) is discussed, the evidence sifted, and Barber's solution presented. (Barber says Arthur was relatively a minor figure made mythically great.) Leslie Alcock's *Arthur's Britain: History and Archaeology* (New York: St. Martin's Press, 1971/ibp) is a book in which much the same thing is done, Alcock's "solution" being that Arthur was "not a mere figment of myth or romance." Geoffrey Ashe's contribution is *Camelot and the Vision of Albion* (London: Heinemann, 1971); the book is breezily written and is a mine of information about the legends and their sources. Ashe's "solution" is not so much a solution as the suggestion that the historical "reality" of Arthur may not be worth believing. Joseph Clancy's *Pendragon: Arthur and His Britain* (New York: Praeger, 1971/ib) is a piecing together of the evidence of poets and chroniclers as a way of giving us a nice brief survey of fifth century Britain, Arthur's world within it, and the Arthur of that world. Jack Lindsay's investigative mind has also turned toward Arthur (as it has toward Helen of Troy and others) in *Arthur and His Times* (London: Muller, 1958/i). Leslie Alcock's *By South Cadbury Is That Camelot* (London: Thames and Hudson, 1972/i) is largely archaeological in its orientation, but it is also broadly concerned with the history and culture, legends as such included. "The Sarmatian Connection: New Light on the Origins of the Arthurian and Holy Grail Legends," an article by C. Scott Littleton and Ann C. Thomas in *Journal of American Folklore*, 91 (January–March 1978), pp. 513-27, provides some evidence that the Arthurian legend may not be Celtic in origin and may not even be historical. The authors suggest that it may well have evolved in the Steppes of what is now southern Russia, the Sarmatians the originators. An old but still useful historical/cultural work—representative of a fair group like it but, in my estimation, the only one that has enough of value left to be worth mentioning—is E.K. Chambers' *Arthur of Britain* (London: Sidgwick and Jackson, 1927; reprinted in Cambridge by Speculum Historiale in 1964).

Other histories that may be of use should also be accounted for here. Geoffrey Ashe's *From Caesar to Arthur* (London: Collins, 1960); *Christianity in Early Britain* (Leicester: Leicester University Press, 1968), ed. M.W. Barley and R.P.C. Hanson; Gilbert Sheldon's *The Transition from Roman to Christian England: A.D. 368-664* (London: Macmillan, 1932); and Beram Saklatvala's *Arthur: Roman Britain's Last Champion* (New York: Taplinger, 1967) all cover roughly the same time period—if in quite different ways. *Christianity in Early Britain* is a collection of essays, some of which are very helpful as background to Arthurian times. The other three books are straight history, the most useful one being Saklatvala's since there is some discussion of Arthurian legends and since the space devoted to Arthur's times is pretty generous.

Other books that might be considered for historical/cultural background are books that deal with knights and chivalry, two examples of which are R. Rudorff's *Knights and the Age of Chivalry* (New York: Viking Press, 1974/i) and *The Age of Chivalry* (Washington, D.C.: National Geographic Society, 1969/i). Both offer some coverage of Arthur and his knights, and they're well illustrated. Also, as I mentioned in the section on Celtic mythology, and earlier in this section, the connection of Arthur and the Celts is, in theory at least, strong enough that books dealing with the Celts occasionally have something of value to offer on Arthur's realm. For example, the chapter entitled "The Celtic Court of King Arthur," pp. 274-86 in Gerhard Herm's *The Celts* (New York: St. Martin's Press, 1977) is well worth looking into.

Works on Geography and Archaeology

Just how far it is possible to talk of the geography and archaeology of Arthur's realm remains a matter for conjecture. J.M.M. Forster's "Questing for Camelot" is an interesting little article on one aspect of the conjecturing; it can be found in *Folklore*, 77 (Winter 1966), pp. 253-56. Several chapters in *Myth or Legend?* (New York: Capricorn Books, 1968/i), ed. Glyn E. Daniel, deal with the fact or fiction of characters and certain Arthurian places in England. "Glastonbury and the Holy Grail" and "Tristan and Isolt" are two of the more interesting ones. Also, because Stonehenge is recorded in Arthurian legend, don't overlook the books on Stonehenge and the other monuments listed in the Celtic section; the same holds for some of the noted mounds and monuments in England even though they predate Arthur.

Primary Sources

The number of what may be *called* primary sources on Arthurian legends, even though not all really are primary, is pretty extensive, so not all will be listed. Also, a great many editions exist of some of them, so rather than offer publication information intended to be exhaustive, selected publication information is given—a single

edition of each source in most cases. Richard L. Brengle edited a
controlled research materials volume called *Arthur, King of
Britain* (New York: Appleton-Century-Crofts, 1964/b) which, if
you can find it, is an ideal starting point since it has excerpts from
chronicles, romances, and other medieval sources as well as some
fine critical essays, many of which afford good background. John
Jay Parry's "The Historical Arthur" and Kenneth Hurlstone
Jackson's "The Arthur of History" are just two of them. Richard
Barber has also edited a marvelous anthology that includes excerpts
from principal Arthurian sources, excerpts from later literary
adaptations, and a fine complement of seventy-two illustrations
(twenty-six in color) of paintings and other works of art. Called
The Arthurian Legends: An Illustrated Anthology (Totowa, N.J.:
Littlefield Adams, 1979/ib), the book also lists the major works
not included in it. Among the "primary" sources available today,
certainly you'll want to use Sir Thomas Malory's *Le Morte d'Arthur*,
which has a long history of editions since the first Caxton edition
in the fifteenth century. A good modern translation of eight
Malory tellings is Eugene Vinaver's *King Arthur and His Knights*
(Boston: Houghton-Mifflin, 1956/p). John Steinbeck used the
Winchester manuscript of Malory and other sources for his *The
Acts of King Arthur and His Noble Knights*, ed. posthumously by
Chase Horton (New York: Farrar, Straus and Giroux, 1976).
Then, there are the works by Chrétien de Troyes. *Eric and Enid*,
Cligés, *Yvain*, and *Lancelot* of Chrétien are all included in *Arthurian
Romances*, trans. W.W. Comfort (New York: Dutton, 1914). The
Roman de Brut of Wace and *Brut* of Layamon are all included in
Arthurian Chronicles (New York: E.P. Dutton, 1912) and should
be considered, along with Geoffrey of Monmouth's *Historia
Regnum Britanniae*, as most important sources. Also, Wolfram von
Eschenbach's *Parzival*, trans. Helen M. Mustard and Charles E.
Passage (New York: Random House, 1961) is a several-times-
removed "primary" source to consider. The Tristan and Iseult
story is best told, in my estimation, in Gottfried von Strassburg's
Tristan, trans. A.T. Hatto (Harmondsworth, G.B.: Penguin,
1960/p), although that telling is a long way from "primary" in the
real sense. *Sir Gawain and the Green Knight* in Marie Borroff's
translation (New York: W.W. Norton, 1967/p) is an important
source, as is *The Mabinogion* in, for example, Jeffrey Gantz's
translation (Harmondsworth, G.B.: Penguin, 1976/p). There are
other short poems (particularly grail poems), romances, and even
earlier sources that could be gone into, but this is a fair start.

Later Artistic Adaptations

Although it is inconsistent of me to include here adaptations of the Arthurian stories done by even later artists, I cannot resist since they include works I myself have had love affairs with. First and foremost is Alfred Lord Tennyson's *Idylls of the King* (begun in 1842 and added to for 45 years), the classic poetic telling of the stories of Arthur, Guinevere, and the grail quest. Then there's that great novel by T.H. White *The Once and Future King* (New York: Berkeley Medallion, 1966/p) which inspired Lerner and Loewe's musical *Camelot* (1959). It is, to my way of thinking, one of the greatest of all historical romances despite its "iffy" historical base. The University of Texas Press at Austin in 1977 published *The Book of Merlyn*, which White intended as the final section of *The Once and Future King*. Also, who could overlook that excellent work by Mark Twain, *A Connecticut Yankee in King Arthur's Court* (published first in 1889; many reprint editions). A broad farce as well as historical romance, it's bound to be fun for those who know the Arthurian stories since it's even fun for those who don't. Merlin's viewpoint is gotten in Mary Stewart's two "historical" novels *The Crystal Cave* and *The Hollow Hills* (New York: Wm. Morrow, 1970/p, 1973/p). They are both superb, well-crafted looks into Arthur's world, through Merlin's eyes. Finally, there are a number of relatively recent novels which should be mentioned as representative of scores of still other works based on Arthurian legend: Thomas Berger's *Arthur Rex: A Legendary Novel* (New York: Dell, 1979/p), Gil Kane's and John Jakes' *Excalibur!* (New York: Dell, 1980/p), Hannah Closs' *Tristan* (New York: Popular Library, 1978/p), Richard Monaco's *Parsival or a Knight's Tale* (New York: Macmillan, 1977) and *The Grail War* (New York: Pocket Books, 1979/p), Nicole St. John's *Guinevere's Gift* (New York: Random House, 1977), John Gloag's *Artorius Rex* (New York: St. Martin's Press, 1977).

Other European Mythologies—Ancient and Medieval

In addition to the mainstream European mythologies—the Greek and Roman, Celtic, Arthurian (legends), and Norse/Teutonic—there are a few others which span between them the same broad sweep in time covered by the major myth systems and groups in Europe. The Etruscan is actually one of these, but the fact that Etruscan civilization has received so much attention in English, even if its mythology is still largely a mystery, made it possible to devote a brief section to it. The others are, in no particular geographical or chronological order: Slavic, Baltic, Thracian, Finno-Ugric, and medieval legends other than Arthurian.

With the Slavs, we are into prehistoric mythology that has been reconstructed through more recent vestiges, mainly folklore. Linguists surmise that the separation of the Slavs from the ancient Indo-European community took place in the second millenium B.C. It wasn't until much later—the sixth century A.D.—that an identifiable Slavonic community emerged in eastern and central Europe and that its mythology as we know it must have been at its high point. Isolated in a heavily forested land broken up only by rivers and swamps, the Slavs were a rustic people who lived in close harmony with the land, a fact rather convincingly attested to in Slavic mythology.

Archaeologists and linguists are of the opinion that as early as 1300 B.C., the Slavs and the Balts were a single community located on the southeastern coast of the Baltic Sea. Gradually, but probably not until the early middle ages, the Baltic peoples became an identifiable group apart from the Slavs, settling in Prussia, Lithuania, and Latvia—all in northern and northeastern Europe. Interestingly enough, it was the Balts who last came under the sway of Catholicism in Europe, the Latvians and Prussians first in the thirteenth century and the Lithuanians last in the fifteenth century, but despite this late conversion, their older mythology and religion is, with the exception of the Latvian version, relatively little known about. It seems that the medieval recorders of the older mythology and religion did a good deal of mis-recording and, probably, intentional distorting. As a result, Baltic mythology is a relatively small package.

Thracian mythology is an even smaller one. Only in the past few years have archaeologists in Romania, Bulgaria, Jugoslavia, and Russia uncovered the main Thracian finds in those countries, finds that haven't done a great deal to enlarge our knowledge of the mythology even though what we now know about the Thracians generally has ballooned enormously in the last twenty years. The ancient Greeks knew the Thracians well enough that some details of their ferocious character and warlike exploits were recorded by the historians Herodotus and Thucydides, and there is little doubt that the Thracians date back into the Bronze Age as an identifiable people. Their territory varied over the years but included parts of Asia Minor as well as the rest of the Balkan region of southeastern Europe, Greece included. The Thracians endured on into the Christian era, but beginning with northern Thrace passing to the Bulgarians in the seventh century A.D., various parts of Thrace came under the control of other countries and groups. The Ottoman Empire after the fall of Constantinople in 1453 was perhaps the main contributor to the Thracians' demise as an independent, relatively far-flung people.

While the Thracians occupy a prominent and long-enduring place in the history of southeastern Europe and adjacent parts of western Asia, the Finno-Ugric peoples are more to be viewed as widespread, different tribes speaking different dialects of the same original language. Four groups typically identified with the Finno-Ugric parent group that dates back into the fourth millennium B.C. are the Magyars (Hungary), the Permians (western Russia and eastern Europe), the Voguls and Ostyaks (western Siberia), and the Cherenis-Mordvin (Volga River region of Russia). As widespread as these people were, it is no surprise that Finno-Ugric mythology is really a mixed bag that shows the influence of other cultures—the Iranian, Scandinavian, and Slavic particularly. Very little has been done to clarify the separate strands beyond a conjectural stage of investigation. During the spread of Christianity in the middle ages and later, the Magyars converted to Catholicism, the northern Finns and Estonians to Lutheranism, and the Russian branches to what was to become Russian Orthodoxy. The embracing of Christianity marked the end of Finno-Ugric mythology, needless to say, but remnants of that mythology are present even today in the regional folklore of a number of places.

The one remaining "mythology" for consideration in our potpourri called "Other European" is the broad group of legends aside from Arthurian that have been passed down from the middle ages. It includes the stories of epic heroes like Roland (France), Igor (Russia), and others; mixed tales in cycles like the Langobardian; and loose tales like those of St. George and the Dragon, William Tell, the Piper of Hamelin. Obviously much of what we're dealing with here is folklore and not mythology in the normal sense of the word. However, these are important stories that have been disseminated far beyond national boundaries, in fact gaining the kind of prominence internationally that place them alongside Arthurian legends as *almost* mythology.

Collections of the Myths

If there are not *many* sources for the mythologies just introduced, there are at least some sources of value. The *Larousse World*

Mythology (New York: Putnam, 1965/i), ed. Pierre Grimal,
trans. Patricia Beardsworth, has sections on the Slavic, Baltic,
Finno-Ugric, and Siberian mythologies, all of them reasonably
good introductions to the myths and historical/cultural background to them. For Slavic and Finno-Ugric mythologies, I frankly
prefer the sections in the *Larousse Encyclopedia of Mythology*
(London: Paul Hamlyn, 1959/ip), ed. Felix Guirand, trans.
Richard Aldington and Delano Ames. They are both nicely organized and written, with more on the myths than in the *World
Mythology* volume. Cultural/historical background is better in the
World Mythology than in the *Larousse Encyclopedia*. There are
very colorful, if too brief, sections in the *Encyclopedia of World
Mythology* (New York: Galahad Books, 1975/i) on "Finnish
Mythology" and "Slavonic Mythology," the latter including a
brief discussion of the Thracian "Rider" god. In the second
volume of the *Pears Encyclopedia of Myths and Legends* (London:
Pelham Books, 1977/i), the chapter on northern Europe includes a
short section on Finno-Ugric myths and some background discussion of both Finno-Ugric peoples and the Balts and Slavs. Jan
Machal's sizable selection of Slavic myths in Volume III of *The
Mythology of All Races* (New York: Cooper Square Press reprint
of the earlier Marshall Jones edition, 1964, etc.) is definitely a
source worth looking into for those myths—as is Uno Holmberg's
Volume IV in that series for Finno-Ugric and Siberian mythologies. The series is over sixty years old now, but still has usefulness,
particularly in areas like these where other more recent sources
are so few in number.

An excellent work on one aspect of Finno-Ugric mythology is
Geza Roheim's *Hungarian and Vogul Mythology* (Locust Valley,
N.Y.: J.J. Augustin, 1954). In addition to covering the myths
as well as is done anywhere else, there are good chapters on
Hungarian history and myth, themes in common with those found
in North American mythology, and on shamanism and totemism.
Rafael Karsten's *The Religion of the Samek* (Leiden: E.J. Brill,
1955) deals with the "ancient beliefs and cults of the Scandinavian
and Finnish Lapps" and includes myths, deities, kinds of worship,
and a discussion of shamanism, making it an excellent sidelight for
any study of Finno-Ugric mythology. Jeremiah Curtin's *Myths
and Folk-tales of the Russians, Western Slavs, and Magyars* (New
York: Benjamin Blom, 1974; reprint of the 1890 edition) includes
thirty-one stories, the bulk of them folktales and legends, but it is
a valuable auxiliary source. So, too, is Y.M. Sokolov's *Russian*

Folklore (New York: Macmillan, 1950); it's more an introduction to the study of Russian folklore than a collection of stories, but it will be great as help alongside better sources of the Finno-Ugric myths.

Far and away the best and most up-to-date source available on the Thracians generally and on Thracian religion and mythology specifically is *Thrace and the Thracians* (New York: St. Martin's Press, 1977/ib) by Alexander Fol and Ivan Mazarov. It is a big and beautiful book which has over 110 pages of photographs, 32 of them in color. Mazarov's chapter on the religion and mythology is as good as possible, given the limited information available.

Romance and Legend of Chivalry (London: Gresham Publishing Co., 1919/i, later reprint editions, too), by A.R. Hope Moncrieff, is an excellent source of medieval legends of the sort associated with heroes and kings. So, too, is Thomas Bulfinch's *Mythology*, the sections included in *The Age of Chivalry* and *The Legends of Charlemagne*, that is (published separately in New York by New American Library Mentor, 1962/p). Bulfinch's *Mythology* remains an excellent source, especially for the medieval material. Helen A. Guerber's *Legends of the Middle Ages* (New York: American Book Co., 1909; Corner House reprint, 1977) contains the great medieval legends in condensed form for high school students and includes Teutonic and Arthurian as well as Spanish (Cid), French (Charlemagne), and others. Norma Lorre Goodrich's *Medieval Myths* (New York: New American Library Mentor, 1961/p) is also meant for that age group and includes only Beowulf, Peredur, Roland, Berta, Sifrit, Igor, and Cid.

Other medieval legends are included in Sabine Baring-Gould's *Curious Myths of the Middle Ages* (New Hyde Park, N.Y.: University Books, 1967; plus other later reprint editions), a volume that has been around almost as long as Bulfinch's *Mythology* but, like the Bulfinch, still valuable as a source. Here you'll find the stories of William Tell, Prester John, St. George, the Wandering Jew, the legend of the cross, and a number of others. For the legend of the cross, two old books you'll also possibly want to look into are W.C. Prime's *Holy Cross: A History of the Invention, Preservation and Disappearance of the Wood Known as the True Cross* (New York: A.D.F. Randolph & Co., 1877) and John Ashton's *The Legendary History of the Cross* (London: Fisher Unwin, 1887). Relics were very much the foundation of interesting legends during the Middle Ages especially; the "Holy Grail" and fragments of the cross on which Jesus was crucified were two of the more popular varieties. James George Frazer's *Myths of the Origin of Fire* (London: Macmillan & Co., 1930) has an interesting chapter on European myths of that type, some of them from mainstream mythologies but including offbeat ones as well.

Works on Historical/Cultural Background

Some background works deserve mentioning as being of special interest for this rather disparate "Other European" category.

Many books on magic have excellent coverage of the middle ages in them, that time being one of particular richness where magic is concerned, but none that I know of is better than Kurt Seligmann's *Magic, Supernaturalism and Religion* (New York: Pantheon Books, 1971). The chapters on magic and the devil in the Middle Ages are both quite good. (Since the devil concept and much that has been part of Christianity are both largely medieval in origin, you might wish to look under "Biblical Mythologies" earlier in this guide for appropriate references.)

In "The Voyage of Brendan," *National Geographic*, 152 (December 1977), pp. 770–97, an article on Ireland's medieval saint who in legend crossed the Atlantic, Timothy Severin attempts to verify the possibility of that crossing. Dealing with possibilities of Finno-Ugric myth is Istvan Fodor's "Are the Sumerians and the Hungarians or the Uralic Peoples Related?" *Current Anthropology*, 17 (March 1976), pp. 115–18. It's a philological argument for early contact between the proto-Hungarians and the Sumerians —either directly or through intermediaries.

Since a main source of Finno-Ugric mythology is the Finnish epic *Kalevala*, Wilfred Bouser's article "Kalevala—The National Epic of Finland" in *Folklore*, 76 (Winter 1965), pp. 241–53, will be worthwhile reading. It introduces nicely both the epic and some main points of Finno-Ugric mythology. William A. Wilson's *Folklore and Nationalism in Modern Finland* (Bloomington: Indiana University Press, 1976/b) is another work on the *Kalevala* that will provide helpful background to (and further bibliography for) Finno-Ugric mythology. That epic, by the way, is available in English translation: *The Kalevala or Poems of the Kaleva District* (Cambridge: Harvard University Press, 1963), compiled by Elias Lonnrot, trans. Francis Peabody Magoun, Jr. It's an essential source *and* good reading for the Finno-Ugric myth student.

Some works that deal with medieval history will be of help as background. The *Larousse Encyclopedia of Ancient and Medieval History* (New York: Harper & Row, 1963/i), though too broad to be of very specific help, does put all of the pieces in our "Other

European" category nicely into place. Other works which do that pretty well are available, too. One of my personal favorites for quick reference is C. McEvedy's two-volume *The Penguin Atlas of Ancient History* and *The Penguin Atlas of Medieval History* (Harmondsworth, G.B.: Penguin, 1967/ip, 1975/ip). For more comprehensive treatment, the multi-volume *Cambridge Medieval History* will no doubt prove useful, as possibly will the multi-volume *Cambridge Economic History of Europe.* UNESCO's thousand-page *The Great Medieval Civilizations* (by Wiet, Elisseeff, Wolff, and Naudou/b) covers more than Europe, but there's much in it that should serve a useful purpose as background to myths and legends of the Middle Ages. Philip Dixon's *Barbarian Europe* (London: Elsevier Phaidon, 1976/ib) is a pretty book that shouldn't be overlooked. Such works as Robert Payne's *The Christian Centuries: From Christ to Dante* (New York: W.W. Norton, 1966/i) and W.G. DeBurgh's *The Legacy of the Ancient World* (Harmondsworth, G.B.: Penguin, 1961/p, originally 1923) are more specialized in approach, but they do offer some useful historical and cultural information. So, too, with two books in the Time-Life *Great Ages of Man* series, *Barbarian Europe*, (New York: Time-Life Books, 1968/ib), by Gerald Simons and the editors of Time-Life Books, and *Age of Faith* (New York: Time-Life Books, 1965), by Anne Fremantle.

Where medieval legends are concerned, two books that will serve nicely as background are R. Rudorff's *Knights and the Age of Chivalry* (New York: Viking Press, 1974/i) and *The Age of Chivalry* (Washington, D.C.: National Geographic Society, 1969). Along those lines, also consider *Concepts of the Hero in the Middle Ages and the Renaissance* (Albany, N.Y.: State University of New York Press, 1975), ed. Norman T. Burns and Christopher J. Reagan. Several of the essays in it (such as Bernard F. Huppe's "The Concept of the Hero in the Middle Ages") are quite good.

Of some help, particularly with medieval legends also, are histories of literature and the like. W.T.H. Jackson's *Medieval Literature: A History and A Guide* (New York: Collier Books, 1966/p) is excellent, as is the section devoted to the Middle Ages in *Backgrounds of European Literature*, 2nd edition (Englewood Cliffs, N.J.: Prentice-Hall, 1975/p). Also, since some national literatures are involved, see histories of French literature—such as L. Cazamian's *A History of French Literature* (New York: Oxford University Press, 1960/p)—for help with the legends of Charlemagne, histories of Spanish literature for help with the legend of the Cid, and histories of Finnish literature for help with the legends of the *Kalevala*.

American Indian Mythologies

Ever since the fifteenth and sixteenth century arrivals in "the new world" of white Europeans, knowledge of the Indians of the Americas has been progressing impressively. The systematic study of contemporary tribes has been a particularly rich source of information in recent years, yielding important facts and theory about many areas of past and present Indian life. What archaeologists in the past hundred years or so have uncovered about ancient Indian groups, in Middle America especially, has added to the store of information enormously. However, as always seems to be the case where an investigation deep into the past is concerned, for all the facts and theory we have, there remains a complex tangle of puzzles which, for as long as they remain unsolved, will no doubt bedevil the serious student of the mythologies of the Americas.

At the head of the list is that old bugbear of a puzzle behind many a culture around the world, that concerning origins. Did the Indians of the Americas travel from afar at some time in the distant past, making the Americas their home, or was there, rather, indigenous origin somewhere in the Americas? A majority of scholars are now inclined to favor the theory that at some time far back in prehistory there were migrations from northeastern Asia into northwestern North America across the Bering land bridge, thus accounting for the Indians of all three Americas. Geologists agree that such a bridge probably existed at one time. Anthropologists have pointed to pertinent physiological and cultural similarities among some Asians and American Indians as corroborative evidence. Archaeologists have presented prehistoric artifacts of like sorts and styles from both places as additional evidence. And all the while, mythologists have noted some similarities in the content of Asian and American Indian myths. Although none of the evidence *proves* the migrations theory, there is more of it than there is evidence in support of the indigenous origin theory.

The following symbols will be found, where applicable, in the bibliographic citation, usually following the date of publication: i = has useful illustrations; b = has a useful bibliography; p = has been published in paperbound edition.

The temptation is thus great, for those in myth study, to specu-
late on "original" myths held by ancient Asians and Americans
and, therefrom, to work comparatively with the various mythologies
involved toward breakthroughs in understanding—not only of the
"why" of myths but of the "where from" as well. The problem, of
course, is that such work is never free from complicating factors—
which leads us to the second of the puzzles. Whom did the ancient
inhabitants of the Americas know from other continents, and in
what ways was contact with other peoples influential? The answers
to these questions may ultimately be more easily arrived at than
the answer to the origins question if only due to the fact that the
contacts, assuming they occurred, happened at a more recent time
and are therefore more easily gotten at and "proven." Artifacts
and inscriptions have, as a matter of fact, been found just about
everywhere in the Americas to lend support to the belief that in
ancient times the Celts, Phoenicians, Hebrews, Romans, Norse,
and Egyptians *could have* been visitors, maybe even settlers. Final
proof is far from at hand—and maybe always will be—but there are
some dazzling maybes in the mill.

Take, for example, the matter of the ancient Olmecs of Middle
America. The pyramids and other architectural wonders of Middle
America have long been the source of inspired guesswork as to the
role of peoples of ancient Egypt and Near Eastern countries in their
construction. Were they built by Egyptians? By Mesopotamians?
Were the Middle Americans really settlers from these regions?
Some have even speculated that ancient astronauts had a hand in
all of the pyramids of the world (the Orient included). However, it
is only recently that even a partially substantiated case has been
made for the Olmecs either being in origin Egyptian or having at
some time been in contact with ancient Egypt. Massive stone heads
with negroid features, some of them showing helmets not unlike
those worn by Nubian soldiers of Egypt's twenty-fifth dynasty,
comprise one small piece of evidence. The fact that the earliest
Middle American pyramid dates from 800 or 700 B.C. is another.
That Columbus reported in his journals that the Indians of the
new world told him they'd traded with black men at an earlier time
can be construed as still another. If indeed any of this sundry
grouping of evidence can be relied upon and more conclusive evidence turns up, just imagine the possibilities for myth students!
One of them has already jumped the gun and gone so far as to
attempt demonstration that much of the Middle American pantheon was Egyptian in origin! There are a great many ifs, ands, and

buts in such "demonstrations," to be sure, but anyone who puts much stock in the *Bible* and its diffusion of the races after Noah or in the *Book of Mormon* and its stories of ancient migrations from the Near East must certainly be among the more interested spectators these days.

There are other examples, too. Those 1800-year-old Hebrew coins found in Tennessee and Kentucky must surely suggest possibilities for those who have wondered about some of the things they've found in North American Indian myths. So, too, must the numerous findings in the United States of Roman coins dating from the fourth century A.D. Not to be dismissed here is the fact that at least one was found in an Indian burial mound! What, then, about the numerous ancient Phoenician relics and inscriptions that have been found as far apart as New England and Brazil, a number of them dating from the sixth century B.C.? Or Norse inscriptions and runes that have been found as far into North America as Oklahoma and, possibly, Utah? What about the fairly recent discovery in Ecuador of ancient pottery that matches closely in artistic style with ancient pottery uncovered by archaeologists in the Orient? What about the many Celtic inscriptions and artifacts discovered in the northeastern United States?

Less a puzzle perhaps but nonetheless important for consideration by myth students is the matter of possible interrelationships right within the Americas. The clear similarities between ancient Middle and South American Indian architectural and artistic styles has long been observed. To what extent, and with what consequences, were the ancient Indians of Middle and South America related and/or in contact with one another? What does the discovery in Tennessee of an example of ancient North American Indian art that is stylistically the duplicate of Middle American art of the same time period mean where the respective mythologies are concerned?

More such examples could be cited. The question of what one who studies the mythologies of the Americas is in for has other answers *in addition to* the obvious ones. The excitement of sensing that there's more behind, say, the myth of Quetzalcoatl-Kukulcan than meets the eye is one thing. Being aware of what anthropology, archaeology, and epigraphy are seemingly daily presenting as supportive evidence is quite another. Together they promise to make the study of the mythologies of the Americas the source of as much excitement in the years ahead as will be found in connection with any mythology anywhere.

Collections of the Myths

There are a number of sources in which North, Middle, and South American mythologies are handled together in an introductory way. The *Larousse World Mythology* (New York: Putnam, 1965/i), ed. Pierre Grimal, trans. Patricia Beardsworth, has fine introductory sections on all of them, for instance, as does the *Larousse Encyclopedia of Mythology* (London: Paul Hamlyn, 1959/ip), ed. Felix Guirand, trans. Richard Aldington and Delano Ames. The latter work handles the three Americas in a single section and is, overall, a bit briefer than the *World Mythology* is in its coverage of the myths. Volume IV of the *Pears Encyclopedia of Myths and Legends* (London: Pelham Books, 1978/i) has fairly useful, if only introductory, coverage of the myths of the three Americas, too. The space devoted to textual coverage of the myths of North, Central, and South America in Veronica Ions' *The World's Mythology in Colour* (London: Paul Hamlyn, 1974/i) is not nearly as extensive as that devoted to related pictures, but for *very* brief introduction, the book will do. Pages 70–85 are devoted to myths of the Americas in *Encyclopedia of World Mythology* (New York: Galahad Books, 1975/i). An older volume with fair usefulness still is Donald A. Mackenzie's *Myths of Pre-Columbian America* (London: Gresham Publishing Co., 1925/i); it's a volume mainly concerned with Middle and North America, though.

Other than these few broader mythographies, two other works should be mentioned. Maria Leach's *The Beginning: Creation Myths Around the World* (New York: Funk and Wagnalls, 1956) includes a total of fourteen North American Indian myths, six Central American, and seven South American. Chapters eleven through thirteen in James George Frazer's *Myths of the Origins of Fire* (London: Macmillan, 1930) are devoted to the Americas.

Works on Historical/Cultural Background

Background works that deal with all three Americas are not readily available. Only one book that I'm aware of, for instance, handles religion in all of the Americas, and that deals with pre-Columbian religions only—*Pre-Columbian American Religions* (New York: Holt, Rinehart and Winston, 1968), by Walter Krickeberg *et al*, trans. Starley Davis. It is useful enough on its subject, however, and should be considered a first-rate background work. Also first rate is John Collier's *Indians of the Americas: The Long Hope* (New York: N.A.L. Mentor, 1947/p), one of the few works around that does a respectable job of dealing with the Indians of the three Americas from earliest time through the twentieth century. *The New World* (London: Elsevier Phaidon, 1975/ib), by E. Swanson, W. Bray, and I. Farrington, is a beautiful book that covers the archaeology and cultural history of the three Americas in pre-Columbian times. As such, it is quite useful. Leo Deuel's *Conquistadors Without Swords: Archaeologists in the Americas* (New York: St. Martin's Press, 1967/ibp) is a fine volume in which the archaeologists involved tell their own stories—usually pretty fascinating ones, to say the least. *Chronologies in New World Archaeology* (New York: Academic Press, 1978), ed. R. E. Taylor and Clement W. Meighan, has sections on all three Americas, each devoted to theoretical and practical discussions about dating archaeological finds. Barbara A. Leitch's *Chronology of the American Indian* (St. Clair Shores, Mich.: Scholarly Press, 1975) covers the Americas from 25,000 B.C. to the present.

The matter of origins of the American Indian has received a lot of attention. For a good general discussion of theories and the author's own position, see Robert Wauchope's *Lost Tribes and Sunken Continents* (Chicago: University of Chicago Press, 1962/ib). Lee Eldridge Huddleston's *Origins of the American Indians: European Concepts, 1492-1729* (Austin: University of Texas, 1967) is more localized in time but is also well worth looking into. Miles Poindexter's *The Ayar-Incas: Asiatic Origins* (New York: Liveright, 1930/i) makes interesting reading if only because Poindexter's proposals are not necessarily commonplace—and he does deal with the Americas generally, not just the Incas. Betty J. Meggers's "The Transpacific Origin of MesoAmerican Civilization: A Preliminary Review of the Evidence and Its Theoretical Implications," an article in *American Anthropologist*, 77 (March 1975), pp. 1-27, is a provocative approach to the subject of origin *and* influence—it provoked a rejoinder in the March 1976 issue of the same journal, pp. 106-10. The section called "Special Studies" in *Prehistoric Man in the New World* (Chicago: University of Chicago Press, 1964), ed. Jesse D. Jennings and Edward Norbeck, is comprised of three articles that also deal generally with the problem of contact and origins. Cyrus H. Gordon's *Before Columbus* (New York: Crown Publishers, 1971/p) is an excellent source for speculation on contact and convergence. *Man Across the Sea: Problems of Pre-Columbian Contacts* (Austin: University of Texas Press, 1971), ed. Carroll L. Riley *et al*, is an excellent source, too, as are James A. Ford's *A Comparison of Formative Cultures in the*

Americas: Diffusion or the Psychic Unity of Man (Washington,
D.C.: Smithsonian Institution, 1969) and the collection of articles
from *Scientific American* called *Early Man in America* (San Fran-
cisco: W. H. Freeman, 1973). An excellent summary article is
Carroll L. Riley's "Interhemispheric Contacts? Comments on a
Controversy," which you'll find in *Archaeology*, 31 (November-
December 1978/b), pp. 59-61.

For art of the Americas, the best volume by far to my knowledge
is Frederick J. Dockstader's *Indian Art of the Americas* (New York:
Museum of the American Indian, 1973/i). The illustrations are
mainly black and white, but there's good representation of the arts
of all three Americas.

North American Indian Mythologies

When the Dutch and English first encountered the North American
Indian in the seventeenth century, there were some 600 Indian
societies in that territory alone which was much later to become
the "lower forty-eight." Not all of these societies were *fully* separate
from one another, it is true; ties were created by the loose organi-
zations of several tribes. Reports sent by the trans-Atlantic emigrants to their fellows in the old world—as well as diaries, journals,
and other works kept here in the new—indicate that the Indian
was viewed both with horror and great interest as a phenomenon
inseparable from the wildness that was the land. While the relationship that developed between white man and red was far from love-
hate most of the time, instead exhibiting more regularly one of
mutual tolerance, there is no question that the Indian and frontier
were so intermixed as something alien to the European sensibility,
something continually to be pushed out of the way and replaced
with civilized orderliness, that the Indian was only rarely seen as
racially one *and* culturally many. The Indian to our present day,
in fact, is understood by very few non-Indians, some anthropologists
and other adventursome souls among them, in a way that would
reflect a knowledge of 600 societies, in a way that would indicate
an appreciation of the finer distinctions in beliefs, myths, and
rituals across the spectrum called "North American Indian."

What I am driving at, of course, is that when most of us speak
of "North American Indian mythology," we are levelling in much
the same way we do when we speak of "Christianity." In the latter
case, though, a great many people are keenly aware of differences

even if not knowledgeable of all of them, whereas in the case of Indians, very few are even at this late date aware sufficiently to recognize anything of the variety that exists from Indian nation to nation and tribe to tribe.

This causes some problems for the myth student, needless to say. Fortunately, books and articles have appeared in abundance over the past fifty years or so that have begun the process of clarifying the differences. However, they are largely anthropological histories and cultural surveys rather than individual collections of myths—although some of these also now exist—and it is necessary to turn to them for particularized information, information that as a rule includes discussions of religion and mythology.

Collections of the Myths

Cottie Burland's *North American Indian Mythology* (London: Paul Hamlyn, 1965/ib), a colorful volume in the *International Mythology* series, has some organization on regional lines, but tribal distinctions are generally overlooked. It is a first-rate source among general mythographies, though, and does include some historical/cultural background information. *The Red Swan: Myths and Tales of the American Indians* (New York: Farrar, Straus and Giroux, 1976/ibp), ed. John Bierhorst, is organized by topic and has in it good examples of hero myths and eschatological myths. There's a useful glossary of information about tribes, languages, and cultures, too. Susan Feldmann's *The Storytelling Stone: Myths and Tales of the American Indians* (New York: Dell, 1971/bp) is divided into three sections—"In the Days of Creation," "Trickster," and "Tales of Heroes, Supernatural Journeys, and Other Folktales"—and each story is identified by tribe and region as is the case in Bierhorst's book. Alice Marriott and Carol K. Rachlin have divided the three dozen or so myths and folktales in their *American Indian Mythology* (New York: New American Library Mentor, 1972/bp) into four sections and have also identified tribes of origin. Ellen R. Emerson's *Myths and Legends of the Indians,* also called *Indian Myths* (Minneapolis: Ross & Haines reprint edition, 1965), Lewis Spence's *The Myths of the North American Indians* (London: Harrap, 1914; Multimedia Reprint, 1975/ip), and Daniel G. Brinton's *The Myths of the New World* (London: 1868; reprinted as *Myths of the Americas* by Multimedia, 1976/p) are all old books, but each has its useful side still. Emerson's is organized thematically, and Indian myths are compared with myths elsewhere throughout its pages. Spence's is quite comprehensive to the year of its initial publication and includes a marvelous introduction. It should not be overlooked, also, that Spence was a first-rate myth scholar in his day. Brinton was, too, though he subscribed heavily to the naturalist theory of interpretation.

Works concerned with more than North American Indian mythology alone may also prove to be of use. Volume X in *The Mythology of All Races* (Boston: Marshall Jones, 1916-32; reprinted in New York by Cooper Square Press, 1964, etc.) is Hartley Burr Alexander's *American (North of Mexico)*. While it is older and limited in its overall usefulness compared with a volume compiled during recent years, it is a valuable source nonetheless. So, too, is *Myths of Pre-Columbian America* (London: Gresham Publishing Co., 1925/i) in Gresham's *Myth and Legend in Literature and Art* series. Written by Donald A. Mackenzie, it is, like Daniel Brinton's *The Myths of the New World*, concerned with Middle American myths as well as North American, but there are plenty of myths in it overall. Volume IV of the *Pears Encyclopedia of Myths and Legends* (London: Pelham Books, 1978/i) has a respectable introduction to the myths of the North American Indians as do both the *Larousse World Mythology* (New York: Putnam, 1965/i), ed. Pierre Grimal, trans. Patricia Beardsworth, and the *Larousse Encyclopedia of Mythology* (London: Paul Hamlyn, 1959/ip), ed. Felix Guirand, trans. Richard Aldington and Delano Ames. The *Larousse World Mythology* has sections on the Eskimos' and North American Indians' myths. These are covered also in the *Encyclopedia of World Mythology* (New York: Galahad Books, 1975/i) on pp. 76-85. The section devoted by Veronica Ions to North American Indian myths in her *The World's Mythology in Colour* (London: Paul Hamlyn, 1974/i) is filled with pictures but has too little in the way of text to be of special value other than for the pictures.

Stith Thompson's *Tales of the North American Indians* (Cambridge: Harvard University Press, 1929; reprinted at Bloomington by Indiana University Press, 1966/p) is more in the folklore category than myth, but there are *plenty* of tales in the collection, many of them origin myths, heroic myths, and trickster stories. It also has a particularly useful section called "Tales Borrowed from Europeans." Vladimir Hulpach's *American Indian Tales and Legends* (London: Paul Hamlyn, 1965/i) is also better categorized as folklore, but it too has many myths—most of them pretty familiar ones to Americans. Jaime de Angulo's *Indian Tales* (New York: Ballantine Books, 1976/p; reprint of the earlier Hill and Wang edition) is less a collection of stories than a look at Indian folklore and ritual, but there are enough stories in it to make it useful as a collection. W. Schmidt's *High Gods in North America* (Oxford: Clarendon Press, 1933) is a broad Indian mythography that focuses on the stories of gods and includes some interesting theoretical angles as to the origins of those gods. The three-volume work called *Traditions of the North American Indians* (bound as one volume—Upper Saddle River, N.J.: Gregg Press, 1970; reprint of the 1830 edition called *Tales of an Indian Camp*) can still be useful for myths and folktales not found readily elsewhere. Its author, James Athearn Jones, was a good friend of Washington Irving. Tristram Potter Coffin's *Indian Tales of North America: An Anthology for the Adult Reader* (Philadelphia: American Folklore Society, 1961/p; reprinted by University of Texas Press at Austin) is a useful little collection of forty-five tales along with a good introduction on reading them. It is divided into three thematic parts, and not all of the stories are myths.

Plains Indian Mythology (New York: Thomas Y. Crowell, 1975; N.A.L. reprint, 1977/p), by Alice Marriott and Carol K. Rachlin, is a pretty sparse collection considering its geographical spread, but it is meant for a popular audience. It's divided into four parts: mythology, legends, folklore, and explantory-historical tales. Ella E. Clark's *Indian Legends of the Pacific North-West* (Berkeley: University of California Press, 1953/ibp) is filled with all kinds of myths, has a good glossary, and is, in general, a valuable volume for North American Indian myth study. Katharine Berry Judson's *Myths and Legends of California and the Old Southwest* (Chicago: A.C. McClurg, 1912) is, too, despite its early date, and Joseph H. Wherry's *Indian Masks and Myths of the West* (New York: Funk and Wagnalls, 1969/ib) is a fine, well illustrated collection of Indian myths of western America categorized thematically.

There are also a number of works in which the myths of smaller regions still, tribes at the narrowest, are collected. Ruth Benedict's two-volume *Zuni Mythology* (New York: Columbia University Press, 1935; A.M.S. reprint, 1969), for instance, is an excellent collection of myths that includes only Zuni myths, most of them types common to North American Indian mythology generally. Ruth L. Bunzel's *Zuni Origin Myths* (Washington, D.C.: Bureau of American Ethnology Annual Report, 1929–30), pp. 545–609, is a good discussion as well as retelling of the origin myths involved. Franz Boas' *Tsimshian Mythology* (Washington, D.C.: Bureau of American Ethnology Report, 1909–10), pp. 29–1037, is a highly valuable work which includes not only a great many myths but information on the Tsimshian culture also. It is an excellent composite collection/background source as a result. Katharine Berry Judson's *Myths and Legends of Alaska* (Chicago: A.C. McClurg, 1911/i) includes Tsimshian, Tlingit, Eskimo, and others—a fine collection of myths and legends. Victor Barnouw's *Wisconsin Chippewa Myths and Tales—And Their Relation to Chippewa Life* (Madison: University of Wisconsin Press, 1977 /p) includes an abundance of stories and analysis from both sociological and psychological perspectives. E.A. Smith's *Myths of the Iroquois*, which is the second annual report of the Bureau of American Ethnology (Washington, D.C., 1881), is a valuable collection and study of the myths. Martha Warren Beckwith's *Myths and Ceremonies of the Mandan and Hidatsa* (Poughkeepsie, N.Y.: Vassar College Press, 1932) is a good off-beat collection, with much background information included. Two books by Hamilton A. Tyler will also be valuable resources: *Pueblo Gods and Myths* (Norman: University of Oklahoma Press, 1964/b) and *Pueblo Animals and Myths* (Norman: University of Oklahoma Press, 1975/b). The first volume is, start to finish, on Pueblo myths, and it includes some historical, ethnographic, and interpretative information; the second focuses on theriomorphic stories. Silas Tertius Rand's *Legends of the Micmacs* (London: Longmans, Green, and Co., 1894; reprinted in 1971 by Johnson Reprint Service of New York) is a useful older work, as are James Mooney's *Myths of the Cherokee* (Washington, D.C.: Bureau of American Ethnology Report, 1902; reprinted later by the Blue and Gray Press of Nashville, Tennessee) and Jeremiah Curtin's *Myths of the Modocs: Indian Legends of the Northwest* (Boston, 1912; reprinted in 1974 by Benjamin Blom of New York). Grace F. Kane's *Myths and Legends of the Mackinacs and the Lake Region*, 2nd edition (Grand Rapids, Mich.: Black Letter Press, 1972/i), and Cora Clark's and Texa Bowen Williams' *Pomo Indian Myths* (New York: Vantage Press, 1954) are both excellent little volumes to consider. William Rees Palmer's *Why the North Star Stands Still and Other Indian Legends* (Englewood Cliffs, N.J.: Prentice-Hall, 1957/i) is a good collection of Pahute Indian stories that includes beautiful illustrations, a glossary, and a

Pahute time-telling chart. Also excellent collections of tribal
myths are Gladys A. Reichard's *An Analysis of Coeur d'Alene
Indian Myths* (Philadelphia: Memoirs of the American Folklore
Society, Vol. 41, 1947), Morris Edward Opler's *Myths and Legends
of the Lipian Apache Indians* (New York: Memoirs of the American
Folklore Society, Vol. 36, 1940), Opler's *Myths and Tales of the
Chiricahua Apache Indians* (New York: Memoirs of the American
Folklore Society, Vol. 37, 1942), and Melville Jacobs' *The People
Are Coming Soon: Chinook Myths and Tales* (Seattle: University
of Washington Press, 1960). All are filled with myths and legends,
only minimal background and other information otherwise in-
cluded. John P. Harrington's *Karuk Indian Myths* (Ramona,
Calif.: Ballena Press, 1972/p; originally published by the Smith-
sonian Institution in 1932 as Bulletin no. 107 of the Bureau of
American Ethnology) is a pamphlet-size work with only twelve
myths in it, but its value lies in its having very literal translations
of the myths and the original Indian texts side-by-side. A.L.
Kroeber's *Seven Mohave Myths* (Berkeley: University of California
Publications in Archaeology and Anthropology, Vol. 11/p) is also
small—unlike his *Yurok Myths* (Berkeley: University of California
Press, 1976/p), which is a 528-page volume packed with myths
and background information. Margaret Bemister's *Thirty Indian
Legends of Canada* (North Pomfret, Vt.: David and Charles,
n.d.) provides some useful stories. Myths from the Queen Charlotte
Islands in Canada are covered nicely in Marius Barbeau's *Haida
Myths* (Ottawa: National Museum of Canada, 1953/ibp), a sizable
and thorough volume. Charles M. Barbeau's *Huron and Wyandot
Mythology in Canada* (Ottawa: Government Printing Bureau,
1915) is also a sizable and thorough collection of myths—with
some background, too.

Jeremiah Curtin's *Creation Myths of Primitive America* (Boston:
Little, Brown and Co., 1898; reprinted in New York by Benjamin
Blom, 1968) is a marvelous collection of North American Indian
creation myths—including origins of the world, man, animals and
fire. The retellings are excellent, and there's a pretty interesting
variety of interpretation in the introduction. A total of fourteen
creation myths from various tribes are included in Maria Leach's
The Beginning: Creation Myths Around the World (New York:
Funk and Wagnalls, 1956/p), a book that is one of the major
sources for creation myths around the world. Aileen O'Bryan's
The Dine: Origin Myths of the Navajo Indians (Washington,
D.C.: Smithsonian Institute, Bureau of American Ethnology

Bulletin no. 163, 1956) is a good source of both the myths and information about them. George B. Grinnell's *Pawnee Hero Stories and Folk Tales* (Lincoln: University of Nebraska Press, 1961) is a highly selective group of Pawnee myths fitting the heroic myth category (with some folktales otherwise). Despite its title, Daniel G. Brinton's *American Hero Myths: A Study in the Native Religions of the American Continent* (Philadelphia: H.C. Watts & Co., 1882; reprinted by Johnson Reprint Corp. in 1970) is less concerned with hero myths than it is North American Indian myths generally. It's both a good collection of the myths and an elaborate interpretation of the religions. Chapter thirteen in James George Frazer's *Myths of the Origin of Fire* (London: Macmillan, 1930) is devoted to North American myths. A useful thematic grouping of trickster myths of the Winnebago (as well as one each from the Assiniboine and Tlingit) is included in Paul Radin's *The Trickster: A Study in American Indian Mythology* (New York: Bell, 1956; revised edition Schocken Books, 1972). There are three fine interpretative sections in the book, too. There are sixty-eight narratives included in Barry Holstun Lopez's *Giving Birth to Thunder, Sleeping with His Daughter: Coyote Builds North America* (Mission, Kan.: Sheed Andrews and McMeel, 1977), a fine topical collection of coyote trickster tales. Katherine Luomala's *Oceanic, American Indian, and African Myths of Snaring the Sun* (Millwood, N.Y.: Kraus Reprint of the 1940 edition, 1975) has some interesting North American Indian myths.

Translations

Quite a few books have appeared in recent years in which native American literature is gathered. While not all of the selections included in these volumes are useful in myth study, there are poems and tales that are—particularly ones in which myths are told, either as primary source or as retold versions. *American Indian Prose and Poetry* (New York: Capricorn Books, 1962/p), ed. Margot Astrov, is one such volume, as is *Shaking the Pumpkin: Traditional Poetry of the Indian North Americas* (Garden City, N.Y.: Doubleday Anchor, 1978/p), ed. Jerome Rothenberg. Both are good sources of myths in native form. *The Portable North American Indian Reader* (New York: Viking Press, 1973/p), ed. Frederick W. Turner III, includes a section entitled "Myths and Tales" (part one, pp. 19–232) which has a healthy selection of Iroquois, Blackfeet, and other myths and folktales in native form.

The Way: An Anthology of American Indian Literature (New York: Alfred A. Knopf, 1972), ed. Shirley Hill Witt and Stan Steiner, is more useful as background to North American Indian myth study than for myths even though a few are included. *Coyote Was Going There: Indian Literature of the Oregon Country* (Seattle: University of Washington Press, 1977), ed. Jarold Ramsey, has over a hundred stories, poems, songs, and myths in it, but its main value is as a folklore collection. John Bierhorst's *Four Masterworks of American Indian Literature* (New York: Farrar, Straus and Giroux, 1974) has two works that could be of use, the Iroquois "Ritual of Condolence" and the Navajo "Night Chant." Both are nicely introduced by Bierhorst (though translated by others), and good notes are provided. For further works that may be helpful, look into Anna Lee Stensland's fine *Literature By and About the American Indian: An Annotated Bibliography*, 2nd edition (Urbana, Ill.: National Council of Teachers of English, 1979/p). There's even a section on myths and legends in it.

Studies of the Myths

Studies of North American Indian mythology, analyses and interpretations of individual myths, and general help *with* the myths are also available. The problem here is similar to the problem involving all North American Indian mythology—the narrowness of many of the studies that limit their usefulness. Among the broader, helpful studies, Franz Boas' "The Mythology and Folktales of the North American Indians," which can be found in his book *Race, Language and Culture* (New York: Macmillan, 1940), and "The Growth of Indian Mythologies," which is included in *Studies in Mythology* (Homewood, Ill.: The Dorsey Press, 1968 /p), ed. Robert A. Georges, must be considered high on any list since they are sufficiently general and contain useful information of an introductory sort. A.G. Rooth's broad theoretical article entitled "The Creation Myths of the North American Indians," *Anthropos*, 52 (1957), pp. 497-508, is well worth looking into as well. Ruth Benedict's "Introduction to Zuni Mythology," also in *Studies in Mythology*, is excellent as an introduction. R.H. Lowie's "The Test Theme in North American Mythology" in the *Journal of American Folklore*, 21 (April–September 1908), pp. 97-148, is partly an exercise in debunking the solar naturalist theory and in comparative analysis of myths exhibiting the test scheme. As a grouping of those myths and an interesting interpretation of their spread and meaning, the article is excellent. Orpheus-type myths are also distributed broadly in North American Indian mythology and have received a good deal of attention as a result. A.H. Gayton's "The Orpheus Myth in North America," included in *Journal of American Folklore*, 48 (July–September 1935), pp. 263–86, is a good source and comparative analysis that demonstrates the motif's pervasiveness in North America. Ake Hultkrantz's *The North American Indian Orpheus Tradition: A Contribution to Comparative Religion* (Stockholm: The Humanistic Foundation of Sweden, 1957) deals with the religious uses of the myth and with the motif's origins and distribution. Guy E. Swanson's "Orpheus and Star Husband: Meaning and the Structure of Myths," in *Ethnology*, 15 (April 1976), pp. 115–33, is a good discussion of questions about the meaning and structure of myths; it analyzes two well-known myths and their global—but mainly North American—variants. Three articles in *Indian Tribes of Aboriginal America* (New York: Cooper Square Press, 1967), ed. Sol Tax, are also broadly useful: Earl W. Count's "The Earth Diver and the Rival Twins: A Clue to Time Correlation in North-Eurasiatic and North American Mythology" (pp. 55–62), Marius Barbeau's "The Old World Dragon in America" (pp. 115–22), and Geza Roheim's "Culture Hero and Trickster in North American Mythology" (pp. 190–94). Count's article is good on west to east diffusion, Barbeau's covers only northeastern and northwestern occurrences, and Roheim's article is a psychoanalytic analysis.

Some specialized studies should be consulted, also. Thomas G. Blackburn's *Flowers of the Wind: Papers on Ritual, Myth and Symbolism in California and the Southwest* (Socorro, N.Mex.: Ballena Press, 1977) is not a large work, but it has many insights pertinent to the southwestern Indian mythologies (some of them "translatable" to other North American Indian mythologies in general). A.L. Kroeber's *A Mohave Historical Bible* (Berkeley: University of California Publications in Archaeology and Anthropology, Vol. 11) offers the "epic" and some good analysis of it in terms of mythmaking, history in myth, and other features. Elaine Jahner's "The Spiritual Landscape," in *Parabola*, 2 (Fall 1977), pp. 32–38, uses Lakota myth to illustrate an interesting look at how world view and myth are shaped by journey, quest, and the landscape. "The Wife Who Goes Out Like a Man, Comes Back as a Hero: The Art of Two Oregon Indian Narratives" is a fine narrative analysis by Jarold W. Ramsey in *PMLA*, 92 (January 1977), pp. 9–18. Ramsey's aim is promotion of "long overdue reclamation of native American literature," but it is particularly useful to myth students for demonstrating analysis of Indian myth. Frederica Delaguna's "Geological Confirmation of Native Traditions, Yakutat, Alaska," in *American Antiquity*, 23 (1958), p. 434, is barely more than a note, but it has importance in that geological confirmation of information contained in a myth is given—something *always* important for understanding of the mythmaking process and its complexity. Two articles in *Source Book in Anthropology*, revised edition (New York: Harcourt, Brace and Co., 1931), ed. A.L. Kroeber and T.T. Waterman, are useful also: R.B. Dixon's "The Creation According to the Maidu" (pp. 458-63), which gives the myth and an interpretation, and W. Thalbitzer's "Shamans of the East Greenland Eskimo" (pp. 430-36), which while dealing with shamanic practices there also gives insights concerning the mythmaking process. A fascinating comparative study of North American Eskimo mythology with that of interior Canadian, northwest coastal, and northeastern Asiatic can be found in F.J. Essene, Jr.'s *A Comparative Study of Eskimo Mythology* (Ph.D. dissertation, University of California at Berkeley, 1947). Essene arrives at the conclusion that all of the groups were once in intimate contact, lending reinforcement to the theory that the Indians of North America at one time were emigrants from eastern Asia. S. Parker's analysis of "Motives in Eskimo and Ojibwa Mythology," in *Ethnology*, 1 (October 1962), pp. 516-23, is well worth looking into, too, when you're about studying Eskimo mythology. L.B. Boyer's "Stone as a Symbol in Apache Mythology," in *American Imago*, 22 (Spring 1965), pp. 14-39, is a most interesting psychoanalytic investigation, and Katherine Spencer's *An Analysis of Navaho Chantway Myths* (Philadelphia: American Folklore Society, 1957/p) and Sam D. Gill's "The Trees Stood Deep Rooted," in *Parabola*, 2 (Spring 1977), pp. 6-12, both offer excellent insights into Navaho myth and ritual. Spencer's book "proposes to explore a portion of Navaho mythology to see what light it throws on the life view and values of the people whose literature it represents"; an anthropological investigation principally, it offers a 50/50 split between myths re-told and analyses of them. Gill's essay is on the Navaho creation myth and the rituals that keep it alive. Finally, Clyde Kluckhohn's "Myths and Rituals: A General Theory," is a good overview of the ritual theory of myth interpretation and uses Navaho materials as the major examples. It first appeared in *The Harvard Theological Review*, 35 (January 1942), pp. 44-79, but has, because it *is* excellent on the ritual theory as such, been reprinted often, including in the book mentioned earlier, *Studies in Mythology* (Homewood, Ill.: The Dorsey Press, 1968/p).

Two essays by Claude Lévi-Strauss—since we're on the subject of myth interpretation—are relevant to North American Indian myth study: his famous "Four Winnebago Myths: A Structural Sketch" and "The Story of Asdiwal." The latter has been included in a number of places, perhaps the most accessible being *The Structural Study of Myth and Totemism* (London: Tavistock Publications, 1968/p), ed. Edmund Leach. "Four Winnebago Myths" can be found in *Myth and Cosmos* (Garden City, N.Y.: Doubleday Natural History Press, 1967/p), ed. John Middleton, and *Culture in History: Essays in Honor of Paul Radin* (New York: Columbia University Press, 1960), ed. Stanley Diamond.

Works on Religion and Related Matters

The best place to find useful discussions of North American Indian religions is in general works on the history and culture of the Indians and in such works devoted to specific tribes and larger groups. These are covered fully below. There are, though, some good works devoted solely to the topic of religion. One of the best general ones is Ruth M. Underhill's *Red Man's Religion: Beliefs and Practices of the Indians North of Mexico* (Chicago: University of Chicago Press, 1972). An excellent group of essays by such noted writers as N. Scott Momaday, *Seeing with the Native Eye: Contributions to the Study of Native American Religion* (New York: Harper Forum, 1976/p), ed. Walter H. Capps, is useful, too, if often specialized rather than general. Speaking of N. Scott Momaday, his "A First Man Views His Land" in *National Geographic*, 150 (July 1976/i), pp. 12-19, is a good, brief look at native American attitudes toward the land and at Indian world view generally. *Teachings from the American Earth: Indian Religion and Philosophy* (New York: Liveright, 1975), ed. Dennis and Barbara Tedlock, is divided into two parts, the first largely on the shamanic experience and the second on the thought behind North American Indian religion, ritual, and myth. Carl Starkloff's *People of the Center: American Indian Religion and Christianity* (New York: Seabury, 1974) is a comparative work showing well the nature of syncretism North American style, but there's much in it on the nature of myth, ritual, and belief in native Indian cultures. *Pre-Columbian American Religions,* trans. Starley Davis (New York: Holt, Rinehart and Winston, 1968) covers only earliest manifestations and in all the Americas, but it is a good background source nonetheless. Part three is devoted to North American religion. Ivar Lissner's *Man, God, and Magic*, trans. Maxwell Brownjohn (New York: G.P. Putnam's Sons, 1961) is really concerned with primitive belief and worship in general, but because Lissner's special focus is North American, there's much useful background in the book for students of North American Indian mythology. Robert H. Lowie's *Primitive Religion* (New York: Boni & Liveright, 1924) is also general in that same way, but chapter one, for instance, includes an excellent discussion of Crow religion. Weston LaBarre's *The Ghost Dance: The Origins of Religion* (New York: Dell Delta Book, 1972/p) is a grand psychological and anthropological study of religion—particularly, as the book's title indicates, of the "origins" of religion. However, LaBarre is a specialist in North American Indian religions, and the book's main examples and longer illustrations are drawn from those religions, making it a useful source.

Three chapters in *Ancient Religions* (New York: Citadel Press, 1965; originally published as *Forgotten Religions* in 1950/bp), ed. Vergilius Ferm, are on individual North American Indian religions: chapter nineteen is Margaret Lantis' "The Religion of the Eskimos"; chapter twenty is Leland Clifton Wyman's "The Religion of the Navaho Indians"; and chapter twenty-one is Micha Titiev's "The Religion of the Hopi Indians." The "dogma, ritual, and symbolism in the religion of the Navaho" is the subject of Gladys A. Reichard's *Navaho Religion: A Study of Symbolism* (Princeton: Princeton University Press, 1963/ip; originally Pantheon Books, 1950). An in-depth study of two Navaho myths and rituals, The Great Star Chant and The Coyote Chant, can be found in Mary C. Wheelwright's *The Myth and Prayers of the Great Star Chant and the Myth of the Coyote Chant* (Santa Fe: Museum of Navaho Ceremonial Art, 1956/i), which is Volume IV in the museum's Navaho Religion series. Elsie Clews Parsons' *Pueblo Indian Religion* (Chicago: University of Chicago Press, 1939) and William K. Powers' *Oglala Religion* (Lincoln: University of Nebraska Press, 1976/i) are both excellent on their respective subjects, Powers' being a comparative study, past practices and beliefs with present. Robert F. Spencer's "Native Myth and Modern Religion among the Klamath Indians," in *Journal of American Folklore*, 65 (July–September 1952), pp. 217-26, is a particularly good study of how a traditional religion comes in contact with, then adapts to, the new, while retaining vestiges of the old. Erna Fergusson's *Dancing Gods: Indian Ceremonials of New Mexico and Arizona* (Albuquerque: University of New Mexico Press, 1957) has, along with a good chapter on Navaho religion, a good array of ritual dances of the Navaho, Hopi, and others. Medicine men of the North American Indians are the focus in C.A. Weslager's *Magic Medicines of the Indians* (New York: New American Library Signet, 1974/p); it is "a condensed account of Indian medicines—both herbal and non-herbal," and includes much that will serve as background to the religions involved. Peter H. Knudtson's "Flora, Shaman of the Wintu," in *Natural History*, 84 (May 1975), pp. 6-17, focuses on a woman shaman in California and, in so doing, presents some interesting and useful information on Indian ritual and belief. Hartley Burr Alexander's *The World's Rim: Great Mysteries of the North American Indians* (Lincoln: University of Nebraska Press, 1953) offers a broad spectrum of rituals and related practices, beliefs. And finally, Vine Deloria, Jr.'s *God Is Red* (New York: Dell Delta Book, 1973) calls for a return to the North American Indian religions since, as he says, Christianity has failed. He provides much in the way of general background to the Indian religions along the way.

Works on Historical/Cultural Background

A number of books afford broad cultural and historical background to the North American Indians, and often including chapters on myth, ritual, and/or religion. *The North American Indians: A Sourcebook* (New York: Macmillan, 1967), ed. Roger C. Owen, James J.F. Deetz, and Anthony D. Fisher, has sections devoted to separate geographical groupings of Indian tribes. Especially interesting is Ruth Underhill's "Religion Among American Indians" (pp. 96-108), A. Irving Hallowell's "Ojibwa World View" (pp. 208-35), and Wellard Z. Park's "Paviotso Shamanism" (pp. 259-70). Clark Wissler's *Indians of the United States*, revised edition (Garden City, N.Y.: Doubleday Natural History Library, 1966/ip; originally 1940) is a broad introduction to the topic. Part two covers the great Indian families and details the geography of the North American Indians in the United States and the differences and similarities between tribes and regional groups. Harold E. Driver's *Indians of North America*, second edition (Chicago: University of Chicago Press, 1969) is a good overall survey of the North American Indians since prehistory, concentrating on the ethnographic and archaeological rather than on the purely differential characteristics. Chapter twenty-three, "Religion, Magic, Medicine," is especially valuable reading. John Collier's *Indians of the Americas: The Long Hope* (New York: W.W. Norton, 1947; N.A.L. Mentor, 1952/p) covers the history of the Indians of the Americas generally (Aztecs and Incas included) from earliest times to the present and is good, brief background. *American Epic: The Story of the American Indian* (New York: N.A.L. Mentor, 1969/ibp), by Alice Marriott and Carol K. Rachlin, is a fine, sweeping look at the Indian in North America, the confrontation with European whites, and the effects of that confrontation. It's good as a historical survey but is even more impressive on value systems and beliefs.

There are also some older works that are still valuable. For instance, there's E.S. Curtis' *The North American Indian* (Cambridge: Harvard University Press, 1908–30), a twenty-volume survey that is, needless to say, pretty comprehensive. Henry Schoolcraft's *History of the Indian Tribes of the United States: Their Present Condition and Prospects* (1975 reprint of the 1851–57 edition published by the Historical American Indian Press/i) runs six volumes and 4700 pages, but it was, in its time, a distinguished work produced under government auspices. In 1775, James Adair's *History of the American Indians* first appeared in London. It is a quaint but curiously informative volume still and has been reprinted by Johnson Reprint Corporation (New York, 1969). *The Indians of North America* (New York: Harcourt, Brace & Co., 1927), ed. E. Kenton, is a collection of papers that may yet be of value as background.

Some colorfully illustrated volumes ought also to be useful. *The American Heritage Book of Indians* (New York: American Heritage Publishing Co., 1961/i), ed. Alvin M. Josephy and William Brandon, is beautifully done all the way—in research, in writing, in illustrations (500 of them). *The World of the American Indian* (Washington, D.C.: National Geographic Society, 1974/i), ed. Jules B. Billard, has 448 illustrations, 362 in color, and is a useful cultural history, mainly modern but including chapters on origins and migrations. There's useful material here on beliefs and religion, too, but it's scattered throughout rather than enclosed in a chapter or two. *America's Fascinating Indian Heritage* (Pleasantville, N.Y.: Reader's Digest, 1978/i) is organized historically and geographically, is filled with pictures, maps, charts, and even includes a guide to sites, museums, and attractions. Oliver LaFarge's *A Pictorial History of the American Indian* (New York: Crown Publishers, 1956/i) is well illustrated in black and white and covers the history in a general way. The chapter entitled "Ghosts and Drugs" is useful as brief background to shamanism and the use of peyote. Bruce Grant's *American Indians Yesterday and Today: A Profusely Illustrated Encyclopedia of the American Indian* (New York: E.P. Dutton, 1958/i) has many helpful sections but is more to be used as reference than for sustained reading. Royal B. Hassrick's *The Colorful Story of North American Indians* (Secaucus, N.J.: Derbibooks, 1975/ip) is thin treatment, but like a number of other volumes which could also be mentioned, it might be helpful. It has 180 photographs, quite a few in color.

Other valuable general works are Barbara A. Leitch's *Chronology of the American Indian* (St. Clair Shores, Mich.: Scholarly Press, 1975) and John L. Stoutenburgh's *Dictionary of the American Indian* (New York: Philosophical Library, 1960). Leitch's book covers the entire time spectrum from 25,000 B.C. through recent times and is useful in locating the "when" of the history of North America's Indians. Stoutenburgh's book is by no means complete, but it has names, terms, and the like that make it a satisfactory reference tool for the nonspecialist.

Books which deal with cultural/historical background on a regional or tribal basis form a pretty sizable group. Robert H. Lowie's *Indians of the Plains* (Garden City, N.Y.: Doubleday Natural History Press, reprint of the 1954 edition/ibp) is topically organized with sections on material culture, social organization, art, supernaturalism. William K. Powers' *Indians of the Northern Plains* and *Indians of the Southern Plains* (New York: Capricorn Books, 1969/ibp and 1972/ibp) cover the same region as Lowie's volume and are well illustrated introductions that include much on culture, values, and religion. Similary good coverage is afforded in *Indians of the Northwest Coast* (Garden City, N.Y.: Doubleday Natural History Press, 1963/ibp) by Philip Drucker; and Gordon C. Baldwin does the same for *Indians of the Southwest* (New York: Capricorn Books, 1970/ibp).

The Navaho, revised edition (Garden City, N.Y.: Doubleday Natural History Library, 1962/ibp; originally published in 1946), by Clyde Kluckhohn and Dorothea Leighton, is a superb book which includes four perspectives on the Navahos—the historical and spiritual most important for myth purposes. On the subject of the Navaho, Geza Roheim has written "The Oedipus Complex of the Navaho" in *Psychoanalysis and Anthropology: Culture, Personality and the Unconscious* (New York: International Universities Press, 1950). Frank Waters' *Masked Gods: Navaho and Pueblo Ceremonialism* (New York: Ballantine Books, 1970/p) is a fine ethnographic and historical study of the two tribes. It's divided into three parts: one on history, one on myths and rituals, and the third on late happenings, including the coming of Christianity. Edward Dozier has written extensively on the Pueblos, his *The Pueblo Indians of North America* (New York: Holt, Rinehart and Winston, 1970) a classic. You can also find an article of his in *Perspectives in American Indian Culture Change* (Chicago: University of Chicago Press, 1961), ed. E.H. Spicer; entitled "Rio Grande Pueblos," it is excellent on change brought to an Indian society by white men. George Bird Grinnell's *The Cheyenne Indians, Their History and Ways of Life* (New Haven: Yale University Press, 1924), a two-volume work, is good, complete coverage of the Cheyenne, with some attention paid to their myths, beliefs, ceremonies, and culture heroes. Frank Waters' *Book of the Hopi* (New York: Ballantine Books, 1974/ip) is equally complete on the Hopi Indians, their history, worldview, art, and myths. *The Zunis of Cibola* (Salt Lake City: University of Utah Press, 1978/ib) is an excellent cultural history of the Zunis from their discovery by whites in the mid-sixteenth century to date and is especially good on the effects of the white man and his beliefs on their society. The final chapters of Carobeth Laird's *The Chemehuevis* (Banning, Calif.: Malki Museum Press, 1976/p) are devoted to myths, and there's a good deal in the rest of the book on Chemehuevi culture, belief, and ritual. *The Indians of Puget Sound* (Seattle: University of Washington Press, 1930/p) by Hermann Haeberlin and Erna Gunther is an ethnographic study principally of the Snohomish, Snuqualmi, and Nisqually tribes. Chapters six through nine are devoted to religion, ritual, and mythology in Franz Boas' posthumous *Kwakiutl Ethnography*, ed. Helen Codere (Chicago: University of Chicago Press, 1966), a fine, comprehensive study of the Kwakiutl. Basil Johnston, himself an Ojibway, wrote *Ojibway Heritage* (New York: Columbia Univeristy Press, 1976), a volume which "sets forth the broad spectrum of his people's beliefs, life, legends." Close to 50 pages are devoted to Menomini myths and 30 to their folktales in an old but quite useful volume by Walter James Hoffman, *The Menomini Indians* (originally published in 1896; reprinted in 1970 by Johnson Reprint Service of New York). Chapters nine and ten in part one are on "Religion" and "The Supernatural," respectively, and all of part two is devoted to folktales and myths in *The Micmac Indians of Eastern Canada* (Minneapolis: University of Minnesota Press, 1955) by Wilson D. and Ruth Sawtell Wallis. The book is a comprehensive study of the Micmacs that runs to better than 500 pages. O.M. Salisbury's *Customs and Legends of the Tlingit Indians of Alaska* (New York: Bonanza Books, 1962), a fine ethnographic study, focuses on the Tlingit in transition from ancient Indian to modern, white-influenced society in the 1920s. Kaj. Birket-Smith's *The Eskimos,* trans. W. E. Calvert (London: Methuen, 1936) is an excellent work for cultural/historical background; chapter eight, "View of Life," and nine, on the issue of independent origin versus diffusion, are of special use to myth students. Edward Moffat Weyer's *The Eskimos: Their Environment and Folkways* (New Haven: Yale University Press, 1932) attempts "to portray the life of the Eskimos as revealed through their customs and beliefs and to describe the environmental conditions under which they live." There are also some good sections on myth and religion in Franz Boas' *The Central Eskimo* (Lincoln: University of Nebraska Press, 1964/p). Hans-Georg Bandi's *Eskimo Prehistory*, trans. Ann E. Keep (College, Alaska: University of Alaska Press, 1969/b) and J. Louis Giddings' *Ancient Men of the Arctic* (London: Secker and Warburg, 1968/i) are both concerned with the archaeology of ancient Eskimo centers.

Works on Archaeology

There are some excellent general works on North American archaeology. C. W. Ceram's *The First American: A Story of North American Archaeology*, trans. Richard and Clara Winston (New York: N.A.L. Mentor, 1971/ibp) is supurb. Written by the author of *Gods, Graves, and Scholars,* a classic overview of archaeological discoveries around the world, *The First American* covers various theories, archaeological finds, and ethnographic information enroute to providing the best single-volume source of information about archaeology involving early Americans. Dean Snow's *The Archaeology of North America* (New York: Viking Press, 1976/ib) is more recent, more colorfully illustrated, and would serve well instead of or alongside Ceram's book. Gordon C. Baldwin's *America's Buried Past: The Story of North American Archaeology* (New York: G.P. Putnam's, 1962/i) is a short survey covering the same general territory. Leo Deuel's *Conquistadors Without Swords: Archaeologists in the Americas* (New York: St. Martin's Press,

1967/ibp), which has the archaeologists telling their own stories, has a sizable section on archaeology north of the Mexican border. *New World Prehistory: Archaeology of the American Indian* (Englewood Cliffs, N.J.: Prentice-Hall, 1970/i), by William T. Sanders and Joseph P. Marino, and *An Introduction to American Archaeology: North and Middle America* (Englewood Cliffs, N.J.: Prentice-Hall, 1966/i), by Gordon R. Willey, are both also usable for archaeological information. Frank Folsom's *America's Ancient Treasures: Guide to Archaeological Sites and Museums* (New York: Rand McNally, 1971/ip), is a book you'll want to look into should you decide to travel around the country to sites and museums; it's divided geographically, and each site and museum is nicely described.

"Who Were the Mound Builders?" is a provocative article on the mysterious prehistoric, man-made mounds found at various places in the East and Midwest that fits into the archaeological category. It's by Brian Fagan in *Mysteries of the Past* (New York: American Heritage Publishing Co., 1977/i), ed. Joseph J. Thorndike, Jr. John A. Eddy's "Probing the Mystery of the Medicine Wheels," in *National Geographic*, 151 (January 1977/i), pp. 140–46, deals with another "mystery," this one found high in the Bighorn Mountains of Wyoming and dating back in origin to 4,000 or more years ago. Such articles are becoming more and more common, particularly in the lay press, so you may wish to be on the lookout for them.

Works on the Origins of North American Indians; Contacts

Investigations of early man in North America have been high on the list of activities concerning North American Indians for at least fifty years now. *Indians Before Columbus* (Chicago: University of Chicago Press, 1947/ib), by Paul Sydney Martin, George I. Quimby, and Donald Collier, is a good survey of the prehistoric Indians of North America for the nonspecialist. It has an excellent chronological chart. Peter Farb's *Man's Rise to Civilization: The Cultural Ascent of the Indians of North America*, revised 2nd edition (New York: E.P. Dutton, 1978/ib) is not so much a cultural survey as an anthropological investigation of the Indians' migration(s) to the new world, their adaptation to the environment, and their assimilation of borrowed cultures. In every way, it's a provocative book. G.H.S. Bushnell's *The First Americans: The Pre-Columbian Civilizations* (New York: McGraw-Hill, 1968/i) surveys all of the Americas and is therefore quite superficial (especially for 144 pages of book!), but it is well illustrated, has a good chronology, and would serve as a brief introduction to the topic. *Discovering Man's Past in the Americas* (Washington, D.C.: National Geographic Society, 1969/i), by George E. and Gene S. Stuart, is a beautifully illustrated volume that covers just Middle and North American Indians; a major concern is their origins and spread. E. H. Sellards' *Early Man in America: A Study in Prehistory* (Austin: University of Texas Press, 1952) is a look at what archaeology has shown us about these origins and spread. *Early Man in the New World* (Garden City, N.Y.: Doubleday Anchor, 1962/p; originally 1950), by Kenneth MacGowan and Joseph Hester, Jr., is a fine "prehistory" that includes a good chapter entitled "Did the Indian Invent or Borrow His Culture?" Robert Wauchope's *Lost Tribes and Sunken Continents: Myth and Method in the Study of American Indians* (Chicago: University of Chicago Press, 1962/ibp) is an especially good book for its survey of theories of the origin of the Indians of all the Americas. It covers Egyptian, Phoenician, Hebrew, and other possibilities, making it obviously a great work for the diffusionist buff, even though Wauchope himself is not in that camp. *Early Man in America* (San Francisco: W.H. Freeman, 1973/i) consists of a series of articles from *Scientific American*— all of them having to do with archaeological finds that help us better understand the origins of American Indians in both continents. It's a well-illustrated collection good for controversy. *Prehistoric Man in the New World* (Chicago: University of Chicago Press, 1964), ed. Jesse D. Jennings and Edward Norbeck, is a collection of papers delivered at a Rice University symposium; of most use in it are the papers dealing with philological/diffusion/contact problems: Gordon F. Ekholm's "Transpacific Contacts," Betty J. Meggers' "North and South American Cultural Connections and Convergences," and Morris Swadesh's "Linguistic Overview." Folsom and Sandia man are the main concern in Frank C. Hibben's *The Lost Americans* (New York: Thomas Y. Crowell, 1946), a book in which the author traces the finds to show that the first Indians in North America got here by way of the Bering land bridge. Charles Berlitz's *Mysteries from Forgotten Worlds* (Garden City, N.Y.: Doubleday, 1972) surveys diffusionist theories of the origins of the earliest Indians and disputes the Bering land bridge origins. *Man Across the Sea* (Austin: University of Texas Press, 1971) includes articles by David E. Kelley, Alice B. Kehoe, and others in which diffusionist versus native origins are discussed, making it a good primer on the matter. James A. Ford's *A Comparison of*

Formative Cultures in the Americas: Diffusion or the Psychic Unity of Man (Washington, D.C.: Smithsonian Institution, 1969) is also good on the controversy—if one man's version. Ivan Van Sertima's position in *They Came Before Columbus: The African Presence in Ancient America* (New York: Random House, 1977) is that Africans visited the Americas as early as 600 B.C., his "proofs" being several, philological included. Barry Fell's controversial *America B.C.: Ancient Settlers in the New World* (New York: Quadrangle Books, 1976/ip) explores the possibilities that such peoples as the Norse, Celts, and Phoenicians arrived in North America at an early time; and Cyrus H. Gordon's *Before Columbus* (New York: Crown Publishers, 1971/ib) and *Riddles in History* (New York: Crown Publishers, 1974/ib) both deal with diffusion possibilities, too, the latter work through epigraphic evidence. O. G. Landsverk's *Runic Records of the Norsemen in America* (Rushford, Minn.: Erik J. Friis, 1974/i) deals with the epigraphic evidence of the Norse presence in ancient North America, eight inscriptions from Oklahoma perhaps the most startling of the finds dealt with. "Pre-Columbian Old World Coins in America: An Examination of the Evidence," an article by Jeremiah F. Epstein in *Current Anthropology*, 21 (February 1980), pp. 1–20, surveys the bulk of the evidence concerning the discovery of ancient old-world coins in North American sites. The article is followed by comments by anthropologists and other experts. A popular theory as early as the sixteenth century was that North and Middle American Indians derived from one of the lost tribes of Israel. Many works were written in an attempt to prove this theory—which still has currency with some groups, by the way—one of the more interesting being Charles Even's *The Lost Tribes of Israel: Or, The First of the Red Men* (originally published in Philadelphia in 1861; reprinted by the Arno Press of New York in 1977). For a particularly good summary article on the matter of origins, see Carroll L. Riley's "Interhemispheric Contacts? Comments on a Controversy," *Archaeology*, 31 (November–December 1978/b), pp. 59–61.

Works on Art

There are a great many works currently available on Indian art. *Indian Art of the United States* (New York: The Museum of Modern Art, 1969/ib; reprint of the 1941 edition), by Frederick H. Douglas and Rene D'Harnoucourt, is a most interesting book, for it includes some pictures of works of art found by archaeologists that substantiate contact between Indians as far removed from one another as the Maya in the Yucatan and Indians in Tennessee. A particularly well illustrated volume is *Sacred Circles: Two Thousand Years of North American Indian Art* (Seattle: University of Washington Press, 1977/i); it has over 800 pictures, and the works date from 1500 B.C. to the present. G. H. S. Bushnell's *Ancient Arts of the Americas* (New York: Frederick A. Praeger, 1965/i) is a good survey with numerous illustrations, some in color. Tlingit, Haida, Kwakiutl, and other northwest tribes are covered in Robert Bruce Inverarity's *Art of the Northwest Coast Indians* (Berkeley: University of California Press, 1950/i), a volume with many photographs (some in color) and good accompanying text. *Images: Stone: B.C.: Thirty Centuries of Northwest Coast Indian Sculpture* (Seattle: University of Washington Press, 1972/i), by Wilson Duff, is a good catalog of sculpture of the northwest Indians, and it's well illustrated. There's a chapter on the artifacts of the tribes of the Pacific northwest in David Attenborough's fine *The Tribal Eye* (New York: W.W. Norton, 1977/i)—a book based on the excellent BBC television series that was aired over PBS stations in this country. Dorothy Jean Ray's *Eskimo Masks: Art and Ceremony* (Seattle: University of Washington Press, 1967/i) is loaded with pictures—as are these other books dealing with Eskimo art: George Swinton's *Sculpture of the Eskimos* (Toronto: McClelland and Stewart, 1971/i), which has both black and white and color photographs; Ernst Rock's *Arts of the Eskimo: Prints* (Barre, Mass.: Barre Publishers, 1975/i), which has about 100 pictures of prints in full color; *Sculpture/Inuit* (Toronto: University of Toronto Press, 1971/i), which has 405 illustrations of works done by Hudson's Bay Eskimos. Over 2,000 North American stone age tools, pieces of equipment, and personal possessions are illustrated in Charles Miles' *Indian and Eskimo Artifacts of North America* (Chicago: Henry Regnery, 1963/i) and over 500 are illustrated in Louis A. Brennan's *Artifacts of Prehistoric America* (Harrisburg, Pa.: Stackpole Books, 1975/i) should you want some pictures of utilitarian objects dating from prehistoric times.

Finally there are some books which go beyond the bounds of myth study. Francisco Guerra's *The Pre-Columbian Mind* (New York: Seminar Press, 1971) is a psychoanalysis of descendents of the Pre-Columbians to see what the acculturation's extent might be, what vestiges remain of the ancestral ways, and the like. It's fascinating if, as mentioned, some distance from what is most germane to myth study involving North American Indians. Also, there are two books that treat the matter of white domination of red. Elemire Zolla's *The Writer and the Shaman: A Morphology of the American Indian*, trans. Raymond Rosenthal (New York: Harcourt, Brace, Jovanovich, 1973), chronologically surveys the attitudes towards and myths about the Indians held by whites from prior to European settlement of North America through the twentieth century. Robert F. Berkhofer's *White Man's Indian* (New York: Alfred A. Knopf, 1978) covers related territory in that the author's concern is how white dominance was established by the ideology of white superiority—a kind of mythmaking that worked.

Middle American Indian Mythologies

No one who has walked the length of the "Avenue of the Dead" at San Juan Teotihuacan and seen, or perhaps climbed, the pyramids of the sun and moon, and been awed by the magnificence of the Temple of Quetzalcoatl, is likely to be unimpressed by the technical and artistic know-how of their builders. Nor is anyone who has visited the jungle ruins at Palenque, climbed to the top of the Temple of the Inscriptions and then descended inside to the great tomb, likely to walk away unaffected. Nor could anyone who has seen the stunning ball courts at Chichen Itza and Copan, the Building of the Columns at Mitla and Magician's Temple at Uxmal, the Great Plaza at Monte Alban and the Atlantes of Tula, or the splendid murals at Bonampak and the enormous Olmec heads of Vera Cruz fail to sense the importance of the peoples who lived so long ago in what are now central and southern Mexico, Guatemala, Belize, Honduras, and other countries to the south but above the border of South America. Seeing good collections of the artifacts that have been recovered at the many sites—say, the ones in the National Museum of Anthropology in Mexico City or in the Regional Museum in Oaxaca—can do nothing less than harden the conviction that the pre-Columbian natives of Middle America were sophisticated in ways quite unlike those of their neighbors to the north—or, maybe alternatively, prompt a conviction that they had help their northern neighbors didn't have.

Going to the ancient Indian myths of Middle America (sometimes they're called Central American or just Mexican, by the way) is of some help in reinforcing either conviction. However, it is unfortunately the case that the Spanish conquest of the Aztec (Mexica) capital at Tenochtitlan, a site now almost totally buried beneath Mexico City, during the first quarter of the sixteenth century, and the earlier mysterious decline of the Maya, Olmec, Toltec, Zapotec, and other ancient cultures of Middle America, left too little in the way of records to draw any firm conclusions. There are records in stone, even books (codices) written by pre-Columbians; there are the important records and books of the Spanish conquerors; and then there are those too often enigmatic ruins and artifacts that attest to a "new world" greatness unimagined in Europe before Cortes. But despite the accumulated evidence, what is missing makes ancient Middle America very much a puzzle still.

Even the matter of where the various cultures there came from and to what extent they were acquainted with one another (or related) is disputed. Rough dates and general regions can be supplied for each of the major cultures. For instance, we know that the Olmecs lived in what are now the Mexican states of Vera Cruz and Tabasco from about 800 B.C. through the late fifth century A.D. The Maya had their start before 2,000 B.C. and had abandoned most of their principal centers in southeastern Mexico and the countries of Guatemala and Honduras by A.D. 900 (despite their existence in decreasingly impressive circumstances to the present day). The Zapotecs, major residents in the Oaxaca Valley and at Monte Alban in Mexico from about A.D. 300, declined in their region, first under Mixtec pressure and then Spanish, but they have persisted, too, if in less grandeur, to the present day. The Toltecs flourished from late in the eighth century A.D. through the end of the twelfth century, their influence obvious at Teoti-huacan, Xochicalco, Tula, and the far distant Mayan center at Chichen Itza. The Aztecs (or Mexica) were relative late-comers compared with the others, their capital city of Tenochtitlan in Lake Texcoco an almost new city (dating from the thirteenth century at earliest) when Cortes, believed by Montezuma and his Aztec people to be the god Quetzalcoatl returning as prophecized, led his Spanish troops to the edge of the lake and to splendor he couldn't in his wildest dreams have believed existed across the Atlantic from Europe.

For each of these cultures there are varying degrees of other kinds of information—from quite a bit in the case of Aztec to almost none in the case of Olmec—and, as with all cultures where the records are incomplete, reconstruction has been attempted to whatever extent the existing evidence will allow. Beyond that there are guesses and imaginings. This poses special problems for the myth student who tackles Middle American mythology seriously, the greatest ones being (1) that there were no doubt mythologies (plural) rather than the mythology (singular) that available collections of the myths usually imply and (2) that there hasn't really been a great deal done *with* the myths that we have.

Collections of the Myths

Be that as it may, there are collections of the myths. Far and away the best single-volume source is Irene Nicholson's *Mexican and Central American Mythology* (London: Paul Hamlyn, 1967/ib). While it has the distinct disadvantage of treatment of the myths as though they all derived from the same system—or from two, Aztec and Mayan—the book has much good background information, the myths are nicely told, and there are plenty of illustrations of places and artifacts. Cottie A. Burland's *The Gods of Mexico* (New York: G.P. Putnam's Sons, 1967/ib) is another good single-volume source, its particular assets being excellent elaboration of the myths, detailed descriptions where necessary, information on codices, and a guide to pronunciation (not to be overlooked where names like Huitzilopochtli are involved!). The section on Middle American mythology in the *Larousse World Mythology* (New York: G.P. Putnam's Sons, 1965/i), ed. Pierre Grimal, trans. Patricia Beardsworth, isn't bad, the book's space limitations considered, but it does focus on Aztec and Mayan alone. The *Larousse Encyclopedia of Mythology* (London: Paul Hamlyn, 1959/ip), ed. Felix Guirand, trans. Richard Aldington and Delano Ames, has a section entitled "Mythology of the Two Americas" that includes too much geographical coverage and too few pages, just about five well illustrated pages devoted to Middle America. The *Pears Encyclopedia of Myths and Legends*, Volume IV (London: Pelham Books, 1978/i) suffers from about the same problem. Miguel Leon-Portilla's "Mythology of Ancient Mexico" in *Mythologies of the Ancient World* (Garden City, N.Y.: Anchor Books, 1961/bp) is an excellent general discussion of Toltec and Aztec mythology, but there is much left unsaid in it, the number of myths covered being few. The *Encyclopedia of World Mythology* (New York: Galahad Books, 1975/i) has a very brief section entitled "South America" that includes terse coverage of Aztec and Mayan mythology. If you can stand that *faux pas*, it will suffice as a briefest of introductions. With sources of the myths so few, the section devoted to them in Veronica Ions' *The World's Mythology in Colour* (London: Paul Hamlyn, 1974/i) comes off pretty well in that many of the myths are retold, and the color pictures are simply magnificent (even though they are, incidentally, the same ones that appear in the Nicholson volume mentioned above). A volume suitable for junior high age and up is Roy Cal's *The Serpent and the Sun: Myths of the Mexican World* (New York: Farrar, Straus and Giroux, 1972), a basic retelling of twelve Aztec and Mayan myths, among them "Brother Sun and Sister Moon" and "The Monster We Live On."

Older and therefore not quite as reliable volumes—mainly due to translations and findings of the past fifty years—are also ones you may wish to consider. Lewis Spence, in his day a fine mythologist, wrote *The Myths of Mexico and Peru* (London: A. Constable & Co., 1907/i), which has in it a fair run of the myths, useful information on the Indians involved, and over fifty full-page illustrations. Volume XI in *The Mythology of all Races* (New York: Cooper Square Press reprint of the 1929 edition) is Hartley Burr Alexander's *Latin American Mythology*. Covering both Middle and South America, it has a pretty good-sized selection of Middle American myths. Donald A. Mackenzie's *Myths of Pre-Columbian America* (London: Gresham Publishing Co., 1918/i) covers all of the Americas but does have enough of the Middle American myths to make it a worthwhile source. Daniel G. Brinton's *Myths of the Americas: Symbolism and Mythology of the Indians of the Americas* (Blauvelt, N.Y.: Multimedia, 1976/p; reprint of the 1868 edition entitled *The Myths of the New World*) is topically organized, and if you can handle his naturalist interpretations, you'll find it has a fair selection of the Middle American myths.

There are six Middle American Indian creation myths included in Maria Leach's *The Beginning: Creation Myths Around the World* (New York: Funk and Wagnalls, 1956), a lovely topical collection of myths. Chapter XII of James George Frazer's *Myths of the Origin of Fire* (London: Macmillan, 1930) is devoted to Middle American myths and although you'll have to use the index to find them, there are quite a few Middle American myths in Cottie A. Burland's *Myths of Life and Death* (New York: Crown Publishers, 1974/i). Also, one of the better collections of folklore useful as well in myth study is Mary Shaw's *According to Our Ancestors* (Norman: University of Oklahoma Press, 1971). It contains "folktexts" from Guatemala and Honduras, modern folktales *thought* to be ancient by the present-day Mayans from whom they were received. Certainly worth mentioning, although neither a collection of myths nor one of folktales, is Jose Lopez Portillo's superb fictional retelling of the life of Quetzalcoatl, a novel called *Quetzalcoatl,* trans. Eliot Weinberger and Diana S. Goodrich (New York: Seabury Press, 1976). It is filled with echoes from other mythologies—Christian primarily, but Greek and Indian as well—and may remind you, as it did me, of the simplicity of Hermann Hesse's *Siddhartha.* Portillo, incidentally, became president of Mexico in 1976.

Translations

Fortunately, there are a number of works available that, while not collections of myths as such, have enough myths in them to make them also worth considering. Fray Diego Duran's *Book of the Gods and Rites* and *The Ancient Calendar,* trans. and ed. Fernando Horcasitas and Doris Heyden (Norman: University of Oklahoma Press, 1975) is one of them. Duran, a sixteenth-century Spanish priest who lived among the Aztecs recorded many of the myths and rituals he heard and observed in his *Book of the Gods and Rites,* making it pretty much a primary source for us. Although *The Ancient Calendar* is not as useful, it does provide good background concerning Aztec time reckoning. Mainly Aztec, but with some Mayan, and Mixtec, *Pre-Columbian Literature of Mexico* (Norman: University of Oklahoma Press, 1969), by Miguel Leon-Portilla, trans. Grace Lobanon and the author, has a good selection of literature introduced by Leon-Portilla. There are myths, religious poetry, and chronicles of conquest. John H. Cornyn's *The Song of Quetzalcoatl* (Yellow Springs, Ohio: Antioch Press, 1930) is a book of pre-Columbian Aztec poems, among which are many references to and stories about divinities. Hugh Fox's *First Fire: Central and South American Indian Poetry* (Garden City, N.Y.: Doubleday Anchor, 1978/bp) has numerous poems that are myth-related and is in general an excellent collection—this despite some interpretations by Fox that you may not agree with. Jerome Rothenberg's *Shaking the Pumpkin: Traditional Poetry of the Indian North Americas* (Garden City, N.Y.: Doubleday Anchor, 1972/bp) is also a useful anthology of the same sort, this one including North American Indian poetry along with Aztec and Mayan. Abraham Arias-Larretta's *Pre-Columbian Masterpieces* (Kansas City, Mo.: Library of the New World, 1967) doesn't have too much in it that is directly useful to myth study, but it does have the *Popol-Vuh,* a Mayan epic of sorts that tells of the adventures of the demigods Hunahpu and Ixbalamque. The complete text of that work is included in *Popol-Vuh: The Sacred Book of the Ancient Quiche Maya* (Norman: University of Oklahoma Press, 1950/b), ed. Delia Goetz and Sylvanus G. Morley. There are a number of Mayan myth texts in *The Book of Chilam Balam of Chumayel*, trans. Ralph L. Roys (Norman: University of Oklahoma Press, 1967), and *Chorti (Mayan) Texts* (Philadelphia: University of Pennsylvania Press, 1972), by John G. and Sarah Fought. *Ancient Nahuatl Poetry* (New York: AMS Press reprint, 1969), a collection of translations made by Daniel G. Brinton in the nineteenth century, has some myths in essentially native form. The Aztec "Quetzalcoatl" and the Mayan prophecy from the *Chilam Balam* called "Cuceb" are translated, with introductions and notes, in John Bierhorst's *Four Masterpieces of American Indian Literature* (New York: Farrar, Straus and Giroux, 1974). Finally, don't overlook the codices, many of which are available in English translations, *The Codex Nuttall* (New York: Dover Press, 1975/ip), by Zelia Nuttall, and, by the same author, *Codex Magliabecchi: The Book of Life of the Ancient Mexicans, Containing an Account of Their Rites and Superstitions* (Berkeley: University of California Press, 1903) among them.

Works on Religion and Related Matters

As is the case with collections of myths, there really aren't in English as many works dealing with the religions of Middle America as might be desired. Part one of *Pre-Columbian American Religions* (New York: Holt, Rinehart and Winston, 1968), by Walter Krickeberg *et al*, trans. Starley Davis, offers useful *broad* coverage of the religions as does Laurette Sejourne's *Burning Water: Thought and Religion in Ancient Mexico* (Berkeley, Calif.: Shambhala, 1976/p; originally Vanguard Press, 1956), which focuses on Toltec civilization and does much to clarify Quetzalcoatl's place in the symbolic and religious lives of the people. Karl W. Luckert's *Olmec Religion: A Key to Middle America and Beyond* (Norman: University of Oklahoma Press, 1976/ib) is a provocative discussion of the oldest known religion in the Americas that includes enough speculation on the possible influences of Olmec religion on later Middle American cultures to make it useful both as general reading for Middle American religions and specific for Olmec alone. A good work to use along with it is P. D. Joralemon's *A Study of Olmec Iconography* (Washington, D.C., 1971). *Death and the After Life in Pre-Columbian America* (Washington, D.C.: Dumbarton Oaks Research Library and Collections, 1975), ed. Elizabeth P. Benson, is a collection of eight conference papers, all of them having to do with the eschatological in ancient Middle and South American cultures. Michael D. Coe's "Death and the Ancient Maya" is an example of the contents. Frank J. Neumann's "The Flayed God and His Rattle-Stick: A Shamanic Element in Pre-Hispanic Mesoamerican Religion," in *History of Religions*, 15 (February 1976), pp. 251-63, focuses on the rattle-stick associated with the deity Xipe Totec toward analysis of the possibilities for shamanic activity in Meso-america. Finally, Hugo G. Nutini looks at syncretism and accultura-tion among the Tlaxcalan in the first century and a half after the Spanish conquest in his "Syncretism and Acculturation: The Historical Development of the Cult of the Patron Saint in Tlaxcala, Mexico (1519-1670)," an article carried in *Ethnology*, XV (July 1976), pp. 301-21.

Studies of the Myths

Although there haven't been many works that help with analyses of Middle American myths, rituals, and religious beliefs and prac-tices as such, there are a few which will be worth considering. Mario Monteforte-Toledo's "Old Myths of the New World," in *Chimera*, 4 (Spring 1946), pp. 25-32, is excellent in the first place for its discussion of Mayan and Aztec myths through their motifs and, in the second, for the idea of diffusion put in its *maybe* proper place, that is, as unimportant. A good general essay on syncretism in Mexico is Jacques Lafaye's "Mexico According to Quetzalcoatl: An Essay of Intra-History," in *Diogenes*, no. 78 (Summer 1972), pp. 18-37. The way the former beliefs and myths reemerge in the context of the new religion is Lafaye's general focus. Miguel Leon-Portilla's *Time and Reality in the Thought of the Maya*, trans. Charles L. Boiles (Boston: Beacon Press, 1973/i) bears close enough relation to Mayan myths that it will serve as a useful background to the study of those myths. F. Toor's *A Treasury of Mexican Folkways* (New York: Gordon Press reprint of the earlier edition, 1976/i) has a sizable amount of myth analysis and other useful material.

Some works that deal with modern-day Mexican Indians are of value, if indirectly, in understanding ancient Middle American ritual. For instance, Antonin Artaud's *The Peyote Dance*, trans. Helen Weaver (New York: Farrar, Straus and Giroux, 1976/p) records in detail the author's experience with the primitive Tara-humara Indians of Mexico and is especially good for its extensive detailing of rituals. The ritual uses of hallucinogens in ancient and modern Mexico are discussed at length in Richard Heffern's *Secrets of the Mind-Altering Plants of Mexico* (New York: Harcourt, Brace, and Jovanovich, 1974). In Fernando Benitez's *In the Magic Land of Peyote*, trans. John Upton (Austin: University of Texas Press, 1975/i), the author's travels with the Huicholes to the land of peyote and his observations about the ritual use of the drug are thoroughly documented. A shamanic ritual involving death is part of James Norman's "The Tarahumaras: Mexico's Long Distance Runners," in *National Geographic*, 149 (May 1976), pp. 702-18. Possibly of use also are Carlos Castaneda's several books documenting his time with the Yaque Indian sorcerer, Don Juan. The principal ones are *The Teachings of Don Juan, A Separate Reality, Journey to Ixtlan*, and *Tales of Power* (New York: Simon and Schuster, 1968, 1971, 1972, and 1975/p, respectively). Just how far any of them reflects ancient practices and beliefs is debatable, but there could be value in looking into them and surmising.

A bibliography that still has some value ought also to be included here. Ralph Steel Bogg's *Bibliography of Latin American Folklore* (New York: H.W. Wilson, 1940/b) is now on the old side, and many of the entries are Spanish-language works, but it does include quite a few entries that *will* be valuable if you get deeply enough into the myths of Middle and/or South America.

Works on Historical/Cultural Background

The ancient civilizations of Middle America have been popular enough that there are now a good many books which treat them in a broad way, several of them including South America too. One of the most interesting for general readers is Victor W. von Hagen's *The Ancient Sun Kingdoms of the Americas* (New York: World Publishing Co., 1957/ib), which has also been published as three separate paperbacks by New American Library under the titles *The Aztecs: Man and Tribe, World of the Maya*, and *Realm of the Incas.* Von Hagen is a lively writer, and the background of the historical and cultural sort that he offers is general, only some of it relating directly to mythology or religion as such. Each volume is well illustrated, has good maps, and includes a comparative chronology. Jonathan Norton Leonard's *Ancient America* (New York: Time-Life Books, 1967) is an even more beautifully illustrated volume covering the civilizations of Middle and South America. The history and culture it discusses have been well researched, and there's a chapter called "Gods and Empires" that myth students will find particularly useful. Cottie A. Burland's *Peoples of the*

Sun: The Civilizations of Pre-Columbian America (New York: Praeger Publishers, 1976/ib) is also a helpful background work covering Middle and South America. It's colorfully illustrated and smoothly written; its main concern is cultural rather than historical, though. Friedrich Katz's volume in the *History of Civilization* series, *Ancient American Civilizations* (New York: Praeger Publishers, 1974/ib), is also a colorful overview, in this case with focus about equally historical and cultural. A. Hyatt Verrill and Ruth Verrill provide good background to Aztec, Mayan, and Incan myth study in their *America's Ancient Civilizations* (New York: G.P. Putnam's Sons, 1953), but the book is not as colorfully illustrated as some other volumes. John Collier's *Indians of the Americas: The Long Hope* (New York: N.A.L. Mentor, 1947/p) covers the history of the Indians of all the Americas in a general way and is probably the best single-volume *introductory* source around. Volumes which broadly survey ancient civilizations may also be useful for introductory purposes: Stuart Piggott's *The Dawn of Civilization: The First World Survey of Human Cultures in Early Times* (New York: McGraw-Hill, 1961/i) includes pretty cursory but nonetheless informative coverage of the pre-Columbian Americas.

Sol Tax edited a collection of essays, *The Civilizations of Ancient America* (New York: Cooper Square Publishers reprint, 1967). The comparative articles at the end are especially interesting ones on the origins of Middle and South American cultures. Barbara A. Leitch's *Chronology of the American Indian* (St. Clair Shores, Mich.: Scholarly Press, 1975) covers all the Americas from 25,000 B.C. to recent times and is a handy volume for reference. Francisco Guerra's *The Pre-Columbian Mind* (New York: Seminar Press, 1971) is an interesting psychoanalytic study of the descendents of the pre-Columbian natives in the three Americas; it examines the nature and extent of acculturation, vestiges of morals and the like that remain—a pretty unusual but useful background work.

Works dealing with the culture and history of Middle America alone are also available. Michael D. Coe's *Mexico* (New York: Praeger Publishers, 1962/ib) is a volume in the fine *Ancient Peoples and Places* series that covers the culture and history of Middle America from the Olmecs through the Spanish conquest. John Eric Thompson's *Mexico Before Cortez* (New York: Charles Scribner's Sons, 1933) is somewhat older, but as with Coe, in Thompson we have a first-rate Middle Americanist (in this case, archaeologist). Because chapter seven in Frederick A. Peterson's

Ancient Mexico: An Introduction to the Pre-Hispanic Cultures (London: Allen & Unwin, 1959/p) is excellent on the matter of Middle American religion generally, you may want to consider the book for cultural/historical background. It has a useful key to pronunciation, too. Richard E. W. Adams' *Prehistoric Mesoamerica* (Boston: Little, Brown, 1978/ib) is a highly readable "synthesis of the prehistoric cultures of Mexico, Guatemala, Belize, and Honduras" that is written by an expert in the archaeology and history of Middle America. *Middle Classic Mesoamerica: A.D. 400–700* (New York: Columbia University Press, 1978/i), a collection of essays by experts edited by Esther Pasztory, has narrower focus in time, but it emphasizes nicely the political, religious, economic, and artistic interrelationships of Middle American cultures during that important time. The writings of renowned Middle American scholars are collected in a volume called *The Maya and Their Neighbors* (Irvington, N.Y.: Herbert Shprentz, 1976/i), ed. Clarence L. Hay *et al*, a volume broad enough in coverage to be quite useful. Henry Bamford Parkes' *A History of Mexico*, 3rd edition (Boston: Houghton Mifflin, 1960) goes beyond the bounds of ancient civilizations, but there's enough on them to make it a helpful introductory work. Finally, don't overlook as a major source the *Handbook of Middle American Indians* (Austin: University of Texas Press, 1964), ed. Robert Wauchope. It has long been an influential work in which can be found a great range of information, including useful details on mythology and religion.

Ignacio Bernal's *Mexico Before Cortez: Art, History and Legend*, revised edition, trans. Willis Barnstone (Garden City, N.Y.: Doubleday Anchor, 1975/ip), in addition to having an excellent pronouncing glossary-gazeteer, is a marvelous introduction to the history that went into the making of Tenochtitlan, the Aztec capital. Bernal, the director of the National Museum of Anthropology in Mexico City, does a fine job here of bringing together the various cultures that were antecedent to the Aztecs and making clear how Aztec greatness came about. *Feathered Serpent and Smoking Mirror: The Gods and Cultures of Ancient Mexico* (New York: G.P. Putnam's Sons, 1975/ib) is a lovely volume in which the text by Cottie A. Burland and photographs by Werner Forman are well paired off in retelling the history of ancient Mexico; it focuses on the beliefs and events that led to the Aztec fall at the hands of the Spanish. There's a great deal here on religion, mythology, and belief. Alfonso Caso's *The Aztecs: People of the Sun* (Norman: University of Oklahoma Press, 1958/i) is beautifully illustrated from various codices as well as with interesting photographs. There's much in it on religion, ritual, and myth. G. C. Vaillant's *Aztecs of Mexico: Origin, Rise and Fall of the Aztec Nation* (Harmondsworth, G.B.: Penguin Books, 1952/ip) is also well illustrated and constitutes an excellent historical source. Miguel Leon-Portilla's *Aztec Thought and Culture* (Norman: University of Oklahoma Press, 1963) is worthwhile for its cultural focus as is Jacques Soustelle's *Daily Life of the Aztecs*, trans. Patrick O'Brian (London: Weidenfeld & Nicolson, 1961/i; New York: Macmillan, 1962). With Caso's, Leon-Portilla's and Soustelle's books behind you, your background to the Aztecs would be pretty impressive.

Among older books, William H. Prescott's classic *The History of the Conquest of Mexico* (originally published in three volumes by Harper & Brothers, 1853; abridged edition, Chicago: University of Chicago Press, 1966) is really a history of more than the conquest, including much on prior history, culture, and religion. Part of the contents of the original work comprises the text of *The World of the Aztecs* (Geneva: Minerva Editions, n.d./i), probably the best volume in Minerva's *The World of . . .* series. It is well illustrated with pictures of ruins and artifacts, Toltec, Zapotec, and others included, and it has Prescott's interesting chapter on correspondences between old and new world myths, culture, and architecture. Fray Diego Duran's *The Aztecs: The History of the Indies of New Spain*, trans. Doris Heyden and Fernando Horcasitas (New York: Orion Press, translated reprint of the sixteenth century work, 1964) was lost until the mid-nineteenth century but is indeed a major source on Aztec history, belief, and customs since Duran lived among the Aztecs and saw first-hand. There're also modern-day descendents of the Aztecs you may wish to look into. James Norman's "The Huichols: Mexico's People of Myth and Magic," in *National Geographic*, 151 (June 1977/i), pp. 832–53, includes details of interest concerning the Huichols' beliefs, rituals, and shaman.

The Maya have also received a good deal of attention. John Eric Thompson's *The Rise and Fall of Maya Civilization* (Norman: University of Oklahoma Press, 1956/i) has the distinct advantage, as a history, of having been written by one of the principal archaeologists involved in excavating Mayan sites. His *Mayan History and Religion* (Norman: University of Oklahoma Press, 1970/ib) devotes equal attention to the history and mythology/religion. Sylvanus Griswold Morley's *The Ancient Maya* (Stanford, Calif.: Stanford University Press, 1946/i) is also a fine, rich history of the Maya, well illustrated and with a good chapter on religion and the gods. Michael D. Coe's *The Maya* (London: Thames and Hudson, 1966/ib), a volume in the *Ancient Peoples and Places* series, is a nicely written and illustrated survey of the Maya, their history and culture, as is Charles Gallenkamp's *Maya: The Riddle and Rediscovery of a Lost Civilization*, revised and expanded edition (New York: David McKay, 1976/ib). Elizabeth P. Benson's *The Maya World* (New York: Apollo Editions, 1972/ip; originally Thomas Y. Crowell) is a lively, if brief, introduction to the Maya written by an expert. G. W. Brainerd's *The Maya Civilization* (Los Angeles: Southwest Museum, 1954/i) would also serve as a brief introduction. *The Mysterious Maya* (Washington, D.C.: National Geographic Society, n.d.) is a beautifully illustrated and interesting volume that can be read profitably by anyone from junior high on up. So, too, with *Monuments of Ancient Civilization: Maya* (New York: Madison Square Press, 1973/i), a nicely done, up-to-date suvey. R. Karen's *The Maya: The Song of the Quail* (New York: Scholastic Book Service, 1972/i) is a colorful introduction to the Maya meant for fifth to eleventh graders. Vittoria Calvani's *The Maya* (Geneva: Minerva Editions, 1976) is illustrated, but it hasn't the good text many of the preceding volumes have. David Grant Adamson's *The Ruins of Time: Four and a Half Centuries of Conquest and Discovery Among the Maya* (New York: Praeger Publishers, 1975/ib) deals with just about every facet of the western world's discovery of the Maya from the sixteenth century through the later archaeological finds. Not every site is dealt with, but most are—and in lively manner. Richard E. W. Adams' *The Classic Maya Collapse*, ed. T. Patrick Culbert (Albuquerque: University of New Mexico Press, 1973) covers just about all that is known concerning the Mayan decline and abandonment of centers at a time well before the Spanish conquest. You'll also find that Brian Fagan's "What Caused the Collapse of the Maya" covers the subject well enough for most purposes. It's an article in *Mysteries of the Past* (New York: American Heritage Publishing Co., 1977/i). Findings in Belize indicate that "The Earliest Maya" lived there in 2,500 B.C.; Norman Hammond's article with that title can be found in *Scientific American*, 236 (March 1977), pp. 116-23, 126-28, 130, 133. A simply lovely series of four articles on the Maya—from ancient to modern, with numerous photographs of artifacts and sites, as well as paintings depicting ancient activities—can be found in *National Geographic*, 148 (December 1975/i), pp. 728-811. It is well enough done to serve as brief, extravagantly colorful introduction to the Maya. And if you're interested in looking into modern descendents, try the article by Louis de la Haba entitled "Guatemala, Maya and Modern," *National Geographic,* 146 (November 1974/i), pp. 661–89.

Where the relation between Aztec/Mayan myths and those of the other cultures is concerned, collections of Middle American myths do not as a rule provide much insight. However, Ignacio Bernal's *The Olmec World,* trans. Doris Heyden and Fernando Horcasitas (Berkeley: University of California Press, 1969/ip) is an exceptionally interesting and informative survey. So are Joseph W. Whitecotton's *The Zapotecs: Princes, Priests, and Peasants* (Norman: University of Oklahoma Press, 1977/ib) and Nigel Davies' *The Toltecs: Until the Fall of Tula* (Norman: University of Oklahoma Press, 1978/ib). Whitecotton's book covers both ancient and modern Zapotecs, and while Davies' book is concerned only with the Toltecs through their habitation of the site known as Tula, a sequel volume is planned in which the Toltecs will be covered to more recent times. Another book, Ronald Spores' *The Mixtec Kings and Their People* (Norman: University of Oklahoma Press, 1970/i) is a good examination of Mixtec culture and political order. Miguel Covarrubias' *Mexico South: The Isthmus of Tehuantepec* (New York: Alfred A. Knopf, 1947/i) focuses on a major settlement area in Mexico, ancient and modern, and as in Bernal's, Whitecotton's, and Davies' books, there is some attention paid to religion, myth, and allied practices.

Works on the Origins of Middle American Indians; Contacts

Where the numerous cultures in Middle America came from originally is, as I mentioned earlier, disputed, but perhaps the greater and more important matter concerns their contacts. At this stage, it would appear that influence could well have included contact with ancient Mediterranean cultures, East Asian cultures, and maybe even Norse and African. A good way to get into the subject is through Lionel Casson's "Who First Crossed the Oceans?" in *Mysteries of the Past* (New York: American Heritage Publishing Co., 1977/i). It is a general article involving other places and instances, but much of it is devoted to Middle America's possible contacts. Thoroughgoing and up-to-date treatment of the issues and evidence can be found in Nigel Davies' *Voyagers to the New World* (New York: William Morrow, 1979/ib). Davies is level headed and a well-known Middle Americanist. Carroll L. Riley's "Interhemispheric Contacts? Comments on a Controversy," an article in

Archaeology, 31 (November–December 1978/b), pp. 59–61, is a
good summary article in which the pro's and con's of diffusionism
are completely discussed. Robert Wauchope's *Lost Tribes and
Sunken Continents* (Chicago: University of Chicago Press, 1962/
ibp) is a good overview in which the various theories of origin and
diffusion are looked into—Egyptian, Phoenician, Hebrew, and
others. *Early Man in America* (San Francisco: W. H. Freeman,
1973/i) is a series of articles from *Scientific American* that work
through the archaeological evidence on the origins of Middle
American cultures. Gordon F. Ekholm's "Transpacific Contacts,"
Betty J. Meggers' "North and South American Cultural Connections and Convergences," and Morris Swadash's "Linguistic
Overview" are three especially good articles on the contacts problems. They're included in *Prehistoric Man in the New World*
(Chicago: University of Chicago Press, 1964), ed. Jesse D. Jennings
and Edward Norbeck. Articles by David E. Kelley, Alice B. Keyhoe,
and others in *Man Across the Sea* (Austin: University of Texas
Press, 1971) will also be worth looking into, as will James A. Ford's
*A Comparison of Formative Cultures in the Americas: Diffusion
or the Psychic Unity of Man* (Washington, D.C.: Smithsonian
Institution, 1969). Charles Berlitz's *Mysteries from Forgotten
Worlds* (Garden City, N.Y.: Doubleday, 1972) is more concerned
with the issue over original migration from Asia, but there is a
good review of diffusionist arguments in the book. Volume IV of
Handbook of Middle American Indians (Austin: University of
Texas Press, 1966), ed. Gordon F. Ekholm and Gordon R. Willey,
focuses on contacts with the old world, China included. Especially
useful are the contrasting articles by Philip Phillips, "The Role of
Transpacific Contacts in the Development of the New World Pre-
Columbian Civilizations," and Robert Heine-Geldern, "The Prob-
lem of Transpacific Influences in Mesoamerica." Ekholm's article
"Is American Indian Culture Asiatic?" in *Natural History*, 59
(October 1950), pp. 344–51, 382, is also quite useful, as is Betty J.
Meggers' "The Transpacific Origin of MesoAmerican Civilization:
A Preliminary Review of the Evidence and Its Theoretical Implica-
tions," in *American Anthropologist*, 77 (March 1975), pp. 1–27.
A book fairly heavy on the deduction and short on proof, but
certainly provocative, is R. A. Jairazbhoy's *Ancient Egyptians and
Chinese in America* (London: George Prior Associated, 1974). The
same kind of comment can be made about Ivan van Sertima's
*They Came Before Columbus: The African Presence in Ancient
America* (New York: Random House, 1977), which pushes as its

premise that Africans visited the Americas as early as 600 B.C. Of course, Thor Heyerdahl made more substantial the thinking that crossing the Atlantic in small boats was at least a possibility; see his *The Ra Expeditions*, trans. Patricia Crampton (Garden City, N.Y.: Doubleday, 1971) for the full account. His *Early Man and the Ocean: A Search for the Beginnings of Navigation and Seaborne Civilization* (Garden City, N.Y.: Doubleday, 1979/b) is concerned with more than just Middle America, but it will be worth looking into.

A book I personally found to contain pretty convincing evidence of the diffusionists' claims is Alexander von Wuthenau's *Unexpected Faces in Ancient America: 1500 B.C.-A.D. 1500* (New York: Crown Publishers, 1975/ib). The book is loaded with pictures of faces in ancient Middle American art, which show various ethnic origins as well as differing artistic styles. Von Wuthenau, an art historian, provides excellent background to the different diffusionist theories as well as making his case for contact. Michael D. Coe's *The Jaguar's Children: Pre-Classical Central Mexico* (New York: The Museum of Primitive Art, 1965/i) covers the years 800–300 B.C., the heyday of Olmec culture. Principally concerned with Olmec art and culture, there's much here to fire diffusionist arguments since much of the art shows rather remarkable similarities to that of trans-oceanic cultures, Near and Far East alike. Constance Irwin's *Fair Gods and Stone Faces* (New York: St. Martin's Press, 1963/i) is a fascinating, if highly speculative, book that deals with the precursors of the Aztecs, Incas, and Mayans. It is a popularized discussion that suggests Phoenician-Carthaginian voyages across the ocean to Middle America. One of the most colorful of the diffusionist polemics—pictures, maps, diagrams, slick text—is James Bailey's *The God-Kings and the Titans: The New World Ascendancy in Ancient Times* (New York: St. Martin's Press, 1973/ib). It relies heavily on the evidence of mythology and archaeology, making it one of the better books for myth students, but be aware it *is* pretty speculative! The same diffusionist zeal is evident in Hugh Fox's *Gods of the Cataclysm: A Revolutionary Investigation of Man and His Gods Before and After the Great Cataclysm* (New York: Harper's Magazine Press, 1976/ib), and there's even a touch of von Daniken euhemerism. Fox's interest is broader than just Middle American cultures, but there's a good deal on them in the book nonetheless.

If you're interested in the diffusion of Middle American culture northward into the southwestern United States, some of the works

included in the section on North American Indian mythology will
be helpful. As a starter, though, I recommend two articles by A. H.
Schroeder: "Unregulated Diffusion from Mexico into the Southwest Prior to A.D. 700," which you'll find in *American Antiquity*,
30 (1965), pp. 297-309, and "Pattern Diffusion from Mexico into
the Southwest after A.D. 600," which is in *American Antiquity*,
31 (1966), pp. 683-704.

Works on Archaeology

Much of what constitutes the diffusionist argument is archaeological in basis, of course. Middle America has not been the scene
of quite as much archaeological work as some regions in the
Middle East and Europe, but what has been done has had results
at least as spectacular. Muriel Porter Weaver's *The Aztecs, Maya,
and Their Predecessors: Archaeology of MesoAmerica* (New York:
Seminar Press, 1972/i) is a history of Middle America through
archaeology, making it a good overview and "way in" to what has
been done there in archaeology. Ignacio Bernal's *A History of
Mexican Archaeology* (London: Thames and Hudson, 1979/i)
may be even better as a source for such information, given the
renown of its author. Claude F. Bandez's *Central America*, trans.
James Hogarth (London: Barrie & Jenkins, 1970/i), a lovely
volume in the *Archaeologia Mundi* series, is a good survey of
archaeological finds. Robert Wauchope's *They Found the Buried
Cities* (Chicago: University of Chicago Press, 1965/ip) is an excellent book in which the great archaeologists of Middle America
tell about their work, problems, and discoveries. Part six of *Hands
on the Past: Pioneer Archaeologists Tell Their Own Stories* (New
York: Alfred A. Knopf, 1966/ip), ed. C.W. Ceram, has ten excerpts
from the writings of archaeologists who worked in Middle and
South America. Another good source of primary accounts, are
parts two through four of Leo Deuel's *Conquistadors Without
Swords: Archaeologists in the Americas* (New York: St. Martin's
Press, 1967/ibp). Ceram's *Gods, Graves, and Scholars*, 2nd edition,
trans. E.B. Garside and Sophie Wilkins (New York: Bantam Books,
1972/ip; originally in shorter hardbound edition published by
Knopf). Peter Tompkins' *Mysteries of the Mexican Pyramids*
(New York: Harper & Row, 1976/ib) is concerned with the total
history of what has been said about the pyramids of Middle
America. Whatever discoveries have been made, whatever theories
have been ventured, and whatever comparisons of the pyramids

with those elsewhere that can be made will probably be found in this superbly illustrated volume.

Guides to Mexican ruins are readily available. Roman Pina Chan's *Guide to Mexican Archaeology* (Claremont, Calif.: Ocelot Press, 1975/ip) is a useful general work, but an even better volume is C. Bruce Hunter's *A Guide to Ancient Mexican Ruins* (Norman: University of Oklahoma Press, 1977/ip), which is a companion volume to his earlier *A Guide to Ancient Maya Ruins* (also University of Oklahoma Press, 1976/ip). Hans Helfritz's *Mexican Cities of the Gods: An Archaeological Guide* (New York: Praeger Publishers, 1970/ip) is a colorful and helpful guide, too. There's also a series of inexpensive "Easy" guides published in English in Mexico that should be mentioned. The series includes *The Easy Guide to Monte Alban*, *The Easy Guide to Palenque* (ibp), and a number of others, all by Richard Bloomgarden, all running thirty-odd pages in length, with maps and plenty of illustrations. They're published by Ammex Asociados, S.A., Lago Silverio No. 224, Mexico 17, D.F., Mexico.

Works dealing with the archaeology of specific cultures or places may be worth looking into as you get more deeply into Middle American myth study. J. Eric Thompson's *Maya Archaeologist* (Norman: University of Oklahoma Press, 1963/ip), for instance, includes the author's reminiscences as an archaeologist in the Yucatan and elsewhere. Thompson is a colorful writer and affords many insights into Mayan life, ideals, culture that make it quite a useful bit of reading. William M. Ferguson's lovely *Maya Ruins of Mexico in Color* (Norman: Univeristy of Oklahoma Press, 1977/i) surveys all of the major Mayan sites within Mexico's borders—a visually exciting volume if ever there was one. Robert L. Brunhouse's *In Search of the Maya: The First Archaeologists* (Albuquerque: University of New Mexico Press, 1973/ib) describes, chapter by chapter, the pioneering archaeological work of eight men in Mayan Mexico, Honduras, and Guatemala. George F. Andrews' *Maya Cities: Placemaking and Urbanization* (Norman: University of Oklahoma Press, 1975/ib) is a large, superbly illustrated volume you'll possibly find of greatest use for pictures of ruins, diagrams, and plans. Francis Robicsek's *Copan: Home of the Mayan Gods* (New York: Museum of the American Indian, 1972/i) is also a beautiful book, this one dealing with one of the most famous Mayan sites in Honduras. There's much on the Temple of the Inscriptions in Alberto Ruz Lhuillier's "The Mystery of the Temple of the Inscriptions" in *Archaeology*,

6 (March 1953/i), pp. 3-11. While Evan Connell is interested in showing how adult preoccupations—as with ruins—can be traced to childhood interests in his "The Aztec Treasure House: Our Passions Are Never Accidental," *Harper's*, 255 (October 1977), pp. 80-84, the article is a pretty fair introduction to the archaeological finds of Middle America, principally Olmec. Lawrence Elliott's "Monte Alban, City of the Gods," *Reader's Digest*, 3 (May 1977/i), pp. 202-08, is an introduction to the Zapotec-Mixtec ruins located high above the Oaxaca Valley in western Mexico. Richard MacNeish's "Ancient Mesoamerican Civilization," in *Science*, 143 (February 7, 1964), pp. 531-37, is an analysis of the phases of civilized occupation of the Tehuacan Valley in Mexico, much the same as is his article entitled "The Origin of New World Civilization" in *Scientific American*, 211 (November 1964/i), pp. 29-37. Susan W. Miles uses myth and other evidence to establish how long man lived at a location in Guatemala in her "Mam Residence and the Maize Myth," in *Culture in History: Essays in Honor of Paul Radin* (New York: Columbia University Press, 1960), ed. Stanley Diamond. Also, you'll find some interesting information on Middle American themes and sites in Gerald S. Hawkins' *Beyond Stonehenge* (New York: Harper & Row, 1973/i), but you'll have to use the index to do so.

Works on Art

In addition to the art discussions and photographs you'll find in some of the books included above, there are many other works that can be looked to for art. There's minimal text in Maria Antonieta Cervantes' *Treasures of Ancient Mexico: From the National Anthropological Museum* (New York: Crescent Books, 1978), but it's loaded with excellent color photographs of the art (and crafts) of the ancient Toltecs, Maya, Zapotecs, Olmecs, and others. G.H.S. Bushnell's *Ancient Arts of the Americas* (New York: Frederick A. Praeger, 1965) is a good introduction that includes all of the ancient Americas. Miguel Covarrubias' *Indian Art of Mexico and Central America* (New York: Alfred A. Knopf, 1957/ib) has fine text and over 200 illustrations, many in color, covering pre-Columbian art from most ancient to Spanish conquest. Hasso von Winning's *Pre-Columbian Art of Mexico and Central America* (New York: Harry N. Abrams, 1968/i) is also a beautiful book loaded with superb illustrations and informative text. *The*

Art of Ancient America (New York: Crown Publishers, 1961), by H.D. Disselhoff and Sigvald Linne, covers Middle and South America and is particularly useful for pictures and also has a fairly good textual complement. *Art in Ancient Mexico* (New York: Oxford University Press, 1941/i), by Gilbert Medioni and Marie-Therese Pinto, is useful for its 258 black and white photos only, the text being no more than brief descriptions of the book's photographs. Pal Keleman's *Medieval American Art* (New York: Macmillan, 1943/i), is a two-volume set, one volume devoted to discussions of pre-Columbian art and the other to pictures alone. George Kubler's *Art and Architecture of Ancient America* (Harmondsworth, G.B.: Penguin, 1962) is a brief survey of Middle American art, architecture included; the text, in this case, is more valuable than the comparatively few pictures. S.K. Lothrop's *Treasures of Ancient America: The Arts of the Pre-Columbian Civilizations from Mexico to Peru* (Cleveland: World Publishing Co., 1964/i) is a big and beautiful art book divided into four sections: Mexico, Maya, Intermediate Area, Peru. Bradley Smith's *Mexico: A History in Art* (Garden City, N.Y.: Doubleday, 1971/i) is also a beautifully illustrated book in large format; it tells the history of Mexico from Olmec to modern through text and pictures (240 in full color). Cottie A. Burland's *Art and Life in Ancient Mexico* (Oxford: Bruno Cassirer, 1947/i) is a little book in which pictures and text are meshed to describe life in ancient Mexico. A. Emmerich's *Art Before Columbus* (New York: Simon and Schuster, n.d./ip) is a brief art history with 150 illustrations. Jacques Soustelle's *Mexico: Prehispanic Paintings* (New York: New York Graphic Society in cooperation with UNESCO, 1958/i) is a pretty comprehensive survey.

More specialized still are such books as Herbert Joseph Spinden's *Maya Art and Civilizations* (Indian Hills, Colo.: Falcon's Wing Press, 1957/i), a sweeping review of the motifs, styles, and purposes of Mayan art; Ferdinand Anton's *Art of the Maya* (New York: G.P. Putnam's Sons, 1970/i), a colorful survey and history of Mayan art in its many forms; and Tatiana Proskouriakoff's *Classic Maya Sculpture* (Washington, D.C.: Carnegie Institution Publication #593, 1950/i), a brief look into Mayan sculpture of the classical period. Cottie A. Burland's *Magic Books of Mexico* (originally Harmondsworth, G.B.: Penguin, 1953; reprinted in Mexico City by Ediciones Lara, 1966/ip) has in it great color plates depicting mainly Aztec deities as painted by the Aztecs

themselves. Finally, there's a section in David Attenborough's
The Tribal Eye (New York: W.W. Norton, 1977/i) devoted to
Mixtec art.

Should you need further help with both the art and archaeology
of Middle America, Aubyu Kendall's *The Art and Archaeology of
Pre-Columbian Middle America: An Annotated Bibliography of
Works in English* (Boston: G.K. Hall, 1977/b) is a first-rate work
to turn to.

Works on Decipherment

A good place to start with the decipherment of Middle American
Indian glyphs, Mayan especially, is Leo Deuel's *Testaments of
Time: The Search for Lost Manuscripts and Records* (New York:
Alfred A. Knopf, 1965). There are three chapters in the book
which cumulatively cover the history of decipherment in Middle
America, with Mayan and Mixtec glyphs the principal focus.
David Humiston Kelley's *Deciphering the Maya Script* (Austin:
University of Texas Press, 1976/i) is a summary of what is known
about Mayan writing to date; it's a large book with many illustra-
tions of the writing. For a briefer survey, see his "A History of the
Decipherment of Maya Script" in *Anthropological Linguistics*,
4 (1961). J. Eric Thompson's *Maya Hieroglyphic Writing: An
Introduction* (Norman: University of Oklahoma Press, 1960/i),
like Kelley's book, is excellent for its text and illustrations, but
Kelley's is more up-to-date in an area that needs constant updating
as new texts and inscriptions are translated. Sylvanus G. Morley's
An Introduction to the Study of the Maya Hieroglyphics (New
York: Dover Publications, 1975/ip; reprint of the 1915 edition)
is now pretty dated. Thompson's *A Commentary on the Dresden
Codex* (Philadelphia: American Philosophical Association, 1972/i)
is a good example of deciphering a codex; it presents facing pages
of codex and commentary/translation. William Edward Gates' *An
Outline Dictionary of Maya Glyphs* (Baltimore: Johns Hopkins
Press, 1931) is now dated by later translations and finds, but it is
interesting for neophyte readers of Mayan. Michael D. Coe's *The
Maya Scribe and His World* (New York: Grolier Club, 1973/i), a
large, well illustrated book, tells about scribes during the classic
period and has, along the way, *much* that is directly related
to myth study.

South American Indian Mythologies

It has been said that the typical Mercator Projection of the world—
you know the map, rectangular and flat, with the Americas right
about in the middle—is in part responsible for a distorted view of
our importance in the world that we United States Americans
have. There we are stage center, only Mexico more exactly so.
If we are to follow this line of thinking further, it should follow
that we U.S. Americans ought to know quite a bit more about
the rest of the Americas, given their relative Mercator centrality
than most of us do.

I can't account for what constitutes your knowledge, but
the world history that I was exposed to in school, to my recollec-
tion, did nothing in particular to enlighten me about Ecuador's
history or Brazil's, and the "world" literature I read was European,
Russian, and token Oriental when it wasn't British or U.S. American in origin. As a matter of fact, until I got fairly far into myth
study just a few years ago, my knowledge of South America
was a sad hodge-podge of unrelated facts and oddments headed
by a reasonably complete list of countries, a few names of cities,
the location of Cape Horn, the importance of two rivers (the
Amazon, of course, and the Orinoco), a belief that the Incas and
Peru were best thought of together, the names of a handful of
writers (Pablo Neruda, Gabriela Mistral, and a number of other
international prize winners), and the knowledge that one of the
world's great films is the Brazilian *Black Orpheus.* There may well
have been more then in my understanding of South America, but
the fact that nothing more comes to mind must mean something.
All I know is that had it not been for a seventh grade geography
teacher, an interest in postage stamps, a fair reading knowledge of
Spanish, and a couple of college courses in cinema, heaven surely
knows that the sad hodge-podge would have been sadder still!

It is fact that South American Indian mythology (mythologies,
more exactly) has not been treated very extensively in English.
Compared with what has been done with North American Indian
mythology, the South American counterpart comes off very
poorly indeed, so poorly as to make this section of the guide one
of the less satisfying ones. Despite the fact that anthropological
work has been progressing with the contemporary "primitive"
groups in South America and that archaeologists have turned up
two especially rich zones of ancient finds—one in the Andes and

along the adjacent Pacific coast from just above Chiclayo in Peru south to La Paz in Bolivia, the other in northern Venezuela and Colombia—little in the way of publications in English has emerged. If anything, getting into South American Indian mythology without a reading knowledge of Spanish is a catch-as-catch-can affair.

Collections of the Myths

Fortunately there's the *International Mythology* series and an excellent volume in it, Harold Osborne's *South American Mythology* (London: Paul Hamlyn, 1968/ib). This beautifully illustrated book is divided into five major sections: Introduction, Inca, Collao, Myths and Legends of the Coast, and Marginal, Forest and Southern Andean Peoples. The introduction offers fine general background, covering as it does the peoples and regions of South America. This coupled with the regional handling of the myths makes the book first rate where no other even remotely like it can be found—written in English, that is. There's a short twelve-page chapter on South American Indian mythology in the *Larousse World Mythology* (New York: G.P. Putnam's Sons, 1965/i), ed. Pierre Grimal, trans. Patricia Beardsworth. It is topically organized but too-brief in its coverage of the myths overall to make it more than a quick introduction. Only eight pages are devoted to the myths in the *Larousse Encyclopedia of Mythology* (London: Paul Hamlyn, 1959/ip), ed. Felix Guirand, trans. Richard Aldington and Delano Ames. The organization here is regional, but with fewer than three pages devoted to myths of the Incas, fewer yet to other groups. The situation is at least as bad in Volume IV of the *Pears Encyclopedia of Myths and Legends* (London: Pelham Books, 1978/i) and is even worse in the *Encyclopedia of World Mythology* (New York: Galahad Books, 1975/i). In the latter work, the section entitled "South America" has in it Middle American (!) myths and there is only a single column devoted to myths of the Incas, but four columns for "Brazilian"; no other groups are represented. Veronica Ions' *The World's Mythology in Colour* (London: Paul Hamlyn, 1974/i) has less than three pages on South American Indian mythology but does have the saving grace of almost ten pages of lovely pictures.

Apart from these few modern sources, there are some older ones. Volume XI of the old standard *Mythology of All Races* series (Boston: Marshall Jones Co., 1916–32; reprinted in New York by Cooper Square Press, 1964, etc.) is Hartley Burr Alexander's

Latin American Mythology. Although it has more on Middle American mythology than it does South American, in lieu of all else, the book is a useful source. Donald A. Mackenzie's *Myths of Pre-Columbian America,* in the series called *Myth and Legend in Literature and Art* (London: Gresham Publishing Co., 1918/i), has only a few South American myths in it, its principal focus being North and Middle American. Lewis Spence's *The Myths of Mexico and Peru* (London: A. Constable & Co., 1907/i) has a reasonable selection of myths of the Incas and other ancient Peruvian cultures, but no more on South American Indian myths. Daniel G. Brinton's *Myths of the Americas: The Symbolism and Mythology of the Indians of the Americas* (Blauvelt, N.Y.: Multimedia, 1976/p; originally published as *The Myths of the New World* in 1868) is mainly naturalist analytical, but there are a few South American Indian myths told in it.

Also, there are seven South American Indian creation myths included in Maria Leach's fine *The Beginning: Creation Myths Around the World* (New York: Funk and Wagnalls, 1956), and chapter eleven of James George Frazer's *Myths of the Origin of Fire* (London: Macmillan, 1930) is devoted to South America.

You'll find a number of South American Indian myths told in what amounts to primary works in Hugh Fox's *First Fire: Central and South American Indian Poetry* (Garden City, N.Y.: Doubleday Anchor, 1978/bp). Although Fox's interpretations and commentaries are sometimes to be questioned, the copious notes he provides are generally quite helpful. You'll find many myths of the Brazilian Xingu Indians in essentially primary form also in O. and C. Villas-Boas' *Xingu: The Indians, Their Myths* (New York: Farrar, Straus and Giroux, 1974). Alfred Metraux's *Myths of the Toba and Pilaga Indians of the Gran Chaco* (Philadelphia: American Folklore Society, 1946) is chock-full of myths from these two Argentinian tribes—in primary form, too. Clements Markham translated two works that will be useful in your study of the myths of the Inca: Cristobal de Molina's *The Fables and Rites of the Yncas* (London: Hakluyt Society, 1873) and *Apu Ollantay* (Lima: Ediciones Markham, 1964). Molina's work is on the "Rites and Laws of the Yncas," so its concern is broader than just conveying myths, but there are plenty of them included. *Apu Ollantay* is supposedly an Incan dramatic work which was performed in Peru right through the eighteenth century, and although it is a background work rather than clearly a source of myths, so many are inherent that it is useful for the myths, too. *The Singing Mountaineers—Songs and Tales of the Quechua People* (Austin: University of Texas Press, 1957), collected by J.M. Arguedas and edited by R. Stephen, has lots of myth-related material of the Quechua, a Peruvian/Bolivian mountain tribe. L.C. Faron's *Hawks of the Sun* (Pittsburgh: University of Pittsburgh Press, 1964) has a good many native Chilean myths in it.

Studies of the Myths

Studies of the South American Indian myths—analyses, comparisons, interpretations, and the like—are particularly hard to come by. The renowned anthropologist Claude Lévi-Strauss has worked extensively with some of the South American myths, and two volumes of his *Introduction to a Science of Mythology* have been published in English: *The Raw and the Cooked* and *From Honey to Ashes* (New York: Harper & Row, 1970/p and 1973/p respectively). Both are difficult reading for those not acquainted with the Lévi-Strauss structuralist system, but the "Overture" to the former volume is something of an introduction to his methodology. In *The Raw and the Cooked*, selected Amazonian myths are worked with, and in *From Honey to Ashes*, only South American Indian myths having to do with tobacco are investigated. The "Overture" to *The Raw and the Cooked*, by the way, has been reprinted elsewhere, in *Studies on Mythology* (Homewood, Ill.: The Dorsey Press, 1968/p), ed. Robert A. Georges, among other places. Other than those two books by Lévi-Strauss, though, the pickings are slim to nonexistent. The beliefs of the Huarochiri, a Peruvian highland tribe, were picked apart handily—a kind of myth analysis, to be sure—by Father Francisco de Avila in his *A Narrative of the Errors, False Gods and Other Superstitions and Diabolical Rites in Which the Indians of Huarochiri Lived in Ancient Times* (London: Hakluyt Society, 1873). You may wish to look into it at some time—mainly for laughs. Ralph Steele Boggs' *Bibliography of Latin American Folklore* (New York: H.W. Wilson, 1940), is now dated but still useful, especially if you care to go into Spanish language works.

Works on Religion and Related Matters

Works that deal specifically with religion and ritual are also pretty hard to come by, and, once again, the best sources for information on this subject will be found among the collections of myths discussed earlier and in the cultural/historical sources covered further on. There is, however, a useful discussion of ancient South American Indian religions in parts two and four of *Pre-Columbian American Religions* (New York: Holt, Rinehart and Winston, 1968), ed. Walter Krickeberg, *et al*, trans. Starley Davis. Also, Julian H. Steward's "South American Indian Religions," is a brief overview that should be helpful; you'll find it in *Ancient Religions* (New York: Citadel Press, 1965/p; originally published as *Forgotten Religions*, 1950), ed. Vergilius Ferm. A few useful sections on religion can be found in *Death and the After Life in Pre-Columbian America* (Washington, D.C.: Dumbarton Oaks Research Library and Collections, 1975), ed. Elizabeth P. Benson, and two articles in *Culture in History: Essays in Honor of Paul Radin* (New York: Columbia University Press, 1960), ed. Stanley Diamond, are worth considering—John V. Murra's "Rite and Crop in the Inca State" and John Howland Rowe's "The Origins of Creator Worship Among the Incas." G. Reichel-Dolmatoff's *Amazonian Cosmos: The Sexual and Religious Symbolism of the Tukano Indians* (Chicago: University of Chicago Press, 1971) is certainly a worthwhile book on the myths of Amazonian Indians. So, too, is Irving Goldman's "The Structure of Ritual in the Northwest Amazon," in *Process and Pattern in Culture* (Chicago: Aldine Publishing Co., 1964), ed. Robert A. Manners. The function of ritual in culture is really the subject of the essay, but there's much on its local uses. Louis C. Faron's "Shamanism and Sorcery Among the Mapuche (Araucanians) of Chile" is in that same book.

Works on Historical/Cultural Background

Works that deal with cultural/historical background to the study of South American Indian myth are numerous and should also be considered as sources for myth, art, and religion since works that deal specifically with these areas of study are at such a premium.

Mariano Picao Salas' *A Cultural History of South America* (Los Angeles: University of California Press, 1965) is a fine, broad work that may well be the best way to get general background. So, too, is Hubert Herring's *A History of Latin America*, 2nd edition (New York: Alfred A. Knopf, 1962), but its major emphasis is on modern history and coverage of *all* the Latin American countries. *Handbook of South American Indians* (Washington, D.C.: Bureau of Ethnology, 1947), ed. Julian H. Steward, is much more to the myth student's immediate purposes since it deals extensively with both ancient and modern South American Indians. *Native Peoples of South America* (New York: McGraw-Hill, 1959) is intended by its authors, Julian H. Steward and Louis C. Faron, as a summary of and speculative addition to the *Handbook* and is well worth looking into once you've seen the *Handbook*. *Peoples and Cultures of Native South America* (Garden City, N.Y.: Doubleday Anchor, 1977), ed. Daniel R. Gross, is a good collection of essays on South American archaeology and culture especially. John Collier's *Indians of the Americas: The Long Hope* (New York: N.A.L. Mentor, 1947) covers all the Americas and is too brief to be very helpful, but it *is* good background to such matters as the origins of the Indians and their interrelationships. Barbara A. Leitch's *Chronology of the American Indian* (St. Clair Shores, Mich.: Scholarly Press, 1975) is a good reference volume which covers the Indians of all the Americas from 25,000 B.C. to recent times.

Works concerned with just the ancient cultures include a few that are quite colorful. Jonathan Norton Leonard's *Ancient America* (New York: Time-Life Books, 1967/ib) covers the pre-Columbian civilizations of Middle and South America. It is a volume in the *Great Ages of Man* series, has marvelous illustrations, useful charts, and even a chapter directly useful to the myth student, "Gods and Empires." Cottie A. Burland's *Peoples of the Sun: The Civilizations of Pre-Columbian America* (New York: Praeger Publishers, 1976/ib) is another lovely volume, in this case by a known expert, which focuses on ancient Mexico, Central America, and Peru. *America's Ancient Civilizations* (New York: G.P. Putnam's Sons, 1953), by A. Hyatt and Ruth Verrill, provides helpful background to Aztec, Mayan, and Incan myth and includes some discussion of the religions and gods involved. Friedrich Katz's *Ancient American Civilizations* (New York: Praeger Publications, 1972/ib), a work in Praeger's *History of Civilization* series, is beautifully illustrated coverage of Middle and South American ancient cultures. Also, don't overlook ancient histories which might include some help on South American cultures; for instance, Stuart Piggott's *The Dawn of Civilization: The First World Survey of Human Cultures in Early Times* (New York: McGraw-Hill, 1961) has a concise but most informative section on the pre-Columbian Americas. Also valuable, Francisco Guerra's *The Pre-Columbian Mind* (New York: Seminar Press, 1971) is a psychoanalysis of the descendants of the pre-Columbians that examines their acculturation and vestiges of ancestral ways that remain in their lives and character.

There are a great many works on the ancient Andes and Peru generally. *The Andes* (New York: Grosset and Dunlop, 1977/ib), by Robert Magni and Enrico Guidoni, trans. Mondadori, is a magnificent, oversized volume in the *Monuments of Civilization* series. It covers the major ancient Peruvian cultures, including the Incas, the Chavin, the Nazca, and many others, making it a valuable resource. *An Ancient World Preserved: Relics and Records of Prehistory in the Andes* (New York: Crown Publishers, 1976/i), revised and updated by Frederic Andre Engel, trans. Rachael Kendall Gordon, is also a lovely volume, as is Philip A. Means' *Ancient Civilizations of the Andes* (New York: Scribner's, 1931, 1964/i). The latter volume has over ninety pages devoted to religion, myth, ritual, and philosophy among the Incas principally. *Andean Culture History*, 2nd edition (Garden City, N.Y.: Doubleday Natural History Press, 1960), by Wendell C. Bennett and Junius Bird, is both a cultural history and archaeological survey of ancient Andean cultures. It doesn't have many pictures, something that pertains also to G.H.S. Bushnell's *The Ancient People of the Andes* (Harmondsworth, G.B.: Penguin Books, 1949/p), but both volumes are excellent background sources that include at least some discussion directly useful in myth study. John Alden Mason's *The Ancient Civilizations of Peru*, revised edition, (Harmondsworth, G.B.: Penguin Books, 1964/ip) is, in contrast, well illustrated in black and white. It covers just about all of Peru's ancient history (which is considerable, as you may know); part three is devoted to the Incas, with chapter thirteen in that part on Incan religion. Victor W. von Hagen's *The Desert Kingdoms of Peru* (London: Weidenfeld and Nicolson, 1965/ib) covers the Mohicas and Chimus especially and is a most useful historical and archaeological survey which includes, in chapter four, some discussion of beliefs and religion. *The Mohica: A Culture of Peru* (New York: Praeger Publishers, 1972/i), by Elizabeth D. Benson, covers the Mohica very well, by the way. Hans Baumann's *Gold and Gods of Peru*, trans. Stella Humphries (London: Oxford University Press, 1963/i) covers broadly the culture, history, beliefs, and customs of ancient Peruvian cultures—with beautiful illustrations. R.J. Owens' *Peru* (London: Oxford University Press, 1963/i) and G.H.S. Bushnell's *Peru* (New York: Frederick A. Praeger, 1957/i) aren't quite as colorfully illustrated, but they too are broad surveys.

With more on the Spanish conquest of Peru than other sources, William H. Prescott's *History of the Conquest of Peru*, two volumes (Philadelphia: Lippincott, 1874; London: Everyman Library,

1963) is the authoritative history. Pedro Pizarro's *Relation of the Discovery and Conquest of the Kingdoms of Peru*, trans. and ed. P.A. Means, two volumes (New York: Macmillan, 1967) is the primary source.

One of the best illustrated works on the Incas alone for general readers is Loren McIntyre's *The Incredible Incas and Their Timeless Land* (Washington, D.C.: National Geographic Society, 1975/i). It is well researched and is loaded with beautiful color pictures and paintings portraying Inca life. Cottie A. Burland's *Peru Under the Incas* (New York: G.P. Putnam's Sons, 1967/i) is also nicely illustrated and should be considered a first-rate background source to the study of Incan mythology. The chapter entitled "The Divine Sanctions" will be particularly helpful. Louis Baudin's *A Socialist Empire: The Incas of Peru*, trans. Katherine Woods and ed. Arthur Goddard (New York: D. Van Nostrand, 1961) is principally a political/economic history. Hans Dietrich Disselhoff's *Daily Life in Ancient Peru*, trans. Alisa Jaffa (New York: McGraw-Hill, 1967/i) is a nice large-format book, well illustrated in color and black and white, which will serve as useful, specialized background to the study of myths of the Incas. The same can be said of Bertrand Flornoy's *The World of the Inca* (Garden City, N.Y.: Doubleday Anchor, 1958/ip), which has a good chapter on Incan mythology entitled "Children of the Sun." Flornoy's *Inca Adventure* (London: Allen and Unwin, 1956/i) is also worth looking into, as is the magnificent photographic journey *The Route of the Incas* (New York: Viking Press, 1977/i), by Hans Silvester (photographs) and Jacques Soustelle (text). *Realm of the Incas* (ibp) is the New American Library version of Part III of Victor W. von Hagen's *The Ancient Sun Kingdoms of the Americas* (New York: World Publishing Co., 1957/bp), a volume covering the Aztecs, Mayas, and Incas. Von Hagen is a "slick" writer who has studied his subject matter at length, making the text both informative and pleasant to read. A good brief introduction to the Incas, their history, culture, myths, and religion can be found in Charles W. Mead's *Old Civilizations of Inca Land* (New York: American Museum of Natural History Press, 1935); it's an older volume but has much to offer the beginner in matters Incan. And speaking of older books, try Garcilaso de la Vega's *The Incas: The Royal Commentaries of the Inca*, trans. Maria Jolas (New York: Orion Press, 1961/i). These are chronicles written over 400 years ago that tell of the Incas from their first king through the Spanish conquest. Huaman Poma's *Letter to a King: A Peruvian*

Chief's Account of Life Under the Incas and Under Spanish Rule,
trans. Christopher Dilke (New York: E.P. Dutton, 1978), was
written at a later time (between 1567 and 1615). It recounts
Poma's journey through Peru recovering the memories of Inca
life and evaluating life under Spanish rule. The first part, dealing
as it does with Inca life, will be of most use in myth study, but
all three parts could be of interest.

Works on contemporary "primitive" cultures in South America
are not as yet overly abundant in English, but they are showing
up. An ethnographic study of a small group of Colombian Indians,
mentioned earlier in connection with works on religion, is Gerardo
Reichel-Dolmatoff's *Amazonian Cosmos: The Sexual and Religious
Symbolism of the Tukano Indians* (Chicago: University of Chicago
Press, 1971). It is a particularly rich source of myths and information on religious beliefs and practices, but it is a general cultural
survey as well. There's a lot on shamanism, religious belief and
practice, and ideas of the soul in another ethnographic survey,
Michael J. Harner's *The Jivaro* (Garden City, N.Y.: Doubleday
Anchor, 1973/ip). The Jivaro are Indians of the Ecuadorian
Amazon. Curt Nimuendaju's *The Apinaye*, trans. R.H. Lowie
(Oosterhout: Anthropological Publications, 1967) is still another
ethnographic account which has in it much the myth student
will find directly useful—in this case on a Brazilian tribe—as
are Charles Wagley's *Welcome of Tears: The Tapirape Indians
of Central Brazil* (New York: Oxford University Press, 1977/ip),
Ellen B. Basso's *The Kalapalo Indians of Central Brazil* (New York:
Holt, Rinehart and Winston, 1973) and two articles "Requiem for
a Tribe" and "Good-Bye to the Stone Age," both in *National
Geographic*, 147 (February 1975), pp. 254–83. Irving Goldman's
The Cubeo (Urbana: University of Illinois Press, 1963), which is
Illinois Studies in Anthropology no. 2, is careful treatment of a
northwestern Amazon tribe, Colombian mainly. Adolfo Vienrich's
Fabulous Quechuas (Lima: Ediciones Lux, 1961) concerns a tribe
of the Peruvian/Bolivian mountains, and Paul Fejos' *Ethnology of
the Yagua* (New York: Viking Fund Publications in Anthropology,
1943) is excellent coverage of a northeastern Peruvian tribe
of Indians.

Works on the Origins of South American Indians; Contacts

Although the solution to the problem of the origin of the South
American Indians is far from at hand, there are many theories and
quite a bit of accumulated evidence. Lionel Casson's "Who First

Crossed the Oceans?" is concerned with the problem in a broad way. The article is included in *Mysteries of the Past,* ed. Joseph J. Thorndike, Jr. (New York: American Heritage Publishing Co., 1977). Two highly speculative books, but ones which deal more fully with the evidence of myths than do any others, are James Bailey's *The God-Kings and the Titans: The New World Ascendancy in Ancient Times* (New York: St. Martin's Press, 1973/ib) and Hugh Fox's *Gods of the Cataclysm: A Revolutionary Investigation of Man and His Gods Before and After the Great Cataclysm* (New York: Harper's Magazine Press, 1976/ib). Each has larger scope than just the South American Indians, but the books are to be considered required reading as background to the study of the mythologies of any of the Americas. Robert Wauchope's *Lost Tribes and Sunken Continents* (Chicago: University of Chicago Press, 1962/bp) is a good overview of the theories involved and, also, covers the Americas generally. Betty J. Meggers' "The Transpacific Origin of MesoAmerican Civilization: A Preliminary Review of the Evidence and Its Theoretical Implications," in *American Anthropologist,* 77 (March 1975), pp. 1–27, reviews the evidence controversially enough to have generated a rejoinder article you can find on pp. 106–10 of *American Anthropologist,* 78 (March 1976). *Early Man in America* (San Francisco: W.H. Freeman, 1973) is a collection of articles from *Scientific American,* all of them having to do with archaeological finds bearing on the problem of the origin of the Indians of the Americas. Miles Poindexter's early contribution to the subject was the second volume of *The Ayar-Incas, Asiatic Origins* (New York: Liveright, 1930/i). Poindexter, who didn't have the advantage of much later research and discoveries, thinks many possibilities exist for answers, Hindu and Egyptian origins among them. Thor Heyerdahl took the problem more or less in reverse in his balsawood boat excursion from Peru to the Polynesian Islands, a journey recounted in *Kon-Tiki: Across the Pacific by Raft,* trans. F.H. Lyon (Chicago: Rand McNally, 1951/ip). Heyerdahl's *Early Man and the Ocean* (Garden City, N.Y.: Doubleday, 1979/b) has many chapters of use, too. Several other books on contact with other cultures made by the South American Indians and/or their origins from elsewhere are: *Prehistoric Man in the New World* (Chicago: University of Chicago Press, 1964), by Jesse D. Jennings and Edward Norbeck; *The Civilizations of Ancient America* (Chicago: University of Chicago Press, 1951; reprinted by Cooper Square Publishers of New York in 1967), ed. Sol Tax; *Man Across the Sea: Problems of Pre-Columbian Contacts* (Austin: University of Texas Press, 1971), ed. Carroll L. Riley *et al;* and James A. Ford's *A Comparison of Formative Cultures in the Americas: Diffusion or the Psychic Unity of Man* (Washington, D.C.: Smithsonian Institution, 1969). All will be useful to varying degrees as you deepen your background to South American mythologies—just as they will be for deepening your background to other American mythologies.

Works on Archaeology

Needless to say, archaeology is as important to understanding the ancient cultures of South America as anthropology is to understanding the contemporary primitive ones. The stretch of coastal and mountainous land from Chiclayo, Peru, to La Paz, Bolivia, has been most written about due to the great number of Incan and pre-Incan finds there. A beautifully illustrated volume that covers just about all of that area is Rafael Larco Hoyle's *Peru*, trans. James Hogarth (Cleveland: World Publishing Co., 1966/i), a volume in the *Archaeologia Mundi* series. It is divided into six major epochs in ancient Peruvian history. Part I of Leo Deuel's *Conquistadors Without Swords: Archaeologists in the Amercias* (New York: St. Martin's Press, 1967/ibp), a work in which the archaeologists involved tell their own stories, is on the Andean sites and offers some pretty exciting reading. Robert Wauchope's *They Found the Buried Cities* (Chicago: University of Chicago Press, 1965/ip), a collection of writings also by the archaeologists involved in great finds, covers Middle America and Peru. Heinrich Ubbelohde Doering's *On the Royal Highways of the Inca: Archaeological Treasures of Ancient Peru*, trans. Margaret Brown (New York: Frederick Praeger, 1967/i) is valuable mainly for its hundreds of black and white photographs of artifacts and ruins from most of the ancient cultures of Peru, Inca included. Hiram Bingham's *Lost City of the Incas: The Story of Machu Pichu and Its Builders* (New York: Duell, Sloan & Pearce, 1948/i) is, in addition to being a good account of the discovery in 1911 of the Inca stronghold high in the Andes called Machu Pichu and of the ensuing excavations there, a fine background history of the Incas. Also useful mainly for its pictures of work done at an Incan site near Cuzco, in fact not very far from Machu Pichu, is Pal Fejos' *Archaeological Explorations in the Cordillera Vilcabamba,*

South-eastern Peru (New York, 1944/i). The story of the six people
who in the winter of 1952 began work of an archaeological-
ethnographic sort along the Inca road (known as Capac Nan)
from Cuzco to Quito is contained in Victor W. von Hagen's
Highway to the Sun (New York: Duell, Sloan & Pearce, 1955/i).
It is great for its descriptions of the environment and remains of
the Incas as well as for speculations on their culture and way of
life—and it *is* well illustrated in black and white. Paul Kosok's
Life, Land and Water in Ancient Peru (New York: Long Island
University Press, 1965/i) is a fine book of black and white photographs and text relating the discoveries and "mapping of ancient
pyramids, canals, roads, towns, walls, and fortresses of coastal
Peru." Robert Charroux's *The Mysteries of the Andes* (New
York: Avon Books, 1977/ip) deals with the discovery and meaning
of some 11,000 engraved stones at Ica in Peru; while a little over
enthusiastic with the evidence, Charroux does provoke thought
about the importance of such finds. James A. Ford's "The History
of a Peruvian Valley," an article in *Scientific American*, 191
(August 1954/i), pp. 28-34, relates the history of Peru's Viru
River Valley from the origins of man there about 12,000 B.C.
through conquest by Pizarro's army in 1532.

It should also be mentioned that the Nazca Plain in Peru,
with its mysterious markings—roads or runways running this
way and that, shapes visible in their entirety only from the air—has
generated a great deal of speculation about the ancient Nazca
people. Erich von Daniken and a host of his followers surmise
ancient astronauts and landing fields. Thomas Bridges' "The
Nazca Markings," which can be found in *Parabola*, 3 (Winter
1978/i), pp. 48-53, contains a review of the theories concerning the markings and the conclusion that we ought to give the
Peruvians credit instead of suggesting outside influence and
help. Loren McIntyre's "Mystery of the Ancient Nazca Lines,"
in *National Geographic*, 147 (May 1975/i), pp. 716-28, relates a
German mathematician's quest to solve the riddle and is also a
good example of the kinds of arguments that have been mounted
against the idea of outside influence and help. Gerald S. Hawkins'
Beyond Stonehenge (New York: Harper & Row, 1973/i) deals
with these and other prehistoric mysteries from the astronomer's
point of view. *Pathway to the Gods: The Mystery of the Andes
Lines* (New York: Harper & Row, 1978/ib) includes evaluations
of various theories and is perhaps the best illustrated guide to
the markings and the puzzles they continue to pose.

Works on Art

Quite a few books deal with ancient South American art. Wendell C. Bennett's *Ancient Arts of the Andes* (New York: The Museum of Modern Art, 1954/i) has many black and white glossy photographs of the art of pre-Columbian civilizations of the Andes. Miguel Mujica Gallo's *The Gold of Peru*, 1st edition, trans. Roger Perriston-Bird (Recklinghausen: A. Bongers, 1959/i; reprinted, 1967) is a beautifully illustrated survey of pre-Incan and Incan jewelry and other art that includes an introductory section in which the story of gold in ancient Peru and of Spain's use of that gold are discussed. Heinrich Ubbelohde Doering's *The Art of Ancient Peru* (New York: Frederick A. Praeger, 1952/i) is an excellent survey, too. Samuel K. Lothrop's *Inca Treasure as Depicted by Spanish Historians* (Los Angeles: The Southwest Museum, 1938/i) is a slip of a book, but it is most interesting in that it relates what the conquering Spanish thought of Incan gold and craftsmanship. According to Cieza de Leon, quoted in the book, at one of the great festivals of the Incas, there was an area of ground 600 x 300 feet "where the clods were pieces of fine gold, and it was artificially sown with corn fields which were of gold, as well as the stems as the leaves and the cobs. . . . Besides all this they had more than 20 sheep (llamas) of gold with their lambs, and the shepherds with their slings and crooks to watch them, made of this metal." Who says prehistoric peoples were necessarily primitive?

Almost half of another book by Lothrop, *Treasures of Ancient America: The Arts of the Pre-Columbian Civilizations from Mexico to Peru* (Cleveland: World Publishing Co., 1964/i), is devoted to ancient South American art and ruins. It has excellent photographs and accompanying text. Pal Keleman's *Medieval American Art*, two volumes (New York: Macmillan, 1943/i) covers only Incan art in addition to Middle American, but the discussion and illustrations make it a worthwhile source. *The Art of Ancient America* (New York: Crown Publishers, 1961/i), by H.D. Disselhoff and Sigvald Linne; *Ancient Arts of the Americas* (New York: Frederick A. Praeger, 1965/i), by G.H.S. Bushnell; and *Art and Architecture of Ancient America* (Harmondsworth, G.B.: Penguin Books, 1962/i), by George Kubler, are all works which devote some space to ancient South American art, the ones by Disselhoff/Linne and Bushnell being especially well illustrated.

African Mythologies

The history of the African continent—the second largest continent and present-day home to more than 400,000,000 people—is surely one of the most interesting histories in the world. On the one hand, we find the fifth century B.C. Greek historian Herodotus discoursing at length on his pleasant travels among a civilized and literate people of northeastern Africa, the Egyptians. On the other, we find Edgar Rice Burroughs' fictional Lord and Lady Greystoke, parents-to-be of Tarzan, standing alone at the edge of the jungle on the shore of West Africa more than 2,300 years later, watching the ship they'd been on sail off, and hear Lady Greystoke confront their prospects in such primitive and terrifying surroundings with ". . . all that I can see is too horrible, too unthinkable to put into words." How odd that such long-range contrasts, the reverse in chronology from what one would expect, could be the case on a single continent. Further, how odd that the earliest fossil remains of primates, from whom some argue both man and modern apes are descended (as Tarzan, in effect, was descended from both man and ape), should be found on the same continent where both man and ape live today. Further still, how odd that traces of stone age culture dating back close to two million years should be found in the same general area of that continent as contemporary, twentieth-century stone age cultures are to be found.

Africa, a continent of contrasts and paradox, so long the "dark continent," yet once home to a high civilization dating back 5,000 years in time, has only in the most recent 200 years begun slowly to yield the essential secrets of its past. When Napoleon Bonaparte and his men entered Egypt in 1798, they found the colossal sphinx at Giza buried neck-deep in sand, just as they had found ancient Egyptian civilization as much as buried by time, its history obscure save for the reports of Near-Eastern contem-

---

The following symbols will be found, where applicable, in the bibliographic citation, usually following the date of publication: i = has useful illustrations; b = has a useful bibliography; p = has been published in paperbound edition.

poraries and others like Herodotus. Except for the northern coast, where groups of ancient Phoenicians, Greeks, and Romans had settled before the Christian era, the continent either rebuffed all comers—from Hanno of the Phoenicians, who may well have sailed around Africa in the fifth century B.C. while Herodotus travelled in Memphis and Thebes, to later explorers like Vasco da Gama, who in 1498, after himself sailing around most of the continent, was apparently found wanting by the inhabitants of advanced towns on the east coast—or it swallowed them up the way it temporarily did the explorer-missionary David Livingstone. The massive colonializing, missionary activities of Europeans in the nineteenth century finally began breaking down the impenetrability of the continent. Moving up from the south and in from the west and north, white missionaries, opportunists, and settlers gradually succeeded in knowing "darkest" Africa, that vast area inland from coastal regions, and opening it to the revealing investigations of ethnologists much the way Napolean and his men at the end of the eighteenth century had probed deep into Egypt to comprehend that ancient "black land" and pave the way for the future retrieval and translation of its literature and history.

Historians (and mythographers) have long been accustomed to dealing with ancient Egypt as though it were somehow part of ancient Western Asia rather than a complex civilization lodged anomalously in time and place in northeastern Africa. Partly this is due to a fact of another sort—that no written African history existed until very recently, while ancient Egyptian history, however fragmentary and second-hand, has existed in written form continuously since the Egyptians lived. Also, there is no question that the commerce and contacts of dynastic Egypt mark it as part of the broad ancient civilization of the Mediterranean region. The great change that occurred in Egypt late in its prehistory (prior to about 3100 B.C.) has additionally suggested, to archaeologists and historians alike, outside influence—possibly the settlement in Egypt of Mesopotamians, for instance. These reasons alone may be enough to warrant dealing with ancient Egypt as though the map were quite different from the way it really is. The fact that ancient Egypt was African, though, despite the way just about all of Africa otherwise developed apart from it into pastoral or hunting cultures, makes it imperative that we who study myth do two things simultaneously: (1) regard ancient Egypt as part of the ancient world while we (2) understand that it *was* African. The time may yet come when we see, more than we now can, greater connection between indigenous African peoples elsewhere and the ancient civilization Herodotus called "the gift of the Nile."

The two separate sections that follow in the guide, one on ancient Egyptian, the other on later African, are really as close as we can get, for the present, to approaching all African mythologies collectively. With the exception of a few histories and some of the worldwide collections of myths, there are very few individual volumes or series which handle ancient Egypt and the rest of Africa together.

Ancient Egyptian Mythologies

Perhaps we are all at present *too* aware of the splendors of ancient Egypt to appreciate that prior to the nineteenth century the only sources of information on Egyptian history, culture, art, religion, and mythology were the *Bible* and classical writers like Herodotus. Perhaps with all the films we've seen, magazine articles we've been exposed to, shelf on shelf of scholarly and popular books on Egypt available in libraries, and even treasures brought to our very doorsteps—as in museum collections of artifacts and in the Tutankhamen road show—we find it hard to imagine how little was known, until very nearly our own era, about the civilization that probably developed at an earlier time than any, except possibly the ones in Mesopotamia and Indus Valley of India, and for a longer continuous period than even these.

It is to Napoleon Bonaparte and his grand expedition to Egypt at the end of the eighteenth century that we owe the start of our acquisition of reliable knowledge of things Egyptian. With his army and an entourage of scholars, he went to Egypt with ambitions of both a military and scholarly sort, and among the more important outcomes was the discovery and eventual translation of the famed Rosetta stone, a large rock slab inscribed in Egyptian hieroglyphic and demotic and, fortunately enough, in Greek.

Now with the translating of a great many important Egyptian works, not to mention a great deal of archaeological work, largely behind us, we know much about the history of ancient Egypt. From about the year 3400 until the first century B.C., well into Roman times, Egypt flourished, though in the years following 1075 decaying gradually for a variety of reasons, not the least of which were invasions by the Assyrians, Persians, Greeks and

Romans. That is more than three thousand years of history as a single civilization! The Mesopotamians—Sumerians, Akkadians, Assyrians, and Babylonians—came and went in that time. Old Testament history is swallowed up in those three thousand years, representing but little more than half of Egypt's duration. The civilization of the ancient Greeks lasted but a third as long as that of the Egyptians—if we are generous and count some pre-history in our reckoning. The heydays of the Minoans, the Hittites, the Phoenicians, and the splendid Persian Empire each account for even smaller fractions of that time. As a matter of fact, only if we count all of the history of western civilization—from the rise of the Greeks and from the period of Exodus in the *Bible* to the present—do we come up with a similar figure, more than three thousand years.

During what is called the Gerzean Period (c. 3400–3200 B.C.), separate kingdoms grew in the upper and lower Nile regions. The earliest hieroglyphs date from these centuries, and the renown Egyptian architectural achievements began appearing. Menes, a ruler from upper Egypt, unified the two kingdoms in about 3200 B.C. From that time until about 2686 B.C. (the Archaic Period), the time during which the epic hero Gilgamesh probably ruled in Mesopotamia, the first two dynasties of Egyptian pharaohs ruled. The Old Kingdom, incorporating the third through sixth dynasties (and including Cheops as one of the rulers), was the period from about 2686 through 2181 B.C. The First Intermediate Period, from c. 2181–1991 B.C., a time during which the famed Cretan labyrinth was built, includes the seventh through eleventh dynasties. The Middle Kingdom, c. 1991–1786 B.C., the twelfth dynasty only, saw active trade begin with Near Eastern centers and Crete. It was a period of building—forts on the Asian front, magnificent structures in Thebes and other cities—and a period when the cult of Osiris became popular. In Mesopotamia, Hammurabi ruled and gave the world his monumental code of laws. The thirteenth through seventeenth dynasties in Egypt, about 1786 through 1567 B.C., known as the Second Intermediate Period, saw bronze working introduced to Egypt by the "Hyksos," Semitic immigrants in the Nile Valley. The New Kingdom, c. 1567–1075 B.C., the eighteenth through twentieth dynasties, was a long and most impressive span of time in Egypt. There were conquests in Asia, and many great achievements in art, architecture, and religion were made—extravagant paintings and works in glass, magnificent temples at Karnak, and Akhenaten's solar monotheism among them. Elsewhere, the great Minoan Empire collapsed, the Hittites reached their peak and faded, the Trojan War was fought and the legendary Greek heroes lived (if indeed they did), and Moses led the Israelites from Egypt and later brought from Sinai the Ten Commandments. Thereafter in Egypt—a thousand-year period when Greece rose to greatness and fell to the Romans, when the Phoenicians established their African colonies (Carthage included), when Babylon fell, when Persia rose to power and fell to Alexander, and when great biblical rulers like Saul, David, and Solomon lived—the falling off occurred, culminating with the Ptolemies, Cleopatra, and Roman rule.

Collections of the Myths

For the myth student, the legacy is a great and interesting one. We are happily past the time when the influential historian Charles Rollin could say with reasonable impunity, "Never were any people more superstitious than the Egyptians. They had a great number of gods, of different orders and degrees, which I shall omit, because they belong more to fable than to history." A look into Egyptian mythology will reveal the great variety one would assume of more than three thousand years of history; to the serious student, nothing much will be worth omitting, much less worth castigating as "superstitious."

E.A. Wallis Budge, keeper, when he lived, of Egyptian and Assyrian antiquities at the British Museum, was the author of what remains after seventy years the most important collection of Egyptian myths, *The Gods of the Egyptians*, two volumes (New York: Dover Publications, 1969/ip; originally London, 1904). It has in it all that you will probably find useful among Egyptian myths, save what little Egyptologists have come up with in the succeeding years, and it is filled with excellent examples of hieroglyphics and art work of the Egyptians. J. Viau's *Egyptian Mythology*, trans. Delano Ames (London: Paul Hamlyn, 1965/ib) is probably the most useful collection of the myths otherwise. It includes plenty of background information and over a hundred excellent illustrations. Also beautifully illustrated is Richard Patrick's *All Color Book of Egyptian Mythology* (London: Octopus Books, 1972/i). The text is brief, though, and fragmented to accompany pictures. Anthony S. Mercatante's *Who's Who in Egyptian Mythology* (New York: Clarkson N. Potter, 1978/ibp) is a handy, alphabetically organized dictionary that is well worth

owning. T.G.H. James' *Myths and Legends of Ancient Egypt*
(New York: Grosset and Dunlop, Bantam, 1971/ip) is in a series
called "All Color Guides" and is written at a level that would
make it suitable for fifth graders and up. James Baikie's *Wonder
Tales of the Ancient World* (London: A&C Black, 1915/i) is similarly meant for younger readers and includes just a sampling of
Egyptian myths. Lewis Spence's *Myths and Legends: Ancient Egypt*
(London: Harrap and Company, 1919), another older volume, is
still an excellent source of the myths—perhaps not as copious and
heavily explanatory as Budge's *The Gods of the Egyptians* but
relatively complete—as is Donald A. Mackenzie's *Egyptian Myth
and Legend*, a volume in Gresham Publishing Company's *Myth and
Legend in Literature and Art Series* (London, 1920/i).

L.W. King's *Legends of Babylon and Egypt* (London: Oxford
University Press, 1918) has a good proportion of the Egyptian
myths and is, after sixty years, quite useful still. The same can be
said of Volume XII in *The Mythology of All Races* (Boston:
Marshall Jones, 1916-32; reprinted in New York by Cooper
Square Press, 1964, etc.), the volume called *Egypt, Far East*,
but the reader must read through Max Müller's solar naturalism
in the process of getting the myths.

Also possible sources of the Egyptian myths are several volumes
which focus on a number of the ancient world's myth systems.
Rudolf Anthes' "Mythology in Ancient Egypt," pp. 15-92 in
Mythologies of the Ancient World (Garden City, N.Y.: Doubleday
Anchor, 1961/bp) is quite good both as a source of the myths and
for its explanations. As with all of the collections which include
more than a single myth system, though, it cannot match for
completeness such volumes as Budge's or Viau's. S.H. Hooke's
Middle Eastern Mythology (Harmondsworth, G.B.: Penguin,
1963/ip) has an even briefer section on Egyptian mythology and
is probably better for its handling of the continuity of Middle
Eastern mythologies than for its handling of any one of them
singly. That is definitely the case in Gerald A. Larue's *Ancient
Myth and Modern Man* (Englewood Cliffs, N.J.: Prentice-Hall,
1975/bp), which has in it many Egyptian myths but which emphasizes the biblical and is topically rather than geographically
organized. Fred Gladstone Bratton's *Myths and Legends of the
Ancient Near East* (New York: Thomas Y. Crowell, 1970) covers
Egyptian mythology in good introductory fashion in part two.

In the worldwide mythographies category, the *Larousse World
Mythology* (New York: Putnam, 1965/i), ed. Pierre Grimal, trans.

Patricia Beardsworth, has one of the better sections on Egyptian mythology. The section in the *Larousse Encyclopedia of Mythology* (London: Paul Hamlyn, 1959/ip), ed. Felix Guirand, trans. Richard Aldington and Delano Ames, is by J. Viau, the author of the Hamlyn volume praised earlier, *Egyptian Mythology*. It seems Viau—or the Hamlyn editorial staff—adapted the latter volume from the section in the *Larousse Encyclopedia*, enlarging it substantially in the process. There's a very nice section on Egyptian myths in Volume I of the *Pears Encyclopedia of Myths and Legends* (London: Pelham Books, 1976/i), too, space limitations considered, and although shorter still, the section in *Encyclopedia of World Mythology* (New York: Galahad Books, 1975/i) is sufficient as brief introduction. With three-and-one-half pages of text and twenty of pictures and captions, Veronica Ions' *The World's Mythology in Colour* (London: Paul Hamlyn, 1974) delivers what the book's title promises but is too brief a source to be used other than for the pictures.

Studies of the Myths

In addition to the analyses of Egyptian myths you'll find in many of the collections just covered, there are a number of other works valuable for analyses. Joseph Kaster's *The Literature and Mythology of Ancient Egypt* (London: Allen Lane, 1970) is excellent for discussions of myths, but it is mainly an anthology of Egyptian literature in translation. H.T. Velde's *Seth, God of Confusion* (reprint of the 1967 edition by E.J. Brill of Leiden, Netherlands, 1978) is a useful examination of the role of Set(h) in Egyptian mythology and religion. A highly useful background work in which an attempt is made to disentangle the myth of the conflict of Horus and Set from the myth of Osiris is John Gwynn Griffiths' *The Conflict of Horus and Set: From Egyptian and Classical Sources* (Liverpool: Liverpool University Press, 1960). Griffiths pays attention to known versions of the myths and deals especially well with the political and historical origins of the conflict myth. The final section of the book includes a most interesting interpretation of the myth, particularly as related to possible historical background. Worthwhile on the subject of Set is A.F.J. Klijn's *Seth in Jewish, Christian and Gnostic Literature* (Leiden: E.J. Brill—*Novum Testamentum* no. XLVI, 1977). C.J. Bleeker's *Hathor and Thoth: Two Key Figures of the Ancient Egyptian Religion* (Leiden: E.J. Brill, 1973/b) is, as the author says, an attempt "to fathom the character and significance of Hathor and Thoth," whom he compares to Dionysus and Apollo as embodiments of enthusiasm and thoughtful relfection respectively. There's a chapter devoted to discussion of the Egyptian creation myth in Samuel G.F. Brandon's *Creation Legends of the Ancient Near East* (London: Hodder and Stoughton, 1963). Hans. J. Klimkeit's "Spatial Orientation in Mythical Thinking as Exemplified in Ancient Egypt: Considerations Toward a Geography of Religions," in *History of Religions*, 14 (May 1975), pp. 266–81, is an excellent discussion of mythmaking and the factors that enter into the shaping of myths, Egyptian myth the principal model. A first-rate analytic source, particularly for myths current in Egypt between 2700 and 1700 B.C., is Robert Thomas Rundle Clark's *Myth and Symbol in Ancient Egypt* (London: Thames and Hudson, 1959/ip). In it, myths are presented in the words of the texts from which they are derived, each one interpreted—sometimes rather idiosyncratically—with religious and symbolic context in mind. Some interpretations of Egyptian myths are included in Don Cameron Allen's *Mysteriously Meant: The Rediscovery of Pagan Symbolism and Allegorical Interpretation in the Renaissance* (Baltimore: Johns Hopkins Press, 1970), all of them interesting though now largely refuted. It is an interesting book nonetheless and should be looked into. J.C. Prichard's *An Analysis of the Egyptian Mythology* (London: John and Arthur Arch, 1819), is also interesting but highly unreliable inasmuch as the myths available to Prichard were few at the time when, in the 1820s, translation of Egyptian texts had just begun.

Two books more in the realm of mythmaking than works in which Egyptian myths are analyzed and interpreted are Richard Roche's *Egyptian Myths and the Ra Story: Based on the Edgar Cayce Readings* (Virginia Beach, Va.: A.R.E. Press, 1975/p) and Rudolf Steiner's *Egyptian Myths and Mysteries*, trans. Norman Macbeth (New York: Anthroposophic Press, 1971/p). In Roche's book, the myths of the Egyptians—at least many of the principal ones—are gone over, with additions and modifications made to many of them based on Cayce's readings while in a self-induced hypnotic state. In effect, this is a "correcting" of Egyptian myth with some suggestions given to archaeologists for future excavations—such as at Jebel Barkal. Steiner accounts for the way we look at the world today by postulating the possibility of our soul's prior existence in ancient Egypt. All sectors should be heard from when myth is being investigated interpretatively, hence my inclusion of these two unusual works here.

Works on Religion and Related Matters

Egyptian myth and religion are as closely aligned as they can be; in fact the overwhelming majority of the Egyptian myths are sacral. Therefore, serious study of the myths must also include a good deal of work with the religion, and because of the alignment, much that you read in studies of the religion will incorporate myth analysis and interpretation. Among the best general surveys of Egyptian religion—and there are many—are Henri Frankfort's *Ancient Egyptian Religion* (New York: Harper Torchbooks, 1961/ip; originally published by Columbia University Press, 1948) and E.A. Wallis Budge's *Egyptian Religion* (Secaucus, N.J.: University Books, 1959/i; originally London, 1900). Frankfort takes into account the historical spectrum, noting changes and modifications in the religion over the years. Budge's book is in a sense a capsule version of many of his other works since the individual chapters cover the same territory. Religious beliefs and practices are rehearsed in it, a special emphasis being Egyptian ideas of the afterlife. His book entitled *From Fetish to God in Ancient Egypt* (London: Oxford University Press, 1934) is concerned mainly with the predynastic period, but there are many hymns, legends, and the like included to make it a valuable companion to his *Egyptian Religion*. Alan W. Shorter's *An Introduction to Egyptian Religion* (London: Kegan Paul, 1931) concentrates on the eighteenth and earlier nineteenth dynasties in arriving at the conclusions that all of Egyptian religion may be seen as "the struggle for supremacy between two great elements of Nature, the sun (Ra, Atum, Horus) and the god of the soil, vegetation and Nile (Osiris)"; and that the death and resurrection of Osiris prepared the way for Christian belief in Egypt. Cerny Jaroslav's *Ancient Egyptian Religion* (London: Hutchinson House, 1952) is a book written for the "inquiring layman" and contains good brief coverage of the religion, gods, and cults. Siegfried Morenz's *Egyptian Religion* (Ithaca, N.Y.: Cornell University Press, 1973), S.A.B. Mercer's *The Religion of Ancient Egypt* (London: Luzac, 1948), and Adolf Erman's *A Handbook of Egyptian Religion* (London: Archibald Constable, 1907) may all also be used profitably even though none is quite up to the calibre of Frankfort's or Budge's surveys.

For highly condensed surveys of Egyptian religion, many general works can be referred to. Robert J. Ellwood's *Many Peoples, Many Faiths: An Introduction to the Religious Life of Man* (Englewood Cliffs, N.J.: Prentice-Hall, 1976) is one of the more recent examples. Samuel Alfred Browne Mercer's "The

Religion of Ancient Egypt," in *Ancient Religions* (New York: Citadel Press, 1965/ip; originally published as *Forgotten Religions* in 1950), ed. Vergilius Ferm, is also a brief but reliable introduction. One of the prefatory chapters in Cornelius Loew's *Myth, Sacred History and Philosophy: The Pre-Christian Religious Heritage of the West* (New York: Harcourt, Brace & World, 1967) deals with Egyptian religion briefly.

William Flinders Petrie's *Religion and Conscience in Ancient Egypt* (London, 1898; reprinted by Benjamin Blom of New York, 1972) is very much of a survey of Egyptian religion, but more importantly a study of religious thought. S.A.B. Mercer's *Growth of Religious and Moral Ideas in Egypt* (Milwaukee, 1919) is another older book with particular value since Mercer traces the development of the religious mind into Egypt's prehistory. James H. Breasted's *Development of Religion and Thought in Ancient Egypt* (New York: Charles Scribner's Sons, 1912/p; reprinted as a University of Pennsylvania paperback in 1972) does much the same thing and is equally strong as a cultural history. John A. Wilson's "Egypt" in *The Intellectual Adventure of Ancient Man* (Chicago: University of Chicago Press, 1946; reprinted in 1949 by Penguin as *Before Philosophy*/p), ed. H. and H.A. Frankfort *et al*, covers generally Egyptian thought on the universe, life values, and the state. It is highly recommended as a brief and provocative introduction to these matters. Samuel G.F. Brandon's *Religion in Ancient History* (New York: Scribner's, 1969; originally 1961) has in it several articles you'll find interesting. Chapters eight and nine respectively deal with Osiris and Akhenaten; chapter seven deals with "The Judgment of the Dead" in Egypt, Mesopotamia, and Christian religion; and parts of other articles will be helpful in the study of Egyptian religion. Brandon's "The Weighing of the Soul" in Egyptian as well as Christian myth and religion is included in *Myths and Symbols: Studies in Honor of Mircea Eliade* (Chicago: University of Chicago Press, 1969). *The Legacy of Egypt*, 2nd edition (Oxford: Clarendon Press, 1971), ed. J.R. Harris, has a number of articles in it that you might find useful, too, including A.A. Bark's excellent discussion of Egyptian religion, "Mystery, Myth, and Magic."

Another of E.A. Wallis Budge's monumental works on Egyptian religion is *Osiris: The Egyptian Religion of Resurrection* (New Hyde Park, N.Y.: University Books, 1961; reprinted as two volumes in New York by Dover Press, 1973/ip). It is a mammoth and scholarly work on just one facet of Egyptian religion, Osiris cult worship. In it Budge shows us how this indigenous African

religion worked, what its liturgy and ritual were, and what its god
was envisioned to be. His equally grand *Tutankhamen: Amenism,
Atenism, and Egyptian Monotheism* (New York: Arno Press Reprint of the 1923 edition) is broadly concerned with Tutankhamen's
reign, but a great deal of it is devoted to Egyptian religion of the
time, monotheism one facet of it. The development of monotheism in the ancient world, largely due to the pervasive influence
of Egypt, is the topic of William Foxwell Albright's great *From
the Stone Age to Christianity: Monotheism and the Historical
Process* (Garden City, N.Y.: Anchor Press, 1957/p), a work
you may wish to read once you've dealt with Akhenaten's
monotheistic reform of Egyptian religion. Cyril Aldred's *Akhenaten and Nefertiti* (New York: The Viking Press, 1973/ib) would
also be very useful at that point. It is by one of the foremost
Egyptologists of our day and deals extensively with the reform.
Immanuel Velikovsky's controversial *Oedipus and Akhnaton:
Myth and History* (Garden City, N.Y.: Doubleday, 1960/i) suggests
that the Greek Oedipus and Akhenaten were one and the same
person—an iffy premise but interesting in much the same way
that Sigmund Freud's premise that Moses learned monotheism
from Akhenaten is (see his *Moses and Monotheism*). Finally,
Eberhard Otto's *Egyptian Art and the Cults of Osiris and Amon*
(London: Thames and Hudson, 1968/i) is an excellent, mainly
photographic, investigation of Egyptian religion at the two cult
centers of Abydos and Thebes. Another potentially useful work
on Osirian worship, J.G. Griffiths' *The Origins of Osiris and His
Cult* (Leiden: E.J. Brill, forthcoming).

Egyptian Ideas of the Future Life (London: Kegan Paul, 1908)
is still another of E.A. Wallis Budge's works on Egyptian religious
beliefs and practices. It remains the classic work on Egyptian
eschatology—except for one other work, that, too, by Budge,
The Egyptian Heaven and Hell (LaSalle, Ill.: Open Court, 1974/p;
reprint of the 1925 edition). Monistic and dualistic conceptions
of death in ancient Egypt are the subject of Jan Zandee's *Death
as an Enemy According to Ancient Egyptian Conceptions*, trans.
Mrs. W.F. Klasens (Leiden: E.J. Brill, 1960; reprinted in New
York by Arno Press, 1976). Paul Carus devoted a chapter to Egypt
in his *The History of the Devil and the Idea of Evil* (New York:
Bell Publishing Co., 1969/i; reprint of an earlier edition); it focuses
on Set as evil.

Closely related to religion in ancient Egypt and in fact part of
it in practice was magic. Once again, the classic work on it is by
E.A. Wallis Budge, specifically his *Egyptian Magic* (New York:

Dover Publications, 1971/p; originally London, 1901). The book is actually not a bad introduction to magic generally, but for coverage of the uses of amulets, spells, names, and the like in Egypt, it is excellent. P. Ghalioungui's *Magic and Medical Science in Ancient Egypt* (London: Hodder and Stoughton, 1963) does much to extend Budge's work and is especially useful for the author's handling of the development of medical science in Egypt as distinct from magic. There are also a number of encyclopedic works on magic. Kurt Seligmann's *Magic, Supernaturalism and Religion* (New York: Pantheon Books, 1971) is one of them with a chapter devoted to ancient Egypt.

Probably as closely related to magic as magic was to religion in ancient Egypt was the development of science. There are good discussions of Egyptian science in George Sarton's *History of Science* (Cambridge: Harvard University Press, 1952; reprinted by W.W. Norton in 1970/p) and Otto Neugebauer's *The Exact Sciences in Antiquity*, 2nd edition (Providence: Brown University Press, 1957). Inasmuch as there's a general chronological movement from myth to philosophy to science—at least in theory— these two works could be useful.

Ritual, too, ties closely to religion, needless to say. The book *Myth and Ritual* (London: Oxford University Press, 1933) has an excellent chapter on ancient Egypt by the editor, S.H. Hooke. The first chapter, also by Hooke, is a good overview of myth-ritual as a concept. H.W. Fairman's "The Kingship Rituals of Egypt," one of the chapters in *Myth, Ritual and Kingship* (Oxford: Clarendon Press, 1958), edited by Hooke, is quite informative. That same subject is dealt with by Henri Frankfort in his *Kingship and the Gods: A Study of Ancient Near Eastern Religion as the Integration of Society and Nature* (Chicago: University of Chicago Press, 1948/ib), in this case as concerns the incarnate god, pharaoh. Some attention is also paid to Egypt in Percival Hadfield's *Traits of Divine Kingship in Africa* (London: Watts & Co., 1949), but the book is largely concerned with other African groups.

The remains of seasonal drama-rirtual are investigated by Theodor H. Gaster in his *Thespis: Ritual, Myth, and Drama in the Ancient Near East*, revised edition (Garden City, N.Y.: Doubleday, 1961; Norton, 1977/p). It has in it much on Egypt. E.O. James' *Seasonal Feasts and Festivals* (New York: Barnes & Noble, 1963/bp) includes a chapter devoted to Egypt, and is a good introduction to the general subject as well. C.J. Bleeker's *Egyptian Festivals: Enactments of Religious Renewal* (Leiden:

E.J. Brill, 1967/b) is a fine study of religious festivals in ancient Egypt—festivals of the dead, of the gods, and of the king. Lewis Spence's *Mysteries of Egypt: Secret Rites of the Nile* (Blauvelt, N.Y.: Multimedia-Steiner Books, 1972/p; a reprint of the earlier edition) also has much to offer that will be helpful.

Since a great deal of the impetus for the myth-ritual school came from the work of James George Frazer and since much of his work deals with relevant activity in ancient Egypt, you might wish to look into his *Adonis, Attis, Osiris: Studies in the History of Oriental Religion* (London: Macmillan and Co., 1906/p) and the classic twelve-volume work, *The Golden Bough*, which is commonly available in Theodor H. Gaster's abridgment, *The New Golden Bough* (Garden City, N.Y.: Doubleday Anchor, 1961).

Finally, Leopold Sabourin's *Priesthood: A Comparative Study* (Leiden: E.J. Brill, 1973/b) includes some information on Egyptian priesthood, and Serge Sauneron's *The Priests of Ancient Egypt* (New York: Grove Press, 1959) is an excellent, thoroughly researched study.

Works on Historical/Cultural Background

Works of all sorts and shapes are available on the culture and history of ancient Egypt, many of them with chapters or sections devoted to religion and mythology. Lionel Casson's *The Horizon Book of Daily Life in Ancient Egypt* (New York: American Heritage Publishing Co., 1975/i) is one of them—in this case colorfully illustrated and with a most useful chapter nine on religion. Pierre Montet's *Everyday Life in Egypt*, trans. A.R. Maxwell-Hyslop (London: Edward Arnold, 1958/i) is not nearly as colorful but it is excellent on the time period 1320–1100 B.C. and includes two pertinent chapters, "In the Temples" and "The Rites of Burial." Jon Manchip White's *Everyday Life in Ancient Egypt* (New York: Capricorn Books, 1963/ip) covers home life, life in cities, the professions, and education. Barbara Mertz's *Red Land, Black Land: Daily Life in Ancient Egypt* (New York: Dodd-Mead, 1978/ip) is a recent volume that has much to commend it as a recreation of the everyday in Egypt, not the least reason being Mertz's graceful and witty prose. Waley-el-dine Sameh's *Daily Life in Ancient Egypt*, trans. Michael Bullock (New York: McGraw-Hill, 1964/i) is a nicely illustrated, large-format volume that also covers the offbeat nicely—handicrafts, food and drink, dress, and many others. Three chapters of the ten in the book by Jacques Champollion, *The World of the Egyptians*, trans. Joel Rosenthal (Geneva: Minerva, 1971/i), are concerned with belief-religion, the balance with culture and the arts primarily.

Lionel Casson and the editors of Time-Life collaborated on another volume I can highly recommend. In the Time-Life *Great Ages of Man* series, *Ancient Egypt* (New York: Time-Life Books, 1965/ib) is loaded with pictures, maps, drawings, and charts. Chapter four is entitled "Gods and the Afterlife." A. Rosalie David's *The Egyptian Kingdoms* (New York: Elsevier Phaidon, 1975/ib) is at least the equal of the Time-Life book for beauty and does have lots of nice features, a helpful glossary among them. It is in *The Making of the Past* series. An even bigger and more beautiful book is Claudio Barocas' *Egypt* (New York: Grosset and Dunlop, 1977/ib), an excellent cultural/historical volume in the series called *Monuments of Civilization.* Equally impressive in size and price—and, if possible, even more lavishly illustrated—is *Ancient Egypt* (Washington, D.C.: National Geographic Society, 1978/i). Typical of National Geographic Society books, it is a splendid accomplishment. Cyril Aldred, a famed Egyptologist, wrote *The Egyptians* (New York: Praeger, 1961/ib) for the *Ancient Peoples and Places* series done jointly by Thames and Hudson in London and Frederick Praeger in New York. It is smaller in format but has eighty-two photographs and numerous drawings, maps, tables. It is superb background to Egyptian myth study, with much on mythology and religion spread throughout. Paul Jordan's *Egypt: The Black Land* (New York: E.P. Dutton, 1976/ip) is a lovely, smaller volume that includes chapters on the archaeological discoveries in Egypt, decipherment of hieroglyphics, everyday life in ancient Egypt, history, and achievements in science and technology. There's even a good chapter on "Religion and Morality." Margaret A. Murray's *The Splendour That Was Egypt* (New York: Hawthorne, 1963/i; Philosophical Library, 1949) is a fine survey of the history and culture arranged topically, including a chapter on religion. It has ninety-five black and white photographs.

Eternal Egypt (New York: New American Library, 1964/ib), by Pierre Montet, trans. Doreen Weightman, is a fine history of Egypt, with a couple of chapters concerned with myth study. John A. Wilson's *The Burden of Egypt: An Interpretation of Ancient Egyptian Culture* (Chicago: University of Chicago Press, 1951/ib) is a good history as well as cultural survey. Myth/religion information is scattered throughout. Hermann Kees' *Ancient Egypt*, trans. Ian F.D. Morrow (Chicago: University of Chicago

Press, 1961), is one of four books with that title that I'm aware of, the others being by Christiane Desroches Noblecourt (Greenwich, Conn.: New York Graphic Society, 1960/i), Jon Manchip White (New York: Thomas Y. Crowell, 1952; Dover Paperback, 1970/ip), and William Stevenson Smith (Boston: Museum of Fine Arts, 1942; Beacon Press, 1961/ip). All are well illustrated, particularly Noblecourt's, and all will serve well as introductions to ancient Egyptian culture and history. *When Egypt Ruled the East*, revised edition (Chicago: University of Chicago Press, 1957/i), by George Steindorff and Keith C. Seele, is meant to be a basic introduction. It's slick, nicely illustrated in black and white, and covers everything in almost superficial ways, the chapter on religion included. Barbara Pradal's *Ancient Egypt from A to Z* (New York: Bobbs-Merrill, n.d./i) is likewise pretty basic. Barbara Mertz calls her *Temples, Tombs and Hieroglyphs* (New York: Dodd-Mead, 1978/ ip) "a popular history of Ancient Egypt." Alan Gardiner's *Egypt of the Pharaohs* (Oxford: Clarendon Press, 1961) is a good history of ancient Egypt. Its author meant it to replace James A. Breasted's earlier gigantic history, *A History of Egypt from the Earliest Times to the Persian Conquest*, 2nd edition (London: 1948), probably the best known of all the many earlier histories that can be found even today in libraries. Leonard Cottrell's *The Lost Pharaohs* (London: Evans Brothers, 1950) is a good basic introduction to Egyptology that focuses on the archaeological finds and their significance. Yves Naud's *The Curse of the Pharaohs*, two volumes, trans. Clive Drummond (Geneva: Editions Ferni, 1977/i) is more broadly a cultural history than its title would signify, but it does trace the idea of tomb curses rather extensively.

There are quite a number of books concerned with large areas of ancient history or archaeology that ought also to be mentioned. Among them are Jacquetta Hawkes' *The First Great Civilizations: Life in Mesopotamia, The Indus Valley, and Egypt* (New York: Alfred A. Knopf, 1973/ib). It's meant as a popularization, but Egypt is treated within the context of the rise of civilization in the ancient world and India. The same might be said of the treatment of Egypt by Glyn Daniel in his *The First Civilizations: The Archaeology of Their Origins* (New York: Thomas Y. Crowell; Apollo Editions, 1970/ip). Both books make fine reading. J.R. Williams' article entitled "The Egyptians" in *Peoples of the Old Testament* (Oxford: Clarendon Press, 1973), ed. D.J. Wiseman, has a different slant in that it deals only with the cultures known by the Hebrews. L. Sprague de Camp is concerned just with

Great Cities of the Ancient World (Garden City, N.Y.: Doubleday, 1972/i), Thebes, Memphis, and Alexandria among them. Henri Frankfort concentrates on "the political and social innovations" that resulted in Near Eastern civilizations in his *The Birth of Civilization in the Near East* (Bloomington: Indiana University Press, 1951; Garden City, N.Y.: Doubleday Anchor, 1959/p). Egypt is more or less the culmination of the trends he investigates.

Stuart Piggott's *The Dawn of Civilization: The First World Survey of Human Cultures in Early Times* (New York: McGraw-Hill, 1961) is one of the many ancient histories with sections devoted to Egypt. Michael Grant's *The Ancient Mediterranean* (New York: Scribner's, 1969) is another. Richard Mansfield Haywood's *Ancient Greece and the Near East* (New York: David McKay, 1964) has plenty of space devoted to Egypt, and *The Near East: The Early Civilizations* (New York: Delacorte Press, 1967), by Jean Bottero *et al*, treats just Assyria and Egypt. Volume I of the *Cambridge History of Africa* (Cambridge: Cambridge University Press, 1975)—has extensive coverage of ancient Egypt, as does Basil Davidson's *Africa: History of a Continent* (New York: Macmillan, 1966). I mention these few books as representative of many like them that may elude your attention; they are well worth considering.

Works which focus on particular time periods in ancient Egypt include Walter B. Emery's *Archaic Egypt* (Harmondsworth, G.B.: Penguin, 1961/ibp) which deals nicely with only the first and second dynasties. Cyril Aldred's *Egypt to the End of the Old Kingdom* (New York: McGraw-Hill, 1965/p) covers only the Archaic and Old Kingdom periods; it would even be suitable for ninth graders despite the writer's eminence as an Egyptologist. E. Baumgarten's *The Cultures of Prehistoric Egypt* (London: Oxford University Press, 1955) delves into earliest Egypt, and Jack Lindsay's *Men and Gods on the Roman Nile* (London: Frederick Muller, 1968) deals with the more recent end of the historical spectrum in ancient Egypt. It, by the way, has much on myth, belief, and worship under Roman rule.

Additionally worthwhile are John G. Jackson's *Man, God, and Civilization* (New Hyde Park, N.Y.: University Books, 1972) and Cyrus H. Gordon's *Before the Bible: The Common Background of Greek and Hebrew Civilizations* (New York: Harper & Row, 1962). Jackson's is an idiosyncratic work in which it is slowly "proven" that Egyptian civilization, which was the inspiration for later western civilizations, derived from Ethiopian civilization.

There's a great deal in it on religion and myth. Gordon systematically goes about showing the influence of Egypt and other cultures in the Near East on Greece and the *Bible.*

Finally, for background, Georges Posener's *Dictionary of Egyptian Civilization* (New York: Tudor Publishing Co., 1954/i) would be well worth having at hand. It is filled with pictures and has useful entries throughout, including much that is myth related. Each volume of the *Annual Egyptological Bibliography* (Leiden: E.J. Brill, 1947 and on/b) covers all that has been done in Egyptian studies during the preceding year. Two articles in *The Bible and the Ancient Near East: Essays in Honor of William Foxwell Albright* (Garden City, N.Y.: Doubleday, 1961), Thomas O. Lambdin's "Egypt: Its Language and Literature" and John A. Wilson's "Egyptian Culture and Religion," assess the most important findings in Egyptology from the 1920s through late 1950s. The collection also offers a good chronology of the ancient Near East, Egypt included, on pages 220 and following. P. Van Der Meer's *The Chronology of Ancient Western Asia and Egypt,* 2nd revised edition (Leiden: E.J. Brill, 1955) is excellent on the subject of chronology which varies somewhat depending on the scale used and, more importantly, on when the scale was devised. Immanuel Velikovsky is one of many who have suggested that there are features of the general chronologies in use that are to be questioned. His controversial *Peoples of the Sea* (Garden City, N.Y.: Doubleday, 1977) is a book to look into if the problem interests you, for it deals heavily with it while dealing with ancient Egypt. The sea peoples, by the way, were a group of marauders who distressed the Egyptians near the end of the Bronze Age. See N.K. Sandars' excellent *The Sea Peoples* (London: Thames and Hudson, 1978/i) for a less intrepid approach to their activities, times, and origins than that given by Velikovsky.

Translations

Quite a few sources of Egyptian texts in translation are now in existence. One of the primary works for myths is Samuel A.B. Mercer's *The Pyramid Texts in Translation and Commentary,* four volumes (New York: Longmans, Green, 1952/i). Another is E.A. Wallis Budge's *The Book of the Dead* (New York: Bell Publishing Co., 1960/i; reprint of an earlier edition); it has an excellent introduction by Budge and is illustrated throughout with examples of hieroglyphic texts and passages. Still another is N. Rambova's *Mythological Papyri Texts* (New York: Bollingen Series, 1957), a multi-volume work. James H. Breasted's *Ancient Records of Egypt*, four volumes (New York: Russell and Russell, 1962; originally 1906) is a well edited set primarily devoted to history and politics. James Pritchard's *Ancient Near Eastern Texts Relating to the Old Testament*, 3rd edition (Princeton: Princeton University Press, 1969/p; paperbound edition entitled *The Ancient Near East*), has some Egyptian mortuary and other texts. A few useful texts also are included in *Papyrus and Tablet* (Englewood Cliffs, N.J.: Prentice-Hall, 1973), ed. A. Grayson and D. Redford. Several Egyptian creation texts are included in *Origins: Creation Texts from the Ancient Mediterranean* (Garden City, N.Y.: Anchor Books, 1976/p), ed. and trans. Charles Doria and Harris Lenowitz. Several good anthologies of Egyptian literature in translation are also available, many of the texts in them mythological in subject matter: Adolf Erman's *The Ancient Egyptians: A Sourcebook of Their Writings*, trans. Aylward M. Blackman (New York: Harper Torchbooks, 1966/p); Miriam Lichtheim's three-volume *Ancient Egyptian Literature: A Book of Readings* (Berkeley: University of California Press, 1975, 1976, 1980/p); William Kelly Simpson's *The Literature of Ancient Egypt*, new edition (New Haven: Yale University Press, 1973/p).

Somewhere between original Egyptian literature and later adaptation of Egyptian myth is H.W. Fairman's *The Triumph of Horus* (Berkeley: University of California Press, 1974). Fairman, the translator of a number of Horus texts, has reconstructed from Egyptian texts what he feels was a drama of the ritual, religious sort; the result is a short play (42 of the book's 150 pages) which may or may not be what the Egyptians had in mind. Whatever, it is most interesting.

As regards the translation of hieroglyphics specifically, there are good chapters on the original deciphering in any of the following books: Leo Deuel's *Testaments of Time: The Search for Lost Manuscripts and Records* (New York: Alfred A. Knopf, 1965/ib); Maurice Pope's *The Story of Archaeological Decipherment: From Egyptian Hieroglyphs to Linear B* (New York: Charles Scribner's Sons, 1975/i); Ernst Doblhofer's *Voices in Stone: The Decipherment of Ancient Scripts and Writings*, trans. Mervyn Savill (New York: Viking Press, 1961/i). There are also some fine chapters in both books by C.W. Ceram discussed in the paragraph that follows.

Works on Archaeology

T.G.H. James' *The Archaeology of Ancient Egypt* (New York: Henry Z. Walck, 1973/i) is one of the many works you can turn to for explicitly archaeological matters. It would be suitable for any age from junior high on up. Pierre Montet's *Isis, Or the Search for Egypt's Buried Past*, trans. Bradford G. Adams (Geneva: Editions Ferni, 1977/i; originally 1956) is, in a sense, the history of Egyptology from primarily the archaeological point of view. It, too, is lively reading for even younger readers. The archaeology of Egypt, Mesopotamia, and India are dealt with in V. Gordon Childe's excellent *New Light on the Most Ancient East* (New York: W.W. Norton, 1953/ip). A whole section, incorporating many chapters, will be found in each of two of C.W. Ceram's fine books: *Gods, Graves, and Scholars*, 2nd edition, trans. E.B. Garside and Sophie Wilkins (New York: Bantam Books, 1972/ip; originally published in a shorter hardbound edition by Alfred A. Knopf in 1951), and *Hands on the Past: Pioneer Archaeologists Tell Their Own Stories* (New York: Alfred A. Knopf, 1966; Schocken paperbound edition, 1970/ip). Jacquetta Hawkes' *Atlas of Ancient Archaeology* (New York: McGraw-Hill, 1974/i) includes a useful section on individual archaeological sites in Egypt, and the *Larousse Encyclopedia of Archaeology* (London: Hamlyn, 1972/i), ed. Gilbert Charles Picard, trans. Anne Ward, has a fairly long, beautifully illustrated section on archaeology in the Nile Valley. Henri-Paul Eydoux's *In Search of Lost Worlds*, trans. Lorna Andrade (London: Hamlyn, 1972/i) also has a few chapters that are devoted to Egyptology—the archaeological mainly—in it. John Gray's *Archaeology and the Old Testament World* (London: Thomas Nelson, 1962/ip; New York: Harper Torchbooks, 1965) and J. Mellaart's *The Chalcolithic and Early Bronze Ages in the Near East and Anatolia* (Beirut: Khayats, 1966) both have some space devoted to it, as well.

Works on Art

Any concern with Egyptian architecture is a concern with temples and pyramids, in effect a concern, too, with archaeology. Alexander Badawy's *A History of Egyptian Architecture* (Berkeley: University of California Press, 1966/i) is one of the best overall sources; it includes sections on religious and funerary architecture in relation to Egyptian belief and ritual. E.A.E. Reymond's *The Mythical*

Origin of the Egyptian Temple (New York: Barnes & Noble, 1969) has a great deal of value. J. Norman Lockyer's *The Dawn of Astronomy: A Study of the Temple Worship and Mythology of the Ancient Egyptians* (Cambridge: M.I.T. Press, 1964; first published in 1894) begins with a survey of worship of the sun and other heavenly bodies and proceeds to examine temples to deities like Hathor and their relation to heavenly bodies. Barbara Mertz's *Temples, Tombs, and Hieroglyphs* (New York: Coward-McCann, 1964/i) is more worthwhile on architecture than on archaeology *per se*. I.E.S. Edwards' *The Pyramids of Egypt* (New York: Viking Press, 1972/ip; first published by Penguin, 1961) is a visually beautiful book in which Edwards offers his expert theories about the reasons for and manner of construction of the great pyramids. Peter Thompkins' *Secrets of the Great Pyramid* (New York: Harper & Row, 1971/ib) is copious in its coverage of the excavation of Egyptian pyramids, theories about them, and the like. He's also the author of *Mysteries of the Mexican Pyramids* (New York: Harper & Row, 1976/ib), a book I mention here since in it Thompkins deals some with pyramids elsewhere, Egypt included, as a way of explaining the possibility that the ancient Mexicans got their ideas from afar. R.A. Jairazbhoy, to extend this aside, is another of those who sees Egyptian influence when he looks at Middle American pyramids; see his *Ancient Egyptians and Chinese in America* (London: George Prior, 1974/ib) for the details. Philippe Aziz' *The Mysteries of the Great Pyramid*, trans. John Derek Megginson (Geneva: Editions Ferni, 1977/i; originally published much earlier), is concerned with the pyramid of Cheops mainly, but there is also some attention in it to the pyramids of Egypt generally and to others elsewhere.

Works concerned with Egyptian art abound. William S. Smith's all-embracing *The Art and Architecture of Ancient Egypt*, 3rd edition (London, 1948; Harmondsworth, G.B.: Penguin, 1958 /ip) is one you might wish to start with. *Egypt: Architecture, Sculpture, Painting in 3,000 Years*, 3rd edition (London: Phaidon, 1961/i), also takes on just about all that can be described as art in ancient Egypt, but it is largely a pictures volume. The same can be said of *The Art of Ancient Egypt* (Vienna: Phaidon, 1936/i), the only appreciable text in it being Hermann Ranke's introduction. Eberhard Otto's *Ancient Egyptian Art* (New York: Harry Abrams, 1967/ib) is a simply lovely book in which text and pictures are combined well. Three books with the same title, *Egyptian Art*, are all colorful and useful volumes, too: Vagn Poulsen's (Greenwich, Conn.: New York Graphic Society, 1968/i); Francesco Abbate's, trans. H.A. Fields (London: Octopus Books, 1969); and Werner and Bedrich Forman's (London: Peter Nevill, 1962). Irmgard Woldering's *Art of Egypt* (New York: Crown Publishers, 1963/i) has hundreds of illustrations and reasonably good text, and Arpag Mekhitarian's *Egyptian Painting*, trans. Stuart Gilbert (New York: Skira, World Publishing Co., 1954/i), a shorter volume devoted to painting and its long history in Egypt, is filled with lovely color plates. For the most comprehensive overall survey of Egyptian art, K. Michalowski's *Art of Ancient Egypt* (New York: Harry N. Abrams, 1974/i) has to be the one, however. It has 143 color plates and almost 800 illustrations in all.

Some works you might, because of their titles, overlook are also worth mentioning. *The Book of the Dead: Papyri of Ani, Hunefer, Anhai* (New York: Miller Graphics, n.d./i), with commentaries by Evelyn Rossiter, is a beautiful book in which all of the vignettes from the three papyri mentioned in the book's title are illustrated in color in their original order. The book would serve nicely for the art alone or along with works on Egyptian eschatology. Seton Lloyd's *The Art of the Ancient Near East* (New York: Frederick A. Praeger, 1961/i) is really a kind of cultural history using art extensively. Egypt, Mesopotamia, and Persia are the ancient countries most thoroughly dealt with. James B. Pritchard's *The Ancient Near East in Pictures*, 2nd edition (Princeton: Princeton University Press, 1969/ip), the companion volume to his *Ancient Near Eastern Texts Relating to the Old Testament*, has hundreds of pictures, many devoted to things Egyptian, and the section of interpretative notes is particularly good with such short essays as "Gods and Their Emblems" and "The Practice of Religion." There's a lovely portfolio of photographs of art and artifacts from ancient Egypt in Alice J. Hall's "Dazzling Legacy of an Ancient Quest," *National Geographic*, 151 (March 1977/i), pp. 292–311. As a further step toward finding pictures especially, don't overlook books which would seem to be specialized in ways not necessarily relevant to myth study, perhaps the perfect example being the many books that in recent decades have appeared on Tutankhamen. One of the better and more useful ones in that group is Christiane Desroches

Noblecourt's *Tutankhamen: Life and Death of a Pharaoh* (New York: New York Graphic Society, 1963/i). It is loaded with excellent photographs, many of them of characters and scenes from Egyptian mythology.

Later African Mythologies

The mythologies of Africa have for some time been split into two large groups—those that derive from ancient Mediterranean origins and those which derive from the black societies of "traditional" Africa. The former mythologies are to be found largely in northern Africa—north of the Sahara and Sudan—and involve ancient Egyptian, Islamic, and Christian, all of them covered elsewhere in this guide. They are part of the ancient Mediterranean world more than of Africa and, in the cases of Islamic and Christian at least, are "imported" mythologies. The "traditional" African mythologies are found in the black African societies generally south of Mauritania, Algeria, Libya, and modern-day Egypt—although after all the missionary work that has been done and political/social reorganization that has taken place, they are not all current. Unlike the northern mythologies, they are not "book" mythologies. That is, there were no written texts prior to the myths being collected and written down by anthropologists, missionaries, and other field workers. They derive from oral traditions which in many cases date back hundreds of years but which, due to the nature of oral traditions, cannot actually be traced back in time except speculatively. Hence, they are designated as "Later African" whether or not the "later" is always verifiably accurate.

Traditional Africans are a surprisingly diverse and large proportion of the overall population of the continent. It has been said that there are between 25 and 30 broad African "societies" and, within those societies, more than 6,000 tribes. The figure is astounding only when divorced from the facts. It's not astounding, for instance, when one knows that in Zaire alone (formerly the Belgian Congo and Congo Democratic Republic) over 300 languages are spoken!

Beneath the diversity, however, is an easily perceived unity that goes beyond the merely racial or physical. What may broadly be called the "culture" of traditional Africa crosses the boundaries of societies and tribes in important ways, making similarities between the separate groups far more prominent than differences. As you study the mythologies of black Africa, you will be struck by the common concerns, fears, and aspirations; by the repeated motifs and themes; by the general oneness of the myths for all their variety. And just as the stories you read will be uniquely African when viewed collectively, they will quite clearly be stories common to the community of man regardless of time or place of origin.

Collections of the Myths

Of the many thousands of narratives that have been collected in Africa, the *overwhelming* majority are folktales. What is more, a great many of the narratives involve animals and insects. The problem for the myth student is that the narratives won't always classify easily. Telling the sacral myth from the folktale is often impossible without knowing the cultural/religious context of the narrative, and because even the animal and insect narratives may be sacral myths, contrary to what one would expect, it is very often necessary to know a *great deal* about the cultural/ religious setting. Many of the collections of African narratives are apt to be confusing rather than helpful. Folktales, legends, and sacral myths are frequently lumped together, division of narratives more often based on myth type (*i.e.*: animal tale, eschatological tale, etc.) rather than on class of myth (*i.e.*: sacral myth, legend, folktale).

Let none of this deter you from getting into traditional or later African mythology, though, for the stories are, by and large, a fascinating group—to a great extent, and surprisingly since they've only recently been recorded, as *literary* a group as you'll find outside the highly polished myths of the ancient Greeks and Romans.

Geoffrey Parrinder's *African Mythology* (London: Paul Hamlyn, 1967/ib) is the best of the available collections mainly because Parrinder, an expert on traditional African religion, provides excellent background for the reader and has organized the book in such a way that the classification problems are minimized. *African Mythology* is a beautifully illustrated volume in Hamlyn's fine *International Mythology* series. Susan Feldmann's *African Myths and Tales* (New York: Dell Laurel, 1970/ip) is also a fine little collection. Feldmann's introduction is superb, and the narratives included in the book are separated into two larger categories, myths and tales, making the classification adequate. Also, the 108 stories she's chosen are nicely representative as well as highly entertaining. The section on African mythology in the *Larousse World Mythology* (New York: Putnam, 1965/i), ed. Pierre Grimal, trans. Patricia Beardsworth, is nicely illustrated and is reasonably long, the space limitations of a single-volume, worldwide mythography considered. It is organized geographically, however, as is the shorter section in the *Larousse Encyclopedia of Mythology* (London: Paul Hamlyn, 1959/ip), ed. Felix Guirand, trans. Richard Aldington and Delano Ames. Volume II of the *Pears Encyclopedia of Myths and Legends* (London: Pelham Books, 1977/ib) has a good representative section on African mythology that includes a fair amount of background as well. It is organized by content features in the myths largely (though not necessarily by myth type). Somewhat over half of Volume VII in *The Mythology of All Races* series (Boston: Marshall Jones, 1916–32; reprinted in New York by Cooper Square Publishers, 1964, etc.) is devoted to African myths. It's a fair source of myths and folktales, but since 1964 many important myths have been collected for the first time. Just four pages are on African mythology in the *Encyclopedia of World Mythology* (New York: Galahad Books, 1975/i), and only a few tribes— and myths—are represented. Too few pages of text are also the case in Veronica Ions' *The World's Mythology in Colour* (London: Paul Hamlyn, 1974/i), though for illustrations the book is hard to beat. Kathleen Arnott's *African Myths and Legends* (New York: Henry Z. Walck, 1963/i) is a useful collection for younger readers especially (grades four through seven roughly), and there are a fair number of myths included.

Jan Knappert's *Myths and Legends of the Congo* (Atlantic Highlands, N.J.: Humanities Press, 1971/p) is a nice anthology. It's easy-to-read; the tales in it are categorized by tribe and include the run of myth and folktale types—although for the latter no classification is given. You might also be interested in an heroic epic of the Nyanga Congolese, *The Mwindo Epic* (Berkeley: University of California Press, 1969/p), ed. and trans. Daniel Biebuyck and Kahombo C. Mateene. Jan Knappert is also the author of *Myths and Legends of the Swahili* (Atlantic Highlands, N.J.: Humanities Press, 1970/p). Here the organization is by content (but not necessarily by type). It's a good collection made all the more interesting by the inclusion of a group of Old

Testament and Islamic myths and legends in which characters and events are infused with new attitudes and characteristics. Alice Werner's *Myths and Legends of the Bantu* (London: George C. Harrap, 1933/i) is an excellent collection which includes stories of where man came from, how death came about, animal tales, and the like. A.C. Hollis' *The Masai, Their Language and Folklore* (Oxford: Clarendon Press, 1905) contains a nice selection of myths and folktales, "The Beginner of the Earth" among them, but the book's age and later ethnographic work limit its completeness. One of the more stunning accomplishments in African studies has to be the book called *Dahomean Narrative: A Cross-Cultural Analysis* (Evanston, Ill.: Northwestern University Press, 1958), by Melville J. and Frances S. Herskovits. While it contains a good collection of Dahomean narratives nicely classified, it is as much an analytic work as a collection. The part entitled "A Cross-Cultural Approach to Myth" (pp. 81–122) is a classic in myth theory. A.J.N. Tremearne's *Hausa Superstitions and Customs* (London: Staples Printers, 1917/i) and H. Callaway's *The Religious System of the Amazulu* (London: Trubner & Co., 1870; reprinted in Capetown by C. Struik, 1970) are both dated works, of course, but Tremearne's book is an ethnographical work with a great number of narratives, and Callaway's bi-lingual text broadly covers Amazulu religion.

Folktales play a large role in the overall group of narratives comprising African mythology. Paul Radin's *African Folktales* (Princeton: Princeton University Press, 1970/p) is an excellent collection. So, too, is Leo Frobenius' *African Genesis* (New York: Stackpole and Sons, 1937; reprinted in 1966 by Benjamin Blom of New York), done in collaboration with Douglas C. Fox. In addition to including a large group of folktales from northern Africa, it is also a study of the tales' relation to cave paintings and the prehistory of Europe. *African Folktales and Sculpture* (New York: Pantheon, 1964/i), by Paul Radin and James J. Sweeney, is a good collection of folktales made all the better by Radin's excellent introduction on African folktales generally and the 187 black and white plates plus fold-out map. A. Jablow's *Yes and No, the Intimate Folklore of Africa* (New York: Horizon Press, 1961) is a good collection covering many tribes. Romanus Egudu's *The Calabash of Wisdom and Other Igbo Stories* (New York: NOK Publishers, 1973/p) has thirty tales in it that really give insight into Igbo thought. As with many other collections of

African narratives, etiological and trickster tales are prominent in this work. *West African Folk-Tales* (London: Harrap, 1917), by W.H. Barker and Cecelia Sinclair, is now severely dated by much later anthropological field work, but it has a useful selection of the west African tales. A. Fuja's *Fourteen Hundred Cowries and Other African Tales* (London: Oxford University Press, 1962) is comprised of traditional tales of the Yoruba, but if you wish some sacral myths of the Yoruba, you'll have to go to Judith Gleason's *Orisha: The Gods of Yorubaland* (New York: Atheneum, 1971), a pleasant collection suitable for readers from about the sixth grade and up.

Another group of collections is comprised of volumes by topic, but including the run of myth classes. Uui Beier's *The Origin of Life and Death: African Creation Myths* (London: Heinemann, 1966/p) has eighteen myths, all of them broadly creation in type, and includes "How the World Was Created from a Drop of Milk." Each myth is identified as to place of origin, and there's a good introductory chapter. R. Meyrowitz's *Akan Traditions of Origin* (London: Faber, n.d.) has all the known origin myths of the Akan (Ghana). There are, incidentally, eight African creation myths in Maria Leach's *The Beginning: Creation Myths Around the World* (New York: Funk and Wagnalls, 1956). Hans Abrahamsson's *The Origin of Death: Studies in African Mythology* (London: Kegan Paul, 1952; reprinted by Arno Press of New York, 1976), originally a doctor of theology dissertation done in Sweden (1951), is excellent on its subject. Abrahamsson reviews the theories associated with origin of death myths, narrates and discusses the African myths related to the theme, surveys the results, tabulates and correlates them to the theories, and locates the whereabouts of the myths on a series of maps. Uche Okeke's *Tales of the Land of Death* (Garden City, N.Y.: Zenith Books, 1971) is a collection of Igbo folktales about *Ana Mmuo*, the land of the dead. The most famous of the tales, "The Bat," is a dandy, but there are other good ones like "The War of Heaven and Earth" and "The Gift of Fire." And speaking of fire, James George Frazer's *Myths of the Origin of Fire* (London: Macmillan, 1930) has two chapters in it on African myths. K.O. Bonsu-Kyeretwei's *Ashanti Heroes* (New York: Panther House, 1972/p) is a good collection of hero myths and folktales. In Katharine Luomala's *Oceanic, American Indian, and African Myths of Snaring the Sun* (Millwood, N.Y.: Kraus Reprint of the 1940 edition, 1975/p) there are myths of another type you may wish at some time to investigate as part of your study of African mythology.

H. Scheub has fortunately compiled an excellent library reference volume should the preceding collections fall short of fulfilling your needs, a work called *African Oral Narratives, Proverbs, Riddles, Poetry and Song: An Annotated Bibliography* (Leiden: E.J. Brill, 1977).

Studies of the Myths

Besides the collections, there are other sources to look to. One of the most productive of them—for matters of ritual, time, and religion as well as myths—is *Myth and Cosmos: Readings in Mythology and Symbolism* (Garden City, N.Y.: The Natural History Press, 1967/bp), ed. John Middleton. Middleton's "Some Social Aspects of Lugbara Myth" and Thomas O. Beidelman's "Hyena and Rabbit" (the analysis of a Kaguru myth) are two articles concerned with myth. A book having to do mainly with the history of Africa and with anthropological research there, *The African World: A Survey of Social Research* (London: Pall Mall Press, 1965), ed. Robert A. Lystad, has one of the best articles of all, William Bascom's "Folklore and Literature" (pp. 469-90). Louis-Marie Ongoum's "Myth and Literature in Africa," trans. Robert Blohm, in *Diogenes*, no. 80 (Winter 1972), pp. 51-62, is a particularly concise and thoughtful discussion of the range represented by myth, oral tradition, and literature (which are indeed *one*, but which the author sees as the movement from emphasis of the mythic to *logos*). The article is excellent for theory and definition ("Literature is a degeneration of Myth allured to intellect.") as well as useful for the African examples. Wole Soyinka's *Myth, Literature and the African World* (Cambridge: Cambridge University Press, 1976) will prove most useful for seeing how African communities (Yoruba mainly) perceive themselves; myth is one of the principal forms in which that perception is found. Luc se Heusch's "Myths and the Convulsions of History," trans. Robert Blohm, in *Diogenes*, no. 78 (Summer 1972), pp. 64-86, is concerned with the epic of the Bemba as a demonstration of the mythic structure of that people and as an exercise in the relationship of history, myth, and the power/authority sanctions of the culture. G.I. Jones' "Oral Tradition and History," in *African Notes*, 2 (January 1965), pp. 7-11, and Jan Vansina's "Once Upon a Time: Oral Traditions as History in Africa," in *Daedalus*,

no. 100 (Spring 1971), pp. 442-68, are both very useful for understanding African myth. Jones' article is good on how history
and myth may be separated from one another—or at least on
what the problems in separating them may be in African myth.
Vansina's article deals with that problem in greater depth; it
delves into the roles, in orally transmitted tradition, of cliches,
nuances, and the intention and memory of the teller. Daniel
Whitman's article on the power of the word in Africa, "Africa
and the Word," *Parabola*, 2 (Spring 1977), pp. 66-73, goes so
far as to point out what may be our lost creative potential today:
the question being whether or not a written tradition relies on the
word in the same way as an oral tradition. Ivor Wilks' review
article entitled "Do Africans Have a Sense of Time?," *The International Journal of African Historical Studies*, 8 (1975), pp.
279-87, covers, mainly by analogy, mythological time in Africa.
The book reviewed, by the way, is David P. Henige's *The Chronology
of Oral Tradition: Quest for a Chimera* (New York: Oxford
University Press, 1974); since just about every African myth
has been retrieved by anthropologists from an oral tradition,
you might wish to look into that book as a way of deepening
your understanding of African myth. Thomas O. Beidelman's
"Ambiguous Animals: Two Theriomorphic Metaphors in Kaguru
Folklore," in *Africa*, 45 (1975), pp. 183-200, is superb for showing
the problems inherent in analyzing myths and folktales; two
African myths are the examples.

Two items with something to offer, though mainly by analogy
and deduction, are the article by Alfredo Margarido and Francoise
Germaix Wasserman entitled "On the Myth and Practice of the
Blacksmith in Africa," in *Diogenes*, no. 78 (Summer 1972), pp.
87-122, and Melville J. Herskovits' book called *The Myth of the
Negro Past* (Boston: Beacon Press, 1958; originally published in
1941/bp). While the former work is a discussion of the blacksmith
in several African societies and the sanctions for his power and
position there, the article is valid in African myth study for
seeing the *function* of myth in Africa. Herskovits' book, while
explicitly a study of the American black and his/her heritage,
has much to offer *about* what constitutes a mythology and what,
in particular, are the vestiges of black African mythology in the
culture and practices of American blacks. See especially the
chapter entitled "The Contemporary Scene: Africanisms in
Religious Life."

Works on Religion and Related Matters

Works that are principally concerned with African religion and philosophy are not only useful as *background* to the study of African mythology, often they deal with myths in such a way as to make them useful for the analysis and interpretation of myths. For example, in *African Systems of Thought* (London: Oxford University Press, 1965), ed. M. Fortes and G. Dieterlen, myths of the tribes that are dealt with in the book's many essays are frequently analyzed and interpreted. The same holds true for the book called *African Worlds: Studies in the Cosmological Ideas and Values of African Peoples* (London: Oxford University Press, 1954), ed. Daryll Forde, a great collection of essays, all of which get at the world views of various African peoples, including the Lele, Lovedu, Dogon, Mende, and others.

E. Geoffrey Parrinder's "God in African Mythology," pp. 111–25 in *Myths and Symbols: Studies in Honor of Mircea Eliade* (Chicago: University of Chicago Press, 1969), has much to offer. So, too, does the spectacular collection of essays coedited by Edwin Smith and Parrinder, *African Ideas of God* (London: Edinburgh House Press, 1950). It offers a great cross section of African viewpoints on God. Malcolm J. McVeigh's *God in Africa: Conceptions of God in African Traditional Religion and Christianity* (Cape Cod, Mass.: Claude Stark, 1974) is a fine comparative study that will serve to illuminate the myths nicely. As the title indicates, syncretism is a major concern of McVeigh. J.B. Danquah's *The Akan Doctrine of God: A Fragment of Gold Coast Ethics and Religion* (London: Lutterworth Press, 1944) is not as useful overall as is section two, "The Akan Meaning of God." There, God in myth is the subject, whatever the title might otherwise suggest.

There are some excellent broad works on African religion that can be quite helpful. Geoffrey Parrinder's *African Traditional Religion*, 3rd edition (New York: Harper Forum Books, 1976/bp) covers the essential topics in a very general way—the gods, rituals, magic, sorcery, and eschatology. Parrinder's *Religion in Africa* (Harmondsworth, G.B.: Penguin, 1969/bp), a longer work that covers Christianity and Moslem religion in Africa as well as the traditional religions, is also a commendable introductory work. John S. Mbiti's *Introduction to African Religion* (London: Heinemann, 1975) is, too; but for a more comprehensive treatment of African religions, Mbiti's superb *African Religions and Philosophy*

(London: Heinemann, 1969; Garden City, N.Y.: Anchor Books, 1970/bp) should be consulted. Benjamin C. Ray's *African Religions: Symbol, Ritual, and Community* (Englewood Cliffs, N.J.: Prentice-Hall, 1976/bp) is a good description of African religions from prehistory through current Christian and Islamic forms. Noel Q. King's *Religions of Africa: A Pilgrimage into Traditional Religions* (New York: Harper & Row, 1970/b) is a *very* brief introduction, but it can be of help for the beginner. *The Historical Study of African Religion* (Berkeley: University of California Press, 1972), ed. T. O. Ranger and I. N. Kimambo, has many essays that should be useful, among them Merrick Posnansky's "Archaeology, Ritual and Religion" and Michael Gilsenan's "Myth and the History of African Religion." *African Religions: A Symposium* (New York: NOK Publishers, 1977/b), ed. Newell S. Booth, is a marvelous background source that includes thirteen essays, most of them on the religions of particular tribes but including the highly recommended "African Mythology: A Key to Understanding African Religion," a lengthy essay written by Kipng'eno Koech.

There are numerous works on African religions that have a regional or tribal focus. E. Geoffrey Parrinder's *West African Religion* (New York: Barnes & Noble, 1969; first published in 1949) is best described by its subtitle, "A Study of the Beliefs and Practices of Akan, Ewe, Yoruba, Ibo and Kindred Peoples." Myth students will delight in it—if for no further reason than that it contains *four* fine chapters on the gods. *Religion and Civilization in West Africa* (London: World Dominion Press, 1931), by J. J. Cooksey and Alexander McLeish, deals with the colonial and missionary activities in French, British, Portuguese, and Spanish West Africa through the year 1930; for syncretism in Africa, this is certainly one work to check into. O. Lucas' *The Religion of the Yoruba* (Lagos, 1948), E. Bolaji Idowu's *Olodumare: God in Yoruba Belief* (London: Longmans, 1962; New York: Praeger, 1963), and Wande Abimbola's *Ifa Divination Poetry* (New York: NOK Publishers, 1977) all deal with the Yoruba of West Africa. Idowu's book is "a new study of the belief of the Yoruba with the specific aim of emphasizing their concept of deity." Abimbola's work includes sixty poems and a nice introductory discussion of Yoruba mythology and the divination system of Ifa (a major divinity in Yorubaland). Thomas T. S. Hayley's *The Anatomy of Lango Religion and Groups* (Cambridge: Cambridge University Press, 1947) and D. A. Low's *Religion and Society in Buganda* (Kampala: East African Institute of Social Research, 1956) both deal with

East African peoples; Low's work is just a pamphlet in size but nonetheless useful. Canon H. Callaway's "The Religion of the Amazulu of South Africa as Told by Themselves," pp. 420-29 in *Source Book in Anthropology*, revised edition (New York: Harcourt, Brace and Co., 1931), ed. A. L. Kroeber and T. T. Waterman, and Hendrik C. Luttig's *The Religious System and Social Organization of the Herero* (Utrecht, 1933) are both on South African peoples. Finally, three more of many like them that could be included are Godfrey Leinhardt's *Divinity and Experience: The Religion of the Dinka* (Oxford: Clarendon Press, 1961); Robert H. Lowie's discussion of Ekoi religion in chapter two of his book *Primitive Religion* (New York: Boni and Liveright, 1924); and James H. Vaughan, Jr.'s "The Religion and World View of the Marghi," an article in *Ethnology*, 3 (October 1964), pp. 389-97.

Another useful library reference volume, this one on religion and philosophy in Africa, is P. Ofori's *Black African Traditional Religions and Philosophy: A Select Bibliographic Survey of the Sources from the Earliest Times to 1974* (Leiden: E. J. Brill, 1974).

Further works within a broad spectrum of religion-related subjects conclude the discussion of works having to do with African religions. Percival Hadfield's *Traits of Divine Kingship in Africa* (London: Watts & Co., 1949) deals with the rituals, beliefs, and practices associated with divine kingship in a widespread group of African peoples. M. Fortes' *Oedipus and Job in West African Religion* (Cambridge: Cambridge University Press, 1959) is, generally speaking, a Frazerian attempt to demonstrate the unity of mankind. Fortes shows, in reasonable enough fashion, that the religious conceptions evidenced in the myths of Oedipus and Job are also to be found in West African religious systems. A useful work in African myth study—and particularly good on magic—is E. E. Evans-Pritchard's *Witchcraft, Oracles and Magic Among the Azande* (Oxford: Clarendon Press, 1937). A collection of essays on the same general topic, and including several on African tribes, is *Magic, Witchcraft, and Curing* (Garden City, N.Y.: Natural History Press, 1967), ed. John Middleton. "The Evil Eye Belief among the Amhara of Ethiopia," an article by Ronald A. Reminick in *Ethnology*, 8 (July 1974), pp. 279-91, has only tangentially to do with the subjects we're here interested in, but there is no question that what causes and sustains belief of any sort, in the evil eye or in myths, can be usefully studied for myth students' purposes *whatever* the context. Reminick's article, by the way, is included in *The Evil Eye* (New York: Columbia University Press, 1976), ed.

Clarence Maloney, a work in which the incidence of the evil eye belief around the world is investigated pretty thoroughly, including one article on the evil eye belief in Tunisia. C. W. Hobley's *Bantu Beliefs and Magic*, 2nd edition (London: H. F. & G. Witherley, 1938) has a good deal of importance in myth study despite the book's age (1922 originally). What Hobley tells us of Bantu beliefs in spirits and of their natural religion "translates" very well into what the myth student will find valuable. The same holds true of Eduard A. Westermarck's *Ritual and Belief in Morocco*, two volumes (New Hyde Park, N.Y.: University Books, 1968), a work concerned principally with Moslem peoples and including investigations of miracles, superstitions, and even the evil eye. Victor Turner's *Revelation and Divination in Ndembu Ritual* (Ithaca, N.Y.: Cornell University Press, 1975), although packed with information for the specialist in the anthropology of religions, is one of the finest books I know of from which insights can be gained into the purpose and meaning of ritual; the Ndembu of Zambia are the main focus. Also dealing with an African tribe and revealing much about the connection of ritual and belief, as well as with their function in society, is Edward H. Winter's "The Slaughter of a Bull: A Study of Cosmology and Ritual," in *Process and Pattern in Culture* (Chicago: Aldine Publishing Co., 1964), ed. Robert A. Manners. Winter's fine article on "Amba Religion" can be found in *Gods and Rituals: Readings in Religious Beliefs and Practices* (Garden City, N.Y.: Natural History Press, 1967/bp), ed. John Middleton, a book in which several other articles deal mainly with ritual among African peoples; Edward Norbeck's "African Rituals of Conflict" is one of them. A couple of articles on ritual in Africa are also included in *The Interpretation of Ritual* (London: Tavistock Publications, 1974/p). "Animals in Lele Religious Symbolism," by Mary Douglas in her *Implicit Meanings: Essays in Anthropology* (London: Routledge & Kegan Paul, 1975), will be quite useful for Congolese mythology. The importance of a symbolic object to believers is really made clear in William S. Ellis' "A Sacred Symbol Comes Home," *National Geographic*, 146 (July 1974), pp. 140–48. It deals with the return of a statue from Dartmouth College to the people of Cameroon. What happens when two myth systems come in conflict with one another is nicely dealt with in Elizabeth Isichei's "Ibo and Christian Beliefs: Some Aspects of a Theological Encounter," *African Affairs*, 68 (April 1969), pp. 121–34. Robin Horton deals with the shift from traditional religions in Africa to Christianity or Islamic religions in his two-part rebuttal article, "On the Rationality of Conversion," *Africa* 45 (1975), pp. 219–35 and 373–98.

Works on Historical/Cultural Background

If you're after historical/cultural background to the study of African mythology, a good place to look is Basil Davidson's *Africa: History of a Continent* (New York: Macmillan, 1966/ib), a beautifully illustrated history of Africa from ancient times (Egypt included). Robert W. July's *A History of the African People* (New York: Scribner's, 1970/ib) is another fine history, about half of it devoted to ancient times. Unlike either Davidson or July, Roland Oliver and John D. Fage spend a disproportionate amount of time on outside influences on African history in their *A Short History of Africa*, 3rd edition (Harmondsworth, G.B.: Penguin, 1970/p) even though they, too, survey the history of Africa from earliest times on. Contrasted with a "short" history is a long one, the multi-volume *Cambridge History of Africa* (Cambridge: Cambridge University Press, 1970, etc./ib). It is, needless to say, comprehensive. At this writing, though, Volume V, only through the year 1870, was the last in the set.

Concerned more with culture than history alone are a number of other works. Colin Turnbull's *Man in Africa* (Garden City, N.Y.: Doubleday Anchor Press, 1976/i) is an excellent general description of the cultures of Africa, from the north to the south and from the old to the new. Turnbull deals tenaciously and well with the unity he sees as underlying all of Africa's cultures. *Peoples and Cultures of Africa* (Garden City, N.Y.: Natural History Press, 1973/bp), ed. Elliott P. Skinner, is a superb volume that includes a total of thirty-six articles organized into six parts having to do with geography, ecology, prehistory, culture, religion and ritual. The parts entitled "African Social Institutions" and "African Beliefs and Religions" will be of most use. G. P. Murdock's *Africa: Its Peoples and Their Culture History* (New York: McGraw-Hill, 1959/i) is a popularized survey of African history and culture. For a very brief overview of the African people, see Basil Davidson's "Africa: The Face Behind the Mask" in *The Light of the Past: A Treasury of Horizon* (New York: American Heritage Publishing Co., 1959/i).

Speaking of Davidson, he is probably the best known author on African history and culture despite the fact that he is not a trained scholar in the ordinary sense; he has written prolifically about

Africa and, as a stylist, is hard to beat. Some others of his exemplary works are *African Kingdoms* (New York: Time-Life Books, 1966/ib), a simply beautiful book in Time-Life's *Great Ages of Man* series; *The Lost Cities of Africa*, revised edition (Boston: Little, Brown, 1970/i), an outline of what is known "and what it now seems reasonable to believe about some leading aspects and achievements of African life and civilization" during the fifteen hundred years prior to the start of colonialization; and *The African Past* (Boston: Little, Brown, 1964), an anthology of excerpts from the writings of explorers, historians, and others which deal with various cultural phenomena as observed or heard about.

Margaret Shinnie's *Ancient African Kingdoms* (New York: St. Martin's Press, 1966; New American Library paperback, 1970/ip) is a fine work with much about earlier Africa and later primitive societies. H. Alimen's *The Prehistory of Africa*, trans. A. H. Brodrick (London: Hutchinson, 1957) is an attempt at geographic reconstruction of the prehistory of Africa that is especially valuable on the diffusion of cultures there. John G. Jackson, by the way, surmises and tries to prove Ethiopian origins of ancient Egyptian civilization in his *Man, God, and Civilization* (New Hyde Park, N.Y.: University Books, 1972). There are many parts of the book otherwise useful in myth study, for instance, the chapters on "Totemism and Exogamy," "The Worship of Nature," "The Origin of Magic and Religion," and "Myths and Mysteries: Pagan and Christian."

An all-around reference work is *Dictionary of Black African Civilization* (New York: Leon Amiel, 1974/i), by Georges Balandier and Jacques Maguet, both well known Africanists. It is a thoroughly well-illustrated book that includes entries on art, culture, archaeology, anthropology, religious life, social life, places, and other matters.

A great many works that deal with the culture and history of individual regions or societies and tribes have appeared in recent years. A few only will be mentioned here. Kenneth Little's *The Mende of Sierre Leone* (London: Routledge & Kegan Paul, 1951/b) is a paradigm of what can be done with the cultural history of a single African people since it covers just about every facet of Mende life and history possible—and there's a good chapter in which myths and religious beliefs and practices are dealt with. T. G. H. Strehlow's *Aranda Traditions* (Melbourne: Melbourne University Press, 1947) is heavily concerned with religion and ritual, but there's also much in it on other cultural matters. Alexander Alland's work on the Abron of the Ivory Coast, *When the Spider Danced:*

Notes from an African Village (Garden City, N.Y.: Anchor Press, 1976/ip) covers the author's three-year experience with the Abron. Two or three chapters in it will be of special help to the myth student.

Finally, a book which crosses borders, thus defying categorization of a sure sort, is *The Dance, Art, and Ritual of Africa* (New York: Pantheon, 1978/i), by Michael Huet, Jean Laude, and Jean-Louis Paudrat. It is a big, expensive, marvelously illustrated volume covering its subject in three broad sections: The Coast of Guinea, The Sudanese Savannahs, and Equatorial Africa. Myth students will find it most valuable for its 125 color and 136 black and white photographs, needless to say, but what it has to offer on ritual will certainly not be lost on them.

Works on Archaeology and Art

Although archaeology has not played anything like the role in the rest of Africa that it has in the Nile Valley, there are some works that deal with what has been done. For instance, Merrick Posnansky's *Myth and Methodology: The Archaeological Contribution to African History* (Legon, 1964/i) clarifies the role of archaeology in determining the early history of African societies. J. D. Clark's *The Prehistory of Africa* (New York: Frederick A. Praeger, 1970/ib) and *Atlas of African Prehistory* (Chicago: University of Chicago Press, 1967/ib) will be useful in much the same way. Jacquetta Hawkes' *Atlas of Ancient Archaeology* (New York: McGraw-Hill, 1974) has a brief but informative section devoted to archaeology in Africa on pp. 14-23. So does David and Ruth Whitehouse's *Archaeological Atlas of the World* (San Francisco: W. H. Freeman, 1975/ibp) on pp. 50-55. There are also fairly specialized sources on regions and individual countries, such as T. Shaw's *Nigeria: Its Archaeology and Early History* (Leiden: E. J. Brill, 1978), actually a volume in the *Ancient Peoples and Places* series published by Thames and Hudson in London and Frederick A. Praeger in New York, or B. M. Fagan's *Southern Africa During the Iron Age* (New York: Frederick A. Praeger, 1965/i).

There are some excellent souces on African art. Elsy Leuzinger's *The Art of Africa* (New York: McGraw-Hill, 1960/i) remains one of the finer works with 63 color plates, 144 other illustrations and figures, generally good text, and even a brief chapter entitled "Religion." Over 200 pages of the 263 in the book are devoted to African art in *African and Oceanic Art* (New York: Harry N.

Abrams, 1968), by Margaret Trowell and Hans Nevermann, and there's some information in the text on how religious belief shapes art in Africa. There are numerous books on sculpture in Africa, too, since that is the principal art form. *The Sculpture of Africa* (New York: Frederick A. Praeger, 1958/i) is a geographical survey which has 321 black and white illustrations and some, though not much, textual complement. Denise Paulme's *African Sculpture* (New York: Viking Press, 1962/i) and Margaret Trowell's *Classical African Sculpture* (New York: Frederick A. Praeger, 1964/i) are both beautifully done books—as are Jean Laude's *The Arts of Black Africa* (Berkeley: University of California Press, 1971/ip), which is also on sculpture, and James J. Sweeney's *African Sculpture* (Princeton: Princeton University Press, 1970/ip), which has excellent text rather than mainly pictures. Also, don't fail to check into David Attenborough's *The Tribal Eye* (New York: W. W. Norton, 1977/i), for there's a good deal on African art in it.

Oceanic Mythologies

Roughly speaking, Oceania is comprised of all of the islands of the Pacific Ocean south of the Tropic of Cancer, the continent of Australia included. More specifically, the broad divisions of Oceania are Polynesia, Micronesia, Melanesia, Australia, and, for our purposes, the Philippines and Indonesia. Polynesia, the easternmost division, comprises all of the islands from the Hawaiian Islands on the north, south on a line to Samoa, Tonga, and New Zealand, and east as far as Easter Island. Micronesia, the northwesternmost division, includes the Mariana, Marshall, Caroline, and Gilbert Islands. Melanesia, the division just south of Micronesia, stretches from New Guinea on the west about to the Fiji Islands on the east. To the west of Micronesia are the Philippine Islands, to the west of Melanesia is Indonesia, and to the southwest of Melanesia is Australia.

I mention all this geography for a reason. Technically, the total area constituting Oceanic mythology is the largest for any mythology in the world, and nowhere else in the world is there a mythology as fragmented by its geography. There are actually vast differences between, say, the mythologies of the Australian aborigines and the Hawaiian islanders, yet both are considered "Oceanic," sometimes as though the differences did not exist. The great distances between Oceanic cultures and, more importantly, their isolation from one another by a barrier not easily overcome, water, has made the mythologies of Oceania quite varied and independent. It is one thing to say that there are differences between the mythologies of tribes of North American Indians or tribes of Africans, but it is quite another to introduce the kind of barrier to commerce that exists in the Pacific. There the mythologies can *really* be different!

The sources of native Oceanic populations are disputed to some extent. On the one hand, the native racial types seem all to be traceable to Asia, but on the other, artifacts and cultural similarities/

The following symbols will be found, where applicable, in the bibliographic citation, usually following the date of publication: i = has useful illustrations; b = has a useful bibliography; p = has been published in paperbound edition.

dissimilarities have made it likely that there were either sources for the populations other than Asian or influences and intermixings of other stocks to account for the differences. Despite the fact that parts of Oceania have been settled for as much as 20,000 years, it is the last populated large region in the presently inhabitable world. New Zealand would appear to be one of the most recently settled of all the Oceanic group, the Maoris arriving there at some time after A.D. 1000.

The European world did not come in contact with Oceanic peoples until the sixteenth century. Magellan, in his circumnavigation of the globe, stopped at the Marianas Islands, and there were subsequent explorers/travellers who made stops at many of the Oceanic islands—usually only long enough to "rip off" the local populace. It wasn't until the 1770s and Captain James Cook's several Pacific journeys, though, that there was any organized attempt to chart the islands.

With the coming of the Europeans, most local mythologies in Oceania began to change or were displaced by Christianity. Fortunately, explorers, missionaries, and other travellers usually recorded local myths, legends, and customs at length, and it is to them, by and large, that we owe our knowledge of what is called "Oceanic Mythology."

Collections of the Myths

Among the better collections of Oceanic myths is Roslyn Poignant's *Oceanic Mythology* (London: Paul Hamlyn, 1967/ib), a volume in the *International Mythology* series published by Hamlyn. It is nicely organized by divisions—Polynesia, Micronesia, Melanesia, and Australia—and is especially well illustrated. Volume IX of *The Mythology of All Races* (Boston: Marshall Jones, 1916-32; reprinted in New York by Cooper Square Press, 1964 and later) is Roland Burrage Dixon's *Oceanic Mythology*. It, too, is one of the better sources for Oceanic myths. Sheila Savill has included an excellent section on the myths in Volume IV of *Pears Encyclopedia of Myths and Legends* (London: Pelham Books, 1978/ib), a volume which also includes the mythologies of the Americas. Both the *Larousse World Mythology* (New York: Putnam, 1965/i), ed. Pierre Grimal, trans. Patricia Beardsworth, and the *Larousse Encyclopedia of Mythology* (London: Paul Hamlyn, 1959/ip), ed. Felix Guirand, trans. Richard Aldington, have useful introductory sections on Oceanic mythology in them. Since both books are worldwide mythographies, there are space limitations that prohibit extensive coverage of the myths, but as introductions, they are fine. The *World Mythology* employs geographical organization by Oceanic division; the *Encyclopedia* organizes by topic. The space devoted to Oceania in each of three other single-volume world-wide myth collections is minimal at best: the *Encyclopedia of World Mythology* (New York: Galahad Books, 1975/i), Veronica Ions' *The World's Mythology in Colour* (London: Paul Hamlyn, 1974/i), and Derek and Julia Parker's *The Immortals* (London: Barrie & Jenkins, 1976/i). None of these will serve as more than briefest of introductions, but all are beautifully illustrated, Ions' volume especially.

There are several thematically organized books that also should be mentioned. Maria Leach's *The Beginning: Creation Myths Around the World* (New York: Funk & Wagnalls, 1956) has a total of twelve Oceanic creation myths in it. James George Frazer's *Myths of the Origin of Fire* (London: Macmillan, 1930) has six chapters set aside for Oceanic myths. Katharine Luomala's *Oceanic, American Indian, and African Myths of Snaring the Sun* (Millwood, N.Y.: Kraus Reprint Edition of the 1940 printing, 1975/p) will also provide you with an interesting thematic grouping of Oceanic myths. Cottie A. Burland's *Myths of Life and Death* (New York: Crown Publishers, 1974/i) has quite a few Oceanic myths, but use the index to find them.

Quite a few books of Australian myths are available, too. A. W. Reed's *Myths and Legends of Australia* (Sydney: A. H. and A. W. Reed, 1965/ib) is one of the better general works. It includes heroic myths, creation myths, astral myths, and many others, and has some interesting illustrations by Roger Hart. W. Ramsay Smith's *Myths and Legends of the Australian Aboriginals* (London: George Harrap, 1930/i) is well illustrated and includes, along with many myths, discussions of such terms as "totemism." It is divided into five parts: Origins, Animal Myths, Religion, Social, Personal Myths. Roland Robinson's *Aboriginal Myths and Legends* (Melbourne: Sun Books, 1966; Mystic, Conn.: Verry, Laurence, 1968/p) is a smaller volume than Reed's, but it does have a good selection of myths. Reed's *Aboriginal Fables and Legendary Tales* (Sydney: A. H. and A. W. Reed, 1965) is principally folklore, as is H. Drake-Brockman's *Australian Legendary Tales* (Sydney: Angus and Robertson, 1953; reissued by Viking Press, 1966/ib). Both can be useful, though, particularly the latter volume with its helpful glossary and the appendix on "The Aboriginal People and Their

Lives." Louis Allen's *Time Before Morning: Art and Myth of the Australian Aborigines* (New York: Thomas Y. Crowell, 1975/i) is a marvelous introduction to the aboriginal myths of northern Australia through illustrations and text. Charles Percy Mountford's *The Dreamtime* (Adelaide: Rigby, 1965/i) is just a slip of a book (seventy-nine pages) with only thirty-two aboriginal myths in it. However, there are thirty-two accompanying paintings by Ainslee Roberts, most reproduced in color, that make it a fine book to browse through. Ursala McConnel's *Myths of the Munkan* (Melbourne: Melbourne University Press, 1957/i) has few myths, too—thirty-six of them—but includes introductions to the individual myths and general explanatory introduction and conclusion. The Munkan, by the way, live in north Queensland and on the Cape York peninsula.

For Polynesian myths, there are plenty of books to look to also. Antony Alpers' *Legends of the South Seas* (New York: Thomas Y. Crowell, 1970/ib) has about seventy myths in it, all of them Polynesian, and the book has a superb bibliography and editorial apparatus to make it the better of the available sources. Johannes Carl Andersen's *Myths and Legends of the Polynesians* (London: George Harrap, 1928/i; reprinted in 1969 by Charles E. Tuttle, Rutland, Vt.) is a big book with plenty of myths and a nice introduction on the Polynesian peoples. Katharine Luomala's *Voices on the Wind: Polynesian Myths and Chants* (Honolulu: Bishop Museum Press, 1955/i) is an interesting volume which has a good selection of narratives set in the framework of the author's background explanations and settings. It is illustrated with drawings by Joseph Feher. William Wyatt Gill's *Myths and Songs from the South Pacific* (London: H. S. King & Co., 1876/i; reprinted in 1977 by Arno Press of New York) contains mainly myths of the Hervey Islanders and is filled with Gill's commentaries. Despite its age, the book is still a very useful one. George Grey's *Polynesian Mythology and Ancient Traditional History of the New Zealand Race* (London: John Murray, 1855; George Routledge & Sons, 1906) is even older and is, in fact, the classic work on New Zealand's Maori, their beliefs and mythology. Mythographers like A. W. Reed drew heavily on it in composing their own collections of myths.

Some other books on Maori myths, legends, and folklore alone are worth looking into. Anthony Alpers' *Maori Myths and Tribal Legends* (Boston: Houghton Mifflin, 1966/i) is one of the more ambitious of them since Grey's ground-breaker. It is interestingly illustrated, has a glossary of names and terms, and should be adequate for all the Maori myths you might need. James Izett's *Maori Lore: The Tradition of the Maori People with the More Important of Their Legends* (Wellington: John Mackay, 1904/i) and Edward Shortland's *Maori Religion and Mythology* (London: Longmans, Green, and Co., 1882/i; reprinted in New York by A.M.S. Press, 1976) are both helpful older works. A. W. Reed's *Myths and Legends of Maoriland* (Sydney: A. H. and A. W. Reed, 1946) is a good collection, and his *Legends of Rotorua and the Hot Lakes* (Rutland, Vt.: Charles E. Tuttle, 1973; originally published in 1958/ip) augments it nicely with stories originating in a volcanic area of New Zealand. Pauline K. Yearbury's *Children of Rangi and Papa* (New York: International Publications Service, 1976/i) is a beautiful volume in which the Maori creation myth is retold.

Books of myths from other areas in Polynesia and Oceania generally comprise our last group of collections of myths. M. Beckwith's *Hawaiian Mythology* (New Haven: Yale University Press, 1940) is both an excellent anthology of the myths of Hawaii and a fine explanatory work as well. William D. Westervelt's *Hawaiian Historical Legends* (Rutland, Vt.: Charles E. Tuttle, 1977/ip; originally published in 1923) is an attractive volume of historical legends and folklore mainly. His book called *Hawaiian Legends of Volcanoes* (Rutland, Vt.: Charles E. Tuttle, 1963/p; reprint of an earlier edition) has some myths in it as well as folktales and legends. *The Legends and Myths of Hawaii* (Rutland, Vt.: Charles E. Tuttle, 1972/ip; reprint of the 1888 edition), by His Hawaiian Majesty, Kalakalia, ed. R. M. Daggett, is an interesting work. It has in it some excellent myths and legends, "The Apotheosis of Pele" one of them; each narrative is set up with its cast of characters prefacing it, as in a dramatic script. Charles F. Gallagher's *Hawaii and Its Gods* (New York: Weatherhill/Kapa, 1975/i) is really a history of the mingling of religions in Hawaii—from earliest polytheism to latest religions—but the first chapter, "The Ancient Way," is fine as an introduction to Hawaiian gods in ancient times. *Myths and Legends of Fiji and Rotuma* (Wellington: A. H. and A. W. Reed, 1967/i), ed. A. W. Reed and Inez Hames, is a good collection illustrated by Roger Hart. *Myths and Legends of Samoa* (Rutland, Vt.: Charles E. Tuttle, 1976/i; reprint of an earlier edition), by Brother Herman, and *Tongan Myths and Tales* (Millwood, N.Y.: Kraus Reprint of the 1924 edition/ip), by E. W. Gifford, are also good collections. So, too, with another older work, Donald A. Mackenzie's *Myths from Melanesia and Indonesia* (London, n.d.), a lovely anthology. *Religious Texts of the Oral Tradition from*

Western New Guinea, Parts A and B (Leiden: E. J. Brill, 1975, 1978), collected and translated by Freerk C. Kamma, is an excellent source of myths from New Guinea; the notes and glossary provided by Kamma make it useful concerning local religious practices as well. Three books with much explanatory material and commentary are W. A. Lessa's *Tales from Ulithi Atoll: A Comparative Study of Oceanic Folklore* (Berkeley: University of California Press, 1961), Kenelm Burridge's *Tangu Traditions: A Study of the Way of Life, Mythology and Developing Experience of a New Guinea People* (Oxford: Clarendon Press, 1969), and Roy Franklin Barton's *The Mythology of the Ifugaos* (Philadelphia: American Folklore Society, 1955/bp). (In case you're wondering, the Ifugaos live in the mountains near Luzon, Philippines.)

An interesting little volume, William S. Stone's *Idylls of the South Seas* (Honolulu: University of Hawaii Press, 1971), is a collection of tales *based on* islands legends. They're really short stories of sorts as Stone handles them, but with a direct relation they have to myths and folktales.

Studies of the Myths

There are not many works available on Oceanic myth which fit the description "analytic" or "interpretive." Eldon Best's little *Some Aspects of Maori Myth and Religion* (Wellington: Dominion Monograph no. 1, 1954) is a good analytic introduction to Maori thought and myth despite the fact that some of the concepts are dated. In a book edited by Robert A. Georges, *Studies in Mythology* (Homewood, Ill.: Dorsey Press, 1968/p), you'll find three essays that may be of use: A. R. Radcliffe-Brown's "The Interpretation of Andamanese Customs and Beliefs: Myths and Legends," W. H. R. Rivers's "The Sociological Significance of Myth" (which uses Oceanic examples), and Bronislaw Malinowski's "In Tewara and Sanaroa—Mythology of the Kula." Speaking of Malinowski, *do* look into his classic works on the Trobriand Islanders; probably the best place to start is *Magic, Science and Religion* (Garden City, N.Y.: Doubleday Anchor, 1954/p; originally published by the Free Press in 1948). In it is much more than *just* the analysis and interpretation of myth, Malinowski's concerns being the overall culture of the Trobrianders, but his classic statement on myth, its meanings and origins, is included. William A. Lessa's fine "Oedipus-Type Tales in Oceania," in *Journal of American Folklore*, 69 (January–March 1956), pp. 63–73, will be worth looking up, too. Lessa concludes that diffusion was probably the case with some twenty-three variants of the "Oedipus-type" narrative in Oceania. Lessa's *"Discoverer-of-the-Sun:* Mythology as a Reflection of Culture," an article reporting his work on Ulithi Atoll, can be found in *Journal of American Folklore* (1966), pp. 3–51, or in condensed form in *Mythology: Selected Readings* (Harmondsworth, G.B.: Penguin Books, 1972/p), ed. Pierre Maranda, pp. 71–110. Elli Kongas Maranda's "Five Interpretations of a Melanesian Myth," in *Journal of American Folklore*, 86 (January–March 1973), pp. 3–13, uses five different interpretative theories on one myth from the British Solomon Islands to show that the separate interpretations are in fact complementary. Maximo D. Ramos' *Creatures of Philippine Lower Mythology* (Manila: University of Philippines Press, 1971) is interesting for a variety of reasons. The first five chapters deal with several sorts of beings that are folklore types; chapter six, "The Importance of Mythology," is a fair summary of the significance of myths—especially as relates to the creatures—and chapters eight through twelve treat *how* the myths are important in the education of the young.

A valuable reference work is Bacil F. Kirtley's *A Motif-Index of Traditional Polynesian Narratives* (Honolulu: University of Hawaii Press, 1971). It does the same thing for Polynesian narratives that Stith Thompson's *Motif-Index of Folk Literature* does generally for narratives around the world—that is, organizes them by motifs in a cross-referencing system that helps the researcher in his quest for like examples.

Works on Religion and Related Matters

A fine work by the renowned comparative religionist Mircea Eliade, *Australian Religions: An Introduction* (Ithaca, N.Y.: Cornell University Press, 1973), is first in line. Its chapter headings reveal best its contents: "Supernatural Beings and High Gods," "Culture Heroes and Mythical Geography," "Initiation Rites and Secret Cults," "The Medicine Men and Their Supernatural Models," "Death and Eschatology: Conclusions." A book which focuses on iconographic representations, ritual practices, and beliefs is Ronald M. Berndt's *Australian Aboriginal Religion* (Leiden: E. J. Brill, 1974/i). It is made all the better by excellent photographs, glossary, and fold-out maps. If you want just a brief introduction to Australian aboriginal religion, though, you'll find a commendable one in A. P. Elkin's "The Religion of the Australian Aborigines," in *Ancient Religions*

(New York: Citadel Press, 1965/bp; originally published as *Forgotten Religions* in 1950). There's also a good chapter by E. A. Worms in *Australian Aboriginal Studies* (London: Oxford University Press, 1963), a "Symposium of papers presented at the 1961 research conference" edited by Helen Sheils. There are two works on Maori religion and related matters that can be recommended: J. Prytz Johansen's *The Maori and His Religion: Its Non-Ritualistic Aspects* (Copenhagen: Ejnar Munksgaard, 1954) and Eldon Best's *Maori Religion and Mythology* (Wellington: Bulletin 10 of the Dominion Museum, 1924; reprinted by A.M.S. Press of New York, 1976). Robert W. Williamson's *Religious and Cosmic Beliefs of Central Polynesia* (Cambridge: Cambridge University Press, 1933) is first rate and also happens to be a good source of central Polynesian myths. Robert H. Lowie's *Primitive Religion* (New York: Boni and Liveright, 1924) has useful chapters on Polynesian and Bukana (New Guinea) religions. The book by Bronislaw Malinowski referred to earlier, *Magic, Science and Religion* has much in it about Trobriander religion, the Trobriand Islands being located northeast of New Guinea, both of them within Melanesia. R. H. Codrington's "Melanesian Religion," pp. 412-20 in *Source Book in Anthropology*, revised edition (New York: Harcourt, Brace & Co., 1931), ed. A. L. Kroeber and T. T. Waterman, is a useful brief introduction to Melanesian religion. A nicely detailed study of Manus religion (Admiralty Islands in Melanesia) can be found in Reo F. Fortune's *Manus Religion* (Philadelphia: American Philosophical Association, 1935). It is especially good on religious sanctions for social behavior and has quite a bit in it on Manus mythology. Hans Scharer's *Ngaju Religion: The Conception of God Among a South Borneo People*, trans. Rodney Needham (The Hauge: Martinius Nijhoff, 1963/i), is a model of what can be done to examine completely the myth/belief system of one people. It also happens to be an excellent source of Ngaju (Malay Archipelago) myths. Ivor Evans' *Studies in Religion, Folklore, and Custom in North Borneo and the Malay Peninsula* (Cambridge: Cambridge University Press, 1923) is also a possible source, in this case for more than just the religion of the Malay people.

Cargo cults and millenarian movements in general in Melanesia have received a good deal of attention in print. Kenelm Burridge's *Mambu: A Melanesian Millenium* (London: Methuen, 1960/b) is an interesting work on the phenomenon overall even though it focuses on Mambu, a New Guinean who in the late 1930s led the cargo movement there. Peter M. Worsley's "Millenarian Movements in Melanesia," in *Gods and Rituals: Readings in Religious Beliefs and Practices* (Garden City, N.Y.: Natural History Press, 1967/p), is a good brief introduction, just as his *The Trumpet Shall Sound: A Study of "Cargo" Cults in Melanesia* (New York: Schocken Books, 1968) is a fine longer one. The chapter entitled "Phantom Cargo" in Marvin Harris' *Cows, Pigs, Wars, and Witches: The Riddles of Culture* (New York: Random House, 1974) is a useful analysis of the cargo cult. The chapter that follows it, "Messiahs," ties in well, too. Kal Muller's "Tanna Awaits the Coming of John Frum," *National Geographic*, 145 (May 1974/i), pp. 706-15, is a study of one aspect of cargo cultism, and there's a map included which shows the range of cargo cults in Oceania.

Among works on rituals in Oceania Roy A. Rappaport's *Pigs for the Ancestors: Ritual in the Ecology of a New Guinea People* (New Haven: Yale University Press, 1967) is an excellent study of the ritual practices of the Maring of New Guinea that are meant to regulate their environment through supernatural agencies. Gillian Gillison's "Fertility Rites and Sorcery in a New Guinea Village," an article in *National Geographic*, 152 (July 1977/i), pp. 124-46, will be well worth looking into for, in addition to what the title suggests, some discussion of myth reversal. Shelley Mydans' "Balinese Rituals Appease Demons of an Unseen World," in *Smithsonian*, 7 (November 1976/i), pp. 82-91, is useful for its close correlation of myth with ritual practices. Also, there are good sections on puberty rites in Australian primitive society in Bruno Bettelheim's *Symbolic Wounds: Puberty Rites and the Envious Male* (Glencoe, Ill.: The Free Press, 1954).

Works on Historical/Cultural Background

There are many sources to turn to for cultural/historical background to the study of Oceanic myth—too many to offer more than a partial array here. C. Hartley Grattan's two-volume *The Southwest Pacific: A Modern History* (Ann Arbor: University of Michigan Press, 1963/ib) is a fine overview that covers, in Volume I, the early exploration and settlement by Europeans, and, in Volume II, the history of Oceania since about 1900. Alan Moorehead's *The Fatal Impact: An Account of the Invasion of the Pacific* (New York: Harper & Row, 1966/i) is a historical survey of the white man's impact on native Oceanic peoples and environment. It is especially lucid on Cook's three voyages. Andrew P. Vayda's *Peoples and Cultures of the Pacific* (Garden City, N.Y.: Natural History Press, 1968/bp) is filled with articles by scholars on a full range of topics related to Oceanic culture and history, including some on myth and religion there. J. Macmillan Brown's *Peoples and Problems of the Pacific* (London: T. Fisher Unwin, 1927) is an older work but remains a useful two-volume survey of islands cultures, with some attention to religion and myth. A broad over-view of the prehistory of Melanesia, Micronesia, and Polynesia—one that provides good background to the possibility of diffusion of culture (mythology included) there—is Peter Bellwood's "The Prehistory of Oceania," in *Current Anthropology*, 16 (March 1975), pp. 9-28. A special issue of *National Geographic*, 146 (December 1974/i), devoted to the "Isles of the Pacific" has four separate articles, all told, and a large insert map. The migrations of the original islanders, their culture, and beliefs are all gone into briefly. A book called *Isles of the South Pacific* (Washington, D.C.: National Geographic Society, 1971/i) has a great deal in it of value, too—the hundreds of color pictures particularly.

R. C. Suggs' *Island Civilizations of Polynesia* (London: Mentor Books, 1960/i) is a fairly useful survey of some of the cultures of Polynesia. Robert W. Williamson's *The Social and Political Systems of Central Polynesia* (Cambridge: Cambridge University Press, 1924) is a mammoth three-volume older work that is perhaps narrower in scope than all but the deepest background will require. Irving Goldman's *Ancient Polynesian Society* (Chicago: University of Chicago Press, 1974/b) offers an interesting perspective on the origins and nature of Polynesian society. Abraham Fornander's *An Account of the Polynesian Race: Its Origin and Migrations* (Rutland, Vt.: Charles E. Tuttle, 1969; reprint of an earlier edi-tion), Peter H. Buck's *Vikings of the Pacific* (Chicago: University of Chicago Press, 1959/p; originally published in 1938), and Thor Heyerdahl's *Kon-Tiki: Across the Pacific by Raft*, trans. F.H. Lyon (Chicago: Rand McNally, 1951/ip) are three works that treat the original settlement of Polynesia. Heyerdahl's book is his well-known account of a raft trip from Peru to Polynesia attempted in order to prove it could have been done in prehistory by settlers of Polynesia.

A generally good introduction to the history of Australia is Douglas Pike's *Australia: The Quiet Continent*, 2nd edition (New York: Cambridge University Press, 1970/p). *The World of the First Australians: An Introduction to the Traditional Life of the Austra-lian Aborigines* (London: Angus and Robertson, 1964/b), by Ronald M. and Catherine H. Berndt, is probably *the* single-volume work which can serve as background to the study of Australian aboriginal myth, but don't overlook some others which will be of use. A. P. Elkin's *The Australian Aborigines: How to Understand Them* (Garden City, N.Y.: Doubleday Anchor, 1964/p; originally published in 1938) and *Aboriginal Men of High Degree* (Sydney: Australian Publishing Co., 1946) are both highly recommended, the latter especially for its focus on the shaman. W. L. Warner's *A Black Civilization* (New York: Harper & Row, 1964) is a useful brief introduction to the Australian aborigines. Geza Roheim's *Children of the Desert: The Western Tribes of Central Australia*, two volumes (New York: Basic Books, 1974), edited posthumously by Werner Muensterberger, is a comprehensive psychoanalytic ethnography that should be of great use as background to Aboriginal mythology. *The Native Tribes of Central Australia* (New York: Macmillan & Co., 1899; Dover, 1968/p) is filled with information on religion of the tribes, but much of the theory employed by its authors, Baldwin Spencer and F. J. Gillen, has been superseded by later research. Just about the same holds true for another big book, A. W. Howitt's *The Native Tribes of South-east Australia* (London: Macmillan & Co., 1904).

R. Codrington's *The Melanesians: Studies in Their History, Anthropology, and Folklore* (Oxford: Clarendon Press, 1891; HRAF reprint edition, 1957) will still serve as highly useful background to the Melanesians, and it does include a good deal on myth and religion. However, the theory of Codrington's time is not necessarily to be accepted without question. So, too, with W. G. Ivens' *Melanesians of the Southeast Solomon Islands* (London, 1927; reprinted by Benjamin Blom of New York, 1974/i), a sociological study that includes much on myth and religion also. Alphonse Riesenfeld's *The Megalithic Culture of Melanesia* (Leiden: E. J. Brill, 1950) will be of most use to anyone interested in the Melanesians' origins, their migrations, their beliefs, and their rituals. Chapter three, "The Problem of the Sun Cult," goes into astral belief and worship in Melanesia. C. G. Seligman's *The Melanesians of British New Guinea* (Cambridge: Cambridge University Press, 1910) covers many aspects of five different New Guinean cultures, with chapters on the religious beliefs, folktales, and taboos of each. Kenneth E. Read's *The High Valley* (New York: Charles Scribner's Sons, 1965/p) is the author's record of nearly two years of field work among the Gahuku tribes of New Guinea. Read's descriptions of the rituals he witnessed are valuable background for the myth student, and there is some information on Gahuku myths scattered throughout the book. Margaret Mead's *Growing Up in New Guinea* (New York: William Morrow, 1930/p), the famous American anthropologist's discussion of child rearing and character development in New Guinea, is also excellent background since rituals and beliefs are constantly referred to and described. Her *Coming of Age in Samoa* (New York: William Morrow, 1928), as a description of family life and psychological development in Samoa, is at least as useful for the same reason. David M. Davies' *Journey into the Stone Age* (London: Robert Hale, 1969/i) is Davies' account of travels among New Guinean highlands people, a travel book not unlike those that were popular in the eighteenth and nineteenth centuries. It has some information on the animistic religious beliefs of the Oremu and others. *New Guinea: A Journey Through 10,000 Years* (Melbourne: Lansdowne Press, 1969/i), by Robin Smith and Keith Willey, is a beautifully illustrated travelogue that has useful text as well, including some discussion of belief and ritual in the second chapter. Frederick William Christian's *The Caroline Islands* (London: Methuen & Co., 1899) is one of the older travel books you'll still find helpful— particularly the information on religion contained in the appendix. P. D. R. Williams-Hunt's *An Introduction to the Malayan Aborigines* (Kuala Lampur, 1952) is an overview which, among many other things, includes discussion of religious beliefs, rituals, and myths. *Ancient Hawaiian Civilization: A Series of Lectures Delivered at the Kamehameha Schools*, revised edition (Rutland, Vt.: Charles E. Tuttle, 1968/p; reprint of an earlier edition) is an excellent source of information about ancient Hawaii edited by E. S. Craighill Handy *et al.* Herb Kawainui Kane's "A Canoe Helps Hawaii Recapture Her Past," in *National Geographic*, 149 (April 1976/i), pp. 468–89, recounts the successful attempt to sail the type of canoe which was believed to have been used 800 years ago between Hawaii and Tahiti—a 6,000-mile round trip. The article is particularly good background to myth study since the trip was actually the reenactment of what in Hawaiian mythology was the origin of the Hawaiian people. Finally, a work that will provide most unusual cultural background to the study of Oceanic myth is Geza Roheim's *Psychoanalysis and Anthropology: Culture, Personality and the Unconscious* (New York: International Universities Press, 1950). Chapters two, three, four, and seven are all on Oceanic groups— psychoanalytic studies of Central Australians and islands cultures.

Works on Art

The best sources for art of Oceania are, in fact, some of the collections of myths covered earlier—Roslyn Poignant's *Oceanic Mythology* or Veronica Ions' *The World's Mythology in Colour*, for instance. Some of the pictures in the former appear in the latter, but the illustrations overall are excellent. The pictures in the section on Oceanic mythology in the *Larousse World Mythology* are also mainly of Oceanic art. National Geographic's *Isles of the South Pacific*, mentioned earlier, has a good many photographs of Oceanic art in it, as do many of the other illustrated works included above valuable for cultural and historical background to the study of Oceanic mythology.

Beyond such sources as these are others you might find useful. Dacre Stubbs' *Prehistoric Art of Australia* (New York: Charles Scribner's Sons, 1977/i) has 108 illustrations, 50 of them in color. It is a lovely, large-format book. There are quite a few pages devoted to Oceanic art in *African and Oceanic Art* (New York: Harry N. Abrams, 1968/i) despite the fact that the book is mainly on African art. Finally, both Carl August Schmitz's *Oceanic Art*, trans. Norbert Guterman (New York: Harry N. Abrams, 1971/i), and Alberto Cesare Ambesi's *Oceanic Art*, trans. Rachel Montgomery (Feltham, G.B.: Paul Hamlyn, 1970/i), are beautifully illustrated books that should be most helpful.

Appendix:
Contemporary Mythology
— Mainly American

Some time ago, I read an article in which the author lamented the fact that we have no communally held myths in modern American society. A lack of cohesiveness, of group-centeredness is the result, the author said. Amen to a certain degree, I say. Anyone, in fact, who has studied mythology at all seriously for a reasonable length of time is bound to be aware that it is really the group's mythology that holds the group together, gives it purpose and direction. Without a mythology held communally by all members of the group, a higher ordering still is needed to assure the otherwise missing cohesion, purpose, and direction. And as we all know, an ordering higher than traditional religions can provide is hard to come by—especially an ordering which both sanctions the entire group's activities and ideas and carries with it the authority of deity in matters of punishment, revenge, or "justice." Law may well come off a poor second in such an instance.

The problem, though, with assuming that we have no communally held myths at present is that we are seeing the product of a very strong traditional mythology and mistaking it for "no myths." The myths which have persisted longest in this country, and within the largest group possible, are those associated with American freedom, democracy, and free enterprise. Our most recent activities in the areas of civil rights, equal rights for women and gays, equal access and opportunity for all, are clear results that point to the strength of the mythology, however totally effective or ineffective our enactments of it may actually be. And in case you've missed the myths of heroes (founding fathers and champions of freedom and business, largely) and the numerous narratives of personal and group successes that lend support to the democratic endeavor, don't fail to attend some classes at your local elementary school some day soon. That's one place they'll be recited for you in very traditional ways—and often.

The following symbols will be found, where applicable, in the bibliographic citation, usually following the date of publication: i = has useful illustrations; b = has a useful bibliography; p = has been published in paperbound edition.

Perhaps part of the problem behind the feeling that there are today no myths in which we can all believe and abide by is that "freedom and democracy for all" inherently means there will be results of other sorts that will not be as readily accepted by all groups, results which threaten the cohesiveness and, ultimately, the success of some of them. When pornography threatens some religious groups and equal rights for women threatens still others, we are witnessing just such a phenomenon. The threats must be perceived as threats to democracy and its institutions generally in order for action to be taken at a high enough level to eliminate the problem at more than a local level. In traditional, homogeneous societies, there is no such problem, since the sanctions for or against are mutually agreed upon, whatever freedom exists being well defined and defended by the entire group's commitment. In heterogeneous societies, however, there isn't that solidarity—not even to the extent that there is agreement on what constitutes just "freedom and democracy" for everyone. All one has to do is read chapter fourteen, "Opinions, Attitudes, and Beliefs," in *Human Behavior: An Inventory of Scientific Findings* (New York: Harcourt, Brace & World, 1964, etc.) by Bernard Berelson and Gary A. Steiner to see the differences between homogeneity and heterogeneity where the transmission of values from generation to generation is concerned and, even more importantly, where the stability of those values over longer periods of time is at stake. The whole spectrum of one's opinions, attitudes, and beliefs is, in heterogeneous societies, subject to bombardment daily by conflicting viewpoints. The sole viewpoint immune more or less to challenge and/or threat is the larger mythology centered on freedom, democracy, and free enterprise. Even there, though, anyone is free to (peaceably) advocate opposing ideologies such as neo-naziism and socialism. The fact that so few have chosen to do so underscores the broad support the mythology of freedom and democracy has in the United States, support that would no doubt result in an immediate display of unity should any group decide other than peaceably to oppose that mythology. It is obvious that here the United States comes closest to being a homogeneous society.

Works on Mythic "Strands" in American Society

Closely tied to America's pervasive mythology are what may be termed "mythic strands," areas of American history and character which have given rise to myths of lesser sorts. These myths are not quite as obvious and probably haven't the same power for moving us as does the mythology of freedom, democracy, and free enterprise. In *Myth and the American Experience*, abridged edition (New York: Glencoe Press, 1973/p), ed. Nicholas Cords and Patrick Gerster, you'll find some of them discussed in interesting if not always mythological ways. The anthology is organized in ten chronological sections started off with Thomas A. Bailey's "History and Myths," a fine introduction, and concluding with the section entitled "And the Myths Continue . . .". David Brion Davis' "Ten Gallon Hero," Alonzo L. Hamby's "The Liberals, Truman, and FDR as Symbol and Myth," Peter Chew's "Black History, or Black Mythology?," and Henry Steele Commager's "The Search for a Usable Past" are among the book's many fine essays. A book which "has to do with the beginnings and the first tentative outlines of a native American mythology . . . that of the authentic American as a figure of heroic innocence and vast potentialities, poised at the start of a new history" is R.W.B. Lewis' *The American Adam: Innocence, Tragedy and Tradition in the Nineteenth Century* (Chicago: University of Chicago Press, 1955/p). It is essentially a literary study but is easily "translated" into what the myth student is looking for. Lewis continually probes the essence of the American hero as he emerged in the nineteenth century and keys us in to the ways the hero is to appear in the popular imagination later on. Henry Nash Smith's *Virgin Land: The American West as Symbol and Myth* (Cambridge: Harvard University Press, 1950/p; reissued in 1970 with a new preface) is a classic work on the myths of the American west. While Smith does not have the mythologist's perspective and method, the book is scholarly and is highly useful in contemporary myth study. Richard Slotkin's *Regeneration Through Violence: The Mythology of the American Frontier, 1600-1860* (Middletown, Conn.: Wesleyan University Press, 1975 /p) even has chapters such as "Mythogenesis," "The Search for a Hero," "Narrative into Myth," and "Evolution of the National Hero" in its survey and investigation of frontier mythology from a literary point of view. Vernon Louis Parrington's *The Romantic Revolution in America* (London: Harvest Books, 1954/p; originally 1927), which is Volume II in his magnificent *Main Currents in American Thought*, indirectly has much to do with the making of myth in America during the romantic age. The book is a perfect example of the fact that myth study transcends the boundaries of myth books, and that even historical and/or literary surveys may have buried away in them something of value. As a further example of this, on pp. 150–52 in *Backgrounds of American Literary Thought*, 2nd edition (New York: Appleton-Century-Crofts, 1967 /p), by Rod W. Horton and Herbert W. Edwards, there's a brief discussion of the American rags-to-riches myth as exemplified in Horatio Alger's works, and in that same book, pp. 365–76, myths of the South (sectionalism and cavalier) are discussed. Also, don't overlook the two-volume *Myth and Southern History* (Chicago: Rand McNally, 1976/p), by Patrick Gerster and Nicholas Cords, for much more than brief discussion.

Mircea Eliade, that well known comparative religionist, has said, "it is not so difficult to recognize, in all that modern people call instruction, education and didactic culture, the function that is fulfilled by the myth in archaic societies." (*Myths, Dreams, and Mysteries*, trans. Philip Mairet, New York: Harper & Row, 1967.) This is echoed by Varda Langholz Leymore's *Hidden Myth: Structure and Symbolism in Advertising* (New York: Basic Books, 1975), a fascinating study in which it is reasonably proven that advertising has much the same function in modern society that myth does in primitive ones: the preservation of the existing order, "the resolution of conflicts." We have made fun of advertising, been entertained by it, cursed its intrusiveness, and even bought the products whose virtues it has belabored—all the while possibly not suspecting its conservative role in society. Broader examination of contemporary American culture will be found in *The American Dimension: Cultural Myths and Social Realities* (Port Townsend: Alfred Publishing Co., 1976), ed. William Arens and Susan Montague. There are articles on television drama, soap operas, rock music, and other aspects of modern American culture, most of which can be read profitably with an eye toward myth.

Works on the Hero in American Society

The hero has, needless to say, been much studied. Robert Jewett and John Shelton Lawrence, in their book *The American Monomyth* (Garden City, N.Y.: Doubleday, 1977), take their cue from Joseph Campbell's *Hero with a Thousand Faces* and describe at length the evidence for what they see as the monomyth operative in current society. "A community in a harmonious paradise is threatened by evil: normal institutions fail to contend with this threat: a selfless superhero emerges to renounce temptations and carry out the redemptive task: aided by fate, his decisive victory restores the community to its paradisal condition: the superhero then recedes into obscurity." The authors trace this myth in the popular media and culture—from *Star Trek* through *Jaws* and Walt Disney's family of animals—and arrive at the conclusion that it is escapist, its outcome an encouragement of the abdication of personal responsibility and an acceptance of passivity even. Other books which deal with the American version of the hero are Dixon Wecter's *The Hero in America* (New York: Charles Scribner's Sons, 1941/b), Marshall Fishwick's *The Hero, American Style* (New York: David McKay, 1969), and *Heroes of Popular Culture* (Bowling Green, Ohio: Bowling Green University Popular Press, 1972/p), ed. Ray B. Browne, Marshall Fishwick, and Michael T. Marsden. None of the works was written by a mythologist, but all are definitely of great value in myth study. Jerome L. Rodnitzky's *Minstrels of the Dawn: The Folk Protest Singer as a Cultural Hero* (Chicago: Nelson-Hall, 1976/bp) is an interesting book on Woody Guthrie, Joan Baez, Bob Dylan, and Phil Ochs as culture heroes, and there's a good deal in it on how these heroes were "made." Winston Churchill's *Heroes of History* (New York: Dodd Mead & Co., 1968/i) ranges from Alfred the Great to Winston Churchill himself, making it broader than just contemporary, but there are plenty of heroes from recent centuries involved. E. Caruth's "Hercules and Superman: The Modern-Day Mythology of the Comic Book," in the *Journal of The American Academy of Child Psychiatry*, 7 (January 1968), pp. 1-12, is an interesting analytical article, and William J. Bennett's "Let's Bring Back Heroes" will be provocative enough—you'll find it in *Reader's Digest*, no. 668 (December 1977), pp. 91-94, or where it originally appeared, *Newsweek* (August 15, 1977).

Studies of Myth in Modern Society

Some excellent sources to look into as you go about investigating contemporary mythology are a small group of works by mythologists or people heavily involved with mythology. Raphael Patai's *Myth and Modern Man* (Englewood Cliffs, N.J.: Prentice-Hall, 1972) surveys various modern-day myths—from the Nazi myth to myths of the future, from a chapter entitled "The Mickey Myth" to one called "Wanted: A Charter Myth for Democracy." Speaking of the Nazi myth, by the way, two works related to that might be of interest: Henry Hatfield's "The Myth of Naziism," pp. 199-220 in *Myth and Mythmaking* (Boston: Beacon Press, 1969/p), ed. Henry A. Murray, and Marie Bonaparte's *Myths of War*, trans.

John Rodker (London: Imago Publishing Co., 1947). Bonaparte's
work deals with the myths that rose in and around World War II
Germany. Among the many other useful chapters in Joseph
Campbell's overview of myth in the modern world, *Myths to Live
By* (New York: Viking Press, 1972; Bantam/p), there's "Mythol-
ogies of War and Peace," "The Impact of Science on Myth," and
"The Mythology of Love." Perhaps the premier volume for those
interested in modern-day myth, though, is Campbell's *Creative
Mythology* (New York: Viking Press, 1968/p), the fourth volume
in his towering *The Masks of God*. A brief look into Campbell's
views on mythology today will be found in "Living Myths: A
Conversation with Joseph Campbell," *Parabola*, 1 (Spring 1976),
pp. 70–81. David Adams Leeming's *Mythology* (New York:
Newsweek Books, 1976) has a brief chapter entitled "Mythology
Today" (pp. 141–51), and for a really worthwhile investigation of
"the impact of ancient Near Eastern myth on modern society,"
see Gerald A. Larue's *Ancient Myth and Modern Man* (Englewood
Cliffs, N.J.: Prentice-Hall, 1975/p). Although Roland Barthes is a
master semiologist, not a mythologist as such, his *Mythologies*,
trans. Annette Lavers (New York: Hill and Wang, 1972/p), has a
great deal in common with Patai's search for mythology in modern-
day life (French mainly, in this case), and the long section entitled
"Myth Today" is especially commendable.

In his most interesting book *The Myth of the State* (New Haven:
Yale University Press, 1973/p; originally 1946), Ernst Cassirer
deals with political myth, specifically the myth of the state, as it
has evolved from ancient times. Part three, "The Myth of the Twentieth Century," four chapters all told, is particularly relevant to
the way myth functions in the modern world. "Mythical thought"
is, to Cassirer, the underpinning of the modern world. "Our science,
our poetry, our art, and our religion are only the upper layer of a
much older stratum that reaches down to a great depth." Modern
culture could not come about "until the darkness of myth was
fought and overcome. But the mythical monsters were not entirely
destroyed. They were used for the creation of a new universe, and
they still survive in this universe. The powers of myth were checked
and subdued by superior forces. As long as these forces, intellectual,
ethical, and artistic, are in full strength, myth is tamed and subdued.
But once they begin to lose their strength chaos is come again.
Mythical thought then starts to rise anew and to pervade the whole
of man's cultural and social life." To Mircea Eliade, "some forms
of 'mythical behavior' still survive today. This does not mean that

they represent 'survivals' of an archaic mentality. But certain aspects and functions of mythical thought are constituents of the human being." Some of these aspects are investigated in his "Survivals and Camouflages of Myth," which is chapter nine in *Myth and Reality*, trans. Willard R. Trask, (New York: Harper & Row, 1963/p), the source of the quotation, but in the first chapter of his *Myths, Dreams, and Mysteries*, trans. Philip Mairet (New York: Harper & Row, 1967) he deals with the subject at greater length. The chapter can also be found in *Myth and Symbol* (Philadelphia, 1966/p; London: S.P.C.K., 1966), ed. Frederick W. Dillistone, and relevant excerpts from Eliade's writings on modern and older myth (and religion) can be found in *Myths, Rites, Symbols: A Mircea Eliade Reader* (New York: Harper & Row, 1976/p), a two-volume work edited by Wendell C. Beane and William G. Doty.

Donald A. Stauffer reaches the conclusion that belief is an important ingredient in all myths *except* the "modern" myths in his fine article "The Modern Myth of the Modern Myth," which can be found in *English Institute Essays: 1947* (New York: Columbia University Press, 1948; New York: AMS Reprint, 1965), pp. 23-49. Jacques Ellul redefines "myth" against its older definitions to account for the modern myths of western civilization, going through some of the modern myths in the process, in "Modern Myths," trans. Elaine Halperin, *Diogenes* (Fall 1958), pp. 23-40. Eliseo Vivas' "Myth: Some Philosophical Problems," in *Southern Review*, 6, New Series (January 1970), pp. 89-103, is quite interesting in its handling of the need for myth even today. Two articles by Henry A. Murray deal with *future* myth: "A Myth for the Future," in *The Making of Myth* (New York: G. P. Putnam's Sons, 1962/p), ed. Richard Ohmann, pp. 171-73, and "The Possible Nature of a 'Mythology' to Come," the concluding essay in the book he edited, *Myth and Mythmaking* (Boston: Beacon Press, 1969/p; originally published in 1959). The latter article is a long one (pp. 300-53) and is excellent for its handling of the characteristics of myth.

Studies of Religion, Belief, Demythologizing

Religion, it should go without saying, remains a strong contributor to whatever can be considered contemporary mythology. In addition to the traditional western religions which draw upon the *Bible*—and here I include Islamic since the *Qur'an* (Koran) has so much in common with the *Bible*—there are later religions which have sprung up in great numbers, each, to whatever degree, with its own mythology. Jacob Needleman's *The New Religions* (New York: E. P. Dutton, 1977/p; originally published in 1970) is a good introduction to the newer mysticisms in the United States, such as, Zen Buddhism, Meher Baba, Subud, and others. Hans Holzer's *The New Pagans* (Garden City, N.Y.: Doubleday, 1972) is, likewise, a good introduction to ancient cults that have been renewed in modern times—cults of Astarte, Isis, Baal, and others. There's even John C. Lilly's *Simulations of God* (New York: Bantam Books, 1976/bp), "a kind of handbook to start one on his own search for his own Simulations of God"—god as drugs, as righteous wrath, as war, as the computer, and so on. Ian T. Ramsey's "Talking About God: Models, Ancient and Modern," in *Myth and Symbol* (Philadelphia, 1966/p; London, S.P.C.K., 1966), ed. Frederick W. Dillistone, focuses on the Old Testament and on how well the models of that time can be used now. An interesting collection of essays that addresses the matter of the new religions and the older ones that have faded is *Sacred Tradition and Present Need* (New York: Viking Press, 1975), ed. Jacob Needleman and Dennis Lewis. Such questions as what truths are worth keeping? and what is the significance of "myth"? are dealt with in ways that will be useful to the myth student. In fact, Leon Cristiani's *Evidence of Satan in the Modern World* (New York: Avon Books, 1975/p) may well be useful, too, since Cristiani deals with examples of demonic possession through eyewitness accounts, case histories, as well as the transcript of an exorcism. Also, there are two very helpful essays on the secularization of the sacred in Donald R. Cutler's *The Religious Situation: 1968* (Boston: Beacon Press, 1968), a subject surely relevant to contemporary myth study. Many more such works could be included here, but the direction should be clear. In studying contemporary mythology, one has to go well into the religious situation as part of that study.

The coming together of science and religion is a related area of investigation that needs attention. Jacob Needleman's *A Sense of the Cosmos: The Encounter of Modern Science and Ancient Truth* (New York: E. P. Dutton, 1976/p; originally published in 1965) is an exploration of that coming together toward an understanding of the unity which seems to underlie all things. Needleman doesn't deal directly with myth, but the questions he raises will be well thought about by anyone interested in contemporary mythology and religion. There are four provocative articles in "God and Science: New Allies in the Search for Values," a special issue of

Saturday Review, 5 (December 10, 1977), pp. 13, 43. Especially of use is Martin E. Marty's "Science Versus Religion: An Old Squabble Simmers Down." Earl R. MacCormac's *Metaphor and Myth in Science and Religion* (Durham, N.C.: Duke University Press, 1976) is an excellent bit of reading you might wish to indulge in, too; MacCormac deals incisively with the language of religion and the language of science and concludes that the similar uses of metaphor in both make it useless to deal with provability in either case where metaphor is employed. Emerson W. Shideler's *Believing and Knowing: The Meaning of Truth in Biblical Religion and in Science* (Ames: Iowa State University Press, 1966) tackles essentially the same problem from a different angle, that involving their different systems of *thought*. Jacob Bronowski's *Magic, Science, and Civilization* (New York: Columbia University Press, 1978) also has something to offer on the overall conflict of science and religion since Bronowski feels keenly that science is but a strategy, continually modified and adjusted, for understanding the world.

The discussion of works having to do with the coming together of science and religion too could be extended to include many more works. The direction should again be clear, though, it not being out of the question that both science and religion are mythologies unto themselves, each a way of understanding, each a way of assuring tomorrow.

Another shade in the same spectrum is works in which demythologizing is the aim of the author or authors. Ashley Montagu and Edward Darling investigate popular myths—some ancient, most modern—in their book *The Ignorance of Certainty* (New York: Harper & Row, 1970), a heady and entertaining little volume. Their definition of "myth" is hardly the mythologist's, but since they are about debunking what they see as popular misconceptions and erroneous beliefs in the interest of showing how foolish those who are *certain* of their beliefs appear to them to be, their handling of "myth" is clear at all times. Pages 1 through 30 are collectively entitled "Myths from the Bible Laced with Truth," which gives pretty good indication of the book's overall contents. Barrows Dunham's *Man Against Myth* (Boston: Little, Brown, 1947) is another work in which "myth" is equated with "false belief." Dunham lines up popular beliefs in such a way as to make them appear to be modern myths, those that divide people—for instance beliefs in racial superiority, and blue-bloodedness. Charles Wood's *The Myth of the Individual* (New York: John Day, 1927) is a demythologist work, too; Wood's concern is to liberate people from any myth that is restricting. The classic modern demythologist works are those authored by Rudolf Bultmann (or involving Bultmann's demythologist thinking). Bultmann argued long for the demythologizing of the Christian religion—that is, for the removal from the religion of all that is contrary to nature. The miraculous was one element he saw as "mythical" and therefore undermining of faith in a scientific age. Some of Bultmann's works are included in the discussion of works on the New Testament in the earlier section in the guide on Biblical Mythologies, but a brief one useful as an introduction to the controversy he started is *Myth and Christianity: An Inquiry into the Possibility of Religion without Myth*, trans. Norbert Guterman (New York: Noonday, 1958/p), a "debate" between Karl Jaspers and Bultmann. M. Guyau, a French sociologist of the nineteenth century, wrote a book which would seem to be appropriate here as the last work on religion/demythologizing in our discussion of modern mythology. Entitled *The Non-Religion of the Future* (New York: Schocken Books, 1962/p; originally published in 1897), it in itself promoted a kind of modern mythology, a time when metaphysical hypotheses will replace religious dogma while retaining all that is "pure in the religious sentiment."

Works on UFO's, Beasts, and Atlantis

A further and very active area of contemporary mythology involves just about everything from UFO's to creatures with fur or fins. Man has always had a preoccupation with the unknown, a fact verified by every nook and cranny of mythology whether ancient or modern, the numbers of narratives dealing with it now well beyond my capacity to count. The interesting thing about the unknown is that while it is certainly characterized by change over the millenia, our information about land, sea, and air growing and forcing the change, what it is inhabited by tends not to change very much at all. Hercules' hydra is today's abominable snowman (Yeti) or bigfoot (sesquatch), and Gilgamesh's cedar forest was no more feared for its alien Humbaba than a UFO is for its alien helmsman. The subject is a big one even today—pyramid power, astrology, ESP, the Bermuda triangle, and other phenomena are just a few to go along with the UFO's and creatures that lurk.

It has to be somewhat shocking at least to discover that more people around the world today believe in UFO's than *ever* believed in Ea in ancient Mesopotamia, Thor in the lands of the Norsemen, or even Zeus-Jupiter in ancient Greece and Rome. I am not sure more people have *reported* sightings of UFO's than ever believed in any of these deities, but I am inclined to think so. The question that arises is are there myths about UFO's the way there were about the deities?, and my quick answer is yes. Major Donald E. Keyhoe's *Aliens from Space: The Real Story of Unidentified Flying Objects* (Garden City, N.Y.: Doubleday, 1973/i) and Ralph and Judy Blum's *Beyond Earth: Man's Contact with UFO's* (New York: Bantam, 1974/ibp) are two fairly recent books that deal with UFO's informatively, and if you crave more works, the latter book has a good bibliography. You will find both filled with modern myths, some of them not at all unlike a great many traditional myths you might find in, say, the *Larousse Encyclopedia of Mythology.*

The field has been spiced up in the past decade or so by the presence of Erich von Daniken and a host of followers and opponents. Von Daniken suggests that many of the technological achievements and myths of the ancients, not to mention numerous anomalous finds, must be attributed to the presence on earth at some distant time of astronauts from outer space who instructed the ancients, perhaps planted intelligent life here, and whose presence is recorded in the myths of gods as well as in the amazing accomplishments of the past. The bibliography here, too, is long, so mention of some of von Daniken's works and a few others will have to suffice. *Chariots of the Gods* (New York: G. P. Putnam's Sons, 1968/ip) was von Daniken's first work of importance, followed by *Gods From Outer Space* (New York: Bantam, 1972/ip; originally published in 1970 as *Return to the Stars*), *The Gold of the Gods* (New York: G. P. Putnam's Sons, 1973/ip), and *In Search of Ancient Gods: My Pictorial Evidence for the Impossible* (New York: G. P. Putnam's Sons, 1973/ip)—all of them translated by Michael Heron. Among the more interesting books by others is Richard E. Mooney's *Gods of Air and Darkness* (New York: Stein and Day, 1975). Mooney deals more with relevant myths from primitive and/or ancient cultures than even von Daniken does. Gerhard R. Steinhauser's *Jesus Christ—Heir to the Astronauts* (New York: Abelard—Schuman, 1975) is an interesting flower in this flower-filled field, too, since Steinhauser tries to show how Jesus of Nazareth fits into the scheme von Daniken popularized. Adam and Eve are fitted in by Irwin Ginsburg in his *First Man, Then Adam* (New York: Simon & Schuster, 1977).

Scientific repudiation (demythologizing?) of the whole business has been brewing in various sectors, though, and it is possible to

find articles in just about every periodical around in which von
Daniken's views are taken to task. One of the best lengthy sources
is Ronald Story's *The Space Gods Revealed* (New York: Harper &
Row, 1976/ib). In it, Story systematically attacks von Daniken's
logic, proofs, and overall implausibility.

The matter of modern-day beasts is no less busy a subject. Pros
and cons are heard and seen everywhere. Sightings of the abominable snowman were long the rage, and expeditions to Yeti's
Himalayan homeland were undertaken, at least a couple of them
returning with some sort of evidence that the white-furred creature
is more than a mirage. A bill was introduced on the floor of the
Oregon state legislature in 1977 to protect bigfoot even though
the representative introducing the bill didn't know whether it
exists. In the April 6, 1975, issue of *Family Weekly*, Jacques
Cousteau, the oceanographer, was reported as saying he didn't
think the Loch Ness monster exists. "But," he said, "the legend
persists, and will continue to do so, because one human being out
of every four is a mythomaniac." Right on the heels of that statement, though, *The Monsters of Loch Ness* (Chicago: Swallow Press,
1976/i), a 415-page book with 126 photos, drawings, and charts,
and 8 maps, written by Roy P. Mackal, a "research scientist with
a Ph.D. in biochemistry," appeared, its author convinced of the
existence of the Loch Ness monsters. Other waters, too, have their
monsters according to reports. "Is There a Champlain Monster?"
by Brian Vachon in *Reader's Digest*, 112 (April 1978), pp. 9-10,
14, 16, reports numerous sightings of a monster or monsters in
Lake Champlain, upstate New York. An annual trip to *Books in
Print* and the *Reader's Guide to Periodical Literature* will provide
you with plenty of leads for further research into the subject of
modern-day beasts. For a history of the phenomena, look into C.J.S.
Thompson's *The Mystery and Lore of Monsters* (New Hyde Park,
N.Y.: University Books, 1968/i).

Still a reasonably thriving source of modern mythology, though
it too has far older roots, is the subject of mythical places. Plato's
Atlantis is probably the one place with the longest history of interested seekers—mainly because it, if it ever existed, sank into the
ocean, leaving no traces that can easily be found. In May of 1978,
a two-part special entitled *Calypso's Search for Atlantis* was shown
on PBS television. In it, Jacques Cousteau and his men searched
the Mediterranean for whatever traces they could come up with,
the outcome being more fuel for the fires of Atlantis mythology
than even the most fervent believers probably were able to hope

for—although the matter of its actual existence before Plato's time is still not proven. An interesting book on the subject of mythical places, Atlantis included, is Raymond H. Ramsay's *No Longer on the Map: Discovering Places That Never Were* (New York: Viking Press, 1972/i). Among the other places Ramsay investigates is Eldorado, a mythical place in South America. "The Golden Man," by Evan Connell in *Atlantic Monthly*, 241 (June 1978), pp. 65-71, is one of the best summaries of the legend and the activities of those who have sought it. An excellent work on Atlantis is J. V. Luce's *Lost Atlantis* (New York: McGraw-Hill, 1969/ib).

Two recent articles which attack the more or less related areas of astrology, ESP, pyramid power, UFO-logy, and monsters should be mentioned in conclusion: James S. Trefil's "A Consumer's Guide to Pseudoscience," *Saturday Review*, 5 (April 29, 1978), pp. 16-21, and Kendrick Frazier's "UFOs! Horoscopes! (And Other Nonsense)," *Reader's Digest*, 113 (July 1978), pp. 141-44, condensed from the March 1978 issue of *Smithsonian*. These are clearly demythologist works which, as I read them, underscored my own belief in the fact that one of the strongest modern mythologies is that created by the demythologists—a debunking of anything believed in that is unproven their particular mythology. One could alter their writings only slightly to include all religious beliefs.

Studies of American Society—From Sports to Santa Claus

Having gone as far as we have with contemporary mythology, the way has been cleared for a discussion of works not necessarily related to mythology as such but quite clearly useful for any myth student who wishes to investigate other possible mythic strands in the United States. Articles and books are showing up with great regularity that, it seems to me, are well worth considering for what they might trigger in the myth student's mind rather than for what is in them on myth. Conrad P. Kottak's "Rituals at McDonald's," an article in *Natural History*, 87 (January 1978/i), pp. 74-83, is one such article. Or, what about William Arens' "The Great American Football Ritual," also in *Natural History*, 84 (October 1975), pp. 72-81? Sports are so central to American life today that they ought to be fertile territory for the myth student. Two books in this vein are Allen Guttmann's *From Ritual to Record: The Nature of Modern Sports* (New York: Columbia University Press, 1978) and David Q. Voigt's *America Through Baseball* (Chicago:

Nelson-Hall, 1976). Chapter ten in Voigt's book is entitled "New Heroes for Old," but beyond such an obvious excursion into myth as in that chapter, there's very little overt handling of myth by either author. Reading between the lines, inferring, and, in general, donning the cap of the mythologist will be necessary in order to get at whatever mythic strand is to be found. James Wolfe's "Voting on Faith: Myth and Ritual in Presidential Politics," in *Parabola*, 1 (Fall 1976), pp. 26–39, is more directly concerned with myth, for Wolfe deals in the article with how presidential candidates may utilize the myths of the hero, divine king, and others. Wolfe contends that there is a "civil religion" in the United States that is a fundamental part of politics since it legitimizes political authority. Bernard C. Meyer's article "Houdini: The Mythmaker Variations on the Theme of the Family Romance," in *The Psychoanalytic Quarterly*, 45, no. 4 (1976), pp. 588–611, deals with parallels to known myths and mythic events in the achievements and "tricks" of the great escape artist. Ursula K. LeGuin generalizes well on the elements of myth in science fiction in "Myth and Archetype in Science Fiction," *Parabola* 1 (Fall 1976), pp. 42–7. That opens up the whole realm of science fiction and myth, of course, and brings to mind the fantasy fiction of J.R.R. Tolkien, Richard Adams, and many others. What about a modern mythology in these "fantasies" inasmuch as so many go so regularly to the spring? What, too, about popular beliefs other than those we covered earlier (UFO's, pyramid power, etc.), the evil eye one of them which has fair incidence worldwide? Clarence Maloney's *The Evil Eye* (New York: Columbia University Press, 1976/b) is an excellent anthology of essays on that subject.

Americans' capacity for building myth is as great as any other people's is. The long history of myths *about* the American Indian is another piece of evidence to go along with all we've already suggested. Elemire Zolla's *The Writer and the Shaman: A Morphology of the American Indian*, trans. Raymond Rosenthal (New York: Harcourt, Brace, Jovanovich, 1973) is an excellent source for finding out about this American mythology. Zolla delves into the metaphors of the Indian as savage, primitive, noble savage, small child, and so on. Another white American mythology is that about the blacks, and the place to start your investigation of it is Melville J. Herskovits' *The Myth of the Negro Past* (Boston: Beacon Press, 1958/p; originally published in 1941) even though it is focused on the blacks' mythology of their own past—a mythology, too, that is American. On that subject, by the way, *African*

Folklore in the New World (Austin: University of Texas Press, 1977/i), ed. Daniel J. Crowley, is a fine collection of essays by folklorists in which the origins of tales told by blacks in America are debated.

American folklore in general would certainly have to be a source of study for anyone interested in contemporary mythologies, for behind the great body of folklore that has now been collected will be found many of the mythic strands we've mentioned. The area is enormous, though, so I'll refer you to Jan Harold Brunvand's *The Study of American Folklore: An Introduction* (New York: W. W. Norton, 1968/b) for bibliographical direction rather than attempt any here. Also, see Albert B. Friedman's "The Usable Myth: The Legends of Modern Mythmakers" in *American Folk Legend: A Symposium* (Berkeley: University of California Press, 1971) for a good general discussion of the making of myth in America.

Certainly no discussion of contemporary mythology would be complete without mention of Santa Claus. Eric R. Wolf's "Santa Claus: Notes on a Collective Representation," an article on pp. 147-55 in *Process and Pattern in Culture* (Chicago: Aldine Publishing Co., 1964), ed. Robert A. Manners, is a useful introduction to the Santa myth, its origin, purpose, and meaning. Full discussion of St. Nicholas in the western world can be found in George H. McKnight's *St. Nicholas, His Legend and His Role in the Christmas Celebration and Other Popular Customs* (Williamstown, Mass.: Corner House Reprint of the 1917 edition, 1974/i). *The Illustrated Book of Christmas Folklore* (New York: Seabury Press, 1973/i), by Tristram Potter Coffin is a colorful and entertaining work on Christmas tradition, that of Santa Claus included.

Some Sources for Further Study

As should now be clear, there're a lot of sources to look to for the study of contemporary mythology. Because we Americans have a penchant for studying ourselves, our myths, folktales, and legends are constantly exposed in one way or another. Sometimes they're exposed in books which are patent attempts to expose them—as in Patai's, Jewett's and Lawrence's, and others' mentioned above. However, as we've also seen, unlikely sources may well be the places where a good deal of fruitful research and reflection should take place. Don't overlook books on American culture and traditions. In sociology textbooks like Robin M. Williams' *American Society: A Sociological Interpretation*, 3rd edition (New York:

Alfred A. Knopf, 1970), there's plenty of food for thought—
and not alone in the chapters on values and religion. In the popular
sociology of a Vance Packard, also, much can be found, just as it
can in Martin Mayer's works on television or Madison Avenue and
in Marshall McLuhan's many books and articles. McLuhan, like
many of the culture critics and historians seldom deals directly
with myth as such, but occasionally the exception shows up, as
with McLuhan's "Myth and Mass Media," an article he wrote for
Daedalus and which is included in Henry A. Murray's *Myth and
Mythmaking* (Boston: Beacon Press, 1969/p; originally published
in 1959). The material for your research is there, in other words,
for quite an exciting area of myth study.

Author

Ron Smith is Associate Professor of English, Utah State University. His publications include *A Guide to Post-Classical Works of Art, Literature, and Music Based on Myths of the Greeks and Romans* and numerous articles on mythology, college English curriculum, and the preparation of English teachers. Since 1978 he has served on the Task Force on Competency Testing of the Conference on College Composition and Communication and on the Committee on Comparative and World Literature of the National Council of Teachers of English.

BL   Smith, Ron, 1937—
311
S6   Mythologies of the
        world

DATE			
APR 2 5 1984			
SEP 2 2 1989			
JAN 2 6 1990			
FEB 1 9 1990			
DEC 1 6 1992			
DEC 0 1 1994			
DEC 0 9 1994			
DEC 0 9 1994			